Furnace Remelting as the Expression of YHWH's Holiness: Evidence from the Meaning of *qannāʾ* (קנא) in the Divine Context

NISSIM AMZALLAG
nissamz@post.bgu.ac.il
The Ben-Gurion University in the Negev, Beer Sheba 84105, Israel

In the Bible, the human *qannāʾ* (קנא) expresses a negative, self-destructive trait of character mainly related to envy and jealousy. In contrast, the divine *qannāʾ* points to an essential attribute of YHWH, which relates both to divine holiness and to a fiery mode of action frequently imaged by volcanism. The metallurgical affinities of this volcanic representation, together with the designation of the rust accumulating on copper artifacts (verdigris) as *qannāʾ*, suggest that the divine *qannāʾ* is closely related to the recycling of corroded copper through furnace remelting. This assumption is supported by the metallurgical context of meaning of the three wonders performed by Moses in the name of YHWH (Exod 4:1–9), by the evidence that the *qannāʾ* mode of divine action evokes a fiery destroying process that spontaneously promotes a whole rejuvenation, and by the extensive revitalizing powers attributed to furnace remelting in many ancient religions. It is concluded that our understanding of the divine *qannāʾ*, a notion of central importance in Israelite theology, is biased by the extrapolation of the human context of meaning of *qannāʾ* as "jealousy" to the divine sphere.

Very little information is revealed in the Bible about the origin, identity, and nature of YHWH. To clarify these points, special attention should be devoted to the precise meaning of the words expressing YHWH's most essential attributes. Among them, *qannāʾ* holds one of central importance. Considered a name for YHWH in Exod 34:14, it is likened to his whole holiness in Josh 24:19. Walther Eichrodt even considered the divine *qannāʾ* to be "the basic element in the whole Old Testament idea of God."[1] Our current understanding of the divine *qannāʾ* as

---

I want to thank the anonymous reviewers for their helpful comments and Susana Lezra for English revision of the manuscript.

[1] Walther Eichrodt, *Theology of the Old Testament*, trans J. A. Baker (Philadelphia: Westminster, 1961), 210.

jealousy (or its related sentiments) is therefore quite disappointing. Divine jealousy and hubris are sometimes evoked in the mythologies of the ancient Near East, but in no way do they add greatness to the gods.[2] Rather, they crudely reveal limitations of their wisdom and/or powers.[3] Accordingly, the praise of "divine jealousy" by the Israelites is difficult to understand, especially in light of the acknowledged overextended powers of YHWH.[4]

Obviously, such divine sentiment is not interpreted as pettiness or apprehension, and it is not assumed to jeopardize YHWH's status among the Israelites. A problem remains, however: jealousy, in the human context, is far from a positive sentiment. It reduces the autonomy of the subject by introducing dependence on the source stimulating such a feeling.[5] It is even frequently considered to be self-destructive.[6] How can these features be blended, through a common appellation, with an essential attribute of a god acknowledged as the supreme creator, the (only) autonomous being (Exod 3:14), and the god of the gods (Deut 10:17, Ps 82:1)? Many explanations have been proposed to justify this singular situation.

Some scholars have rejected the interpretation of divine *qannāʾ* as jealousy.[7]

---

[2] Jealousy among gods, or even divine jealousy of mortals is acknowledged in Ugaritic and Mesopotamian mythologies. See Johannes C. de Moor, *The Rise of Yahwism: The Roots of Israelite Monotheism*, BETL 91 (Leuven: Peeters, 1990), 228–29.

[3] This feature apparently led Euripides to deny any actual divine status to the Olympian gods. See S. E. Lawrence, "The God That Is Truly God and the Universe of Euripides' Heracles," *Mnemosyne* 51 (1998): 129–46, esp. 132. The gods envying mortals are also mocked by Aristophanes. See John H. Elliott, "God—Zealous or Jealous but Never Envious: The Theological Consequences of the Linguistic and Social Distinctions," in *The Social Sciences and Biblical Translation*, ed. Dietmar Neufeld, SymS 41 (Atlanta: Society of Biblical Literature, 2008), 79–96, esp. 84.

[4] It has been suggested that the divine restriction imposed on Adam concerning the "tree of knowledge" (Gen 2:16–17) was stimulated by jealousy of the deity for Adam's prerogatives, and especially the privilege of immortality. See David Carr, "The Politics of Textual Subversion: A Diachronic Perspective on the Garden of Eden Story," *JBL* 112 (1993): 577–95. However, the term *qannāʾ*, so frequently attributed to YHWH, is curiously absent in this story, as well as any other expression evoking jealousy.

[5] As stressed by E. Reuter, "*qannāʾ*," *TDOT* 13:49: "In the human domain *qnʾ* refers primarily to a violent emotion aroused by fear of losing a person or object."

[6] Elliott attempts to depict jealousy as a positive sentiment: "In Biblical culture (in contrast to contemporary Western culture), jealousy was generally regarded positively as a desirable trait of a personage of honor defending and protecting those under this person's care and protection. In this positive sense, jealousy was attributed also to God" ("God—Zealous or Jealous," 86). However, *qannāʾ*, in the human context, is not viewed especially as a positive sentiment in the Bible. Conjugal jealousy is qualified as "the rage of man" (Prov 6:34); anger is described as "the rottenness of the bones" (Prov 14:30); and the passion of love is equated with a divine fire devouring the lovers (Cant 8:6). Even as zeal for YHWH, *qinʾâ* is described as a passion cruelly devouring the psalmist (Pss 69:10, 119:139). See H. G. L. Peels, "*qanna*," *NIDOTTE* 3:937–40, esp. 938; Reuter, *TDOT* 13:52.

[7] See Peels, *NIDOTTE*, 3:939. H. A. Brongers excludes the idea that YHWH may be jealous of other gods or mortals, considering it to be no more than a crude and misleading

In their opinion, such a misunderstanding results from the wide spectrum of feelings related to *qannāʾ*. They assume that the human *qannāʾ* expresses primarily *envy* and *jealousy*, while its divine counterpart evokes primarily *passion* and *determination*.[8] However, the translation of divine *qannāʾ* as "jealousy" in so many Bible versions reveals that this distinction is not as clear-cut as one might desire.

Other scholars consider that the exclusivity required by YHWH from worshipers led those opposing his cult to call him by the mocking nickname of *ʾēl qannāʾ* (the jealous god), as a play on *ʾēl qōnēh* (the divine creator).[9] One must still justify, however, how such derision may have been transformed into an essential attribute of YHWH and, moreover, into a symbol of divine holiness.

Alternatively, "divine jealousy" is approached as an expression of the intolerant exclusivity of the cult of YHWH.[10] This interpretation is supported by the comparison of idolatry with prostitution and/or adultery, likening the angry reaction of the deity to conjugal jealousy.[11] Though problematic, this association may be justified by the necessary use of metaphors in evoking the divine reality, on the assumption that once humans speak or think about anything beyond direct experience, they do so by analogy.[12] This explanation rests on two presuppositions: (1) the words have the same meaning in human and divine contexts; (2) divine reality systematically transcends direct experience, so that it necessarily belongs to the domain of metaphor.

Concerning biblical Hebrew, the first assumption is far from trivial. For example, the verb קנה (*qal*), in the divine context, evokes demiurgic powers (Gen 14:19, 22; Exod 15:16), whereas it means "to buy" in the human context (see, e.g., Gen 25:10, 33:19, Exod 21:2). So an extrapolation of the human meaning to the divine context leads to the misleading conclusion that, in Israelite theology, YHWH

---

anthropopathism ("Der Eifer des Herrn Zebaoth," *VT* 13 [1963]: 269–84, esp. 276). He concludes (p. 284) that *qannāʾ* in the divine context does not express jealousy but rather the unavoidable consequences of Israel's status as the people of YHWH.

[8] See Elliott, "God—Zealous or Jealous," 84, 93–95.

[9] See de Moor, *Rise of Yahwism*, 229.

[10] See Christoph Dohmen, "'Eifersüchtiger ist sein Name' (Ex 34, 14): Ursprung und Bedeutung der alttestamentlichen Rede von Gottes Eifersucht," *TZ* 46 (1990): 289–304.

[11] See, e.g., Judg 8:33 and Ezek 23:2–9. This is suggested by the parallel in the Decalogue between the prohibition of idolatry (second commandment of the first table, Exod 20:3–6) and the prohibition of adultery (second commandment of the second table, Exod 20:13). This parallel leads Catherine E. Winiarski to conclude, "In this way, the prohibition against idolatry seems to be modeled on a prior injunction against adultery. By implication, the Israelites have to imagine themselves as the wife of a jealous husband" ("Idolatry, Adultery and the Subject of Monotheism," *RelLit* 38 [2006]: 44). See also Jacob S. Licht, "*qanna*," in *Encyclopaedia Biblica* (Jerusalem: Bialik Institute, 1976), 7:196–98; Elliott, "God—Zealous or Jealous," 86.

[12] See Bruce Edward Baloian, *Anger in the Old Testament*, AUS, Series 7: Theology and Religion 99 (New York: Lang, 1992), 160.

"acquired" his status in the world (Gen 14:19), and even his "rights" over the Israelites (Exod 15:16) from another divine being, their previous owner.

The case of כבוד is instructive, too. In the human context, this term evokes honor, wealth, glory, and reputation. However, *kəbôd-YHWH* is a technical term designating a material reality inherent in YHWH's theophany and characterized by a fiery and radiant nature.[13] This singularity is totally dismissed by the translation of *kəbôd-YHWH* as "the glory of YHWH." Furthermore, if *kəbôd-YHWH* reflects a material reality and the human *kābôd* an abstract concept, we may conclude that the theophany of YHWH is not necessarily approached in the Bible through metaphors only but *also* through sensory experiences. This means that the second assumption is not granted either. These observations, together with the problems in understanding divine *qannāʾ* as jealousy or its derivatives, invite us to test whether the meaning of *qannāʾ*, in the divine context, differs radically from its human counterpart. In such a case, the divine *qannāʾ* is expected to reveal an essential characteristic of the Israelite deity currently hidden by such confusion.

I. Differences between Divine and Human qannāʾ

The interpretation of divine *qannāʾ* as jealousy finds a clear expression in the LXX. *Qannāʾ* as an essential attribute of YHWH is translated as ζηλωτόν in Josh 24:19 and as ζηλωτής in Exod 34:14. Exactly the same verb, ζηλόω, is used in the Greek version when translating *qannāʾ* as a human sentiment.[14] In Greek, the verb ζηλόω designates a range of sentiments from passionate emulation to jealousy and destructive zeal, which fits very well the use of *qannāʾ* in the human context. This leads to the conclusion that the meaning of divine *qannāʾ* necessarily falls within the range of feelings evoked in the human context.[15] Accordingly, *qannāʾ*, as an essential divine attribute (Exod 34:14, Josh 24:19) becomes the expression of the exclusivity of the cult of YHWH. By extension, the association of *qannāʾ* with the destructive powers of YHWH expresses the angry reaction of the deity to the violation of the terms of his alliance with the Israelites.[16]

---

[13] For an interpretation of *kəbôd-YHWH* as a technical term, see C. John Collins, "kabod," *NIDOTTE*, 577–87, esp. 581; John F. Kutsko, *Between Heaven and Earth: Divine Presence and Absence in the Book of Ezekiel*, BJSUCSD 7 (Winona Lake, IN: Eisenbrauns, 2000), 80. The fiery and radiant nature of *kəbôd-YHWH* is revealed in Exod 24:17, Deut 4:36, 5:19–20, Isa 60:1–2, Ezek 1:28, 10:4, 43:2–5. See Nissim Amzallag, "The Material Nature of the Radiance of YHWH and Its Theological Implications," *SJOT* 29 (2015): 80–96.

[14] See, e.g., Gen 26:14, 30:1, 37:11, Num 5:14.

[15] According to Peels, *qannāʾ* in the divine context evokes "an energetic state of mind urging towards action. The cause of this *qanna* action is the (possibly imagined) infringement of someone's rights or injury to the subject's honor" (*NIDOTTE* 3:938).

[16] See Peels, *NIDOTTE* 3:938; Baloian, *Anger in the OT*," 156, 160.

The assumption of a parallel meaning of *qannāʾ* in divine and human contexts is challenged, however, by some observations. First of all, the verbal construction קנא + the preposition ב, which in the human context explicitly expresses the negative sentiment of jealousy, is never encountered in the divine context. This prevents any simple extrapolation of *qannāʾ* as jealousy to the divine context. Furthermore, in the Bible, the adjective form (*qannāʾ* or *qannôʾ*) is attested only in the divine context.[17] If this adjective simply designates a jealous-like trait of character, there is no reason why it is not used in the human context. This anomaly is especially significant in light of the designation of the adjective *qannāʾ* as an essential attribute of YHWH.

Finally, an essential difference is attested between the nature of the divine *qannāʾ* and that of the human *qannāʾ*. In the human context, *qannāʾ* is endowed with a multiplicity of meanings (zeal, jealousy, competitive spirit, suffering enmity, animosity, anger, and wrath).[18] All of these may stimulate an action, but its nature cannot in any way be deduced from *qannāʾ* itself. In the human context, therefore, *qannāʾ* is restricted to a psychological dimension. A different situation obtains in the context of divine use. The expression in Isa 63:15, "Where is your *qannāʾ* and your mighty acts," suggests that the divine *qannāʾ* is associated with a specific mode of action expected by the prophet (see also Zech 1:14, 8:2). It is confirmed in Ezek 23:25, where the verb "to give," used in the expression ונתתי קנאתי בך, unambiguously evokes a mode of action.[19] The fact that the prophet does not detail its nature suggests that this specific mode of action was well known by his audience. This conclusion is valuable concerning the locution "The *qannāʾ* of YHWH will do it [תעשה זאת]" (2 Kgs 19:31, Isa 9:6, 37:32) claimed without further details.

These considerations reveal that the divine *qannāʾ* is not only an essential attribute, expressed by an adjective never used in the human context, but it is also a specific mode of action,[20] which has no equivalent in the human context of meaning. The only exception is the intervention of Phinehas related in Num 25:7–8, 14–15. There it is explicitly stated that, by killing Zimri and Kozbi, Phinehas quenched the divine *qannāʾ* and its destructive consequences for the Israelites (Num 25:11). This action, therefore, represents a substitute for divine intervention, a feature justifying its homology with the divine *qannāʾ*.

The repetition of *qannāʾ* in Exod 34:14b ("For YHWH, whose name is *qannāʾ*, is a *qannāʾ* God") remains meaningless as long as it is understood as a sentiment

---

[17] See Exod 20:5, 34:14, Deut 4:24, 5:9, 6:15, Josh 24:19, Nah 1:2.

[18] See *HALOT* 3:1110.

[19] This use is evoked by Koehler and Baumgartner (*HALOT* 3:1111) stressing the other meaning of *qannāʾ* in the divine context as "activity in a punitive sense" or even "activity against foreign (oppressive) peoples and in favor of the people of the covenant."

[20] See Werner Berg, "Die Eifersucht Gottes – ein problematischer Zug des alttestamentlichen Gottesbildes?" *BZ* 23 (1979): 197–211.

more or less related to jealousy.[21] The meaning becomes clear, however, once we assume that here the text evokes *qannāʾ* as an essential attribute (first mention) and as a mode of action (second mention). Their conjunction stresses that the *qannāʾ* mode of action of YHWH is directly derived from the nature of *qannāʾ* as an essential attribute. This reveals that the *qannāʾ* mode of divine action is assumed to reveal the nature of this divine essential attribute. At this point we must clarify its nature.

II. The Fiery Nature of the Divine *qannāʾ*

The divine *qannāʾ* is evoked in Ps 79:5 as something "burning like fire" ("How long, YHWH? Will you be angry forever? Will your *qannāʾ* burn like fire"?). The same fiery imagery is attested in Ezek 36:5 ("Surely in the fire of my *qannāʾ* I have spoken"). These expressions are generally understood simply as metaphors, exactly as jealousy (*qannāʾ*) is evoked in Cant 8:6 as a fiery passion consuming the lovers ("Jealousy [קנאה] is cruel as the grave; its flashes are flashes of fire"). However, further considerations invite us, once again, to dissociate the human and divine domains of meaning.

In the divine context, the fiery component of *qannāʾ* is viewed as a genuine reality. This is revealed in Ezek 38:19: "For in my *qannāʾ* and in the fire of my wrath have I spoken: Surely in that day there shall be a great shaking in the land of Israel." Exactly the same reality is evoked in Num 25:11, where the divine *qannāʾ* is expected to burn the Israelites: "so that I consumed not the children of Israel in my *qannāʾ* [בקנאתי]." This point is confirmed by the parallel explicitly stressed between the divine *qannāʾ* and a devouring fire: "Let them see your *qannāʾ* for your people and be ashamed; yea, let the fire for your adversaries consume them" (Isa 26:11). In addition, Zephaniah evokes the fire of YHWH's *qannāʾ* (אש קנאתי) as something "devouring" the whole earth (Zeph 1:18). Finally, among the mentions of *qannāʾ* as an essential attribute of YHWH (Exod 20:4, 34:14 [2x], Deut 5:9, 6:14, Josh 24:19), Deut 4:24 explicitly associates it with a "devouring fire": "For YHWH your god is a devouring fire, a *qannāʾ* god." All these observations indicate that, in contrast to the human context of meaning, the fiery expression of the *qannāʾ* should be considered to be not a metaphor but rather a genuine mode of divine action.

In Zeph 3:8, the blind-destroying *qannāʾ*-fire (אש קנאתי) of YHWH is represented as something poured upon the earth. This image has been interpreted as a reference to the lava released during volcanic eruptions.[22] Such a volcanic dimension of the divine *qannāʾ* is identified also in the first vision of Nahum. YHWH is first approached as a *qannôʾ* and avenging (*nōqēm*) deity (Nah 1:2). Thereafter,

---

[21] The modification introduced by the Greek translation ("For the lord God, a jealous name, is a jealous god") does not substantially improve the meaning.

[22] See Jean Koenig, "Aux origines des théophanies iahvistes," *RHR* 169 (1966): 1–36, esp. 14.

YHWH's *qannāʾ* mode of action is described as something drying the sea and the rivers and burning everything on the earth (v. 4). The subsequent verse ("The mountains quake before him, and the hills melt") dissipates any doubt concerning the volcanic nature of this divine *qannāʾ*.[23] The same volcanic reality is attested in Deut 32:19-22, where the three stages of the reaction of YHWH to the sins of the Israelites are detailed: he is first spurned (v. 19), then hides his face (v. 20); thereafter his *qannāʾ* is turned against the Israelites (v. 21). The volcanic dimension of this divine *qannāʾ* is revealed in the subsequent verse: "For a fire is kindled in my anger, and it burns unto the lowest hell, and devours the earth with her produce, and sets on fire the foundations of the mountains" (v. 22). These considerations reveal that here volcanism is not introduced as a metaphor evoking an extensively destroying event. It rather appears as a mode of action closely related to the nature of YHWH himself.[24] This essentiality of the volcanic component is supported by the representation of the Sinai theophany as a volcanic eruption (Exod 19:16-19).[25] It is confirmed by the volcanic context of the final day of YHWH, in which the god not only intervenes but also self-reveals to humankind.[26]

III. QANNĀʾ AS FURNACE REMELTING

No volcanic activity is known in Canaan during biblical times; the closest active volcanoes were located far away, in the Arabian peninsula or in the Mediterranean islands (Thera, Sicily).[27] If the volcanic theophany and mode of action of

---

[23] See ibid., 31; Klaas Spronk, *Nahum*, HCOT (Kampen: Kok Pharos, 1997), 42. Kenneth L. Barker and D. Waylon Bailey, *Micah, Nahum, Habakkuk, Zephaniah*, NAC (Nashville: Broadman & Holman, 1998), 175.

[24] Concerning the volcanic dimension of primeval Yahwism, see Jacob Dunn, "A God of Volcanoes: Did Yahwism Take Root in Volcanic Ashes?" *JSOT* 38 (2014): 387-424; Nissim Amzallag, "Some Implications of the Volcanic Theophany of YHWH on His Primeval Identity," *Antiguo Oriente*, forthcoming.

[25] See Martin Noth, *Exodus: A Commentary*, trans. J. S. Bowden, OTL (Philadelphia: Westminster, 1962), 156; Koenig, "Aux origines des théophanies," 15-18, 32-35; Yaakov Bentor, "Geological Events in the Bible," *Terra Nova* 1 (1990): 326-38, esp. 336; Colin J. Humphreys, *The Miracles of Exodus: A Scientist's Discovery of the Extraordinary Natural Causes of the Biblical Stories* (New York: HarperCollins, 2003), 84-87. This volcanic dimension is confirmed in Deut 4:11 and in the Song of Deborah (Deut 5:5).

[26] See Isa 13:9-10; Jer 4:4; Amos 5:8; Joel 2:10; 3:4; 4:15; Zeph 1:5, 15-16; Zech 14:6. The volcanic character of these descriptions is detailed in Koenig, "Aux origines des théophanies," 25-26.

[27] See Viktor E. Camp et al., "The Madinah Eruption, Saudi Arabia: Magma Mixing and Simultaneous Extrusion of Three Basaltic Chemical Types," *Bulletin of Volcanology* 49 (1987): 489-508, esp. 489-90.

YHWH do not correspond to the local geological reality, they may have been introduced in the Bible to describe an essential component of the deity.

The only gods specifically associated with volcanoes in antiquity are the gods of metallurgy.[28] It is not difficult to understand why. The slag flowing from a furnace resembles the lava flowing from a volcano. Furthermore, in antiquity metallurgy was the *only* human activity simulating such a melting of stone. This feature strengthens the symbolic equivalence of metallurgy and volcanism. This homology is also expressed in the Bible, through the comparison of the smoke emanating from Sinai (described as an erupting volcano in Exod 19:16–19) with the smoke of a furnace (Exod 19:18). In addition, in Psalm 18 the poet explicitly describes YHWH inducing the melting of mountains by his anger and even pictures the flow of lava "being emitted" from his "mouth": "Then the earth reeled [ותגעש] and trembled; also the foundations of the mountains moved and were shaken [התגעשו], because he was wroth" (v. 8). The mention of burning coals in the next verse suggests that, here again, this volcanic activity was equated with the work of a furnace ("Smoke arose up in his nostrils, and devouring fire from his mouth; coals flamed forth from him" [Ps 18:9]). The homology between volcanism and furnace activity is suggested also in Ps 21:10. There, the "consuming fire" (אש אוכלת) of YHWH, explicitly compared to the fire of a furnace (תנור אש), "swallows" YHWH's enemies exactly like flowing lava. The conjunction of a volcanic dimension of the *qannāʾ* mode of action of YHWH with a symbolic homology between volcanic activity and smelting suggests that the divine *qannāʾ* may reflect something closely related to metallurgy.

A metallurgical context for the meaning of *qannāʾ* is attested in Arabic, where the cognate term designates "rust."[29] The meaning of *qannāʾ* as "rust" is also explicitly attested in the Wisdom of Ben Sira: "Never trust an enemy; his wickedness is as destructive as rust [קנאה]. Watch out, and be on guard against him, even if he acts ever so humble. He is like a metal mirror that rusts away [קנא] if you don't keep it polished" (Sir 12:10–11 GNB). Since mirrors were made out of copper in antiquity, the rust evoked here by *qannāʾ* clearly refers to verdigris, the green patina of oxidized metal gradually covering copper-made artifacts.[30]

---

[28] Hephaestus, the Greek smith-god was called "the prince of Etna," and his metallurgical activity was supposed to occur at the heart of the volcano. See Alwyn Scarth, "Volcanic Origins of the Polyphemus Story in the Odyssey: A Non-Classicist's Interpretation," *CW* 83 (1989): 89–95. The Etruscan and Roman counterparts of Hephaestus (respectively Sethlans and Vulcan) are also fully identified with active volcanoes. A homology between metallurgy and volcanism is also clearly attested in the mythologies of central and northern Europe. See H. R. Ellis Davidson, "Weland the Smith," *Folklore* 69 (1958): 145–59, esp. 158; Richard L. Dieterle, "The Metallurgical Code of the Volundarkvida and Its Theoretical Import," *HR* 27 (1987): 1–31, esp. 3–6.

[29] See *DCH* 7:266, 602.

[30] From a comparison of the Hebrew text with the Syriac translation, G. R. Driver concluded that *qannāʾ* should be considered to have been originally present in the Hebrew version ("Hebrew Notes on the 'Wisdom of Jesus Ben Sirach,'" *JBL* 53 [1934]: 273–90, esp. 276). An Arabic influence

The combination of the devouring fire of an active volcano (and its furnace counterpart) with the rust accumulating on copper artifacts enables us to identify the meaning of *qannāʾ* in a metallurgical context: the process of *furnace remelting*, by which the copper of corroded metallic artifacts becomes recycled. *Qannāʾ* therefore designates both the rust metal to be recycled and the process of its regeneration by furnace remelting.

IV. The Symbolic Meaning of Furnace Remelting

Identification of the *qannāʾ* mode of action as furnace remelting clarifies why such a destructive process may be viewed as an essential attribute of YHWH, and why it may even express YHWH's holiness. The strong reducing power of furnaces induces a whole reduction of the copper oxides (verdigris), so that furnace remelting produces a complete regeneration of the metal, *without any loss of matter*. From a symbolic perspective, furnace remelting is a process of rejuvenation by fire through destruction of shape. This interpretation is confirmed by the symbolism of the cauldron: this cultic artifact was identified in antiquity both with the furnace and with the mouth of a volcano, and at the same time it was extensively acknowledged as the specific site of rejuvenation.[31]

Furnace remelting was the *only* process in antiquity that made possible such a rejuvenation of matter. It is not surprising, therefore, that the gods patronizing metallurgy were traditionally viewed as divine beings mastering the secrets of life, vitality, and eternity.[32] Nor is it surprising that they displayed strong healing

---

on the author of the book of Sirach is rejected by Driver (p. 290), who concluded that this word, as well as many others he identified there, belongs to a "common stock of pan-Semitic vocabulary and as such might well have found a place in the Hebrew language." This use of *qannāʾ* to designate verdigris (green colored) is apparently ancient, as suggested by the designation of lapis lazuli, a blue-green stone, as *uqnu* in Akkadian. In Ezek 24, the verdigris of the Jerusalem copper cauldron is termed חלאה (v. 6) or חלאתה (v. 12), a feature explaining why the meaning of *qannāʾ* as verdigris in ancient Hebrew is generally ignored.

[31] See Elmer G. Suhr, "The Tripod," *Folklore* 82 (1971): 216–32, http://dx.doi.org/10.1080/0015587X.1971.9716731. Suhr ("The Griffon and the Volcano," *Folklore* 78 [1967]: 212–24, esp. 218–19) clearly established the parallel between the cultic cauldron and the volcano: "The bronze cauldron around which the protomes are placed is similar in shape to the caldera or crater from which the gases and lava are ejected."

[32] In Egypt, Ptah, the patron of metallurgists, is the god who provides the vitalizing *ka* (the source of immortality) to all the other deities. See Peter A. Piccione, "Mehen, Mysteries and Resurrection from the Coiled Serpent," *JARCE* 27 (1990): 43–52, http://dx.doi.org/10.2307/40000072. A similar metallurgical ascendant is attested in Vedic India, where the divine soma, the beverage conferring immortality to the gods, is prepared by the smith-god Tvastar. See Stella Kramrisch, "The Rg Vedic Myth of the Craftsmen (the Rbhus)," *Artibus Asiae* 22 (1959): 113–20, esp. 116.

powers.³³ The frequent use of copper, verdigris, and fragments from furnaces in the preparation of ancient remedies reveals that the healing powers were interpreted in close relation to the process of furnace remelting and its renewing capacity.³⁴

Metallurgy was also closely related to the netherworld for apparently the same reasons. This is revealed by the frequent use in funeral contexts in ancient Egypt of copper ore, charcoals, slag, and furnace residuals.³⁵ These findings suggest that death was conceived of in close relation to the process of furnace remelting. The same metallurgical symbolism of death and afterlife is attested also in cultures from Bronze Age Europe.³⁶ It seems, therefore, that in many ancient societies, ageing was

---

³³ For example, Ptah, the Egyptian smith-god, was considered the main healing god in Egypt, exactly like Ea/Enki, his Mesopotamia counterpart. The Mesopotamian gods Gibil and Nusku also were regarded as healers. Similar healing powers are attributed to the Greek god of metallurgy, Hephaestus, and to Lug, his Celtic counterpart. Also in Vedic India, Tvastar was the main god mastering the healing powers. See Walter A. Jayne, *The Healing Gods of Ancient Civilizations* (1925; repr., New Haven: Yale University Press, 1962), 53, 57, 74–78, 118–21, 126, 161, 176, 327–44, 516, respectively. This extensively acknowledged dimension of healing is confirmed by the role of physician assigned to the smith in traditional African societies. See Walter E. A. Van Beek, "Iron, Brass and Burial: The Kapsiki Blacksmith and His Many Crafts," in *Forges et forgerons: Actes du IVe Colloque Méga-Tchad. CNRS/ORSTOM, Paris, du 14 au 16 septembre 1988*, ed. Yves Moñino, Collection Colloques et séminaires (Paris: Orstom, 1991), 281–310, esp. 284; Philip de Barros, "Iron Metallurgy: Socio-Cultural Context," in *Ancient African Metallurgy—The Socio-Cultural Context*, ed. Michael S. Bisson et al. (Walnut Creek, CA: AltaMira, 2000), 147–98, esp. 175; Gamache T. Kodji, "Traditional Beliefs in Modern Societies. The Case of the Kapsiki Blacksmiths of Mogode, Northern Cameroon" (PhD diss., University of Tromsø, 2009), 34–35.

³⁴ In ancient Egypt, copper/rust is the main component in a panacea mentioned in the Ebers papyrus (12.17–13.1). This reality is attested also in Mesopotamia (see Pablo Herrero, *La thérapeutique mésopotamienne* [Paris: Éditions Recherche sur les civilisations, 1984], 56).

³⁵ This practice is extremely ancient: malachite was found as a deposit and it was apparently spread on the dead before burial in predynastic Egypt. This custom is evidenced by the green color so frequently observed on bones. See Béatrix Midant-Reynes, *Aux origines de l'Égypte: Du néolithique à l'emergence de l'Etat* (Paris: Fayard, 2003), 164, 170, 180–84. For the presence of charcoal in the burials, see ibid., 167, 171, 174. This provides an explanation why green was traditionally considered the color symbolizing resurrection in ancient Egypt. See Manfred Lurke, *The Gods and Symbols of Ancient Egypt: An Illustrated Dictionary* (London: Thames & Hudson, 1980), 127.

³⁶ Also in prehistoric Europe, it seems that the burial mounds of the elite (kurgans) were apparently shaped like a furnace. Dieterle suggests, "The older domed furnaces that preceded the volcanic designs of the Iron age were almost perfect images of the megalithic tombs and, for that matter, of the individual "kurgan" style tomb of the Indo-European peoples" ("Metallurgical Code of the Volundarkvida," 5). Similar practices are observed in traditional societies from India and Africa, where the dead are frequently buried on charcoal. See Nayanjot Lahiri, "Indian Metal and Metal-Related Artifacts as Cultural Signifiers: An Ethnographic Perspective," *World Archaeology* 27 (1995): 116–32, esp. 130; Christian Seignobos, "Les Murgurs ou l'identification ethnique par la forge," in Moñino, *Forges et forgerons*, 43–226, esp. 81; Renate Wente-Lukas, "Fer et forgeron au sud du lac Tchad," *Journal des Africanistes* 47 (1977): 107–22, esp. 117.

equated with a gradual rusting-like process leading to death. The burial was approached as a furnace in which the process of rejuvenation of the soul/body was expected to occur.[37]

These considerations reveal that metallurgy, especially that of copper, was of central cultural importance in antiquity, and that the recycling of copper by furnace remelting deeply influenced the way healing, death, afterlife, and vitality were conceived.[38] The current ignorance of this central reality is probably the consequence of a gradual amnesia of the cultural dimension of metallurgy, which may have been due to the replacement of copper by iron as the main metal during the first millennium BCE. In contrast to copper, iron did not melt in antiquity, its melting point (1538° C) being unattainable in ancient furnaces. This means that the recycling of corroded iron by furnace remelting was totally ignored by the ancient metallurgists. So the gradual ascendance of iron over copper during the course of the first millennium BCE considerably reduced both the practical importance of furnace remelting and its theological consequences. It is likely that this replacement of copper by iron was the source of the progressive disappearance or transformations, during the course of the first millennium BCE, of the metallurgical traditions inherited from Bronze Age religions.

V. Furnace Remelting as an Essential Attribute of YHWH

The above analysis suggests that furnace remelting was viewed in antiquity as the process leading to revitalization through destruction of shape. If *qannāʾ*, in the divine context, truly relates to such a reality, we can expect to find indications supporting the idea that furnace remelting was an essential attribute of YHWH, and that it was closely related to the many processes of vitalization/rejuvenation. Such evidence can be found in the book of Exodus. Moses is requested to perform three wonders to convince the Israelites that he is truly speaking in the name of YHWH (Exod 4:1–9). It is explicitly mentioned that these wonders are related to YHWH. This means that they cannot be simply interpreted as magic tricks performed to

---

[37] A tradition of cremation at elevated temperature (more than 1000° C) is even attested in Bronze Age Scandinavia, a feature clearly expressing a belief in after-death regeneration through furnace remelting. See Joakim Goldhahn and Terje Oestigaard, "Smith and Death—Cremations in Furnace in Bronze and Iron Age Scandinavia," in *Facets in Archaeology: Essays in Honour of Lotte Hedeager on Her 60th Birthday*, ed. K. Childis et al. (Oslo: Oslo Academic, 2007), 215–41.

[38] On the central importance of metallurgy in the elaboration of beliefs and religions of Bronze Age societies, see Kristian Kristiansen and Thomas B. Larsson, *The Rise of Bronze Age Society: Travels, Transmissions and Transformations* (Cambridge: Cambridge University Press, 2005), 52–56.

reinforce the authority of Moses in the eyes of the Israelites, as is so frequently assumed.[39] Rather, it seems that they truly reflect essential attributes of the deity.

These three wonders are not equivalent. The second miracle is introduced to clarify the meaning of the first one (Exod 4:8), and the third miracle is to be performed only for those asking for further clarifications (Exod 4:9). Two conclusions may be deduced: (i) the first wonder, alone, expresses a reality *specifically* related to YHWH; (ii) the genuine meaning of the first wonder was ignored by most of the people, a feature justifying the performance of the two additional wonders to clarify it.

The first wonder, the reversible metamorphosis of a scepter (מטה) into a serpent (נחש) (Exod 4:1–5), may hardly be understood as an instance of "serpent charming," as assumed by some scholars. It occurs after Moses reached the mountain of god not far from the encampment of Jethro, the priest belonging to the tribe of Kenites (metalworkers). This means that the site was probably a Kenite holy place. From the description of intense burning without fire (Exod 3:2), some authors have even concluded that this site was an altar of cultic metallurgy.[40] In such a context, the transformation of the מטה of Moses into a נחש finds a simple explanation: it is the melting of a copper artifact (מטה as scepter) and its transformation into raw material (נחש as copper). The second phase of the miracle, therefore, becomes the formation of a new metallic artifact on the basis of this raw copper.[41] The melting was spontaneously induced once Moses threw his scepter on the ground, near the burning bush. So we may conclude that this melting occurred not in a crucible but directly in contact with the glowing coals. This wonder is therefore nothing other than furnace remelting, a process by which the copper scepter of Moses is renewed through transitory loss of shape, at the serpentine/liquid phase. This metallurgical interpretation clarifies how Egyptian specialists were able to perform the same wonder without difficulties (Exod 7:10–12).

---

[39] See William H. C. Propp, *Exodus 1–18: A New Translation with Introduction and Commentary*, AB 2 (New York: Doubleday, 1999), 226; Cornelis Houtman, *Exodus*, vol. 1, HCOT (Kampen: Kok, 1993), 391–92. According to Umberto Cassuto, these tricks are performed to persuade the Israelites that Moses is not inferior to the Egyptian enchanters (*A Commentary on the Book of Exodus*, trans Israel Abrahams, Publications of the Perry Foundation for Biblical Research [Jerusalem: Magnes,1967], 46).

[40] John C. H. Laughlin concluded that "the 'burning bush' could very well have been a metal altar of the Kenites. The presence of such an altar would explain both the cultic nature of the site prior to Moses, and, of course, the reason why the 'bush' did not burn" ("A Study of the Motif of Holy Fire in the Old Testament" [PhD diss., Southern Baptist Theological Seminary, 1975], 16 n. 41).

[41] See Nissim Amzallag, "YHWH: The Canaanite God of Metallurgy?" *JSOT* 33 (2009): 387–404, esp. 395–96. The copper nature of the scepter (מטה) and the homonymy copper/serpent (נחש) suggest the interpretation of this miracle as the melting of the copper artifact (first stage) and the remaking of a new copper artifact from the liquid copper.

The second wonder is the miraculous healing of Moses's hand after its temporary contact with his bosom. The metallurgical context of the previous wonder stimulates a parallel between the rust accumulating on the surface of a copper artifact and the skin disease covering the hand of Moses. This homology is especially relevant in light of the identification, in ancient medicine, of the heart as the source of the body's heat.[42] Accordingly, positioning the hand on the bosom symbolizes its coming back to the bodily furnace. The second miracle represents, therefore, a medical extrapolation of the process of metal rejuvenation through furnace remelting. It is strictly parallel to the attribution in antiquity of healing powers to the gods patronizing metallurgy.

The third wonder evokes the transformation of water into blood once poured on the ground (Exod 4:9). In the metallurgical context of the first wonder it is supposed to clarify, this third wonder focuses on the liquid element symbolizing the transitory liquid phase in the furnace remelting process. In the Bible, blood is viewed as carrying the "vital force" (Lev 17:14). The transformation of water into blood, once poured on solid ground, signifies that this liquid phase vitalizes the solid state, the shaped universe. This interpretation too fits the vitalizing powers extensively attributed in antiquity to the gods patronizing metallurgy.

These considerations reveal that the three wonders express a unique reality: the process of rejuvenation inherent in furnace remelting (first wonder), its extension to healing (second miracle), and even to vitalization of the entire universe (third wonder). They also explain the hierarchy between these wonders, and why the last one, though being the most persuasive, cannot be performed before the first two. They further indicate that, exactly as in other cultures of antiquity, furnace remelting was conceived in ancient Israel as the source of healing, rejuvenation, and even vitalization of the entire universe. This conclusion supports the interpretation of *qannāʾ* identified here.

The hierarchy of wonders reveals that YHWH was essentially related to the furnace remelting process (first wonder), but that this reality was ignored by most of the Israelites, who acknowledged YHWH only through the consequences of this essential attribute: the power of healing and of vitalization of the universe. This fits precisely the fact that metallurgy was a highly specialized skill in antiquity, so that the process of furnace remelting, though being of central cultural importance, was generally ignored.

---

[42] Before the seventeenth century, it was universally accepted that the heart did not enable the blood to circulate but only heated it. In their opinion, this heating was counteracted by the cooling effect of the breath. This representation of the heart as the bodily furnace is confirmed by ancient Greek medicine, and it is probably rooted long before in the ancient Near East.

VI. The Dimension of Rejuvenation of the Divine QANNĀʾ

Furnace remelting is a process of destruction of shape immediately followed by regeneration of matter. So if the divine *qannāʾ* in the Bible is viewed as a furnace remelting process of rejuvenation, this is expected to be closely related to destruction by fire. This point is examined here.

The rejuvenation of humankind in Zephaniah 3:8–9. The "day of YHWH" is viewed in Zeph 3:8 as the fire of divine *qannāʾ* devouring the earth as a whole. This process is imaged as the pouring of the divine destroying anger upon the nations. Surprisingly, this extensive volcanic-like destruction leads to an improved reality: "For then will I turn to the peoples a pure language, that they may all call upon the name of YHWH, to serve him with one consent" (3:9). The expression "For then" (כי אז) at the beginning of v. 9 specifies that the positive outcome is a direct consequence of the *qannāʾ* destroying event (v. 8). The mention of peoples speaking a pure language evokes the period before the tower of Babel (Gen 11:9). This means that the divine *qannāʾ* is here envisioned as a genuine process of rejuvenation of humankind bringing it back to the early postflood period.[43]

The regeneration of Israel in Isaiah 37. Following the oracle against Sennacherib (vv. 22–29), Isaiah promises that "the remnant that is escaped of the house of Judah shall again take root downward, and bear fruit upward" (v. 31). The description of this renewing event concludes with the following statement: "the *qannāʾ* of YHWH Sebaoth will do this" (v. 32). If *qannāʾ* refers here only to the destroying process, one would expect it to be mentioned in close relation with the promise of the destruction of the Assyrian army (v. 29) and/or the mention of the destruction/defeat of the Judeans. So the mention of divine *qannāʾ* in v. 32 reveals that it evokes the entire process of destruction–rejuvenation, exactly as expected in the context of furnace remelting. It should therefore be translated as "YHWH Sebaoth will perform this through rejuvenation by melting."

Global regeneration in Isaiah 9. The ultimate renewing process in Isaiah 9 is expected to induce a radical transformation on the earth. This process starts with extensive destruction by a devouring fire (v. 4). It is immediately followed by the birth of a "prince of peace" (v. 5) promoting a new wealthy era on the earth. Here again, the mention of the divine *qannāʾ* in v. 6 indicates that this divine process encompasses both destructive (v. 4) and renewing (v. 5) realities. It is noteworthy

---

[43] This pre-Babel period follows the flood, the last widely destructive event revitalizing the earth in response to its total corruption (Gen 6:13). So, from a furnace remelting perspective, following the flood the earth is expected to return to the ideal state: the filling of the entire earth by the sons of Noah. See Carol M. Kaminski, *From Noah to Israel: Realization of the Primaeval Blessing after the Flood*, JSOTSup 413 (London: T&T Clark, 2004), 140–41.

that the mention of this "*qannāʾ* process" is preceded by a long description of a miserable and corrupted reality (8:19–23), a feature apparently introduced to justify the need for revitalization, exactly as rust accumulating on a copper artifact "calls" for its remelting.

The regeneration of Jerusalem in Zechariah 7:11–8:6. The corruption of Jerusalem igniting the anger of YHWH and stimulating its destructive consequences is detailed in Zech 7:11–14. But immediately after that, Jerusalem becomes the "city of truth" (8:3) and happiness (8:4). This metamorphosis is explicitly depicted as a "wonder" (פלא) performed by YHWH (8:6). Its nature is revealed at the middle of the process: "Thus said YHWH Sebaoth: I am *qannāʾ* [קנאתי] for Zion a great *qannāʾ* [קנאה]; and a great wrath [חמה] I am *qannāʾ* [קנאתי] for her" (8:2). In this verse, the mention of the divine *qannāʾ* expresses the two contrasting meanings: the destroying powers of YHWH (wrath) and the "renewing" of Zion. This fits precisely the context of rejuvenation by destruction through furnace remelting.[44]

These examples suggest that the divine *qannāʾ* was not viewed by the Israelites simply as the destructive expression of anger of God. Precisely as in furnace remelting, it was conceived as a wonder leading to a complete rejuvenation of creation through a massive destruction of shape.

VII. Discussion

Divine qannāʾ as Furnace Remelting

The present study stresses the fundamental difference between human and divine *qannāʾ*. While the human *qannāʾ* remains a feeling, the divine *qannāʾ* is a fiery mode of action conceived as a process of destruction immediately followed by rejuvenation/redemption. Such a positive outcome through destruction remains difficult to justify as long as divine *qannāʾ* is understood as jealousy;[45] it becomes clear, however, once the divine *qannāʾ* is identified with furnace remelting.

In antiquity, the only fiery reality leading to entire rejuvenation was the furnace remelting process. This is enough to make it the most probable meaning of *qannāʾ* in the divine context. This conclusion is confirmed by two complementary findings: (i) the volcanic affinities of the *qannāʾ* mode of action, which integrate this notion with the metallurgical sphere; (ii) the designation of rust, and more specifically verdigris, as *qannāʾ*. The simplest way to combine these two elements

---

[44] I propose the following translation of Zech 8:2: "Thus said YHWH Sebaoth: I am performing [קנאתי] for Zion a great rejuvenation by melting [קנאה]; and a great wrath [חמה] I am destroying her by melting [קנאתי]." It is noteworthy that the same term is used in Zech 8:6 and in Isa 9:5 to evoke the outcome of the renewing process: פלא

[45] See Barker and Bailey, *Micah, Nahum,* 169; Trent C. Butler, *Joshua,* WBC 7 (Waco, TX: Word, 1983), 275.

in a context of rejuvenation is to assume that *qannāʾ* designates the process of furnace remelting.

G. R. Driver assumed that metallurgy was probably the primary context of meaning of *qannāʾ* in Semitic languages.[46] This suggests that the divine *qannāʾ* relates to the original meaning of the term, while its human counterpart is an extension of this primary meaning to the psychological domain. This interpretation resolves the problem of the etymology of *qannāʾ* as jealousy.[47] It is supported by John Elliott, who suggests that "the root meaning of *qanna* is 'to become red in the face.' Redness in the face is the external symptom of excitement and intense feelings of various things."[48] The human *qannāʾ* seems, therefore, to be an extrapolation of the redness of metal artifacts thrown into a furnace for remelting, which leads to their self-destruction.[49]

The Parallel between qannāʾ and YHWH's Holiness

The mention of YHWH's dimension of *qannāʾ* in Josh 24:19 is a warning addressed to the Israelites concerning the God who "will not forgive your transgressions nor you sins." At the same time, in this verse *qannāʾ* is likened to YHWH's "holy nature": "For he is a holy God. He is a *qannāʾ* God" (ESV). This homology emphasizes the essential dimension of the divine *qannāʾ*. It also suggests that YHWH's holiness is a concept closely related to the divine process of rejuvenation through destruction.

At Ugarit, the root *qdš* is used to describe the gods themselves as well as everything connected more intimately with them, belonging to them in nature or consecrated and thus associated with them by human beings.[50] This definition fits our understanding of holiness in ancient Near Eastern religions.[51] It is also applicable to ancient Israel, where the root קדש denotes a separation that stems from the consecration of what belongs to the sphere of God's being or activity.[52]

---

[46] See Driver, "Hebrew Notes," 276.

[47] The lack of a satisfying explanation of the etymology of *qannāʾ* as jealousy is signaled by Brongers, "Der Eifer des Herrn Zebaoth," 269–70.

[48] See Elliott, "God—Zealous or Jealous," 85.

[49] It is noteworthy that, in Arabic and Syriac, *qannāʾ* evokes something becoming red by heating. See Elliott, "God—Zealous or Jealous," 85–86.

[50] This definition is formulated by W. Kornfeld, "*qdš*," *TDOT* 12:521–26, esp. 524.

[51] For a general discussion of holiness in the ancient Near East, see Julien Ries, "Expression et signification du sacré: Résultats d'une enquête," in *L'expression du sacré dans les grandes religions*, vol. 1, *Proche Orient ancien et traditions bibliques*, ed. J. Ries et al., Homo religiosus 1 (Louvain: Centre d'histoire des religions, 1978), 293–316.

[52] This view of holiness in the Bible is confirmed by the claim "You shall be holy [קדוש] to me, for I YHWH am holy [קדש] and have separated you from the peoples, that you should be mine" (Lev 20:26). For general considerations, see Philip Peter Jenson, *Graded Holiness: A Key to the Priestly Conception of the World*, JSOTSup 106 (Sheffield: JSOT Press, 1992), 48. Similarly,

The Song of the Sea reveals another dimension to YHWH's holiness. In this hymn, YHWH is praised for being "glorious in holiness" (נאדר בקדש) (Exod 15:11) immediately after the Egyptian army was completely destroyed in the sea (15:10). The same association between holiness and massive destruction is attested in the book of Samuel, where it is reported that the Philistines mourned after the capture of the ark of alliance "because YHWH had smitten the people with a great slaughter. And the men of Bet-Shemesh said: Who is able to stand before YHWH, this holy God [האלהים הקדש הזה]" (1 Sam 6:19–20).

This destructive dimension of YHWH's holiness is confirmed by the frequent use of חרם in the Bible to designate *consecration by total destruction*.[53] This *ḥērem* is explicitly evoked, in the instructions given to the Israelites concerning the sinner city, as a destruction by fire: "You shall gather all its spoil into the midst of its open square and burn the city and all its spoil with fire, as a whole burnt offering to YHWH your God" (Deut 13:17). In the next verse, this sanctification by fire is justified as being necessary in order to quench YHWH's fierce anger and its devastating consequences (v. 18), a feature confirming the parallel between holiness, *qannāʾ*, and *ḥērem* destruction by fire.[54]

The parallel between *qannāʾ* and the destructive dimension of holiness may even be extended. In the Bible, YHWH's holiness is closely related to fire and intense light.[55] Until now, no special attention has been devoted to these singularities because fire and light are general attributes of deities in many ancient religions. However, YHWH's holiness is closely related to a reality defined as *kəbôd-YHWH* (see Exod 29:43, 1 Kgs 8:10–11, Isa 6:3, 10:16–17). As mentioned earlier, this latter expression is a technical term that designates a fiery reality of material nature.[56] This singularity may explain why the radiance specifically emanating from *kəbôd-YHWH* differs from the brilliance generally associated with the holiness of all other

---

William H. C. Propp assumes that קדש mainly designates "YHWH's prerogative, that which properly belongs to him and sets him above his Creation" (*Exodus 19–40: A New Translation with Introduction and Commentary*, AB 2A [New York: Doubleday, 2006], 683).

[53] In the story of the conquest of Jericho (Josh 6), a clear distinction is made between what should be devoted to YHWH by destruction, called חרם (the city and all that is in it, v. 17), and what is consecrated without being destroyed (the metals) and called קדש ("But all silver and gold, and every vessel of bronze and iron, are holy [קדש] to YHWH," v. 19). Accordingly, it seems that חרם and קדש express two antagonistic though complementary expressions of YHWH's holiness.

[54] In this case, *ḥērem* appears as a human initiative performed in order to quench any eventual explosion of divine anger and its blind destructive consequences. Therefore, *ḥērem* is the human counterpart of the divine *qannāʾ*, and it is performed in order to prevent an expression of the latter.

[55] See Helmer Ringgren, *Israelite Religion*, trans David Green (London: SPCK, 1974), 73–74. See also James Muilenburg, "Holiness," *IDB* 2:616.

[56] See n. 13 above. For further examples, see Exod 16:7, Num 14:21–22. The materiality of *kəbôd-YHWH* is stressed in the expression "the *kəbôd-YHWH* was seen/revealed" in Exod 33:22–23; Lev 9:6, 23; Num 16:19; 17:7; 20:6; Isa 35:2; 40:5.

deities.[57] The property of radiance implies that *kəbôd-YHWH* is something very hot. The shapeless nature of *kəbôd-YHWH* (Deut 4:15) even suggests that this notion designates matter in a molten state. In Ezekiel's first vision, this radiant *kəbôd-YHWH* is apparently likened to molten metal through its designation as *ḥašmal* (see Ezek 1:4, 27).[58]

All these considerations reveal a conceptual relation between YHWH's holiness, his destructive dimension, and metal in its molten state (*kəbôd-YHWH*). This association indicates that, exactly as with *qannāʾ*, YHWH's holiness was closely related to the experience of rejuvenation by destruction through furnace remelting. This conception of YHWH's holiness is especially interesting in light of the general considerations about the notion of holiness in ancient religions. As suggested by Mircea Eliade, holiness was in the past a notion closely related to the original status of beings. In this context, ceremonies referring to the "holy time of origins" were viewed as promoting a periodic regeneration and/or vitalization of the world.[59] In such a context, it is not surprising to see the rejuvenation by furnace remelting being understood as the expression of YHWH's holiness: in antiquity it was the *only* process experienced by humankind that enabled a complete rejuvenation of matter.

Divine qannāʾ as an Essential Attribute

If furnace remelting is a wonder essentially related to YHWH (as deduced from Exod 4:1–9), we may conclude that the God of Israel was acknowledged as the smelting god, at least by those well informed about his genuine nature. This conclusion is not as surprising as it may appear at first sight. YHWH originates from Seir (Judg 5:4), the south Canaanite area of copper mining and production.[60] Before Israel, he was apparently worshiped by the Canaanite metalworkers (the

---

[57] See Shawn Z. Aster, "The Phenomenon of Divine and Human Radiance in the Hebrew Bible and in Northwest Semitic and Mesopotamian Literature: A Philological and Comparative Study" (PhD diss., University of Pennsylvania, 2006), 387–427.

[58] Concerning the identification of חשמל as metal in a molten state, see G. R. Driver, "Ezekiel's Inaugural Vision," *VT* 1 (1951): 60–62. The metallic nature of *kəbôd-YHWH* is suggested also in Exod 20:22–23, Isa 42:8, 48:10–11, Pss 19:2, 106:19–20. For more details about the molten-metal nature of *kəbôd-YHWH*, see Amzallag, "Radiance of YHWH," 91–94.

[59] See Mircea Eliade, *Le sacré et le profane*, Collection idées 76 (Paris: Gallimard, 1965), 93–96. This representation was apparently deeply rooted in the ancient Near East. In the Sumerian religion, for example, rituals of purification were performed to bring the "profane universe" back to an initial holy state in order to vitalize it. See Herbert Sauren, "Le sacré dans les textes sumériens," in Ries et al., *Proche Orient ancien*, 105–38, esp. 112, 121.

[60] Tom E. Levy and Mohammad Najjar, "Edom and Copper: The Emergence of Ancient Israel's Rival," *BAR* 32 (2006): 24–37; Juan M. Tebes, "A Land Whose Stones Are Iron, and out of Whose Hills You Can Dig Copper: The Exploitation and Circulation of Copper in the Iron Age Negev and Edom," *DavarLogos* 6 (2007): 69–91.

Kenites).⁶¹ Even after becoming the god of the Israelites, YHWH is revealed in a volcanic theophany. His mode of action and his celestial throne are closely related in the Bible to the metallurgical context.⁶² Moreover, the divine being carrying YHWH's name (the so-called emissary of YHWH) was identified as the Canaanite smith-god.⁶³ So if YHWH, in the Bible, remains acknowledged under his former identity, it is not so surprising that the "wonder" of furnace remelting was viewed as one of his most essential attributes.

Today, the patron gods of metallurgy are generally regarded as artisan deities of lower rank than the patron gods of rain, agriculture, sexuality, war, and kingship. However, the present study invites us to revisit this opinion. The god patronizing furnace remelting was the deity mastering the only process of rejuvenation known in antiquity. He was therefore the only deity providing vitality both to the created universe and to the divine beings. This may easily promote him to the rank of supreme deity, especially in Canaan, a land characterized by a very ancient and extensively developed metallurgical tradition.⁶⁴

Influence on Biblical Theology

Furnace remelting is a process of revitalization of matter through destruction of shape. This linkage between the saving and destroying processes confers a paradoxical dimension on the *qannāʾ* holiness of YHWH.⁶⁵ Such a paradox is reflected in the Bible by the mention of YHWH as a "great and awful" (גדול ונורא) deity (see Deut 7:21, 10:17, Dan 9:4, Neh 1:5, 9:32). Exactly like *qannāʾ*, this ambivalent appellation is explicitly related to the holiness of YHWH: "Let them praise your name, great and awful; Holy is he" (Ps 99:3). This combination of greatness and awfulness

---

⁶¹ See Moshe Weinfeld, "The Tradition of Moses and Jethro at the Mountain of God," *Tarbiz* 56 (1988): 449–60; Israel Knohl, "Cain: The Forefather of Humanity," in *Sefer Moshe: The Moshe Weinfeld Jubilee Volume. Studies in the Bible and the Ancient Near East, Qumran and Post-Biblical Judaism*, ed. Chaim Cohen, Avi Hurvitz, and Shalom M. Paul (Winona Lake, IN: Eisenbrauns, 2004), 63–67; Joseph Blenkinsopp, "The Midianite-Kenite Hypothesis Revisited and the Origins of Judah," *JSOT* 33 (2008): 131–53; Justin Kelley, "Towards a New Synthesis between the God of Edom and YHWH," *Antiguo Oriente* 7 (2009): 255–80; Marlene M. Mondrian, "Who Were the Kenites?" *OTE* 24 (2011): 414–30.

⁶² See Nissim Amzallag, "Copper Metallurgy: A Hidden Fundament of the Theology of Ancient Israel?" *SJOT* 27 (2013): 151–69. For volcanic theophanies of YHWH, see Koenig, "Aux origines des théophanies," and the references therein.

⁶³ See Nissim Amzallag, "The Identity of the Emissary of YHWH," *SJOT* 26 (2012): 123–44. In the Bible, the emissary displays the same relationship with YHWH as the smith artisan with regard to the smelter, this mysterious personage coming from far (mining areas), teaching him his art, and supplying the raw material for his activity.

⁶⁴ See Nissim Amzallag, "From Metallurgy to Bronze Age Civilizations: The Synthetic Theory," *AJA* 113 (2009): 497–519, esp. 502–4.

⁶⁵ Th. C. Vriezen, *An Outline of Old Testament Theology*, 2nd rev. and enl. ed. (Oxford: Blackwell, 1970), 299.

promotes a painful relationship between YHWH and his worshipers, explicitly evoked by the psalmist: "Will you be angry with us for ever? Will you draw out your anger to all generations?" (Ps 85:6).

This paradox finds its ultimate expression in the volcanic representation of the final day of YHWH (Joel 2:11, 3:3–4, Mal 3:23).[66] This great and awful (גדול ונורא) event is expected simultaneously to reveal the deity, to blindly destroy the earth (through volcanic eruptions), and to redeem the earth as a whole (Isa 13:9; Joel 1:15–17; 2:11; Zeph 1:13–15; Mal 3:1–3, 23). This reality explains why Amos, strikingly, does not expect the coming of the day of YHWH: "Woe to you who desire the day of YHWH! Why would you have the day of YHWH? It is darkness, and not light" (Amos 5:18).

These considerations suggest that the depiction of YHWH as a *qannāʾ* God should not be understood simply as presenting an avatar of pre-Israelite Yahwistic metallurgical traditions. Rather, the concepts inspired by the process of furnace remelting seem to be of central importance in biblical theology. They promote the belief that the necessary outcome of a tragic event is the recovery of an improved state, the one closest to the "vitalized origin." They also condition the vision of the final issue as an ultimate remelting event bringing back an entirely renewed earth.

Some of the passages mentioned in this study belong to the latest biblical books. This reveals that the metallurgical dimension of divine *qannāʾ* remained acknowledged, at least partly, at the beginning of the postexilic period. The assimilation of the divine *qannāʾ* to its human counterpart in the LXX, however, indicates that, in the late Second Temple period, this metallurgical dimension was ignored in influential circles among the Jews. We may, therefore, conclude that the metallurgical roots of Yahwism were forgotten, rejected, or intentionally erased during the interval between the redaction of the last prophetic books and the Greek translation of the Bible. Such an amnesic process should, therefore, be regarded as the crucial feature metamorphosing, in late antiquity, biblical theology into a family of new beliefs.

---

[66] The volcanic nature of the day of YHWH is confirmed in Joel 3:3 by the mention of pillars of smoke (תימרות עשן) obscuring the sky, exactly as occurs during a volcanic eruption.

Computerized Source Criticism of Biblical Texts

IDAN DERSHOWITZ
dershowitz@gmail.com
Hebrew University
Jerusalem 9190501, Israel

NAVOT AKIVA
navot.akiva@gmail.com
Bar-Ilan University
Ramat-Gan 5290002, Israel

MOSHE KOPPEL
moishk@gmail.com
Bar-Ilan University
Ramat-Gan 5290002, Israel

NACHUM DERSHOWITZ
nachumd@tau.ac.il
Tel Aviv University
Tel Aviv 6997801, Israel

We have developed an automated method to separate biblical texts according to author or scribal school. At the core of this new approach is the identification of correlations in word preference that are then used to quantify stylistic similarity between sections. In so doing, our method ignores literary features—such as possible repetitions, narrative breaks, and contradictions—and focuses on the least subjective criterion employed by Bible scholars to identify signs of composition. The computerized system is unique in its ability to consider subtle stylistic preferences in aggregate, whereas human scholars are generally limited to cases where a word preference is pronounced. Our method is also less liable to accusations of bias, thanks to its reliance on context-independent criteria. Its efficacy is demonstrated in its successful deconstruction of an artificial book, *Jer-iel*, made up of randomly interleaved snippets from Jeremiah and Ezekiel. When applied to Genesis–Numbers, the method divides the text into constituents that correlate closely with common notions of "Priestly" and "non-Priestly" material. No such corroboration is forthcoming for the classic Yahwistic/Elohistic division.

"We instruct the computer to ignore what we call grammatical words—articles, prepositions, pronouns, modal verbs, which have a high frequency rating in all discourse. Then we get to the real nitty-gritty, what we call the lexical words, the words that carry a distinctive semantic content. Words like love or dark or heart or God. Let's see." So he taps away on the keyboard and instantly my favourite word appears on the screen.

—David Lodge, *Small World* (1984)

We are grateful to Professors Marc Brettler, Shimon Gesundheit, and Avi Shmidman for their valuable assistance and suggestions.

In this article, we introduce a novel computerized method for source analysis of biblical texts. The matter of the Pentateuch's composition has been the subject of some controversy in modern times. From the late nineteenth century until recent years, the Documentary Hypothesis was the most prevalent model among Bible scholars. Since then, scholars have increasingly called into question the existence of some or all of the postulated documents. Many prefer a supplementary model to a documentary one, while others believe the text to be an amalgam of numerous fragments. The closest thing to a consensus today—and it too has its detractors—is that there exists a certain meaningful dichotomy between Priestly (P) and non-Priestly texts.[1]

The various source analyses that have been proposed to date are based on a combination of literary, historical, and linguistic evidence. Our research is a first attempt to put source analysis on as empirical a footing as possible by marshaling the most recent methods in computational linguistics. The strength of this approach lies in its "robotic" objectivity and rigor. Its weakness is that it is limited to certain linguistic features and does not take into account any literary or historical considerations.

Though this work does not address the question of editorial model, we do hope it might contribute to the fundamental issue of literary origins. For cases in which scholars have an idea how many primary components are present, our new algorithmic method can disentangle the text with a high degree of confidence.

The method is a variation on one traditionally employed by biblical scholars, namely, word preference. Synonym choice can be useful in identifying schools of authors, as well as individuals. Occurrences in the text of any one word from a set of synonyms are, however, relatively infrequent. Therefore, synonyms are useful for teasing out some textual units, but not all. Accordingly, we use a two-stage process. We first find a reliable partial source division based on synonym usage. (Only a preference of one term over its alternative is registered; the context in which it is used is ignored.) In the second stage, we analyze this initial division for more general lexical preferences and extrapolate from these to obtain a more complete and fine-grained source division.

As noted, the advantage of a numerical lexical approach is its fundamentally objective nature. While potentially valuable, literary observations and historical reconstructions are prone to controversy. For instance, a repetition may be viewed by one scholar as a telltale sign of multiple sources and by another as an intentional literary device. While our computerized method is objective and powerful, the narrow focus on lexical analysis can occasionally lead to anomalous assignments

---

[1] For a review of the current landscape, see Konrad Schmid, "Has European Scholarship Abandoned the Documentary Hypothesis? Some Reminders on Its History and Remarks on Its Current Status," in *The Pentateuch: International Perspectives on Current Research*, ed. Thomas B. Dozeman, Konrad Schmid, and Baruch J. Schwartz, FAT 78 (Tübingen: Mohr Siebeck, 2011), 17–30.

of provenance that elementary nonlexical considerations (ideology, narrative consistency, repetitions, continuity, etc.) would have precluded.

The algorithm is generic in that it can be applied to any collection of biblical texts (or, for that matter, to other corpora). Apart from the consonantal text, the only information used is Strong's *Concordance*, for the purpose of sense disambiguation and synonymy.[2] No prior knowledge regarding authorship is required. Thus, we will confirm the overall effectiveness of our method by testing it on an *artificial* book, *Jer-iel*, constructed by randomly interweaving the books of Jeremiah and Ezekiel. The algorithm is indeed able to separate this *Jer-iel* composite into its constituents with extremely high accuracy: 96%, as described in detail below. Moreover, when our automated methods are applied to the first four books of Moses, we will see that the results largely correspond to the "consensus" Priestly/non-Priestly (P/non-P) dichotomy (with some notable exceptions, which we discuss below). This suggests that our method may provide a powerful new instrument for the scholar's toolbox.

I. Previous Work

Author attribution is an active area of computer-science research. In the standard problem, which is not the one addressed herein, there is a known list of potential authors for each of whom there are sample writings. Then, the task of the algorithm is to apply automated computational methods to determine who among those is the true author of some anonymous text. Current methods achieve this goal by comparing quantifiable characteristic features of the unknown work to the sample writings. This is called the *authorship attribution* problem.[3] Another problem—closer in spirit to the task at hand, though not identical—is the *author clustering* problem. In this problem, one seeks to divide a collection of writings into a predetermined number of clusters, each written by a distinct author, by identifying shared measurable commonalities among the given works.[4]

What we attempt here is to take a single text and segment it along authorial

---

[2] James Strong, *The Exhaustive Concordance of the Bible* (New York: Abingdon, 1890). We made use of an online edition: http://www.htmlbible.com/sacrednamebiblecom/kjvstrongs/STRINDEX.htm.

[3] Patrick Juola, *Authorship Attribution* (Delft: Now Publishers, 2008); Moshe Koppel, Jonathan Schler, and Shlomo Argamon, "Computational Methods in Authorship Attribution," *Journal of the American Society for Information Science and Technology* 60 (2009): 9–26; Efstathios Stamatatos, "A Survey of Modern Authorship Attribution Methods," *Journal of the American Society for Information Science and Technology* 60 (2009): 538–56, http://dx.doi.org/10.1002/asi.21001.

[4] Robert Layton, Paul Watters, and Richard Dazeley, "Automated Unsupervised Authorship Analysis Using Evidence Accumulation Clustering," *Natural Language Engineering* 19 (2013): 95–120, http://dx.doi.org/10.1017/S1351324911000313.

boundaries and only then cluster the derived segments. This differs from clustering where one begins with single-author units and then simply assigns each such unit to the appropriate cluster. Surprisingly little work has been done in computer science to date on automatically identifying multiple authors within a single text, although some research has been done on identifying language and register transitions.[5] Those who have addressed similar questions, such as plagiarism detection, either assume that there is a single dominant author or that some pairs of units labeled as same-author/different-author are available for training purposes.[6] We make no such assumptions.

Several studies consider the problem of identifying the author of disputed NT books from among a set of known biblical authors.[7] As noted above, this classification problem is quite distinct from the biblical decomposition problem we are considering, where a single text needs to be separated into authorial strands. Other, earlier computational works on biblical authorship questions use various methods to test whether the clusters in a given clustering of some biblical text are sufficiently distinct to be regarded as a composite text.[8] However, it is a simple matter to find some significant differences or similarities between two texts and to point to these

---

[5] An early algorithmic approach is Aravind K. Joshi, "Processing of Sentences with Intrasentential Code-Switching," in *Proceedings of the 9th Conference on Computational Linguistics*, ed. Ján Horecký, North-Holland Linguistic Series 47 (Prague: Academia, 1982), 145–50. See Donald Winford, *An Introduction to Contact Linguistics*, Language in Society 33 (Malden, MA: Blackwell, 2003), 126–67.

[6] For the former, see, e.g., Sven Meyer zu Eissen and Benno Stein, "Intrinsic Plagiarism Detection," in *Advances in Information Retrieval: Proceedings of the 28th European Conference on IR Research*, ed. Mounia Lalmas et al., Logic in Computer Science 3936 (London: Springer, 2006), 565–69; David Guthrie, Louise Guthrie, and Yorick Wilks, "An Unsupervised Probabilistic Approach for the Detection of Outliers in Corpora," in *Proceedings of the Sixth International Language Resources and Evaluation Conference* (Paris: European Language Resources Association, 2008), 28–30. For the latter, see, e.g., Neil Graham, Graeme Hirst, and Bhaskara Marthi, "Segmenting Documents by Stylistic Character," *Natural Language Engineering* 11 (2005): 397–415, http://dx.doi.org/10.1017/S1351324905003694. One recent work similar in spirit to ours is Julian Brooke, Graeme Hirst, and Adam Hammond, "Clustering Voices in *The Waste Land*," in *Proceedings of the ACL Workshop on Computational Linguistics for Literature* (Atlanta: Association of Computational Linguisticw, 2013), 41–46.

[7] David L. Mealand, "Correspondence Analysis of Luke," *Literary and Linguistic Computing* 10 (1995): 171–82, http://dx.doi.org/10.1093/llc/10.3.171; Matthew J. Berryman, Andrew Allison, and Derek Abbott, "Statistical Techniques for Text Classification Based on Word Recurrence Intervals," *Fluctuation and Noise Letters* 3 (2003): 1–10, http://dx.doi.org/10.1142/S021947750300104X.

[8] Yehuda T. Radday and Haim Shore, *Genesis: An Authorship Study in Computer-Assisted Statistical Linguistics*, AnBib 103 (Rome: Biblical Institute Press, 1985); Yehuda T. Radday, "Isaiah and the Computer: A Preliminary Report," *Computers and the Humanities* 5 (1970): 65–73; Ronald E. Bee, "Statistical Methods in the Study of the Masoretic Text of the Old Testament," *Journal of the Royal Statistical Society* 134 (1971): 611–22, http://dx.doi.org/10.2307/2343656; David I. Holmes, "Authorship Attribution," *Computers and the Humanities* 28 (1994): 87–106, http://dx.doi.org/10.1007/BF01830689.

as indicative of separate or identical sources. Such arguments are, therefore, unconvincing, unless it can be shown that observed differences can be exploited to provide the correct split in cases where ground truth is known.[9] This is what we proceed to do next.

II. Synonym-Based Source Division

In this section, we describe an algorithm for automated clustering of single-author textual units, preliminary to the full-fledged source-division method of the next section. By way of illustration, we take the 52 chapters of Jeremiah and the 48 chapters of Ezekiel, two roughly contemporaneous prophetic books, as our corpus. Given their 100 unlabeled, unordered chapters, the task of the algorithm is to separate them out into the two constituent books.[10]

1. Stage 1: Initial Clustering

To obtain a word-based source division, we first employ one of the key features often used to classify different components of biblical literature, namely, synonym choice. The underlying hypothesis is that different authorial components are likely to differ in the proportions with which alternative words from a synonym set (henceforth: synset) are used. As is well known, this hypothesis has played a part in the critical analysis of the Bible since the pioneering work of Jean Astruc, who used a single synonym set—divine names—to divide the book of Genesis.[11] For our purposes, we regard occurrences of distinct words to be "synonymous" if they are identically translated in the KJV. For example, the translations of both נטעתי (lexical form: נטע) and אשתלנו (lexical form: שתל) include the English lemma "plant," and are thus treated as synonyms. It is not necessary for the terms to be identical in nuance (if such a thing exists); rough equivalence in usage is sufficient.[12] This definition yields 517 synsets in the Hebrew Bible, comprising a total of 1,551 individual terms. Most sets consist of only two terms, but some include many more.

---

[9] A. Dean Forbes, "A Critique of Statistical Approaches to the Isaiah Authorship Problem," in *Actes du Troisième Colloque International Bible et informatique: Interprétation, herméneutique, compétence informatique*, Travaux de linguistique quantitative 49 (Paris: Champion 1992), 531–45.

[10] In principle, the clustering algorithm could create any number of clusters, corresponding to any given number of authors; for this example, we take it as given that the correct number of authorial clusters is two.

[11] Jean Astruc (published anonymously), *Conjectures sur les mémoires originaux: Dont il paroit que Moyse s'est servi pour composer le livre de la Genèse* (Brussels: Fricx, 1753).

[12] We manually deleted obvious mistakes, such as unrelated words that are translated to different senses of the same English word. We also merged synsets containing the same word in overlapping senses, including the set of divine names. It is perhaps noteworthy that this synset rarely affects results. (See the discussion of Gen 1 below for a possible exception.)

For example, there are seven Hebrew words corresponding to "fear" (פחד, יראה, מגור, אימה, מורא, ירא, as well as פנים, on account of its co-occurrence with ערץ, חל, etc.).

With these synsets in hand, we can obtain a measure of similarity between any two chapters. Whenever both chapters use words from the same synset, we look to see whether the choice of term is the same or different. The greater the proportion of sets for which the choices are the same, the greater the measure of similarity.[13] Specialized algorithms are then used to cluster the chapters, so that those in the same cluster are as similar as possible, while chapters in distinct clusters are as dissimilar as possible.[14]

We apply this method to separate the 100 chapters of Jeremiah and Ezekiel into precisely two clusters. The result is one cluster of 53 chapters, of which 48 are Jeremiah, and another cluster, with 47 chapters, of which 43 are from Ezekiel. Some concrete examples will help illustrate the process. There are two Hebrew terms (פאה and מקצוע) corresponding to the English word "corner"; two (מנחה and תרומה) corresponding to the word "oblation"; and two (נטע and שתל) corresponding to the word "planted." We find that three choices (מנחה, פאה, and נטע) tend to be located in the same units and, concomitantly, the other three alternatives (תרומה, מקצוע, and שתל) are located in other units; the former are all Jeremiah and the latter are all Ezekiel. The algorithm takes into consideration the combination of synonym choices made in each chapter.

This synonym-based clustering is fairly good, but we can do much better. We observe that some chapters are assigned to one cluster or the other only because it is the nature of the clustering algorithm to classify every unit, however weak the evidence. But in fact borderline chapters may have only a weak affinity to other chapters in that cluster and are not part of what we might think of as its "core" components. We can compute a "center of gravity" of each cluster and use proximity to it as a basis for identifying the core chapters of each of the two clusters. When we formally compute cores in our Jeremiah-Ezekiel experiment, we are left with 74 chapters that split between Jeremiah and Ezekiel with only two misplaced units. Thus, we have a much better clustering, even if only a partial one.

---

[13] Formally, we adapt a similarity measure known as *cosine* (after its analogous use for capturing the magnitude of angles). For details, see Moshe Koppel, Navot Akiva, Idan Dershowitz, and Nachum Dershowitz, "Unsupervised Decomposition of a Document into Authorial Components," in *Proceedings of the 49th Annual Meeting of the Association for Computational Linguistics: Human Language Technologies* (Portland: Association for Computational Linguistics, 2011), 1356–64.

[14] Specifically, we regard each chapter as a node in a graph each edge of which is weighted according to the similarity of the nodes it connects. We then seek a "minimal cut" of the graph into connected components, one component per cluster. Details of the method can be found in Inderjit S. Dhillon, Yuqiang Guan, and Brian Kulis, "Weighted Graph Cuts without Eigenvectors: A Multilevel Approach," *IEEE Transactions on Pattern Analysis and Machine Intelligence* 29 (2007): 1944–57, http://dx.doi.org/10.1109/TPAMI.2007.1115.

2. Stage 2: Learning a Chapter Classifier

Now that we have what appear to be strong representative units for each author, we can use them to classify the remaining unclustered, noncore chapters. Recall that the classification task, in which we wish to assign an anonymous text to one of several potential authors (for whom we have writing samples), is well understood. By analyzing common features of our core chapters, we can automatically formulate rules that best characterize the differences between authors; these rules, aggregately known as a *classifier*, are then used to classify all chapters. Roughly speaking, the method that we use for finding such a classifier assigns to each textual feature some weight in support of one class or the other, according to some predetermined formula.[15] A text is then assigned by the classifier to the class with greater aggregate weight.

The learned rules depend, of course, on the choice of the types of textual features that we are considering. In general, it is known that the best features for textual classification are simply the frequency of use of each word that appears often enough in the corpus. The algorithm finds a variety of words used differentially by the two presumed authors.[16] For example, על, הזאת, and הזה are overrepresented in one of the cluster cores (the one corresponding mainly to Jeremiah), while והנה, אדם, and אחד are overrepresented in the other cluster core. Hence, these words will be assigned considerable weight in support of the respective classes in which they are frequent.[17]

We use our learning algorithm to learn a classifier based on our core chapters. This classifier is then used to classify all chapters, including the other, noncore, chapters. The result is remarkable: we obtain a near-perfect split of the 100 chapters. Even the two Ezekiel chapters that were previously in the Jeremiah core fall to the Ezekiel side; only Ezekiel 42 is incorrectly classified.

3. Testing the Method

To further establish the efficacy of our method, we introduce Isa 1–33 into the mix. From among these three books we have three pairs of books: Jeremiah|Ezekiel, Jeremiah|Isaiah, Ezekiel|Isaiah. For each of the book pairs, the algorithm is given all the chapters in the two books but no information regarding which chapter came from which book, and we ask the algorithm to cluster the chapters of the two books

---

[15] We use support vector machines, as described in Corinna Cortes and Vladimir Vapnik, "Support-Vector Networks," *Machine Learning* 20 (1995): 273–97, http://dx.doi.org/10.1007/BF00994018.

[16] Our definition of "word" here is a series of uninterrupted letters—not necessarily a single lexeme.

[17] The assigned weights for these and a few other relatively significant words are as follows: -14.9 אני, -12.6 אדם, -4.1 והנה, -3.2 וכל, -0.8 אחד, 4.7 הזאת, 4.9 גם, 6.2 על, 10.9 הזה, 15.0 כי. Positive weights are indicative of Jeremiah, and negative weights point to Ezekiel.

to the greatest extent possible. We find that our two-stage method achieves near perfect results for those prophets (94–99%). Moreover, the chapters of each of the three prophetic works are automatically sorted from the chapters of a book in a different genre (Job) with not a single mistake.

III. Artificially Mixed Books

Up until now, we have considered the case where we are given a text that is pre-segmented into chapters, each of which is known to be from a single book. This does not capture the kind of decomposition problems faced in the Pentateuch, where there is no necessary correlation between chapter breaks and crossovers between authorial styles. Thus, we wish now to generalize our two-stage method to handle unsegmented text.

To make the challenge precise, consider how we might artificially create the kind of document that we wish to decompose into sources. We create a composite document, called *Jer-iel*, by first choosing a random number of contiguous verses (between 1 and 100) from the beginning of Jeremiah, then some random quantity from the beginning of Ezekiel, then some from the remaining verses of Jeremiah, and so on until one of the books is exhausted, at which point we take the remaining verses of the other book. We wish to find an algorithm that, given no information beyond the composite document itself, can split the verses of the composite document into two sets, ideally with one consisting of Jeremiah and the other of Ezekiel.

We adapt the two-stage method described above in the following way. First, we "chunk" the text into segments of forty verses each, in order to create artificial "chapters." Of course, each such segment is not homogeneous and is likely to include verses from both Jeremiah and Ezekiel. In fact, in our composite *Jer-iel*, about 30% of the segments are mixed and the rest are either pure Jeremiah or pure Ezekiel.

We then run the two-stage method on the segmented text, just as we did on the homogeneous chapters above. Specifically, we encode the segments as lists of synonym occurrences and cluster them. Then we identify the cores of each cluster. The key is for the cores to consist primarily of pure segments.

In fact, when we apply this part of our algorithm to *Jer-iel*, we find that all of the pure Jeremiah segments are in one core and all the Ezekiel segments are in another core. In addition, there are some mixed segments in each core.

Following our algorithm as described above, we now use these cores to learn a classifier that automatically identifies *verses* as more similar to the first cluster core or more similar to the second cluster core. Unlike for the earlier case, at this stage, we are classifying not whole segments (which might be of mixed origin) but rather individual verses. This allows us to obtain a fine-grained division of the text.

The problem with classifying individual verses is that they are short and may contain few or no characteristic features of either book. To remedy this, and also to take advantage of the "stickiness" of classes across consecutive verses (if a given verse is from a certain book, there is a good chance that the next verse is from the same book), we use a "smoothing" procedure. If a verse is not strongly assigned to either class, we check the class of the last assigned verse before it and the first assigned verse after it. If these are the same, the verse is assigned to that class. If they are not, we determine some optimal split point using a formal method and assign all verses before that point to the same class as the last assigned prior verse and all verses following that point to the same class as the first assigned subsequent verse. (In broad terms, we choose the split point that makes the verses on its two sides as different as possible.)

Employing this optional procedure generally gives somewhat stronger overall results, but it papers over certain very interesting observations regarding small pockets of verses that are not from the same class as surrounding verses. This phenomenon will become more apparent below, when we consider the division of the first four books of the Pentateuch.

Using our method, with smoothing, on *Jer-iel*, we obtain a split of verses in which 96% of the verses are correctly assigned.

When applying the same method to other same-genre merged books, we obtain 83% accuracy for Isaiah-Jeremiah and 88% accuracy for Isaiah-Ezekiel. When we create merged books by combining each of the three prophetic works with Job, we are able to sort out the verses with accuracy ranging from 89% to 95%. In other words, our algorithm can successfully tease apart components of an artificially merged document, whether of the same genre or not, with quite high accuracy.

IV. Automated Source Division of the Pentateuch

Having demonstrated the efficacy of our method, we wish to apply it to the Pentateuch. While there is little agreement among Bible scholars regarding the composition of the Pentateuch, there exists a common denominator among most experts: the first four books are made up of Priestly and non-Priestly material. We therefore endeavor to find the optimal binary split of Genesis–Numbers.[18]

---

[18] We obtain similar results and nearly identical accuracy levels when applying the method to all five books of the Pentateuch. However, given that there is little agreement regarding the boundaries of the edited composition, and since our experiment is a binary split, we opted to examine Genesis through Numbers for the purpose of this article. It may be interesting to run similar experiments in the future with different bounds: Gen–Josh, Deut–2 Kgs, etc. We omitted poetry from our analysis, due to its distinct language register.

We now show intermediate results for our method as it progresses through each step of the algorithm.

1. Stage 1: Initial Clustering

Initially, we encode each chapter in terms of the synonyms used (or not used) in that chapter for each of the synsets, as described above. We then measure the difference/similarity of every pair of chapters and use this information to cluster the chapters into two clusters. (Note that this is a crude clustering in which chapters are treated as coherent units; in the next stage, we drop this assumption.) We then consider the cores of each of these two clusters.

At this stage, we obtain the following two cores:

Cluster Core 1 (53 chapters)
 Exodus 16, 25, 28–31, 36–39
 Leviticus 1–12, 14, 16, 19, 22–25, 27
 Numbers 1–3, 5–10, 13–15, 17–19, 26–29, 31, 33–34, 36
Cluster Core 2 (37 chapters)
 Genesis 4–5, 12–13, 16, 18, 21, 26, 29–34, 36–37, 41–47, 50
 Exodus 2, 3, 8, 17–19, 22–24, 34
 Numbers 21–23

It is already clear that Cluster 1 corresponds roughly with Priestly (P) sections, and Cluster 2 with non-Priestly sections. Since at this stage we treat chapters as though they were coherent units, a number of mixed chapters are assigned to one cluster or another.

In table 1, we show synonym choices that characterize the respective cluster cores. For each synonym, we show in the left column the percentage of chapters of the P core in which the synonym appears, and in the right we show the same for the non-P core.

We note that the two cluster cores make consistent lexical choices over a number of apparently unrelated synsets. In some cases, such as names of God, there are synonyms that are used in both clusters, while others are used in only one of the clusters.[19] In other cases, such as בגד and שמלה, each cluster is characterized by a particular choice of synonym. Thus, for example, we have וכבס בגדיו (Lev 13:6) but וכבסו שמלתם (Exod 19:10).

---

[19] Note that with regard to names of God, our method does not take advantage of potentially relevant thematic material, such as Exod 6.

Table 1. Synonyms that characterize the cluster cores and the percentage of core chapters with that word choice

Synonym		P Core (%)	Non-P Core (%)
captain	נשיא	19	3
	שר	2	30
clothes	בגד	19	3
	שמלה	0	19
earth	אדמה	0	22
	ארץ	47	86
go	בא	15	14
	הלך	8	78
God	א-ל	0	19
	א-להים	2	57
	י-הוה	96	65
man	אדם	30	11
	איש	21	59
manner	דבר	0	8
	משפט	9	0
meat	לחם	6	0
	אכל	2	14
midst/among	קרב	9	16
	תוך	49	11
near	נגש	6	24
	קרב	15	11
offer	הקריב	45	0
	זבח	4	11
put	נתן	49	5
	שת	0	8
	שם	17	41
said	אמר	85	95
	דבר	87	59
sin	חטאה	9	14
	חטא	11	0
south	נגב	9	8
	תימן	6	0
stone	סקל	0	8
	רגם	6	0

Most of the distinguishing terms picked up by our algorithm are well known among Bible scholars.[20] The less-pronounced synsets, however—דבר/אמר, for instance—are not widely appreciated. This is to be expected, as a weak predilection of a source in one direction or the other requires precise counts of word occurrences—something better left to a machine. Our method's ability to grapple with subtle tendencies of this nature is one of its most salient advantages.

2. Stage 2: Learning a Verse Classifier

All the above core chapters are now used as the basis for a second round of classification. The method automatically identifies relatively frequent words (not necessarily in our synsets and often made up of multiple undivided lexemes) that are found with widely differing frequencies in the two cluster cores. These words are used to construct the best possible classifier for distinguishing Type 1 (P) texts from Type 2 (non-P) texts, and this classifier is used to classify *every* individual verse in Genesis–Numbers as one type or the other.

As described in section III.2 above, the computed classifier assigns "weights" to words, thus designating them as markers of one class or the other. In table 2, we list the thirty words to which the classifier assigned the most weight for each of the respective classes. For each word, we show in the left column the weight given by the classifier to each occurrence of the word, with positive weights for P and negative weights for non-P. The middle column shows the frequency of the word's occurrence relative to the total number of words in the P core chapters, and the right column gives the same for the non-P core.

We make three primary observations about this list. First, we note that it is interesting that an initial clustering based solely on synonym choice, with no thematic criteria, should result in a division that so clearly splits the text along certain thematic lines. Most conspicuously, of course, the word הכהן appears quite frequently in the core chapters of what turns out to be the P cluster but not at all in the non-P core. Second, it is noteworthy that the Tetragrammaton is frequent in both cores, but its *absence* turns out to be a marker of the non-P cluster; though not obvious from this table, there are virtually no core P chapters in which it does not appear.[21] Third, we find that clustering according to synonym choices reveals yet other differences in lexical choice regarding words that are not obviously related to the synsets considered earlier. Thus, unexpectedly, we find that the function word עליו appears four times as often in the P core, while לי occurs four times as often in the non-P core.

---

[20] See, e.g., Joseph Estlin Carpenter and George Hartford-Battersby, *The Hexateuch: According to the Revised Version*, 2 vols. (London: Longmans, Green, 1900), 185–221; Heinrich Holzinger, *Einleitung in den Hexateuch* (Freiburg im Breisgau: Mohr Siebeck, 1893), 93–110, 181–91, 283–91, 338–49.

[21] Likewise the plural construct form בני. Similarly, כי and ויאמר appear in almost all core chapters of the non-P cluster.

Table 2. Words to which our learned classifier assigned the highest weights for the respective classes, along with their frequencies (as a percentage of total words) in each class

Word	Weight	P (%)	Non-P (%)	Word	Weight	P (%)	Non-P (%)
הכהן	8.9	0.64	0.00	ויאמר	-16.1	0.20	1.70
י-הוה	8.3	1.76	1.04	כי	-10.7	0.66	1.70
בני	7.3	1.32	0.55	העם	-7.0	0.13	0.39
ואת	6.7	1.44	0.71	יעקב	-6.6	0.00	0.64
אהרן	6.3	0.59	0.06	פרעה	-6.4	0.00	0.57
בן	6.0	0.71	0.39	אם	-6.3	0.13	0.15
לכם	5.8	0.44	0.15	אלוף	-6.1	0.00	0.20
זהב	5.6	0.39	0.02	יוסף	-6.0	0.05	0.71
לפני	5.5	0.54	0.13	בארץ	-6.0	0.05	0.43
העדה	5.4	0.18	0.00	שם	-5.9	0.07	0.43
אני	4.9	0.24	0.11	א-להים	-4.8	0.01	0.46
למטה	4.8	0.17	0.00	אברם	-4.7	0.00	0.16
ויסעו	4.8	0.19	0.04	ויקרא	-4.6	0.02	0.29
ישראל	4.7	0.98	0.46	הא-להים	-4.3	0.00	0.20
עליו	4.7	0.32	0.08	לי	-4.3	0.11	0.43
צוה	4.7	0.29	0.03	ההר	-4.0	0.04	0.13
לי-הוה	4.4	0.70	0.10	עשו	-3.9	0.06	0.27
משפחת	4.1	0.37	0.01	נא	-3.8	0.01	0.33
מועד	3.9	0.37	0.00	מצרים	-3.5	0.11	0.46
יהיה	3.9	0.37	0.07	ויבא	-3.5	0.02	0.25
קדש	3.9	0.34	0.02	גם	-3.4	0.02	0.29
וידבר	3.8	0.33	0.07	אלי	-3.4	0.00	0.22
איש	3.8	0.38	0.32	אנכי	-3.4	0.00	0.25
ויחנו	3.8	0.17	0.04	חמור	-3.4	0.00	0.10
המזבח	3.7	0.34	0.01	הנה	-3.3	0.03	0.29
הקדש	3.6	0.26	0.00	את	-3.1	3.10	3.48
הוא	3.5	0.51	0.47	ויהי	-3.0	0.08	0.34
אהל	3.5	0.31	0.01	לנו	-3.0	0.02	0.17
המשכן	3.3	0.17	0.00	ישלם	-2.9	0.00	0.08
לאמר	3.3	0.46	0.34	עם	-2.9	0.02	0.20

Of course, this is only a partial list, and, while numerous distinguishing words familiar to Bible scholars are present, others are found farther down the full list. Sometimes, this is because the word tends to co-occur with other significant words, and therefore each of the co-occurring words is assigned a lower weight. Other times, it is because the word's distribution across the chapters in the class is not sufficiently uniform.

Many interesting words are found just slightly farther down the full list and are worth mentioning. For instance, words that contribute to the assignment of a verse as P include צבא, במים, ואל, לכל, and שקל, while התער, ותאמר, מאד, ארצה, חן, and גדול, among others, contribute to a non-P classification.

More interesting, perhaps, are the "generic" terms, like ויאמר, which is eight times more likely to appear in the non-P core than in P (a similar ratio holds for noncore verses), versus וידבר, which is five times more likely in P. The algorithm takes quite subtle differences into account, too; for example, את, which is only slightly less common in the P core, is assigned a nonnegligible weight by the classifier. The combination of all these features—strong markers and weaker ones, each with the appropriate weight—is what gives the classifier its discriminative strength.

In the next step, we use our learning algorithm to establish a classifier that is then used to categorize each verse in Genesis–Numbers. After smoothing (explained above), the algorithm proposes a split of verses, presented in table 3.[22]

Table 3. Verses assigned to each class by our classifier (with smoothing)

P	Non-P
Gen 9:18–10:31, 15:18–16:1, 19:23–27, 22:21–23:20, 25:1–18, 34:24–30, 35:20–36:39	Gen 1:1–9:17, 10:32–15:17, 16:2–19:22, 19:28–22:20, 24, 25:19–34:23, 34:31–35:19, 36:40–50:26
Exod 5:13–21, 6:4–7:8, 9:4–7, 12:2–28, 12:40–13:1, 13:21–14:3, 14:8–10, 14:27–16:36, 20:9–17, 24:2–31:17, 34:3–7, 34:21–40:38	Exod 1:1–5:12, 5:22–6:3, 7:9–9:3, 9:8–12:1, 12:29–39, 13:2–20, 14:4–7, 14:11–26, 17:1–20:8, 20:18–24:1, 31:18–34:2, 34:8–20
Lev 1:1–25:6, 25:30–27:34	Lev 25:7–29
Num 1:1–10:28, 10:33–11:7, 12:16–13:26, 13:32–14:10, 14:25–20:25, 25:5–33:56	Num 10:29–32, 11:8–12:15, 13:27–31, 14:11–24, 20:26–25:4

Now we wish to compare the smoothed results with those obtained by scholars using traditional methods. We use Theodor Nöldeke's seminal source analysis as our initial point of reference.[23] As can be seen in the table, the results correspond quite closely with Nöldeke's P/non-P division. To be precise, our method's split (after smoothing) aligns with Nöldeke for 86.6% of the verses. While this figure is already noteworthy, it turns out that despite the comparative resilience of Nöldeke's analysis, our algorithm has a tendency to disagree with his classification specifically where it deviates from the subsequent majority opinion. For instance, Nöldeke

---

[22] The full results prior to smoothing are too long to include here but can be found online at http://www.dershowitz.net/summary and http://www.dershowitz.net/results.

[23] Theodor Nöldeke, *Untersuchungen zur Kritik des Alten Testaments* (Kiel: Schwers, 1869), 143–44. Nöldeke of course uses different terminology.

takes Exod 17 to be Priestly, whereas our method classifies it as non-P. As it happens, nearly all Bible scholars agree that the bulk of that chapter is non-P. Similar examples abound. Therefore, we compare the algorithm's results against both Nöldeke's division and a "consensus" of various scholars, which we use as our primary benchmark.[24] We find that for those verses for which all these scholars agree, the algorithm's split corresponds with the consensus split for 91.4% of the verses.[25]

We visually display the correspondence between the respective divisions in figure 1. Each of the "barcodes" represents a division of the text. A horizontal line represents a single verse, the first verse of Genesis lying at the bottom and the last verse in Numbers lying at the top. A line is black if the corresponding verse is assigned to P and white if the verse is assigned to non-P. Gray indicates that there is no consensus.

VI. Discussion

It might be noted that our method's split corresponds to a considerable extent with that between narrative and legal sections of the Pentateuch. In fact, many of the sections for which our method's split does not correspond with the benchmark P/non-P split are narrative sections in P and legal sections in non-P.[26] Nevertheless, there are numerous examples where our method's split corresponds perfectly with the benchmark P/non-P split within a narrative section or, alternatively, within a legal section.

To appreciate this point, let us consider in some detail Num 13–16, where there are numerous transitions between legal and narrative sections. At Num 13:32, the return of the spies to the desert, there begins a string of verses assigned by our method, as by the benchmark division, to P. It is important to recall that our method's assignments are based on an optimal aggregation of small bits of evidence. Thus, these verses are assigned to P because of the presence of words such as בני and the Tetragrammaton, both highly weighted for P. As in the benchmark division, our method finds a transition to non-P at 14:11. The indicators of non-P in this section, a dialogue between Moses and God that extends through 14:24, are

---

[24] It would be impossible—technically and fundamentally—to establish a true consensus vis-à-vis pentateuchal source analysis. In addition to Nöldeke, we currently include the analyses of Samuel Rolles Driver, *An Introduction to the Literature of the Old Testament*, 9th rev. ed., International Theological Library (Edinburgh: T&T Clark, 1913), and Richard Elliott Friedman, *The Bible with Sources Revealed: A New View into the Five Books of Moses* (San Francisco: HarperCollins, 2003). The selection of these scholars was dictated largely by accessibility; we intend gradually to update our benchmark to account for as many opinions as possible.

[25] Without smoothing, the method obtains a correspondence of 85.2%.

[26] Perhaps unsurprisingly, P passages generally ascribed to the Holiness stratum are disproportionately likely to be classified by our method as non-P.

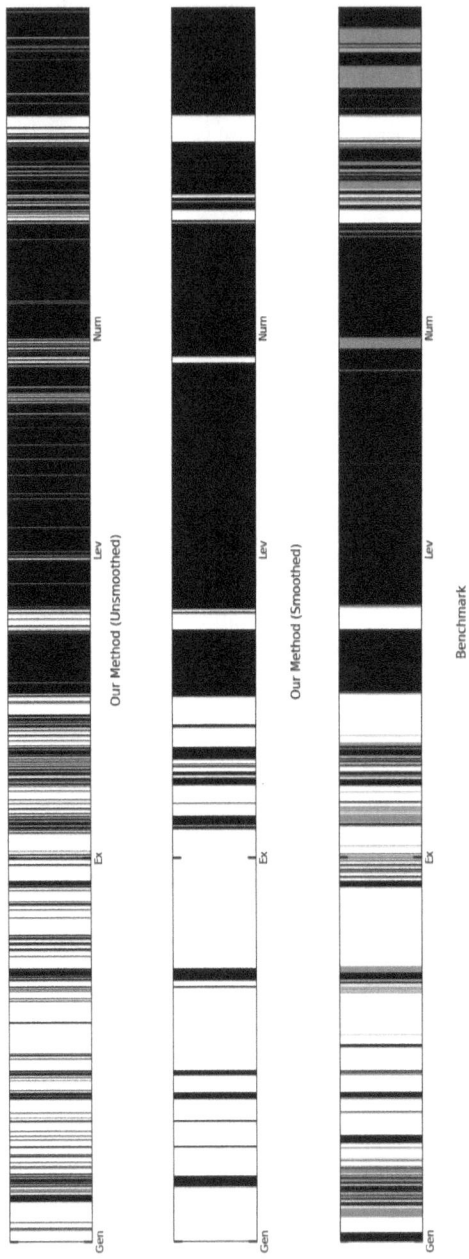

Figure 1. A visual display of the correspondence between our division—both unsmoothed (leftmost "barcode") and smoothed (center)—and the benchmark division (right).

נא, העם, כי, and ויאמר. Numbers 14:25–38, God speaking to Moses and Aaron, is assigned, approximately as in the scholarly benchmark, to P, the main indicators being בני, לכל, לכם, and the Tetragrammaton.

The algorithm assigns Num 15 to P as in the benchmark. Numbers 16, the story of Korah, is a narrative section that is regarded by many as an amalgamation of (perhaps multiple strata of) P and non-P. Our smoothed method assigns the chapter to P, but the unsmoothed method tells a more nuanced story. Among the strong P words in this section, we find לכל, ואל, לפני, לכם, and the Tetragrammaton. Among the strong non-P words, we find כי, גם, לנו, מאד, נא, and אם. Overall, vv. 1–11 and 16–25 are assigned to P and vv. 12–15 and 26–30 are assigned to non-P, corresponding almost perfectly with the benchmark—despite the fact that our considerations are entirely lexical and we do not take into account thematic or ideological considerations at all. One point of interest may be Num 16:33. Whereas some scholars see marks of P or redaction in the previous verse, v. 33 is generally considered to be wholly non-P. Our unsmoothed method, however, clusters the verse with P, due in part to the words קהל and תוך, which appear at the end of the verse. Given the possibly fragmentary account of Korah's death in P, with some attributing the orphaned passage ואת כל האדם אשר לקרח ואת כל הרכוש to that source (or a harmonizing editor), it may in fact be worth considering the possibility that the phrase ויאבדו מתוך הקהל is external to the non-P narrative.

The most prominent case in which our division departs from the benchmark opinion is Gen 1:1–2:4a. Our method places the section in the predominantly non-P cluster, despite Bible scholars' nearly unanimous agreement that it is Priestly in origin. Our divergent results, in this case, can perhaps be attributed to a few factors that conspire to mislead the computer algorithm. One issue is the prevalence of the word א-להים, which our method considers to be a strong indicator of non-Priestliness, as is quite evident in table 2. As noted above, our method does not account for any transition in Exod 6 (P). A second factor is the repeated appearance of the verb ויאמר. This word is also associated with the non-Priestly texts, since P generally prefers the verb וידבר, as mentioned above. However, ויאמר in Gen 1 does not take an indirect object, whereas in the vast majority of cases in which P opts for וידבר, it is followed by אֶל, etc. Therefore, ויאמר here is not truly indicative of non-P, but our method, which is blind to syntax, cannot distinguish between these two usages of ויאמר.[27] All that having been said, the terms that the method identifies as markedly non-P in this section—the aforementioned ויאמר and א-להים, along with כי—feature in the narrative's so-called *Wortbericht* elements, which some scholars indeed believe to be pre-Priestly, or perhaps more accurately, pre-P^g.[28] It may therefore be worth considering our method's results in light of the questions surrounding the literary history of Gen 1:1–2:4a.

---

[27] As we note below, we plan to incorporate syntactical and morphological data in a future version of our method.

[28] See Jürg Hutzli, "Tradition and Interpretation in Gen 1:1–2:4a," *JHebS* 10 (2010), article 12. Regarding the status of the approbation formula, see pp. 19–20.

Another interesting example is Gen 9. Though our method agrees with many scholars that there is a source change at v. 18, the attribution of the two sources is reversed. Whereas most scholars assign the first part of the chapter to P, our method clusters that section with non-P.

There are several cases in which our method's division may have something to contribute to the scholarly conversation. One such example is Gen 18:17–19. Nöldeke considers the passage to be non-Priestly (as do the other scholars), while the unsmoothed version of our method clusters it with P.[29] These three verses were attributed by Julius Wellhausen to a late supplementer, due to perceived similarities with Gen 13:14–17 and 22:15–18—both of which he considered to be redactional—as well as "suspicious language."[30] The status of the passage, together with its broader context, is debated to this day.[31] The fact that our method finds that the three verses stand out from their surroundings indicates that the language is indeed suspicious. The confluence of the words אשר, על, and יהיה—each of which is more prevalent in P than in non-P—is particularly notable in this context. In addition to voicing an opinion regarding debated passages, our method may thus prove useful as a tool for identifying areas worthy of further study wherever it disagrees with scholars in the field.[32]

We have seen thus far that there is a high degree of correspondence between our algorithm's results and previously proposed P versus non-P source divisions. However, when we use the same synonym-driven method to break up the text into three categories, the non-P verses (in the first four books) do not split into anything like the classical J and E sources. Even if we try simply to split the non-P material into two, the resulting subclusters—and even their cores—do not correspond to the classical documents. There appear to be two possible explanations for this: (1) the J and E sources are not sufficiently distinct from one another in terms of word usage for our method to tease them apart; (2) the traditional J/E division is flawed. Either way, we find that while purely word-based classification is a useful new tool, it does not obviate philological analysis.

VII. Conclusions

We have shown that documents can be deconstructed into authorial components with very high accuracy by using an automated two-stage process. First, we

---

[29] We refer here to our unsmoothed results, which are pertinent for questions regarding individual verses. The smoothed results are better suited for identifying broader patterns.

[30] Julius Wellhausen, *Die Composition des Hexateuchs und der historischen Bücher des Alten Testaments*, 3rd ed. (Berlin: Reimer, 1899), 26.

[31] See, e.g., Johannes Unsok Ro, "The Theological Concept of YHWH's Punitive Justice in the Hebrew Bible: Historical Development in the Context of the Judean Community in the Persian Period," *VT* 61 (2011): 406–25.

[32] See, for instance, the brief discussion of Num 16:33b, above. We thank Prof. Jan Christian Gertz for highlighting this additional use for our method.

establish a reliable partial clustering of units by using synonym choice; next, we use these partial clusters as training texts to learn a text classifier using recurring words as features. The learned classifier is then used to classify verses in one authorial thread or another.

We have considered only decompositions into two components, although our method generalizes trivially to more than two components, for example, by applying it iteratively. The real challenge is to determine the correct number of components where this information is not given. We leave this for future work.

Despite this limitation, our success on artificially merged biblical books suggests that the method can be fruitfully applied to the Pentateuch, given that many scholars divide the text into two primary categories—Priestly and non-Priestly. We find that our algorithm's split corresponds to scholarly views regarding P and non-P for over 90% of verses.

Analysis of the disagreements suggests that our method is prone to assigning P narratives and H law to non-P. In some of these cases, such as Gen 18:17–19 and Num 16:33b, our method may contribute to the discussion. Other times, such as Gen 1:1–2:4a, the method's conclusions appear to conflict with the preponderance of evidence produced by other methods.[33]

Among the tools at our disposal for improving our method are the inclusion of measurable morphological and syntactical features (in addition to the lexical features we already use) and disambiguation of polysemic words (such as אל and לך) in the second phase of the algorithm. Likewise, some recent work of ours suggests that the first phase of the algorithm might be performed using binary lexical features (viz., the presence or absence of a common word in the text) rather than synonyms.[34]

For this article, we exploited our new method to explore stylistic features in the Pentateuch. In many ways, this experiment has served as a proof of concept. We set out to establish the method's uniqueness and efficacy, rather than settle long-standing disputes in the field. In the future, we wish to provide more data regarding the strata and sources of the Pentateuch. We also look forward to applying our method to additional biblical books in the hope that it may shed some new light on unsettled questions of authorship.

---

[33] However, see discussion above for an alternative explanation of the discrepancy.
[34] Moshe Koppel and Navot Akiva, "A Generic Unsupervised Method for Decomposing Multi-Author Documents," *Journal of the Association for Information Science and Technology* 64 (2013): 2256–64, http://dx.doi.org/10.1002/asi.22924.

What's Divine about Divine Law?
Early Perspectives
Christine Hayes

"This is a pathbreaking and ambitious study of a topic of crucial importance for Jewish studies in particular and legal philosophy more broadly. The scholarship is first-rate. Hayes convincingly establishes that the rabbinic discourse on divine law in late antiquity was self-consciously distinct from Greco-Roman conceptions as well as a great deal of prior Jewish literature."
—Jonathan Klawans, author of *Josephus and the Theologies of Ancient Judaism*

Cloth $39.50

PRINCETON UNIVERSITY PRESS

See our E-Books at press.princeton.edu

TORONTO JOURNAL OF THEOLOGY

The *Toronto Journal of Theology* is a progressive, double blind, peer refereed journal of analysis and scholarship, reflecting diverse Christian traditions and exploring the full range of theological inquiry: Biblical Studies, History of Christianity, Pastoral Theology, Christian Ethics, Systematic Theology, Philosophy of Religion, and Interdisciplinary Studies. The journal is available in print and online.

COMPLETE ARCHIVE NOW AVAILABLE!
Toronto Journal of Theology Online is a fully searchable electronic resource and now includes the complete archive of 60 issues and over 2000 articles, reviews and commentaries!

TORONTO JOURNAL OF THEOLOGY
Fall 2014

30/2

TJT ONLINE - www.utpjournals.com/tjt

The Bible, Archaeology, and the Practice of Circumcision in Israelite and Philistine Societies

AVRAHAM FAUST
avraham.faust@biu.ac.il
Bar-Ilan University, Ramat-Gan 52900, Israel

The Bible portrays circumcision as having an important role in Israelite culture. Consequently, circumcision has received a great deal of scholarly attention. Some have viewed it as having an "internal" role, for example, for rites of fertility and marriage, whereas others have highlighted its "external" role as an ethnic marker, differentiating the Israelites from "other" groups. Circumcision, however, was practiced by many groups in the ancient Near East, and it is commonly accepted that if circumcision was an ethnic marker, it functioned mainly against the "foreign" Philistines, who did not practice it. Interestingly, all the biblical texts that depict the Philistines as ערלים (uncircumcised) project this reality into the premonarchic period (Iron I), regardless of their date, source, or genre. Not a single text, regardless of genre, uses this pejorative to describe the Philistines in the monarchic period (Iron II). This clear cut dichotomy is supported by additional historical and archaeological lines of evidence (direct and indirect) and is in line with other changes in Philistine culture. All this seems to suggest that the Philistines started to circumcise in Iron II, the time when they ceased to manufacture their Aegean-inspired decorated pottery, adopted the local script, changed their foodways, and so on. This, in turn, gives us a better understanding of the significance of circumcision for the Israelites, and it appears that the "internal" and "external" explanations are not mutually exclusive. Rather, they reflect different perspectives on the practice over time, as well as different views by different social fractions.

The Bible portrays circumcision as having an important role in Israelite culture. Many scholars have stressed the significance of circumcision for rites of fertility and marriage, whereas others have emphasized its role as an ethnic marker.

I would like to thank Dr. Avi Shveka and Dr. Shawn-Zelig Aster for commenting on an earlier version of this article, and the anonymous reviewers for their helpful comments. All mistakes and errors are, of course, mine.

After briefly reassessing the significance of circumcision in Israelite society in the first part of the article, I will argue that the two explanations are not mutually exclusive. In the second part of the article, I will discuss the main group of ערלים (uncircumcised)—the Philistines. An examination of the biblical texts, along with the few available external sources and the detailed archaeological data we possess, seems to indicate that the Philistines were uncircumcised only during the premonarchic era and that during Iron II they practiced circumcision.

I. Circumcision in the Bible

Circumcision has been discussed extensively by biblical scholars.[1] On the basis of references in the Pentateuch and especially in the P source, many scholars adopt such factors as fertility, initiation, and education as explanations for circumcision in ancient Israel. Those scholars, therefore, stress the role of this practice for internal negotiations within Israelite society.[2] Roland de Vaux, for example, concluded that circumcision "is regarded as that which makes a man fit for normal sexual life; it is an initiation to marriage."[3] Howard Eilberg-Schwartz offered an elaborate explanation for the rite and for why it was practiced on babies (rather than at an older age, as is common in circumcision-practicing societies), and even for why it is prescribed for the eighth day after birth.[4] David A. Bernat summarized: "The dynamics of circumcision in the Priestly literature are exclusively internal, and its ramifications are solely upon the relationship between Israel and her deity,"

---

[1] See, e.g., Roland de Vaux, *Ancient Israel: Its Life and Institutions* (New York: McGraw Hill, 1961), 46–48; Erich Isaac, "Circumcision as a Covenant Rite," *Anthropos* 59 (1964): 444–56; Michael V. Fox, "The Sign of the Covenant: Circumcision in the Light of the Priestly ʾôt Etiologies," *RB* 81 (1974): 557–96; Harvey E. Goldberg, "Cambridge in the Land of Canaan: Descent, Alliance, Circumcision, and Instruction in the Bible," *JANES* 24 (1996): 9–34; Robert G. Hall, "Circumcision," *ABD* 1:1025–31; Howard Eilberg-Schwartz, *The Savage in Judaism: An Anthropology of Israelite Religion and Ancient Judaism* (Bloomington, IN: Indiana University Press, 1990); Andreas Blaschke, *Beschneidung: Zeugnisse der Bibel und verwandter Texte*, TANZ 28 (Tübingen: Francke, 1998); Nick Wyatt, "Circumcision and Circumstance: Male Genital Mutilation in Ancient Israel and Ugarit," *JSOT* 33 (2009): 405–31; David A. Bernat, *Sign of the Covenant: Circumcision in the Priestly Tradition*, AIL 3 (Atlanta: Society of Biblical Literature, 2009); Matthew Thiessen, *Contesting Conversion: Genealogy, Circumcision, and Identity in Ancient Judaism and Christianity* (New York: Oxford University Press, 2011).

[2] See, e.g., Helmer Ringgren, *Israelite Religion* (Philadelphia: Fortress, 1966); Fox, "Sign of the Covenant"; Eilberg-Schwartz, *Savage in Judaism*; Hall, *ABD* 1:1026; Goldberg, "Cambridge in the Land of Canaan"; Wyatt, "Circumcision and Circumstance"; see also Bernat, *Sign of the Covenant*; Thiessen, *Contesting Conversion*.

[3] De Vaux notes that "this significance must have died out when the operation was performed soon after birth," but he adds that the adoption of the practice of early circumcision was only gradual and late (*Ancient Israel*, 48).

[4] Eilberg-Schwartz, *Savage in Judaism*, 174–76.

adding, "Nowhere in the P document is circumcision configured as mark of ethnic identity of communal boundaries that distinguished Israelites from the surrounding nations."[5]

One of the main reasons for denying ethnic significance to circumcision is that many groups in the ancient Near East practiced circumcision.[6] As Michael V. Fox noted, "It would not be of much use in distinguishing the Israelites from their neighbors because many of them were also circumcised."[7]

But the overall rejection of circumcision as having an ethnic quality is very problematic. First of all, as admitted, for example, by Fox, "for practical purposes circumcision could at most distinguish the Israelites from the Philistines." Fox claims that this distinction was "not an issue for P," noting that highlighting tribal consciousness was only of secondary importance.[8] Whether it was or could have been an issue for P is a different matter to be addressed briefly below, but Fox seems to have pointed in the right direction here, although he later ignored the implications of his own insight. Fox and many others focused on circumcision in the Pentateuch, while scholars who interpreted circumcision as an ethnic marker based their observation mainly on the many references to the practice in parts of the Deuteronomistic History.[9] Robert G. Hall, for example, writes, "Although many of the surrounding nations practiced it (Jer 9:25–26), circumcision gave Hebrews a sense of national identity,"[10] adding, "This usage peaked when the Hebrews confronted 'uncircumcised' nations." It is quite clear that in some parts of the Bible, circumcision is prominent in contexts that refer to ethnic boundary maintenance,

---

[5] Bernat, *Sign of the Covenant*, 132. Bernat believes that only in the postbiblical Greco-Roman period did circumcision play a role in ethnic boundary maintenance. See also de Vaux, *Ancient Israel*, 48; Ringgren, *Israelite Religion*, 203.

[6] Bernat, *Sign of the Covenant*, 131; see also Jacob S. Licht, "Circumcision" (in Hebrew), *Encyclopaedia Biblica*, 9 vols. (Jerusalem: Bialik Institute, 1950–1989), 4:894–901, esp. 896, 899; de Vaux, *Ancient Israel*, 46–47; Hall, *ABD* 1:1025; Isaac, "Circumcision as a Covenant Rite," 450; Ringgren, *Israelite Religion*, 203; Thiessen, *Contesting Conversion*, 7, 45.

[7] Fox, "Sign of the Covenant," 591 (note that this was not the only reason for his conclusion).

[8] Ibid., 595. See also Bernat, who writes, "A few diverse texts configure the foreskin of the penis and/or of the heart as a sign of foreignness," but he adds, "This foreskin-foreignness equation is not a matter of ethnicity" (*Sign of the Covenant*, 127). In a short footnote (ibid., n. 1), however, Bernat acknowledges that the Philistines are an "exception." See also Ringgren, *Israelite Religion*, 203.

[9] I am referring to the entire Deuteronomistic History, although it appears that much of the books of Samuel, for example, predates this editing. See, e.g., P. Kyle McCarter Jr., *I Samuel: A New Translation with Introduction, Notes, and Commentary*, AB 8 (Garden City, NY: Doubleday, 1980), 15; see also Alexander A. Fischer, "Die Saul-Überlieferung im Deuteronomistischen Samuelbuch (am Beispiel von I Samuel 9–10)," in *Die deuteronomistischen Geschichtswerke: Redaktions- und religionsgeschichtliche Perspektiven zur "Deuteronomismus"-Diskussion in Tora und Vorderen Propheten*, ed. Markus Witte, Konrad Schmid, Doris Prechel, and Jan Christian Gertz, BZAW 365 (Berlin: de Gruyter, 2006), 163–81.

[10] Hall, *ABD* 1:1026.

and especially (although not only) when the Israelites interacted with the Philistines. Indeed, Jacob Licht noted that the Philistines are the only ones who were called "uncircumcised"—עֲרֵלִים, e.g., 2 Sam 1:19, and Erich Isaac states, "The opprobrious epithet 'uncircumcised' was applied apparently only to the Philistines in the Bible."[11] The following verses clearly exemplify the ethnic connotation of circumcision: "Is there not a woman among your kin ... that you must go to take a wife from the uncircumcised Philistines?" (Judg 14:3); "What shall be done for the man who kills this Philistine, and takes away the reproach from Israel? For who is this uncircumcised Philistine?" (1 Sam 17:26); "Tell it not in Gath, proclaim it not in the streets of Ashkelon; or the daughters of the Philistines will rejoice, the daughters of the uncircumcised will exult" (2 Sam 1:20). In all these instances (and others, e.g., 1 Sam 14:6), it is clear that circumcision was viewed as a marker when Israelites and Philistines interacted.[12]

The idea that circumcision could have had such an ethnic role is not without parallels. Ian Hodder observed that circumcision rites served to enhance ethnic solidarity among a group that practiced it (the Mbunda or Wiko), against their main "other" that did not (the Lozi).[13] According to Max Gluckman, the behavior of the Wiko in the lodge—where novices were circumcised and reside before and after initiation—was markedly hostile toward their Lozi and Kwangwa neighbors. Gluckman described how his Lozi attendants, the "true" uncircumcised, were treated: "The men delighted in threatening my Lozi with 'cutting,' and told us stories on how they frightened Lozi intruders into tears."[14] Consider, in this light, the stories of David bringing "a hundred foreskins of the Philistines" (1 Sam 18:25). Regardless of the historicity of the various narratives, Gluckman's description demonstrates that when a group that practices circumcision and one that does not are in a state of hostility, such stories are likely to develop. Gluckman summarized,

---

[11] Licht, "Circumcision," 897; Isaac, "Circumcision as a Covenant Rite," 450; see also Trude Dothan and Robert L. Cohn, "The Philistine as Other: Biblical Rhetoric and Archaeological Reality," in *The Other in Jewish Thought and History: Constructions of Jewish Culture and Identity*, ed. Laurence J. Silberstein and Robert L. Cohn, New Perspectives on Jewish Studies (New York: New York University Press, 1994), 63; Peter Machinist, "Biblical Traditions: The Philistines and Israelite History," in *The Sea Peoples and Their World: A Reassessment*, ed. Eliezer D. Oren, University Museum Monographs 108 (Philadelphia: University Museum, University of Pennsylvania, 2000), 67–68; Wyatt, "Circumcision and Circumstance," 421 n. 51; Ringgren, *Israelite Religion*, 203.

[12] Another example in which circumcision is used to describe ethnic negotiations is Gen 34, traditionally attributed to J (e.g., E. A. Speiser, *Genesis: Introduction, Translation, and Notes*, AB 1 [Garden City, NY: Doubleday, 1964], 266–67; Richard Elliott Friedman, *Who Wrote the Bible?* [San Francisco: HarperSanFrancisco, 1997], 62). The historical context, however, is unclear, and it is possible that the story is meant to explain how (some?) Canaanite groups were circumcised.

[13] Ian Hodder, *Symbols in Action: Ethnoarchaeological Studies of Material Culture*, New Studies in Archaeology (Cambridge: Cambridge University Press, 1982), 116–17.

[14] Max Gluckman, "The Role of the Sexes in Wiko Circumcision Ceremonies," in *Social Structure: Studies Presented to A. R. Radcliffe-Brown*, ed. Meyer Fortes (Oxford: Clarendon, 1949), 151.

"Wiko circumcised probably glorify the lodge additionally against the uncircumcised foreigners because they live among those who despise them." According to him, "the lodge definitely assert Wiko pride and culture against the dominant group among whom they have settled."[15] It is therefore not surprising that in some contexts, when new identities were forced on existing populations, circumcision was forbidden. Thus, Eric R. Wolf noted that "Dingiswayo forbade the circumcision schools that united the members of related homesteads under the jurisdiction of their chief's son."[16] Dingiswayo was aware of the role circumcision played for those people and of the threat that it posed to the attempt to unify all the groups under the Zulu, and acted accordingly.[17]

The fact that many groups in the ancient Near East, including Israel's neighbors, practiced circumcision does not therefore mean that it could not serve as an ethnic marker. Rather, this fact directs us to the specific historical context in which circumcision could become ethnically meaningful—the interaction of the Israelites with the uncircumcised Philistines.

While some of the scholars mentioned above viewed the "internal" and "external" explanations as contradictory and felt it was necessary to disqualify one in order to support the other, it appears that the two are actually complementary.[18] This is all the more significant when one considers that scholars who tended to stress the "internal" explanation for the practice studied the Pentateuch, and mainly P, whereas those who highlighted the role of the practice in boundary maintenance concentrated on the historical books of the Bible.

The fact that one source gives a certain explanation for a practice does not exclude the possibility that other peoples/groups at the very same time had different explanations, nor that even the same group had other explanations in different times. Whatever P had to say about circumcision is both late (regardless of its exact date, in the preexilic period, as many scholars maintain, or in the exilic or postexilic period, as advocated by others) and sectorial (below). Even a practice that was used to demarcate boundaries had an internal resonance. The people who practiced it

---

[15] Ibid., 152.

[16] Eric R. Wolf, *Europe and the People without History* (Berkeley: University of California Press, 1982), 349; see also J. Wright, "Pre-Shakan Age-Groups Formation among the Northern Nguni," *Natalia* 8 (1978): 22–30.

[17] For Zulu expansion, see Leonard M. Thompson, "Co-Operation and Conflict: The Zulu Kingdom and Natal," in *The Oxford History of South Africa*, ed. Monica Wilson and Leonard Thompson (Oxford: Oxford University Press, 1969), 342–45.

[18] Notably, regardless of the exact role a practice might have in the society's internal communication, some practices might teach a great deal about the boundaries of groups, even if as a by-product. Thus, Nicholas David et al., in summarizing their study on pottery decoration among several groups in Cameroon, wrote that the Mafa and Bulahay peoples engage in pottery decoration as a means of transmitting messages within the group, but as a by-product the distribution of those messages "offer[s] not only good but the best evidence of 'ethnicity' generally preserved in the archaeological record" (Nicholas David, Judy Sterner, and Kodzo Gavua, "Why Pots Are Decorated," *Current Anthropology* 29 [1988]: 378).

had to give themselves an explanation as to why it is important to do it, and being different from their adversaries was not always seen as sufficient.

It is likely that the practice preceded its role in ethnic negotiations and resulted from internal factors, whatever they were, when it was practiced. Circumcision was apparently widespread in the ancient Near East long before the Israelites; it is therefore likely that at least some of the various groups that slowly developed into "Israel" practiced circumcision from the beginning.[19] Later, when the Israelites interacted with a group that did not practice it, circumcision became much more important, invested with new a meaning, and canonized. Thus, the *origin* of the custom cannot be attributed to the formation of ethnic boundaries but grows out of other factors, perhaps similar to those attributed (above) to the P-source by some scholars. This practice, however, was chosen as an ethnic behavior because of the interaction with the Philistines.[20]

I am not suggesting that P necessarily preserved those early traditions, but that perhaps the original reasons given for the practice were indeed internal, until the interaction with the Philistines in the (late) Iron Age I. Later, when P was composed, the Philistines were (again?) not an issue (more below), and hence this source stressed, again, internal reasons for the practice. It is likely, therefore, that the two approaches—the one that sees circumcision as an "internal" Israelite issue related to fertility and marriage, and the one that sees it as an ethnic trait—are two facets of the same phenomenon. One explanation was the internal reasoning given within the society for the practice, and the other relates to the fact that the practice did demarcate the boundaries of the group in some historical contexts, especially when Israelites interacted with Philistines. But what of the place of circumcision in the latter society? In the second part of the article I will discuss the significance of circumcision for those the Bible depicts as *the* uncircumcised—the Philistines.

II. The Uncircumcised Philistines

The Philistines were the uncircumcised par excellence in biblical tradition.[21] When reviewing the evidence regarding the Philistines, however, we are facing an interesting anomaly. The Philistines are always described as uncircumcised in

---

[19] For the process, see Avraham Faust, *Israel's Ethnogenesis: Settlement, Interaction, Expansion and Resistance*, Approaches to Anthropological Archaeology (London: Equinox, 2006), and many references.

[20] For the mechanisms through which certain traits were chosen to transmit ethnicity while others were not, see Siân Jones, *The Archaeology of Ethnicity: Constructing Identities in the Past and Present* (London: Routledge, 1997); Faust, *Israel's Ethnogenesis*, 152–54, 183–84; see also Avraham Faust, "The Emergence of Iron Age Israel: On Origins and Habitus," in *Israel's Exodus in Transdisciplinary Perspective: Text, Archaeology, Culture and Geoscience*, ed. Thomas E. Levy et al. (New York: Springer, 2015), 467–82, and references there.

[21] Although the term "uncircumcised" was used to describe other peoples (e.g., Gen 34:14) (more below).

texts pertaining to the premonarchic period (the period of the settlement/judges, or Iron I) and the very beginning of monarchic period (i.e., up to the time of David) but are never described as such in texts pertaining to later eras (the monarchic era, or Iron II).

Philistines and Circumcision in the Premonarchic Era

Almost all the texts that refer to circumcision as an ethnic marker in general—and all the texts that mention the Philistines in such a context in particular—are related to events that took place (or were supposed to have taken place according to the stories) in the premonarchic period, up to the time of David. Those include Judg 14:3; 15:18; 1 Sam 14:6; 17:26, 36; 31:4; 2 Sam 1:20; 1 Chr 10:4; see also 1 Sam 18:25; 18:27; 2 Sam 3:14. While being ערל (uncircumcised) is portrayed in pejorative and negative ways also in texts that relate to later eras, it is striking that the Philistines are described in this way *only* in texts that are meant to depict the reality during Iron I.

Philistine uncircumcision in Iron Age I is not a late invention, nor a projection of a later reality backward in time, and the biblical depiction of the Philistines as uncircumcised is indirectly supported by an extrabiblical source. As Elizabeth Bloch-Smith notes, "In describing Sea Peoples among the Libyan invaders, Merneptah singles out the '[Sher]dan, Shekelesh, Ekwesh, of the countries of the sea, who had no foreskins,' omitting the Pelest/Philistines, in conformance with the biblical characterization of the Philistines as uncircumcised."[22] It is quite clear, therefore, that the Philistines were indeed uncircumcised during Iron I.

Philistines and Circumcision in Iron II

As noted, the Philistines are never described as uncircumcised in texts pertaining to Iron II, although the Deuteronomistic History includes quite a few references to the Philistines at the time, in negative contexts, e.g., 1 Kgs 16:15, 2 Kgs 18:8. None of the texts that refer to a period later than Iron I mentions uncircumcision in reference to the Philistines specifically.[23] This means that the Deuteronomic Historian calls the Philistines uncircumcised only when the stories are projected to the time of David or before, but never in stories about the monarchic period.

This clear dichotomy within the Deuteronomistic History is matched by the picture in other biblical sources, where the Philistines are never called uncircumcised in texts pertaining to the period of the monarchy. Thus, although most

---

[22] Elizabeth Bloch-Smith, "Israelite Ethnicity in Iron I: Archaeology Preserves What Is Remembered and What Is Forgotten in Israel's History," *JBL* 122 (2003): 415. This does not prove, of course, that the biblical texts have credibility; it only shows that the description is not necessarily late (more below).

[23] See Baruch Halpern, *David's Secret Demons: Messiah, Murderer, Traitor, King* (Grand Rapids: Eerdmans, 2001), 457.

prophets mention the Philistines (Isa 2:6; 9:12; 11:14; 14:29; Jer 25:20; 47:1–7; Ezek 16:27, 57; 25:15–17; Amos 1:8; 6:2; 9:7; Obad 1:19; Zeph 2:5), usually in a negative manner, they never call the Philistines uncircumcised. The silence of the prophets is especially surprising when they offer specific prophecies against the Philistines, when we might expect to hear the pejorative "uncircumcised." Its absence in Isa 14:29–32, Jer 47:1–7, and Ezek 25:15–17, is therefore surprising. The lack of references to the uncircumcised Philistines is especially striking in Ezekiel, as on a number of occasions he mentioned "the daughters of the Philistines" (Ezek 16:27, 57), which seems to be an allusion to David's lament (2 Sam 1:20) but the expected "daughters of the uncircumcised" are not mentioned. Moreover, Ezekiel was relatively obsessed with the question of uncircumcision (ערל or ערלים occurs fourteen times in this prophetic book). Still, all those instances fail to connect uncircumcision with the Philistines.

The prophets' surprising avoidance of the term "uncircumcised" when referring to the Philistines fits nicely with the situation in the Deuteronomistic History. The omission of the pejorative "uncircumcised" in texts pertaining to the period of the monarchy is consistent, regardless of which type, source, or biblical genre one is scrutinizing. The Philistines are described as uncircumcised in texts pertaining to Iron I (regardless of the texts' time of authorship) but are never described as such in texts pertaining to Iron II. Furthermore, although these latter texts do mention uncircumcision in general, and uncircumcised groups in particular (below), the term is never applied to the Philistines.

But why did the biblical authors systematically avoid calling the Philistines uncircumcised in texts referring to the monarchic period? Is it possible that the Philistines simply began to practice circumcision during this time? Various lines of evidence suggest that the Philistines were indeed circumcised in Iron II.

Philistine Uncircumcision in Iron Age II

In addition to the internal stratigraphy in the biblical texts, the suggestion that the Philistines started to circumcise in Iron II is supported by textual (biblical and external) and archaeological (both direct and indirect) evidence.

An External Source

Direct support for the suggestion that the Philistines practiced circumcision is found in Herodotus's *Histories* (2.104), where the fifth-century BCE Greek historian claimed that "the Syrians of Palestine" practiced circumcision and further reported that they adopted this custom from the Egyptians (they "confess that they learnt the custom of the Egyptians").[24] Herodotus probably traveled inland to

---

[24] Translation from George Rawlinson, *The History of Herodotus*, Everyman's Library (London: Dent, 1910).

important centers like Egypt and Babylon, but it appears that most of his travels were along the coast,[25] and he most likely was referring to the Philistines, as the term Palestine (derived from Philistia) clearly indicates.[26]

The notion that the Philistines were *the* uncircumcised led many scholars (from Josephus onward) to assume that Herodotus could not have referred to the Philistines, and that he must have meant another group,[27] whether Jews or Arabs.[28] But it appears that we should take Herodotus at face value, as referring to the inhabitants of Philistia. It is even possible that the explicit reference to the origin of this practice suggests that Herodotus's sources knew that the practice was not native to those people. This strengthens the suggestion that he indeed referred to the inhabitants of Philistia, and that, though they had been uncircumcised in the past, they began to practice circumcision at some point.[29]

Biblical Sources

In Ezek 32:17–32, dated to the very end of Iron II, the prophet lists uncircumcised peoples—Assyria, Elam, and some others—but do not mention the Philistines. Some scholars, "knowing" that the Philistines were "the" uncircumcised, saw this omission as an indication that the Philistines were ethnically and politically in decline and were thus not important enough to be mentioned in such a prophecy.[30] This, however, does not cohere with the overall picture that emerges from the texts, as there are quite a few prophecies against the Philistines in the eighth to sixth centuries BCE (including by Ezekiel himself—see the prophecy against the Philistines in 25:15–17; see also Ezek 16:27, 57; Jer 25:20; 47:1–7), indicating that they were important enough to warrant some attention. The omission of the Philistines

---

[25] See John Gould, *Herodotus* (New York: St. Martin's, 1989), 11–12; David Asheri, "General Introduction," in *A Commentary on Herodotus: Books I–IV*, ed. David Asheri, Alan Lloyd, and Aldo Corcella (Oxford: Oxford University Press, 2007), 6.

[26] Seymour Gitin, "Philistines in the Books of Kings," in *The Books of Kings: Sources, Composition, Historiography and Reception*, ed. André Lemaire and Baruch Halpern, VTSup 129 (Leiden: Brill, 2010), 348.

[27] See, e.g., David M. Jacobson, "Palestine and Israel," *BASOR* 313 (1999): 67; see also Israel Eph'al, "The Philistine Entity and the Origin of the Name 'Palestine'" (in Hebrew), in *Tehillah le-Moshe: Biblical and Judaic Studies in Honor of Moshe Greenberg*, ed. Mordechai Cogan, Barry L. Eichler, and Jeffrey H. Tigay (Winona Lake, IN: Eisenbrauns, 1997), 35*.

[28] Some claimed that he referred to Jews (see already Josephus, *Ant.* 8.262; also Jacobson, "Palestine and Israel," 67) or Arabs (Menahem Stern, *Greek and Latin Authors on Jews and Judaism*, 3 vols., Fontes ad res Judaicas spectantes; PIASH, Section of Humanities [Jerusalem: Israel Academy of Science and Humanities, 1976], 1:3–4).

[29] Scholars usually treat Herodotus's testimony seriously; regarding circumcision of Arabs and Phoenicians, see, e.g., Thiessen, *Contesting Conversion*, 7, 53, 56; Jack M. Sasson claims that the origin of this custom is Syrian ("Circumcision in the Ancient Near East," *JBL* 85 [1966]: 476).

[30] Menahem Haran, on Ezek 40:17–32, in *Ezekiel—The World of the Bible*, ed. G. Brin and M. Haran (in Hebrew; Tel Aviv: Davidson-'Ati, 1996), 167.

from lists of the uncircumcised peoples may well be evidence that they were indeed circumcised.[31]

Direct Archaeological Evidence

There is, of course, not much direct archaeological data on circumcision. Still, we do have some archaeological hints that clearly suggest either that in Iron

---

[31] At first, Jer 9:25 appears to pose a problem for the present suggestion. The fact that the Philistines are missing from this verse, which appears to list (in its beginning) a number of circumcised people (see, e.g., de Vaux, *Ancient Israel*, 47), might suggest that they were not circumcised (e.g., F. B. Huey, *Jeremiah, Lamentations*, NAC [Nashville: Broadman, 1993], 122). Such an interpretation seems surprising in light of the above (and especially given Jeremiah's own failure to call the Philistines uncircumcised when mentioning them), and the verse is problematic and seems to exhibit internal contradiction as to whether the nations were circumcised (beginning of v. 25) or not (end of v. 25) (see, e.g., Tremper Longman III, *Jeremiah, Lamentations*, NIBCOT [Peabody, MA: Hendrickson, 2008], 93). One should therefore hesitate to give a single (problematic) verse much weight. Moreover, there might be a simpler explanation for the omission of the Philistines from the verse. Richard C. Steiner has recently suggested that Jeremiah lists people who practiced incomplete circumcision, for example, the Egyptians ("Incomplete Circumcision in Egypt and Edom: Jeremiah [9:24–25] in the Light of Josephus and Jonckheere," *JBL* 118 [1999]: 497–505; see also Isaac, "Circumcision as a Covenant Rite," 453; Sasson, "Circumcision in the Ancient Near East," 474). Jeremiah's aim was, according to Steiner, to warn the inhabitants of Judah that although they practiced full circumcision, "the difference is imaginary; the circumcision of the Jews is also incomplete," and their "real" circumcision will not save them (pp. 504–5; I am grateful to Mark Smith for directing me to Steiner's article). If Steiner is correct, then it is possible that the Philistines are not mentioned because they, too, practiced full circumcision, and hence there was no point in mentioning them (see now also Longman, *Jeremiah, Lamentations*, 93; Thiessen [*Contesting Conversion*, 54–55] accepts the idea that Israelite circumcision differed from non-Israelite circumcision, though he does not accept the difference suggested by Steiner). Notably, others have suggested that the list is referring to a specific political situation, and that the prophet criticized the partners of a certain alliance. Thus, Wilhelm Rudolph suggested that the list of people refers to a specific historical setting, in which a number of peoples joined in a pact against Babylon (*Jeremiah*, HAT [Tübingen: Mohr Siebeck, 1947], 60–61; see also Thiessen, *Contesting Converstion*, 53). William L. Holladay agreed that this reflects an anti-Babylonian coalition led by Egypt (*Jeremiah 1: A Commentary on the Book of the Prophet Jeremiah, Chapters 1–25*, Hermeneia [Philadelphia: Fortress, 1986], 319). He summarized, "The point of the passage is that Yahweh will punish everyone in the coalition, pagans and Jews alike" (p. 320). And Douglas R. Jones explicitly wrote, "The nations specified are not the only ones which practiced circumcision" (*Jeremiah: Based on the Revised Standard Version*, NCB [Grand Rapids: Eerdmans, 1992], 170–71), adding, "It may be that those named have entered into an alliance with Egypt.… It is more likely that the list is rhetorical, and belongs to a time when those nations, which practiced circumcision, were friendly enough to be linked together for the purpose of the preacher." It appears, therefore, that if this interpretation is correct, not much can be learned from those who are not mentioned in the list, which is referring either to a specific political alliance or to a political atmosphere of such an alliance (and given the quick changes in the political circumstances at the time, there is no way we can reconstruct where the Philistines were politically at any given moment, nor can we date the prophecy with great precision).

II the Philistines were circumcised or, at least, that circumcision was important for them. Thus, a few objects unearthed at biblical Gath have been interpreted as phalli.[32] This interpretation is not certain, but, as noted by David Ben-Shlomo, these vessels probably depict circumcised phalli, "on account of their rather flat ends."[33] If Ben-Shlomo is correct, and since the artisans of the time probably differentiated between circumcised and uncircumcised phalli,[34] this might be significant.

Indirect Archaeological Evidence

The suggestion that the Philistines started to circumcise in Iron II is in line with the general acculturation (or fusion, or creolization) process the Philistines went through at the time. It is widely known that Philistine material culture was altered significantly in the course of the Iron Age. Trude Dothan's seminal work *The Philistines and Their Material Culture* deals with Iron I only, and an explanation for this is posited in the last paragraph of the book. After describing the events of the eleventh century, Dothan writes, "It should be stressed that it was during this

---

[32] Aren M. Maeir, "A New Interpretation of the Term ʿopalim (עפלים) in the Light of Recent Archaeological Finds from Philistia," *JSOT* 32 (2007): 28, http://dx.doi.org/10.1177/0309089207083762.

[33] David Ben Shlomo, *Philistine Iconography: A Wealth of Style and Symbolism*, OBO 241 (Fribourg: Academic Press; Göttingen: Vandenhoeck & Ruprecht, 2010), 58. Maeir had suggested that perhaps the objects depict erect phalli and that circumcision might not be visible ("New Interpretation of the Term ʿopalim," 28). But, as we will see below, it is likely that the artisans differentiated between circumcised and uncircumcised phalli.

[34] An erect phallus was depicted on one of the *situlae* uncovered in the Egyptian enclave in Ashkelon (Lawrence E. Stager, "Ashkelon and the Archaeology of Destruction: Kislev 604 BCE," *ErIsr* 25 [1996]: 69*). Interestingly, Maeir interpreted the entire group of *situlae* as uncircumcised phalli ("New Interpretation of the Term ʿopalim," 26). This view goes against the interpretation of the excavator and there is nothing to support it, but if Maeir is correct it shows that the artisans of the time went to the trouble of differentiating circumcised and uncircumcised phalli, hence strengthening the significance of the uncircumcised phalli from Gath. Notably, the artifacts from Ashkelon are Egyptian, and the above-mentioned depiction of an erect phallus is of an Egyptian god, found along with other Egyptian objects in what the excavator regards as an Egyptian enclave (Stager, "Ashkelon," 69*), thus rendering them irrelevant (even if the objects are indeed uncircumcised phalli) for the study of Philistine practices (contra Itzhaq Shai, "Was Circumcision Practiced in Philistia in the Iron Age II?" [in Hebrew], *ErIsr* 30 [Ben-Tor Volume, 2011], 415). We should also note that Ben-Shlomo mentions another object that he interprets as a circumcised phallus from Iron I (!) Ekron (*Philistine Iconography*, 58–59). A look at the photograph, however, casts doubt on the interpretation of the object, and Ben-Shlomo himself noted that the interpretation of all the objects is doubtful, thus suggesting that we should be careful in giving too much significance to the finds. Notably, Philip J. King discussed a circumcised phallus that was found in Gezer but this was a Canaanite site, and hence the find does not contribute to the present discussion ("Gezer and Circumcision," in *Confronting the Past: Archaeological and Historical Essays on Ancient Israel in Honor of William G. Dever*, ed. Seymour Gitin, J. Edward Wright, and J. P. Dessel [Winona Lake, IN: Eisenbrauns, 2006], 333–40).

period of greatest expansion that Philistine culture lost its uniqueness and vitality and slowly became assimilated into the surrounding Canaanite culture."[35] Other scholars followed, and the changes that took place in the Philistine material culture have been widely interpreted as an indication of their assimilation.[36] Following the work of Bryan J. Stone, Seymour Gitin, and others, it is generally accepted today that what we are witnessing is simply a weaker form of acculturation.[37] It seems that the Philistines, while adopting cultural traits of other peoples and losing many of their own traits, retained their identity at least until the late Iron Age.[38] Still, there is agreement that the Philistine material culture was drastically transformed at the time and that the Philistines lost most of their foreign, "Aegean-inspired" traits and adopted many "Levantine" ones.[39] The debate is only what to call this change: accul-

---

[35] Trude K. Dothan, *The Philistines and Their Material Culture* (New Haven: Yale University Press, 1982), 296.

[36] See Shlomo Bunimovitz, "Problems in the 'Ethnic' Identification of the Philistine Material Culture," *TA* 17 (1990): 219; Amihay Mazar, "No More 'Philistine Culture'? A Response to S. Bunimovitz" (in Hebrew), *Archaeologya* 1 (1986): 27; Trude K. Dothan and Moshe Dothan, *People of the Sea: The Search for the Philistines* (New York: Macmillan, 1992), 85–86; Trude K. Dothan, "The Arrival of the Sea Peoples: Cultural Diversity in Early Iron Age Canaan," in *Recent Excavations in Israel: Studies in Iron Age Archaeology*, ed. Seymour Gitin and William G. Dever, AASOR 49 (Winona Lake, IN: Eisenbrauns for ASOR, 1989), 11–12.

[37] Bryan J. Stone, "The Philistines and Acculturation: Culture Change and Ethnic Continuity in the Iron Age," *BASOR* 298 (1995): 7–32; Seymour Gitin, "The Philistines: Neighbors of the Canaanites, Phoenicians and Israelites," in *100 Years of American Archaeology in the Middle East: Proceedings of the American Schools of Oriental Research Centennial Celebration, Washington DC, April 2000*, ed. Douglas R. Clark and Victor H. Matthews (Boston: ASOR, 2004), 57–85; Seymour Gitin, "Philistia in Transition: The Tenth Century and Beyond," in *Mediterranean Peoples in Transition: Thirteenth to Early Tenth Centuries BCE*, ed. Seymour Gitin, Amihai Mazar, and Ephraim Stern (Jerusalem: Israel Exploration Society, 1998), 162–83.

[38] Stone, "Philistines and Acculturation"; Eph'al, "Philistine Entity and the Origin of the Name"; Aharon Kempinski, "Philological Evidence on the Problem of Philistine Assimilation" (in Hebrew), *Archeologya* 1 (1986): 28–30; idem, "Some Philistine Names from the Kingdom of Gaza," *IEJ* 37 (1987): 20–24.

[39] See, e.g., Yohanan Aharoni, *The Archaeology of the Land of Israel* (Philadelphia: Westminster, 1981), 188; Gabriel Barkay, "The Iron Age II–III," in *The Archaeology of Ancient Israel*, ed. Amnon Ben-Tor (New Haven: Yale University Press, 1992), 334; Bunimovitz, "Problems in the 'Ethnic' Identification"; Dothan, *Philistines and Their Material Culture*, 296; idem, "Arrival of the Sea Peoples," 11–12; Carl S. Ehrlich, "'How the Mighty Are Fallen': The Philistines in Their Tenth Century Context," in *The Age of Solomon: Scholarship at the Turn of the Millennium*, ed. Lowell K. Handy, SHCANE 11 (Leiden: Brill, 1997), 190, 198–201; Amihai Mazar, *Archaeology of the Land of the Bible, 10,000–586 B.C.E.* (New York: Doubleday, 1990), 328; idem, "The Iron Age I," in Ben-Tor, *Archaeology of Ancient Israel*, 301; Joe Uziel, "The Development Process of Philistine Material Culture: Assimilation, Acculturation and Everything in Between," *Levant* 39 (2007): 168–69, http://dx.doi.org/10.1179/lev.2007.39.1.165; Gitin, "Philistines in the Books of Kings," 325; see also Benjamin Mazar, *The Early Biblical Period: Historical Studies* (Jerusalem: Israel Exploration Society, 1986), 75–82; and even Shai, "Was Circumcision Practiced?" 414; Aren M. Maeir, "Philistia Transforming: Fresh Evidence from Tell es-Sâfi/Gath on the Transformational

turation, fusion, hybridization, creolization, or another term.[40] Thus, Joe Uziel wrote, "It therefore seems that the process of fusion was not completed until late in the Iron Age I or early in the Iron Age II. From this point on, the changes in the Philistine culture are minimal."[41] Even Itzhaq Shai wrote that "during the transition from the Iron I to the Iron II much of the uniqueness of the Philistine material culture disappeared, and it became quite similar to that of their neighbors."[42] And Maeir summarized: "the overall trend appears to be that during the Iron Age IIA, Philistine culture went through a rather intensive process of change. A large portion of the foreign, mostly 'Aegean' components that typified the Iron Age I assemblages are lost."[43] He referred to those as "deep changes."[44]

The changes include, for example, the complete disappearance of the decorated, Aegean-inspired Philistine pottery at the beginning of the Iron Age II.[45] In addition, most Philistine sites exhibit a drastic decline in the consumption of pork,[46]

Trajectory of the Philistine Culture," in *The Philistines and Other "Sea Peoples" in Text and Archaeology*, ed. Ann E. Killebrew and Gunnar Lehmann, ABS 15 (Atlanta: Society of Biblical Literature, 2013), 240–41. In a recent publication, Maeir, Louise A. Hitchcock, and Liora Kolska Horwitz appear to deny this change, but they do not address most of the relevant data ("The Construction and Transformation of Philistine Identity," *OJA* 32 [2013]: 1–38, http://dx.doi.org/10.1111/ojoa.12000). As all scholars are aware (including Maeir, "Philistia Transforming"), Philistine material culture went through drastic changes at the time, and it is impossible to ignore this overall pattern (see also Avraham Faust, "From a Regional Power to a Peaceful Neighbor: Philistia in the Transition from Iron Age I to Iron Age II," *IEJ* 63 [2013]: 174–204; Avraham Faust and Justin Lev-Tov, "Philistia and the Philistines in the Iron Age I: Interaction, Ethnic Dynamics and Boundary Maintenance," *Hiphil Novum* 1 [2014]: 1–24).

[40] E.g., Stone, "Philistines and Acculturation"; Uziel, "Development Process of Philistine Material Culture"; David Ben-Shlomo, Itzhaq Shai, and Aren M. Maeir, "Late Philistine Decorated Ware 9 ('Ashdod Ware'): Typology, Chronology, and Production Centers," *BASOR* 335 (2004): 1–35.

[41] Uziel, "Development Process of Philistine Material Culture," 169; see also 168.

[42] Shai, "Was Circumcision Practiced?" 414 (my translation); see also 413.

[43] Maeir, "Philistia Transforming," 241.

[44] Ibid.; see also 240.

[45] Dothan, *Philistines and Their Material Culture*, 218; Dothan, "Arrival of the Sea Peoples," 11–12; Barkay, "Iron Age II–III," 334; Bunimovitz, "Problems in the 'Ethnic' Identification"; Uziel, "Development Process of Philistine Material Culture," 169; Mazar, *Archaeology of the Land of the Bible*, 328; idem, "Iron Age I," 301; Aharoni, *Archaeology of the Land of Israel*, 188; also Erlich, "'How the Mighty Are Fallen,'" 198–99; Maeir, "Philistia Transforming," 240. See now the extensive discussion in Avraham Faust, "Pottery and Society in Iron Age Philistia: Feasting, Identity, Economy and Gender," *BASOR* 373 (2015): 167–98.

[46] Brian Hesse and Paula Wapnish, "Can Pig Remains Be Used for Ethnic Diagnosis in the Ancient Near East?" in *The Archaeology of Israel: Constructing the Past, Interpreting the Present*, ed. Neil Asher Silberman and David Small, JSOTSup 237 (Sheffield: Sheffield Academic, 1997), 263; Justin Lev-Tov, "Zooarchaeology and Relations of Power during the Neo-Assyrian Empire: An Example from Tel Miqne-Ekron," paper presented at the ASOR Annual Meeting, Boston, 17–19 November 1999; idem, "The Faunal Remains: Animal Economy in the Iron Age I," in

and this is also the time when the Philistines apparently adopted the Canaanite script.⁴⁷ These are but examples of the material changes the Philistines experienced at the time discussed here.

In a similar vein, during the transition from Iron I to Iron II there were drastic changes in settlement patterns in Philistia, and most of the sites that existed in the

---

Mark W. Meehl, Trude Dothan, and Seymour Gitin, *Tel Miqne-Ekron Excavations 1995–1996: Field INE East Slope, Iron Age I (Early Philistine Period)*, Tel Miqne-Ekron Final Field Report Series 8 (Jerusalem: W. F. Albright Institute of Archaeological Research; Institute of Archaeology, Hebrew University of Jerusalem, 2006), 207–33; Brian Hesse, Deidre N. Fulton, and Paula Wapnish, "Animal Remains," in *Ashkelon 3: The Seventh Century B.C.*, ed. Lawrence E. Stager, J. David Schloen, and Daniel M. Master, Harvard Semitic Museum Publications (Winona Lake, IN: Eisenbrauns, 2011), 624–30; Amihai Mazar and Nava Panitz Cohen, *Timnah (Tel Batash), 2.1: The Finds from the First Millennium BCE: Text*, Qedem 42 (Jerusalem: Institute of Archaeology, Hebrew University of Jerusalem, 2001), 283. The only exception is Gath; see Justin Lev-Tov, "A Preliminary Report on the Late Bronze and Iron Age, Faunal, Assemblages from Tell es-Safi/Gath," in *Tell es-Safi/Gath 1*, ed. Aren M. Maeir, ÄAT 69 (Wiesbaden: Harrassowitz, 2012), 589–612; Avraham Faust and Justin Lev-Tov, "The Constitution of Philistine Identity: Ethnic Dynamics in 12th–10th Centuries Philistia," *OJA* 30 (2011): 14 n. 3, 26 n. 11; see now also Lidar Sapir-Hen, Guy Bar-Oz, Yuval Gadot, and Israel Finkelstein, "Pig Husbandry in Iron Age Israel and Judah: New Insights Regarding the Origin of the 'Taboo,'" *ZDPV* 129 (2013): 11, 13. Maeir, Hitchcock, and Horwitz challenge the idea that pork was ethnically significant at the time ("Construction and Transformation"), but the examples they bring to counter the clear pattern are from Canaanite sites, which they label "Philistines." Thus, the fact that pork constituted less than 1 percent of the diet at Qubur el-Walayda (Edward F. Maher, "Late Iron Age Faunal Remains from Qubur al-Walaydah," *WO* 40 [2010]: 268–72, http://dx.doi.org/10.13109/wdor.2010.40.2.268) is used to "show" that some Philistines did not consume much pork (Maeir, Hitchcock, and Horwitz, "Construction and Transformation," 5–6). But even before the faunal remains were analyzed, the excavator questioned the "Philistine" nature of the site (Gunnar Lehmann, "Cooking Pots and Loomweights in a 'Philistine' Village: Preliminary Report on the Excavations at Qubur el-Walaydah, Israel," in *On Cooking Pots, Drinking Cups, Loomweights and Ethnicity in Bronze Age Cyprus and Neighbouring Regions: An International Archaeological Symposium Held in Nicosia, November 6th–7th, 2010*, ed. Vassos Karageorghis and Ourania Kouka [Nicosia: A. G. Leventis Foundation, 2011], 291). Indeed, the faunal evidence unearthed confirms those suspicions; that is, the site was Canaanite rather than Philistine (see also Faust, "From a Regional Power"; Faust and Lev-Tov, "Philistia and the Philistines"). The only Philistine site in which pork continued to be consumed in significant percentages in Iron II is Gath (see Lev-Tov, "Preliminary Report on the Late Bronze"; Faust and Lev-Tov, "Constitution of Philistine Identity"), but this seems to be the exception rather than the rule (for the reasons for the situation in Gath, see Faust and Lev-Tov, "Constitution of Philistine Identity," 26 n. 11; Faust, "From a Regional Power").

⁴⁷ Itamar Singer, "Egyptians, Canaanites, and Philistines in the Period of the Emergence of Israel," in *From Nomadism to Monarchy: Archaeological and Historical Aspects of Early Israel*, ed. Israel Finkelstein and Nadav Na'aman (Jerusalem: Yad Ben-Zvi, 1994), 332–37; Uziel, "Development Process of Philistine Material Culture," 167; even Maeir, Hitchcock, and Horwitz ("Construction and Transformation," 10–12) had to acknowledge that the Philistines adopted a local language (p. 10; they did not address the adoption of a local script), and this is the significant pattern (see also Maeir, "Philistia Transforming," 241; Uziel, "Development Process of Philistine Material Culture," 167; Faust and Lev-Tov, "Philistia and the Philistines").

region during the late Iron I were destroyed or abandoned in the early Iron IIA (on the basis of data from excavations).[48] The issue is addressed at length elsewhere,[49] and suffice it to note that out of twenty-two late Iron I sites excavated in the region, only eight sites continued to exist in Iron II, and at least two or three of those probably came under Israelite control,[50] and some of the remaining five or six sites declined in area. This is the context for the above-mentioned cultural changes in Philistia.

It is quite clear, therefore, that the Philistines went through a rapid process of culture change at the time, and when they ceased to manufacture their unique, Aegean-inspired ceramics (and adopted locally syntaxed decoration; Ashdod Ware), abandoned the foreign linear script (and adopted the local Phoenician script), reduced the amount of pork they consumed (and increased the percentage of sheep and goats in their diet), they also stopped being "uncircumcised" and began to practice circumcision, like their neighbors.

III. Discussion

In light of all the above, it is quite clear why the later texts (e.g., in the books of Kings or the classical prophets), whose historicity is usually less questioned, cease to use the pejorative term "uncircumcised" to describe the Philistines—the latter were simply not "uncircumcised" anymore, having adopted circumcision in their acculturation process. Interestingly, such a situation is not without an ethnographic parallel. Hodder refers to the Elmolo, who in the past "did not circumcise males or have *moran*, but by 1958 had begun to adopt both these traits from the Samburu"; this was accompanied by the adoption of some other Samburu customs.[51]

---

[48] Regarding the large sites, see already Amihai Mazar, "The Search for David and Solomon: An Archaeological Pespective," in Israel Finkelstein and Amihai Mazar, *The Quest for the Historical Israel: Debating Archaeology and the History of Early Israel. Invited Lectures Delivered at the Sixth Biennial Colloquium of the International Institute for Secular Humanistic Judaism, Detroit, October 2005*, ed. Brian B. Schmidt, ABS 17 (Atlanta: Society of Biblical Literature, 2007), 135; Lawrence E. Stager, "Forging an Identity: The Emergence of Ancient Israel," in *The Oxford History of the Biblical World*, ed. Michael D. Coogan (New York: Oxford University Press, 1998), 171; Carl S. Ehrlich, *The Philistines in Transition: A History from ca. 1000–730 B.C.E.*, SHCANE 10 (Leiden: Brill, 1996), 53–55; for a detailed discussion, see Faust, "From a Regional Power," and many references there.

[49] Faust, "From a Regional Power."

[50] E.g., Mazar and Panitz-Cohen, *Timnah (Tel Batash)*, 274, 277–78; James W. Hardin, Christopher A. Rollston, and Jeffrey A. Blakely, "Biblical Geography in Southwestern Judah," NEA 75 (2012): 24–25, 34.

[51] Hodder, *Symbols iin Action*, 101. For past and present practices, see also W. S. Dyson and V. E. Fuchs, "The Elmolo," *Journal of the Royal Anthropological Institute of Great Britain and Ireland* 67 (1937): 336, http://dx.doi.org/10.2307/2844144; Katherine M. Grillo, "The Materiality of

The present discussion may have implications for the historical credibility of the texts, especially segments of the Deuteronomistic History (e.g., in the books of Samuel). There is a clear dichotomy between early and late in the Deuteronomistic History: texts that refer to the premonarchic era use the term "uncircumcised" to describe the Philistines, whereas texts that refer to the monarchic period do not use the term for such purposes. This distinction is quite consistent, and it is difficult to attribute it to editing, especially as it is not unique to the Deuteronomistic History and corresponds to what we see in other sources. While there is agreement that the texts discussed are (probably much) later than Iron I, the pattern is clear and calls for an explanation. Since we have seen that the dichotomy probably corresponds to historical reality, the usage of "uncircumcised" in relation to Iron I must mean that the author(s) had some ancient texts or other reliable sources or traditions in front of him/them, from which he/they drew both the stories and the term. In light of the accepted view regarding the time of authorship,[52] it appears that the author(s) employed a term that was not used in his/their own time to refer to the Philistines of the premonarchic era.

This can be supported by the fact that 1 Chronicles—written probably during the Persian period—uses the term ערל ("uncircumcised") only once, while 1–2 Samuel use it quite often (above), although the stories told in these works are similar. The editor of Chronicles probably used his own language when rewriting the stories, therefore reducing the usage of this old term significantly. Hence, it is reasonable to claim that some of the stories relating to the premonarchic era in 1–2 Samuel are old and could not have been invented during Iron II or later (regardless of their historicity).[53]

Mobile Pastoralism: Ethnoarchaeological Perspectives from Samburu, Kenya" (PhD diss., Washington University, 2012), 48.

[52] See, e.g., Otto Eissfeldt, *The Old Testament: An Introduction* (Oxford: Blackwell, 1966); Friedman, *Who Wrote the Bible?*; Alexander Rofé, *Introduction to the Composition of the Pentateuch* (in Hebrew; Jerusalem: Academon, 1994); Christoph Levin, *The Old Testament: A Brief Introduction* (Princeton: Princeton University Press, 2001); Thomas Römer, *The So-Called Deuteronomistic History: A Sociological, Historical and Literary Introduction* (London: T&T Clark, 2005); Witte et al., *Die deuteronomistischen Geschichtswerke*.

[53] Notably, Israel Finkelstein claimed recently that the traditions regarding the Philistines can be dated to the late Iron Age ("The Philistine in the Bible: A Late-Monarchic Perspective," *JSOT* 27 [2002]: 131–67). While it is possible that some of the traditions are late, the present discussion shows that some of the traditions could not have been invented that late and either must have been written closer to the time they describe or were based on "old" traditions (for early elements, see also Jeffrey R. Zorn, "Reconsidering Goliath: An Iron Age I Philistine Chariot Warrior," *BASOR* 360 [2010]: 1–22; Lawrence E. Stager, "Biblical Philistines: A Hellenistic Literary Creation?" in *"I Will Speak the Riddles of Ancient Times": Archaeological and Historical Studies in Honor of Amihai Mazar*, ed. A. Maeir and P. de Miroschedji [Winona Lake, IN: Eisenbrauns, 2006], 375–84. See also Itamar Singer, "The Philistines in the Bible: A Short Rejoinder to a New Perspective," in Killebrew and Lehmann, *Philistines and Other "Sea Peoples,"* 375–84.

Interestingly, the fact that in Iron II there were not really uncircumcised groups (עֲרֵלִים) in Israel's immediate vicinity explains why circumcision was not an "issue" for P (or for most other sources for that matter).[54] The only exceptions are some early texts/traditions/memories in the Deuteronomistic History, and all the other sources appear to be later and were probably written, edited, or compiled when the Philistines were indeed circumcised, and therefore it was "not an issue."

IV. Summary

The biblical description of circumcision led scholars to view its significance to ancient Israelite society either as related to rites of fertility and marriage or as demarcating ethnic boundaries, especially with the Philistines. The first view is based mainly on references to the practice in the Pentateuch, and especially in the P source, while the other interpretation relies on some of the references in the historical books, especially the books of Samuel. The two explanations, however, are not mutually exclusive, and it is likely that the various explanations that were deduced from the biblical source material reflect both differing perspectives on the practice over time and different views by different social factions at the same time. The custom that was practiced by many groups in the ancient Near East, including the Israelites, had an internal explanation that members of this society used to justify it. Later, when the Israelites interacted with uncircumcised peoples, the existing practice was useful in delineating boundaries and was invested with a new meaning. At this time it was very sensitive ethnically. The custom continued to be practiced also after its ethnic significance decreased (though it probably still had an ethnic dimension, even if latent), and at this time other meanings or explanations developed (or were reemphasized) and became more important (again).

As far as the ethnic quality of the trait is concerned, since many groups in the ancient Near East practiced circumcision, it is commonly accepted that circumcision played a role as an ethnic marker mainly, or probably only, against the Philistines. The Philistines were a group that was considered to originate (and many of its members probably were) from outside of western Asia who did not practice circumcision, and whose foreignness was a major tool in shaping its identity against the "natives."[55]

The treatment of the Philistines in the biblical texts as uncircumcised, however, is somewhat peculiar. All the texts that depict the Philistines as uncircumcised are projected to the premonarchic era, regardless of their date, source, or even

---

[54] Fox "Sign of the Covenant," 595; also Bernat, *Sign of the Covenant*, 132.

[55] Stone, "Philistines and Acculturation," 23; Faust and Lev-Tov, "Constitution of Philistine Identity"; Faust and Lev-Tov, "Philistia and the Philistines"; Faust, "From a Regional Power." Interestingly, in some books of the LXX Philistines were translated as "foreigners" (Thiessen, *Contested Conversion*, 45).

genre. Not a single text, of whatever nature, uses this pejorative to refer to the Philistines of the monarchic era, and this seems to suggest that the Philistines were practicing circumcision in Iron II. It is not only the clear distinction between the uncircumcised Philistines of Iron I and the not-uncircumcised Philistines of Iron II within the same sources (e.g., within the Deuteronomistic History) that indicates that the Philistines adopted circumcision in Iron II. This is supported also by the fact that all sources of whatever genre never deviate from this division (thus, the Prophets also never call the Philistines uncircumcised). This clear-cut dichotomy seems to suggest that this distinction reflects a historical situation and that the Philistines started to circumcise in Iron II.

Furthermore, there are additional sources that direct us to the same conclusion. The fact that the Philistines were uncircumcised in Iron I is supported by an Egyptian source. That they were circumcised later is supported by Herodotus, as well as by their omission from the list of uncircumcised people in Ezek 32:17–32. The few circumcised phalli unearthed in Iron II Gath might also support the suggestion that they were circumcised at the time (but the interpretation of these objects is very problematic). Finally, the overall process of Philistine acculturation (or fusion, creolization, hybridization, etc.)—a process in which the Philistines lost many of their foreign and unique traits during the early Iron II and adopted Levantine behaviors and traits—seems to suggest that it is very likely that the Philistines adopted circumcision also. Actually, given the scope of this process, it would have been quite surprising if they had not! Hence, the idea that the Philistines began to circumcise should not surprise us and, given the overall changes in Philistine material culture, might even be expected.

A Stratified Account of Jephthah's Negotiations and Battle: Judges 11:12–33 from an Archaeological Perspective

ELIZABETH BLOCH-SMITH
bloch-smith@msn.com
123 Upland Terrace, Bala Cynwyd, PA 19004

The account of Jephthah's battle against the Ammonites in Judg 11:12–33 contains glaring inconsistencies. Negotiations preceding the battle invoke Israelite conflicts with Amorites and Moabites—none of which pertain to Ammon. An archaeological survey of the vacillating fortunes of Transjordanian Moab, Ammon, and Gilead suggests historical contexts and approximate dates for periods of territorial contention between Israel and its neighbors. Reading the invocation of war against Sihon/Moab (early ninth century) in the context of later conflicts with Ammon (late ninth or eighth century) explains some of the apparent inconsistencies and dates the historical contexts invoked in this and other biblical texts that pit Israel against these Transjordanian nations. Archaeological remains from Ḥesban (Heshbon) and Dhiban (Dibon) add datable parameters for texts or the updating of passages that feature these sites. So, for example, in the Judges text, celebrating Heshbon rather than Dibon as Sihon's capital city likely dates this version of events to the seventh or perhaps the sixth century.

I. INTRODUCTION AND METHODOLOGY

Judges 11:12–33 explains the Ammonite invasion of Gilead as retaliation for earlier events. To justify the attack, an unnamed Ammonite king accuses the Israelites en route from Egypt of conquering his territory from the Arnon (Wadi Mujib) to the Jabbok (Wadi Zarqa) (11:13) (fig. 1). In response, Jephthah rehearses

---

This article benefitted from critiques by my life and intellectual partner, Mark S. Smith, of New York University; the 2011 Albright Institute for Archaeological Research fellows; the 2012 Colloquium for Biblical Research participants; and a *JBL* reviewer. I gratefully acknowledge funding from the National Endowment for the Humanities; any views, findings, conclusions, or recommendations expressed in this publication do not necessarily reflect those of the National

Israel's accommodating the kings of Edom and Moab and battling Sihon the Amorite, with no mention of Ammon (11:16–22).[1]

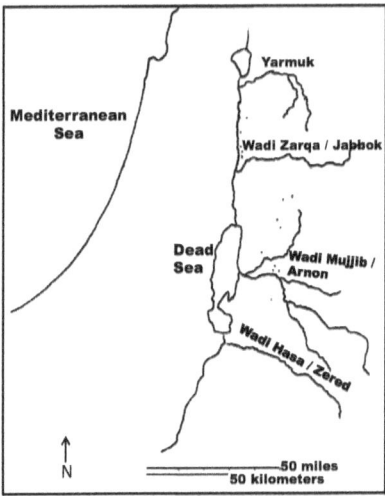

Figure 1. Major Wadis of Transjordan

This version of events is riddled with inconsistencies. First, the Ammonite king claims land between the Arnon and the Jabbok that the Israelites conquered from Sihon the Amorite. Second, YHWH gave the contested region of Ar along the Arnon to Moab as an inalienable possession (Deut 2:9), yet Ammon now makes proprietary claims to the same land.[2] Third, in negotiating with the Ammonite king, Jephthah invokes the Moabite god Chemosh, the Moabite king Balak son of Zippor, and disputed territory including the Moabite heartland along the Arnon (Judg 11:24–26). Fourth, victorious Jephthah routs the Ammonites from Aroer to

---

Endowment for the Humanities. All dates are BCE unless otherwise indicated. For site names, the most common spellings are employed and "Khirbet," "Tall/Tell/Tel," and "Rujm" have been omitted, as all place-names, with exceptions noted, refer to the archaeological site rather than to a contemporary settlement with the same name. Bible translations are from *JPS Hebrew-English Tanakh: The Traditional Hebrew Text and the New JPS Translation*, 2nd ed. (Philadelphia: Jewish Publication Society of America, 1999).

[1] Numbers 21:21–32 and Deut 2:24–36 offer expanded versions of these episodes. The relationship of Judg 11 to Num 21–22 and Deut 2–3 is beyond the scope of this article, but see the Judges commentaries of Baruch Levine (*Numbers 21–36: A New Translation with Introduction and Commentary*, AB 4A [New York: Doubleday, 2000]) and Walter Groß (*Richter*, HThKAT [Freiburg im Breisgau: Herder, 2009], 557–65) for representative discussions and bibliography.

[2] To complicate the picture further, according to Num 32:33–38 and Josh 13:15–28, the same land was also assigned to Reuben and Gad.

Abel-keramim in the Rabbat-Ammon vicinity, to the north of Jahaz and the contested Moabite plateau (Judg 11:32-33).

Various historical explanations for this seemingly confused account have been proffered. Scholars identified Judg 11:19-22 as an insertion into a description of Ammonite aggression against Gilead (Uwe Becker, G. A. Cooke, Otto Eissfeldt, George Foot Moore, J. A. W. Richter, J. Alberto Soggin, Barry G. Webb) or a version of Israelite defeat of Moab (Dieter Böhler, C. F. Burney, Karl Budde, Carl Heinrich Cornill, Walter Groß, H. Holzinger, Charles Foster Kent, Rudolph Kittel, Marie-Joseph Lagrange, Baruch Levine, Wilhelm Nowack).[3] The intersection of the two events—war with Sihon in the context of battle against Ammon—has not been addressed.

An archaeological approach demonstrating changing geopolitics offers historical contexts for Israelite conquest in the territory from the Arnon to the Jabbok (Judg 11:19-22) and for Ammonite aggression directed against Israelite Gilead (11:12-15, 28, 32-33). Physical remains in conjunction with extrabiblical texts situate Israelite combat with Sihon/Moab and with Ammon in the early ninth and later ninth to eighth centuries respectively. Past warfare with Moab is invoked in the context of the present battle with Ammon. Jephthah's speeches in vv. 15 and 23-27 effect the transition from the previous Sihon/Moabite to the current Ammonite arena.

This study distinguishes between the literary construct "biblical Israel" and the archaeological entity "ancient Israel." In recounting biblical Israel's history, textual additions and revisions as well as variant versions may obscure and blur chronological changes and developments, as appears to be the case in Judg 11. In contrast to "biblical Israel," archaeologists reconstructing "ancient Israel" work with physical remains that permit absolute and relative dating of specific features, events, and general historical contexts. "Ancient Israel" constitutes an independent entity—insofar as archaeologists are able to ignore biblical testimony—against which the biblical text may be assessed.

---

[3] Representative works include George Foot Moore, *A Critical and Exegetical Commentary on Judges*, ICC (Edinburgh: T&T Clark, 1895); Marie-Joseph Lagrange, *Le livre des Juges*, EBib (Paris: Librairie Lecoffre, 1903); C. F. Burney, *The Book of Judges: With Introduction and Notes* (London: Rivingtons, 1918); Otto Eissfeldt, *Die Quellen des Richterbuches: In synoptischer Anordnung ins Deutsche übersetzt, samt einer in Einleitung und Noten gegebenen Begründung* (Leipzig: Hinrichs, 1925); Robert G. Boling, *Judges: Introduction, Translation, and Commentary*, AB 6A (Garden City, NY: Doubleday, 1975); and Dieter Böhler, *Jiftach und die Tora: Eine intertextuelle Auslegung von Ri 10,6-12,7*, ÖBS 34 (Frankfurt am Main: Lang, 2008). Most recently, Jack M. Sasson considered the declaration of war an ex post facto literary creation crafted to demean Israel's enemies and draw YHWH into the fray; historical accuracy played no explicit role in the account (*Judges 1-12: A New Translation with Introduction and Commentary*, AYB 6D [New Haven: Yale University Press, 2014], 434-35).

Efforts to correlate archaeological evidence with biblical testimony raise two methodological issues. First, the initial version of an allegedly historical account likely draws on actual geopolitical circumstances and events with resonance for the audience in order to foster credibility and to stoke an emotional response. Accordingly, the earliest accounts of battles against Sihon/Moab and Ammon arguably date from periods within memory of Moabite and Ammonite hostility against Israel. By analogy, fifty years ago portrayals of American conflict and doomsday scenarios, whether historical or satirical, were set in the context of the Soviet–American Cold War. A Soviet spy triggered an emotional response from those who experienced the Cuban Missile Crisis and the arms race between the United States and the Soviet Union. Suggesting that historical reality provides the context and setting for a biblical account is not an argument for the veracity of specific details. Fabricated or manipulated elements may be introduced into an actual historical context for a variety of reasons including to create a sense of "epic distance" and an idealized past, and for entertainment, pedagogic, religious, or political purposes.[4]

In our passage, the inclusion of folkloristic-sounding elements raises the second methodological issue, namely, to identify criteria for determining the veracity of a narrated element. Archaeology and extrabiblical texts bolster arguments for historicity in two ways. First, material finds confirm specific biblical elements ranging from individuals, to battles, to peaceful or contentious foreign relations. Prominent examples include the Jerusalem stamp seals belonging to Yehucal son of Shelemiyahu and Gedaliyahu son of Pashhur, two of King Zedekiah's court officials named in Jeremiah (Jer 37:3, 38:1), and the Nineveh palace reliefs depicting the siege of Lachish by the Assyrian king Sennacherib (2 Kgs 18:17, 19:8).[5] Additionally, archaeology and extrabiblical texts attest to time-bound biblical elements, such as a specific structure in a specified location. Judges 9 refers to the destruction of a Shechem temple capable of accommodating one thousand men and women (Judg 9:46, 49). Excavation unearthed a massive tower-temple destroyed in the late twelfth century (1125/1100 BCE) and replaced by a granary in the ninth or eighth century.[6] Based on this physical evidence, a massacre story likely originated in the period within memory of the temple's late-twelfth-century demise, a memory that would have faded with the construction of the ninth- or eighth-century granary that obscured the earlier ruins.

---

[4] Ian Morris, "The Use and Abuse of Homer," *ClAnt* 5 (1986): 81–138, here 89.

[5] Eilat Mazar, *The Palace of King David: Excavations at the Summit of the City of David Preliminary Report of Seasons 2005–2007* (Jerusalem: Shoham, 2009), 66–71; David Ussishkin, *The Conquest of Lachish by Sennacherib*, Publications of the Institute of Archaeology 6 (Tel Aviv: Tel Aviv University, 1982).

[6] Joe Seger, "Shechem," *OEANE* 5:19–23, here 22–23; Lawrence Stager, "The Shechem Temple: Where Abimelech Massacred a Thousand," *BAR* 29.4 (2003): 26–35, 66–69.

Other criteria may help identify historical elements. In contrast to generalized topographic appellations such as Ramah ("height"), Gibeah ("hill"), or Mizpeh ("lookout"), distinctive names such as Minnith of Judg 11:33 may attest to historical sites. The addition of a second name to orient a later audience indicates a known place or people. Chaldean Ur (Gen 11:31) constitutes the parade example, with the third-to early-second-millennium Sumerian city of Ur referenced by the ninth-century Chaldeans.[7] Finally, etiologies offer an explanation for a putative historical reality. The object of the explanation, rather than the explanation itself, may reflect the reality at the time. In an example from Judges, the naming of Ramath-Lehi, where Samson discarded a jawbone (Judg 15:17), perhaps signifies a locale with that name, regardless of the name's derivation.

Any attempt to identify historical realities behind the Jephthah story must acknowledge the inclusion of elements that belie the chapter's historicity in its current form. Jephthah's lineage as the son of the eponymous Gilead, conferring legendary character, and an unnamed prostitute, denoting marginal status, and his vaguely stated burial "in one of the towns of Gilead" compromise his historical status (Judg 11:1, 12:7). Nameless principal participants, including the king of Ammon and Jephthah's daughter, further undermine the veracity of the received text (Judg 11:12, 34–40). Comparing Judg 11 to the Num 21 and Deut 2 versions of events also raises questions of literary dependence, relative chronology, and historicity.

Jephthah might be just another fish story. Comparable to the prophet Jonah ben Amittai named in 2 Kgs 14:25, who posthumously assumes a starring role in the book of Jonah, Jephthah of 1 Sam 12:11 might have been a forgotten hero resurrected to fight the Ammonites. However, our story was likely not fabricated out of whole cloth. Archaeology and texts, both biblical and extrabiblical, attest to Israelite subjugation of Moabite territory and conflict with Ammon for control of Gilead offering historical contexts for the events related.

Chronological Considerations and Archaeological Caveats

A consideration of archaeological evidence pertaining to the historical contexts for the battles described in Judg 11 requires chronological limits. Foreign empires interacting with our region provide the necessary parameters. Pharaoh Merneptah contributed the *terminus post quem* with his late-thirteenth-century mention of a people "Israel." Moab may date from the thirteenth century as well if the original text of a Luxor depiction of Ramses II's conquest of an abandoned fortified settlement reads "Land of Moab."[8] The name occurs with certainty in the

---

[7] Richard Hess, "Chaldea," *ABD* 1:886–87, here 886.
[8] Timothy Harrison, "'The Land of Mēdeba' and Early Iron Age Mādabā," in *Studies on Iron Age Moab and Neighbouring Areas in Honour of Michèle Daviau*, ed. Piotr Bienkowski, ANESSup

ninth-century stela of Mesha king of Moab. The earliest extrabiblical attestations to an Ammonite kingdom date to the late ninth or early eighth century: a king of Ammon paid taxes to Tiglath-pileser III of Assyria, and the late-ninth- or early-eighth-century Citadel inscription refers to a monumental construction suggestive of a centralized authority able to muster the necessary resources.[9] Assyria supplied the *terminus ante quem*. Late-eighth-century campaigns to the region left the area depopulated and life disrupted; the northern kingdom of Israel ceased to exist. Arguably, "Israel" of our text might represent Israelites broadly rather than the more specific northern kingdom allowing for a later date. However, the book of Judges focuses on northern territory, tribes, and geopolitical relations, with only two explicit references to Judah (1:1–20, 19:1–2), anchoring the precipitating events in northern, Israelite traditions. A Persian-period context is untenable if the account originates with historical interaction between Israel and its Transjordanian adversaries, Moab and Ammon.

This study employs the traditional "high chronology" favored by many Transjordanian excavators in order to facilitate comparisons among Transjordanian sites (though it complicates Cisjordanian correlations).[10] Iron IIA begins with the gradual resumption of settled and urban life in ca. 1000 BCE and ends in ca. 925 BCE with Pharaoh Sheshonq's unsuccessful campaign to restore Egyptian suzerainty.[11] Iron IIB covers the period from Sheshonq's campaign to the Assyrian annexation of the north in 722 BCE. During this period urban life revived with the rise of strong kingdoms. The Aramean Tel Dan inscription, the Moabite Mesha Stela, and the Amman Citadel inscription of the mid-ninth through the early eighth century proclaimed and glorified the new, royal polities. Each nation-state evolved a distinctive material culture sufficiently divergent to delineate its territorial vicissitudes or cultural spheres. Not surprisingly, the growth of the kingdoms led to regional conflicts, an important datum for our study.

---

29 (Leuven: Peeters, 2009), 27–45, here 30 n. 17; Bruce Routledge, *Moab in the Iron Age: Hegemony, Polity, Archaeology*, Archaeology, Culture, and Society (Philadelphia: University of Pennsylvania Press, 2004), 7, 58.

[9] "Tiglath-Pileser III (744–727): Campaigns against Syria and Palestine," trans. John A. Wilson (*ANET*, 282); Burton MacDonald, *"East of the Jordan": Territories and Sites of the Hebrew Scriptures*, ASOR Books 6 (Boston: American Schools of Oriental Research, 2000), 160; Walter E. Aufrecht, *A Corpus of Ammonite Inscriptions*, ANETS 4 (Lewiston, NY: Mellen, 1989), 154–57.

[10] Larry Herr exemplifies the commonly employed Transjordanian chronological scheme ("The Iron Age II Period: Emerging Nations," *BA* 60 [1997]: 114–83). For an introduction to the chronological debates and their repercussions, see Thomas E. Levy and Thomas Higham, "Introduction: Radiocarbon Dating and the Iron Age of the Southern Levant: Problems and Potentials for the Oxford Conference," in *The Bible and Radiocarbon Dating: Archaeology, Text and Science*, ed. Thomas E. Levy and Thomas Higham (London: Equinox, 2005), 3–14.

[11] This historical reconstruction is based on destructions north of the Jabbok. South of the Jabbok, the poorly defined material culture of this period derives largely from tombs.

Turning to the archaeological evidence, a few caveats are necessary. First, certain regions relevant to this study are poorly known, including the plateau north of the Jabbok. Second, pottery typologies are improving, but some excavations and numerous surveys combine Iron IIA and IIB into a single category or distinguish only between Iron I and Iron II, limiting the usefulness of their work for this project. Third, preclassical sites typically have limited exposure, so excavation may not yield a representative picture of the settlement.

II. Historical Contexts for the Warfare of Judges 11:12–33

A. Moab

1. Moab in the Bible and the Mesha Stela

Moab's territory extended from the Arnon south to the Zered (Num 21:13–15, Judg 11:18) and north to encompass the plateau conquered by Sihon and Mesha (Num 21:21–25, 26–30; Isa 15–16; Jer 48:21–24; Mesha inscription (MI), lines 7–26).[12] Jephthah and Ammon contest this northern tableland, as do Moses and Sihon (Num 21:21–32, Deut 2:26–36, Judg 11:13–26).

According to Judg 11, earlier hostilities precipitated the current Ammonite invasion. However, in the recitation of Transjordanian engagements, Israel interacted with Edom, Moab, and the Amorites, but not with the disputant, Ammon (11:16–22). Moabite elements are prominent: an unnamed king of Moab, the deity Chemosh, King Balak son of Zippor, and the Moabite heartland along the Arnon River (11:15–26). This story has literary integrity as an account of an Israelite engagement not with Ammon but with Sihon, who allegedly conquered Moabite territory from the Arnon to the Jabbok (Num 21:26). Invoking Chemosh and Balak may acknowledge a link between Sihon and the Moabites. However, according to Judg 11:17–18 (but not Numbers), Moab rebuffed Israel's request for passage so Israel skirted the region, affording no easy explanation for Moabite elements in an allegedly Ammonite episode.

The mid-ninth century Mesha Stela concedes Omride annexation of Moab's "land of Madaba" (MI lines 7–8). Though the Bible omits mention of the conquest, both Israelite and Moabite sources testify to Mesha's successful rebellion at Ahab's death or during his reign (2 Kgs 1:1, 3:4–5, MI lines 6–9). To allegedly *re*assert control north of the Arnon, Mesha settled and developed towns from Nebo, Atarot, and Madaba in the north to Aroer and Dibon in the south (MI lines 1, 7–11, 26). Israel retaliated. King Jehoram recruited Judah and Edom, but his alliance was repulsed (2 Kgs 3:6–27).

---

[12] Mesha inscription translations are from Routledge, *Moab in the Iron Age*, 135–36.

Omri's early-ninth-century conquest, as claimed by Mesha, violated the injunction in Deut 2:9 forbidding Israelite acquisition of Moabite territory. To avert the transgression, perhaps Sihon served as a ruse or a decoy, deployed to legitimate Omride actions. As early as the 1880s, Eduard Meyer and Bruno Baenisch, and more recently Baruch Levine, considered the Heshbon Ballad to be a ninth-century victory song celebrating the Israelite/Omride conquest of Heshbon.[13] Walter Groß challenges this reconstruction, noting that Heshbon, Sihon's capital according to Num 21:26 and 28, Deut 2:26 and our text, is not mentioned in the Mesha Stela; Dibon, not Heshbon, was Mesha's capital city.[14]

2. Archaeology of Moab

A survey of the archaeological evidence of the region north and south of the Arnon suggests a historical context for Israel's battle against Sihon/Moab. After an apparent twelfth-century (Iron IA) gap or highly diminished settlement, sedentarization gradually resumed in every area surveyed including along the King's Highway.[15] Rather than intensive settlement, the numerous eleventh-century (Iron IB) agricultural settlements on the Kerak plateau (south of the Arnon) likely reflect a transitory population with frequent movement and resettlement.[16] More substantial hamlets situated along the Arnon and its tributaries serving defensive and administrative as well as agricultural functions attest to regional settlement of independent communities adapted to and exploiting localized resources.[17] Mudayna al-Aliya, excavated by Bruce Routledge and Benjamin Porter, exemplifies these eleventh-century farming communities. Thirty-five to forty-five adjacent, pillared houses of varying sizes formed a perimeter (casemate) wall enclosing a central,

---

[13] Levine, *Numbers 21–36*, 40, 44. Exemplifying alternative interpretations, Paul Hanson considers the Heshbon Ballad to be a thirteenth-century Amorite victory song of Sihon's defeat of Moab incorporated by the Elohist to elaborate on his historical note in Num 21:26 ("The Song of Heshbon and David's 'Nîr,'" *HTR* 61 [1968]: 297–320, here 307, http://dx.doi.org/10.1017/S0017816000029229). Thomas D. Petter notes both Moabite and Amorite perspectives in the ballad reflecting "a premonarchic social and cultural context that had disappeared by the later Iron II" (*The Land between the Two Rivers: Early Israelite Identities in Central Transjordan* [Winona Lake, IN: Eisenbrauns, 2014], 55). *Heshbon* refers to the biblical city and *Hesban* to the archaeological site.

[14] Groß, *Richter*, 561. Levine explains Heshbon's absence by restricting Mesha's conquests to south of Heshbon (Levine, *Numbers 21–26*, 131.)

[15] Larry Herr and Mohammed Najjar, "The Iron Age," in *Jordan: An Archaeological Reader*, ed. Russell B. Adams (London: Equinox, 2008), 311–34, here 312, table 10.1.

[16] J. Maxwell Miller, *Archaeological Survey of the Kerak Plateau: Conducted during 1978–1982 under the Direction of J. Maxwell Miller and Jack M. Pinkerton*, ASOR Archaeological Reports 1 (Atlanta: Scholars Press, 1991).

[17] Benjamin W. Porter, *Complex Communities: The Archaeology of Early Iron Age West-Central Jordan* (Tucson: University of Arizona Press, 2013), 134–35.

open plaza. While situated in an agriculturally marginal area, the houses contained installations for food processing and storage such as a tabun (oven), saddle quern, mortar, and collar-rim storejars, and a surprising array of foodstuffs including lentils, wheat, barley, grapes, figs, sheep, goat, pig, and freshwater crab (fig. 2).[18] The hamlets were largely abandoned by the end of the eleventh century, with no evidence of hostilities.[19] In general, sparse tenth-century (Iron IIA) settlement on the Moabite plateau north of the Arnon continued the transitory, agro-pastoral lifestyle of Iron I.[20]

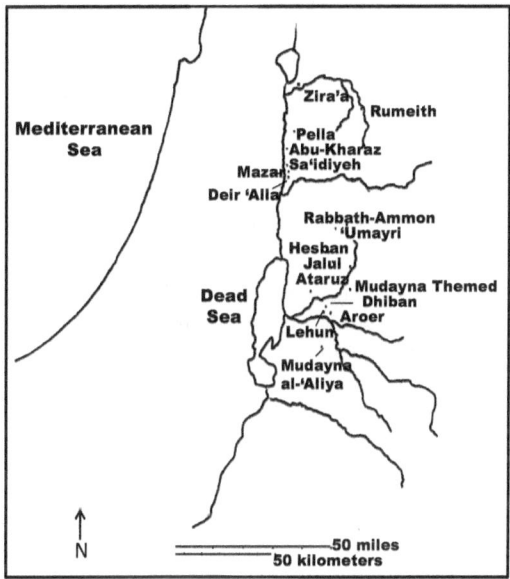

Figure 2. Selected Transjordanian Archaeological Sites Mentioned in the Article

Moab burgeoned in the ninth century as is evident in public constructions and the distribution of "Moabite-style" pottery as far north as Hesban.[21] Forts and

---

[18] Bruce Routledge and Benjamin Porter, "A Place In-Between: Khirbet al-Mudayna al-'Aliya in the Early Iron Age," in *Crossing Jordan: North American Contributions to the Archaeology of Jordan*, ed. Thomas E. Levy, P. M. Michèle Daviau, Randall W. Younker, and May Shaer (London: Equinox, 2007), 323–29; Justin S. Lev-Tov, Benjamin W. Porter, and Bruce E. Routledge, "Measuring Local Diversity in Early Iron Age Animal Economies: A View from Khirbat al-Mudayna al-'Aliya (Jordan)," *BASOR* 361 (2011): 67–93, here 73–78.

[19] This abandonment contrasts with the destruction of contemporary settlements south of Amman such as Jalul, Jawa, and 'Umeiri.

[20] Harrison, "'Land of Mēdeba,'" 33.

[21] James Sauer, "The Pottery of Hisban and Its Relationship to the History of Jordan: An

small nucleated settlements founded along the eastern border in territory largely abandoned since Iron I and the late-ninth-century growth of regional centers from Heshbon to Baluʻa attest to Moabite advances.[22] Mudayna eth-Themed, a center for textile production and exchange, exemplifies such centers. A six-chamber gate in a casemate wall formed by adjacent houses defends the town with industrial buildings.[23] Befitting its royal status as the capital city (MI line 1), Dhiban prospered during or following Mesha's reign in Iron IIB (840/830–785/748).[24] An artificial, fortified podium covering the eastern portion of the tell accommodated a monumental building once dubbed "Mesha's Palace" (at least 21 x 25 m).[25] Following this flourish, Dhiban declined precipitously.

The fortified town of Khirbat Ataruz ("corral"), identified with biblical Atarot (Num 32:3, 34), incorporated a religious compound. Excavations under the direction of Chang-Ho Ji unearthed a multistory and multichamber temple complex built in the tenth century, expanded in the ninth and eighth centuries, and destroyed in the eighth century. The sanctuary consisted of a main room (30 x 13 m), two antechambers, and an open courtyard. Cultic elements and contents of the temple,

---

Interim Hesban Pottery Report, 1993," in *Hesban after 25 Years*, ed. David Merling and Lawrence T. Geraty (Berrien Springs, MI: Institute of Archaeology, Andrews University, 1994), 225–82, here 245; Herr and Najjar, "Iron Age" (2008), 321.

An unprovenienced, octagonal basalt column inscription celebrates a successful Moabite campaign against Ammon. In the preserved lines, the speaker, presumably the king, boasts of "many captives" engaged in construction, including the building of Bet Harosh and a "shaft/ reservoir a mighty/strong gate." "And the Ammonites saw that they were weakened in every...." Similarities to the Mesha Stela in style, content, paleography, and orthography date the inscription to the eighth century, and historical considerations suggest it predates Tiglath-pileser III's campaigns in the region (Shmuel Ahituv, *Echoes from the Past: Hebrew and Cognate Inscriptions from the Biblical Period* [Jerusalem: Carta, 2008], 419–23; J. Andrew Dearman, "Moab and Ammon: Some Observations on Their Relationship in Light of a New Moabite Inscription," in Bienkowski, *Studies on Iron Age Moab*, 97–116). If authentic, this testimony reinforces the archaeological picture of Moab's preeminence in this period.

[22] Routledge, *Moab in the Iron Age*, 191, 193, 200; Gregory Linton and Daniel Hoffman, "Report of 1999 and 2001 Karak Resources Project Regional Survey," *ADAJ* 48 (2004): 267–84; Harrison, "'Land of Mēdeba,'" 34; Piotr Bienkowski, "'Tribalism' and 'Segmentary Society' in Iron Age Transjordan," in idem, *Studies on Iron Age Moab*, 11–12.

[23] P. M. Michèle Daviau and Robert Chadwick, "Shepherds and Weavers in a 'Global Economy': Moab in Late Iron Age II – Wadi eth-Thamad Project (Khirbet al-Mudayna)," in Levy et al., *Crossing Jordan*, 309–14, here 310; Larry Herr, "Mudeina eth-Thamad, Khirbet el-," *NEAEHL* 5:1846.

[24] *Dhiban* refers to the archaeological site and *Dibon* to the biblical city.

[25] Routledge, *Moab in the Iron Age*, 164; Bruce Routledge, Danielle S. Fatkin, Benjamin W. Porter, Katherine Adelsberger, and Andrew Wilson, "Long-Term Settlement Change at Dhībān," *SHAJ* 11 (2013): 131–41, here 123, 139–40. According to Israel Finkelstein and Oded Lipschits, Mesha mimicked the Omride fortress architecture employed for Atarot and Jahaz ("Omride Architecture in Moab: Jahaz and Ataroth," *ZDPV* 126 [2010]: 29–42, here 37).

courtyard, and related structures included two high places/altars, a standing stone, and over three hundred artifacts such as four stone altars, a model two-story temple, and statues of deities, most notably a large, terra-cotta bull.[26] Neither Moabite nor Israelite identity may be conclusively ascertained, though the absence of comparable eighth-century, theriomorphic deity images in Judah is cited in arguments for Moabite rather than Israelite cultural influence and hegemony.[27]

Archaeological and textual evidence pertaining to Ataruz/Atarot illustrates the vicissitudes of peoples and settlements in the Iron IIA–IIB. Mesha informs us that "the men of Gad [ʾš gd] (had) dwelt in the land of ʿAṭarot from of old" (MI line 10). While "men of Gad" and the Israelite tribe of Gad are likely synonymous, as they inhabited the same territory, this Transjordanian tribe need not have affiliated with Israel "from of old." Residence in (formerly, according to Mesha) Moabite territory (MI line 10) identified "the men of Gad" as Moabites. With Omri's conquest of the region and construction of the city of Atarot for the "men of Gad" (MI lines 10–11, 14), Israelite hegemony conferred Israelite affiliation. In the mid-ninth century, Mesha retaliated against those who benefitted from Omride largesse and perhaps adopted Israelite religious practices. He enslaved or massacred the "men of Gad" and settled "men of Šaron and Maḥarot" in the vanquished Atarot thereby decisively ending Gad's Israelite affiliation (MI lines 11–17, 25–26). This sequence of events demonstrates multiple concurrent and sequential identities for resident groups based on lineage/tribe, land, and supratribal authority.[28] It also attests to Israelite and Transjordanian tribes/clans as recognized entities (polities?) concurrent with monarchies.

This interpretation of the Mesha Stela proposes that Gad affiliated with Israel for less than fifty years and only *after* the foundation of the northern kingdom. Yet Israel numbers Gad among the tribes in the premonarchic period (though not in Judg 5) and claims the territory as divinely allocated. Perhaps Israel retrojected Gad's settlement in "the land of Atarot from of old" into the narrative of the premonarchic tribal confederation to bolster Israel's early presence in southern Transjordan in conjunction with the tribe of Reuben. This would explain Jephthah's assertion that Israelites inhabited the region from Heshbon to Aroer for three hundred years (Judg 11:26). Knowing the period of Gad's Israelite affiliation may help date selected textual traditions. For example, Gad's omission from the Judg 5 battle muster may indicate that the list predates the tribe's association in the early ninth century.

---

[26] Chang-Ho C. Ji, "Khirbat ʿAtarūz: An Interim Overview of the 10 Years of Archaeological Architectural Findings," *ADAJ* 55 (2011): 561–79; Donald R. Keller, Barbara A. Porter, and Christopher A. Tuttle, "Archaeology in Jordan, 2010 and 2011 Seasons," *AJA* 116 (2012): 693–750, here 719.
[27] Victor Hurowitz, "Solomon's Temple in Context," *BAR* 37.2 (2011): 46–57, 77–78, here 53.
[28] Routledge, *Moab in the Iron Age*, 149–50.

Might Israel have defeated a formidable "Sihon" prior to the early-ninth-century reign of Omri? Sihon ruled from biblical Heshbon (Num 21:26, 28; Deut 2:26; Josh 12:2, 5; Judg 11:19) but, unfortunately, later construction largely obliterated the Iron Age remains at the archaeological site of Hesban. Based on "copious pottery in a rock-cut trench" in conjunction with faunal and botanical remains, the excavator, Lawrence Geraty, characterized Iron I Hesban as a small, unfortified, agro-pastoral village.[29] Not until the ninth or eighth century (Iron IIB) did the construction of a water reservoir indicate higher-order political and economic organization.[30] By the seventh to sixth centuries, Hesban grew into a prosperous settlement probably built around a fort. Hesban waxed in the seventh and sixth centuries as Dhiban waned. Ashy debris dumped into the reservoir by the second-century builders, the first to return to the site, suggests Hesban met a violent end.[31] The possible fiery demise occurred not earlier than the sixth century, though the definitive date remains elusive. Accordingly, references to Heshbon as Sihon's capital refer to or evoke the city of the ninth to the sixth century. The catastrophic conflagration of the sixth century may provide a *terminus post quem* for the Heshbon ballad, "For fire went forth from Heshbon, Flame from Sihon's city" (Num 21:28a).

Moab fared less well than Ammon and Edom under the Assyrians in Iron IIC (722–586 BCE). As Ammonites pushed south into formerly Moabite territory, archaeological surveys reveal a Moabite retreat to the agriculturally more marginal eastern Kerak plateau and the Wadi Hasa vicinity.[32]

B. Ammon

1. Ammon in the Bible

YHWH instructed the Israelites to honor the divine allocation to Lot's child Ammon, "For I will not give any part of the land of the Ammonites to you as a possession; I have assigned it as a possession to the descendants of Lot" "all along the Wadi Jabbok and the towns of the hill country" (Deut 2:19, 37). At its most expansive, in our chapter, Ammon encompassed not just the Jabbok vicinity but also the plateau and valleys south to the Arnon and west to the Jordan (Judg 11:13). This enlarged Ammon incorporated formerly Moabite territory, including Sihon's Heshbon, explaining its identification as both Moabite (Isa 15:4; 16:8–9; Jer 48:34, 45) and Ammonite (Jer 49:3).[33]

---

[29] Larry Herr, "Jordan in the Iron I Period," *SHAJ* 10 (2009): 549–61, here 555; Lawrence Geraty, "Heshbon," *NEAEHL* 2 (1993): 626–30, here 628.

[30] Paul J. Ray Jr., *Tell Hesban and Vicinity in the Iron Age*, Hesban 6 (Berrien Springs, MI: Andrews University Press, 2001), 99, 107, 110, 115, table 3.

[31] Lawrence Geraty, "Ḥesban" in *OEANE* 3:19–22, here 20–21.

[32] Routledge, *Moab in the Iron Age*, 200.

[33] Strategically situated on the Wadi Hesban, making it a logical border town, Heshbon is also allotted to Reuben (Num 32:1–3, 37; Josh 13:15–23) and Gad (Josh 21:36, 1 Chr 6:66).

The Bible describes contentious relations between Ammonites and Israelites with Israel initially victorious. Saul and David claimed victory near Jabesh-Gilead and at the Ammonite capitol city of Rabbah, respectively (1 Sam 11:11, 2 Sam 12:29). Chronicles adds Judahite subjugation of Ammon by the pious kings Jehoshaphat, Uzziah, and Jotham (2 Chr 20:22, 26:8, 27:5). However, Amos's oracle against the Ammonites for atrocities committed in battle against Gilead during Uzziah's reign (784–742 BCE) contradicts the Chronicler's rosy depiction (Amos 1:13). Amos's testimony dates Ammonite expansion into Israelite Gilead to the mid-eighth century and portrays Israel as sorely oppressed. In Jerusalem's final years, Ammonites in conjunction with Chaldeans, Arameans, and Moabites attacked Jehoiakim's city, likely with Babylonian assent (2 Kgs 24:2).

2. Archaeology of Ammon

Iron I settlement concentrated in the fertile plain immediately to the south and southwest of Rabbat-Ammon (Rabbah).[34] Around 1000 BCE (Iron IC/Iron IIA), destruction and abandonment of a number of sites ringing Rabbah, but not elsewhere in the country, left the area largely uninhabited.[35] Tell el-Umayri, south of Rabbat-Ammon, fortified with the earliest identified casemate-like wall, a massive rampart, and a dry moat, represents the most elaborate of the sites excavated.[36]

Occupation around Rabbat-Ammon did not resume until the middle to late ninth century, from which time Ammon increasingly prospered and expanded its territory and sphere of influence. As in the case of other modern cities built over ancient capitals, limitations in excavating in modern-day Amman restrict our

---

[34] Robert G. Boling, "Site Survey of the el-'Umeiri Region," in *Madaba Plains Project: The 1984 Season at Tell el-'Umeiri and Vicinity and Subsequent Studies*, ed. Lawrence T. Geraty et al., Madaba Plains Project 1 (Berrien Springs, MI: Andrews University Press, 1989), 98–188; Robert D. Ibach Jr., *Archaeological Survey of the Hesban Region: Catalogue of Sites and Characterizations of Periods*, Hesban 5 (Berrien Springs, MI: Institute of Archaeology, Andrews University Press, 1987); Gaetano Palumbo et al., "The Wādi az-Zarqā' ad-Dulayl Excavations and Survey Project: Report on the October–November 1994 Fieldwork Season," *ADAJ* 40 (1996): 375–427; Chang-Ho Ji, "Archaeological Survey and Settlement Patterns in the Region of 'Iraq al-'Amir, 1996: A Preliminary Report," *ADAJ* 42 (1998): 587–608.

[35] Chang-Ho Ji, "Iron Age I in Central and Northern Transjordan: An Interim Summary of Archaeological Data," *PEQ* 127 (1995): 122–40, here 122–26; Elizabeth Bloch-Smith and Beth Alpert Nakhai, "A Landscape Comes to Life: The Iron Age I," *NEA* 62 (1999): 62–92, 101–27, here 111.

[36] Larry Herr and Douglas Clark, "From the Stone Age to the Middle Ages in Jordan: Digging up Tall al-'Umayri," *NEA* 72 (2009): 68–97, here 82; Keller, Porter, and Tuttle, "Archaeology in Jordan, 2010 and 2011," 713–14. Jephthah or Joab and David, who "devastated Ammon and besieged Rabbah" (2 Sam 11:1) could conceivably have perpetrated, claimed, or been credited with devastation in the Rabbah vicinity. However, our story begins with Ammonite incursions into Gilead reflecting an expansionist Ammon, which is not well attested until later centuries.

knowledge of ancient Rabbat-Ammon. Tantalizing bits uncovered in the city (el-Qalʿa, "the citadel") attest to Ammonite kings fortifying a citadel, carving a water system in the bedrock, and erecting official/palatial structures, but beginning dates for these public works have not been determined.[37] Monumental building likely commenced by the late ninth century based on the late-ninth- or early-eighth-century Amman Citadel inscription recording the construction of a royal temple (not yet located). Ammonite hegemony and spreading influence are also evident in the distribution of distinctive statuary such as small ceramic male figurine heads, carved Hathoric heads, and stone statues of males with Egyptian *atef* crowns.[38] Through most of the late ninth and eighth century, Ammon comprised little more than the capital city with satellite villages and towns. Although exhibiting the trappings of a royal polity by Iron IIB, its floruit was to follow.

Ammon attained its greatest extent and prosperity in Iron IIC. Both material culture and religious features show the spread of Ammonite control or influence south into the formerly Moabite Madaba-Jalul region, west to the Jordan River, and north of the Jabbok through the Jordan Valley.[39] Several features reflect and served to foster Ammonite identity: promotion of the national god Milkom; names compounded with the theophoric element *ʾIl* or *ʾEl*; specific pottery forms and decoration such as black burnished pots; figurines with unique features; and a distinctive Ammonite dialect and script known from the proliferation of inscriptions, inscribed seals, and ostraca of the eighth through the fifth centuries.[40] A Hesban administrative ostracon of the late seventh or early sixth century written in Ammonite script demonstrates the influence or presence of Ammonites in this formerly Moabite settlement.[41] Excavations have unearthed an Assyrian-style palace in Rabbah and over thirty heavily fortified towers surrounding and defending the capital.[42] Farm-

---

[37] Fawzi Zayadine, Jean-Baptiste Humbert, and Mohammed Najjar, "The 1988 Excavations on the Citadel of Amman Lower Terrace, Area A," *ADAJ* 33 (1989): 357–63.

[38] P. M. Michèle Daviau and Paul Dion, "Independent and Well-Connected: The Ammonite Territorial Kingdom in Iron Age II," in Levy et al., *Crossing Jordan*, 302.

[39] Larry Herr, "Shifts in Settlement Patterns of Late Bronze and Iron Age Ammon," *SHAJ* 4 (1992): 175–78, here 175; P. M. Michèle Daviau, "Moab's Northern Border: Khirbet al-Mudayna on the Wadi ath-Thamad," *BA* 60 (1997): 222–28; Larry Herr and Muhammad Najjar, "The Iron Age," in *The Archaeology of Jordan*, ed. Burton MacDonald, Russell Adams, and Piotr Bienkowski, Levantine Archaeology 1 (Sheffield: Sheffield Academic, 2001), 323–45, here 335–37; Ephraim Stern, *The Assyrian, Babylonian, and Persian Periods, 732–332 BCE*, vol. 2 of *Archaeology of the Land of the Bible*, ABRL (New York: Doubleday, 2001), 237, 245, 258; Daviau and Dion, "Independent and Well-Connected," 306.

[40] Daviau and Dion, "Independent and Well-Connected," 305; Larry Herr, "Ammon," *OEANE* 1:103–5, here 105; MacDonald *"East of the Jordan,"* 161; Aufrecht, *Corpus of Ammonite Inscriptions*.

[41] Ahituv, *Echoes from the Past*, 370–79.

[42] Khair Yassine, *Archaeology of Jordan: Essays and Reports* (Amman: Department of Archaeology, University of Jordan, 1988), 266; Jean-Baptiste Humbert and Fawzi Zayadine, "Trois

steads, villages (Khilda, Safut, Sahab), fortresses (Rujm Henu, Abu Sayyah), and administrative centers (Umayri, Jalul, Jawa South?) identified and excavated in the Amman vicinity constituted a greater Rabbah.[43] Under Ammonite aegis, northern Jordan Valley sites prospered, though on a much-diminished scale compared to earlier periods. To the east on the plateau, the region remained unoccupied or inhabited by nomadic pastoralists. Based on this archaeological evidence, references to an expansive Ammon, such as Jeremiah's invoking Ammonite Heshbon (49:3), likely originated in late Iron IIB or IIC.

C. Gilead

1. Gilead in the Bible and Assyrian Texts

Biblical "Gilead" refers to the eponymous ancestor of the clan (Num 26:29–32, 36:1), a tribe (Judg 5:17), a town (Hos 6:8),[44] and the geographical region encompassing Transjordan north of the Jabbok (Gen 31:21–32:3, Num 32:39–42, 2 Sam 17:24–26; 1 Chr 6:65), south of the Jabbok (Num 32:1–4, Josh 12:2), both north and south (Deut 3:8–10, 12–16; Josh 22:9, 15; 2 Kgs 10:32–33), and perhaps in Cisjordan as well (Num 26:30–32).[45] The varying biblical ascriptions of Transjordanian territory to Gilead, Machir, Reuben, Gad, "half-Manasseh" (itself an unusual designation), Ammon, and Moab may reflect tribal and national vacillations, a lack of knowledge on the part of the authors/editors, or, likely, a combination of the two. In our story, references to Tob country (Judg 11:3), marching through Gilead and Manasseh to "cross over" (the Jabbok?) to the Ammonites (11:29), and Jephthah's conquests (11:33) situate Israelite Gilead in Transjordan north and just south of the Jabbok. This localization contrasts with the disputed territory to the south on the Moabite plateau and along the Arnon (11:26).

---

campagnes de fouilles à Ammân (1988–1991): Troisième terrasse de la citadelle (Mission Franco-Jordanienne)," *RB* 99 (1992): 214–60, here 247–58; Stern, *Assyrian, Babylonian, and Persian Periods*, 245–46.

[43] For references, see Herr and Najjar, "Iron Age" (2001), 335–36; and Herr and Najjar, "Iron Age" (2008), 323–25, table 10.5.

[44] Israel Finkelstein, Ido Koch, and Oded Lipschits situate the town on a low plateau south of the Jabbok, perhaps Khirbet Jal'ad, located 14 mi/22km south of the river valley or the proximate Tell Hajjaj ("The Biblical Gilead: Observations on Identifications, Geographic Divisions and Territorial History," *UF* 43 [2011]: 131–59, here 138–40).

[45] Neither the Arameans nor the Assyrians refer to a region designated *Gilead*, and Ugaritic *Gilead* was likely located in the vicinity of Ugarit (*KTU* 4.125.2; Magnus Ottosson, *Gilead: Tradition and History*, trans. J. Gray, ConBOT 3 [Lund: Gleerup, 1969], 15–17; idem, "In Quest of the Arameans in Northern Jordan," *SHAJ* 7 [2001]: 331–42). Later eighth-century references by Tiglath-pileser III to a town on the border of the territory of Bit-Humria/Israel are reconstructed as Gal-a(za); however, both the reconstruction and identification with the town of Ramot-Gilead are conjectural (Ottosson, *Gilead: Tradition and History*, 19–22).

As related in the Bible, through the reign of Jeroboam I territory north of the Jabbok constituted an integral part of Israel. Variant texts in the MT and 4QSamᵃ describe Nahash and the Ammonites attacking the Transjordanian Israelites, specified as Gadites and Reubenites in the Dead Sea Scrolls, and besieging Jabesh-Gilead. Saul retaliated, leading combined forces from Israel and Judah, to vanquish the enemy (1 Sam 11:1–11).[46] With this contentious period behind him, Ishbaal son of Saul established his capital city at Mahanaim in a kingdom that encompassed "Gilead, the Ashurites, Jezreel, Ephraim, and Benjamin—all Israel," with Gilead given primacy of place (2 Sam 2:8–9). Gilead's continuing importance is demonstrated by Solomon's two or three Transjordanian administrative districts with Mahanaim and Ramot-Gilead as seats of prefects and Jeroboam I's capital at Penuel (1 Kgs 4:13–14, 19a; 12:25). After Jeroboam I, we hear little of the region in the ensuing roughly twenty-five years until the period of the Omrides.

The books of Kings record wars between Israel and Aram for hegemony over Gilead beginning in the ninth century. Ahab's contemporary Ben-Hadad of Aram controlled Succoth and Ramot-Gilead north of the Jabbok (1 Kgs 20:16, 22:3–36). By the second half of the ninth-century reign of Jehu, Israel allegedly relinquished to Hazael "all the land of Gilead … from Aroer, by the Wadi Arnon, up to Gilead and Bashan" (2 Kgs 10:33).[47] Jeroboam II may have restored Israelite suzerainty in the mid-eighth century (2 Kgs 14:23–29, Amos 6:14), but Gilead suffered foreign incursions from the north and the south. As described by Amos, Damascus and the house of Hazael ravaged Gilead "with threshing sledges of iron," and Ammonites cruelly "ripped open the pregnant women of Gilead in order to enlarge their own territory" (Amos 1:3, 13). With the later eighth-century campaigns of Tiglath-pileser III (2 Kgs 15:29, Calaḫ Annals 18 and 24) and Sargon II (2 Kgs 17:5, Great "Summary" inscription), Israel and the territory of Gilead succumbed to Assyria.[48] Accordingly, the historical context for our Gileadite-Ammonite conflict predates the 722 BCE Assyrian dissolution of Israel.[49]

---

[46] F. M. Cross, D. W. Parry, and R. J. Saley, "4QSamᵃ," in *Qumran Cave 4.XII: 1–2 Samuel*, ed. Frank Moore Cross et al., DJD XVII (Oxford: Clarendon, 2005), 1–216, here 65–69. Saul and Samuel retaliate on behalf of Jabesh-Gilead but not for the tribes of Gad or Reuben.

[47] This description encompasses the territory reclaimed by Mesha of Moab on his victory stela.

[48] "The Calaḫ Annals," trans. K. Lawson Younger Jr. (*COS* 2.117A:286); "The Great 'Summary' Inscription," trans. K. Lawson Younger Jr. (*COS* 2.118E:296–97).

[49] First Chronicles attests to enduring Israelite ties and claims to Gileadite territory through marriage and kin relations: Judean Hezron's family marries into the "sons of Machir" (1 Chr 2:21–22), and Penuel, the father of Gedor, is ascribed Judean lineage (1 Chr 4:4). These claims to northern Transjordan, not our contested territory, may depict actual geopolitical relations of the Achaemenid period or an idealized vision (John W. Wright, "The Borders of Yehud and the Genealogies of Chronicles," in *Judah and the Judeans in the Persian Period*, ed. Oded Lipschits and Manfred Oeming [Winona Lake, IN: Eisenbrauns, 2006], 67–89, here 75–83).

2. Archaeology of Gilead

Settlement and socioeconomic patterns in Gilead during Iron I mirrored developments west of the Jordan River; both experienced a disruption of urban life. In general, early-twelfth-century Egyptian withdrawal from the region ended much of the impetus and infrastructure for commerce and development. Jordan Valley centers gave way to highland, rural, transitory settlements of subsistence agro-pastoralists.[50] As noted by Routledge, this apparent profusion of modest settlements should be interpreted not as a coordinated, large-scale migration into the area but as short-term, transitory habitations repeatedly founded and abandoned.[51] Even this limited settlement declined by the end of the period. Sparse evidence suggests that urban life continued in northern Gilead along the Yarmuk and its tributaries (Fukhar, Abila, Irbid, Ya'amoun) and gradually revived in the central Jordan Valley (Abu Kharaz, Deir 'Alla, Mazar).[52]

Iron II Gileadite settlement paralleled the northern kingdom of Israel from the revival of cities and public architecture in Iron IIA to the disruption and devastation by the Assyrians at the end of Iron IIB. The Iron IIA urban revival attests to an increasingly wealthy and hierarchical society concentrated in the more fertile, northern Transjordan and through the Jordan River rift valley. Monumental and private constructions such as Rumeith's walled village (Ramot-Gilead?); Zira'a's fortification wall, public and residential buildings, and workshops; the palace and temple of Pella; Abu Kharaz's "citadel" (this site and Tell el-Maqlub are proposed identifications for Jabesh-Gilead); the Mazar courtyard building and sanctuary; and the Deir 'Alla fortifications and houses (Penuel/Peniel?) are illustrative.[53]

In Iron IIB, central Jordan Valley settlements prospered (Abu Kharaz, Saidiyeh, Deir 'Alla).[54] Sites farther north along the Yarmuk and its tributaries, including

---

[50] Siegfried Mittman, *Beiträge zur Siedlungs- und Territorialgeschichte des nördlichen Ostjordanlandes*, ADPV (Wiesbaden: Harrassowitz, 1970); Routledge, *Moab in the Iron Age*, 92; Herr, "Jordan in the Iron I Period," 554; Abdel-Naser Hindawi, "The Archaeology of the Northern Jordanian Plateau during the Iron Age ca. Late 13th–6th Centuries BC: Tell Ya'amoun as a Key Site" (PhD diss., Albert-Ludwigs-Universität zu Freiburg, 2006), 229.

[51] Routledge, *Moab in the Iron Age*, 92.

[52] Herr and Najjar, "Iron Age" (2008), 314, 315; Hindawi, "Archaeology of the Northern Jordanian Plateau," 210–11.

[53] All biblical correspondences are from MacDonald, *"East of the Jordan,"* appendix; Herr and Najjar, "Iron Age" (2001), 331; Herr and Najjar, "Iron Age" (2008), 318–19, table 10.3; Peter Fischer, "The Iron Age at Tall Abū-Kharaz, Jordan Valley: The Third Major Period of Occupation. A Preliminary Synthesis," *SHAJ* 7 (2001): 305–16; Gerrit van der Kooij, "The Vicissitudes of Life at Dayr 'Allā during the First Millennium BC, Seen in a Wider Context," *SHAJ* 7 (2001): 295–304; Keller, Porter, and Tuttle, "Archaeology in Jordan," 695. According to 1 Kings, early Israelite monarchs ruled these Jordan Valley cities and administered this prosperous region.

[54] Fischer, "Iron Age at Tall Abū-Kharaz," 307–12; Mo'awiyah Ibrahim, James Sauer, and Khair Yassine, "The East Jordan Valley Survey, 1975," *BASOR* 222 (1976): 41–66, here 63;

fortified Rumeith and Ziraʻa, likely succumbed to Aramean control in the ninth century.[55] Material remains do not reflect the probable shifts in hegemony. By later in the eighth century the more agriculturally marginal plateau was largely abandoned, likely in the wake of Tiglath-pileser III's 734 BCE campaign.[56]

During Iron IIC, Jordan Valley sites in the Jabbok vicinity revived apparently under Ammonite aegis (Abu Kharaz, Mazar, Nimrin, Saidiyeh, Deir ʻAlla), most notably Deir ʻAlla with the Balaam inscription.[57] Yaʼamoun and Johfiyeh represent agricultural sites that prospered under the peace and stability brought by Assyrian hegemony.[58] However, much of the northern Jordan Valley and plateau did not rebound after the Assyrian campaigns and remained sparsely settled or inhabited by nomadic pastoralists.[59] Based on this evidence, an Ammonite campaign against Israelites of Gilead must have preceded the Assyrian subjugation and political reorganization of the region.

III. Judges 11:12–33 in Archaeological Contexts

Ammon's justification for war and subsequent defeat related in Judg 11:13 and 32–33 frame Jephthah's iteration of Israel's earlier Transjordanian negotiations and combat (vv. 14–27). While both these accounts likely date to the seventh century, they originated in historical events of earlier centuries. Based on archaeological evidence in conjunction with biblical testimony and the Mesha Stela, it is clear that during the first half of the ninth century Omri and Ahab conquered and held the Moabite plateau north of the Arnon. An ascendant Moab under King Mesha rebelled at Ahab's death and reasserted Moabite control over the region. Accordingly, biblical references to an expansive Moab (Sihon) encompassing territory north of the Arnon (Judg 11:22 but also Isa 15–16 and Jer 48:21–24) originated in or drew on the political reality of the mid to late ninth century. Ammonite expansion intensified in the late ninth and eighth centuries. This intensification brought Ammon into conflict with Gilead/Israel, perhaps in response to the alleged conquests of Jeroboam II (2 Kgs 14:25), and set the stage for a battle such as Jephthah's.

Jonathan N. Tubb and Peter G. Dorrell, "Tell es-Saʻidiyeh: Interim Report on the Fifth (1990) Season of Excavations," *Levant* 23 (1991): 67–86, here figs. 3, 5, http://dx.doi.org/10.1179/lev.1991.23.1.67; van der Kooij, "Vicissitudes of Life at Dayr ʻAllā," 295–304, table 1; Herr and Najjar, "Iron Age" (2001), 332.

[55] Herr and Najjar, "Iron Age" (2008), 320–21.

[56] Herr and Najjar, "Iron Age" (2001), 335.

[57] Fischer, "Iron Age at Tall Abū-Kharaz," 307–12; van der Kooij, "Vicissitudes of Life at Dayr ʻAllā," table 1; Herr and Najjar, "Iron Age" (2008), 323.

[58] Hindawi, "Archaeology of the Northern Jordanian Plateau," 230.

[59] Mittmann, *Beiträge zur Siedlungs- und Territorialgeschichte*; Herr and Najjar, "Iron Age" (2001), 332–36; Daviau and Dion, "Independent and Well-Connected," 306.

Might these conflicts have occurred before the ninth and eighth centuries? Israelite tribes conceivably settled in Transjordan by the end of the thirteenth century, as claimed by Reuben's primogeniture and Israel's defeat of Sihon. Mesha's mid-ninth-century claim to the plateau north of the Arnon may have been fabricated to justify his expansion north into territory under Israelite dominion for the previous "three hundred years." However, advocates for this early period lack substantiating extrabiblical or archaeological evidence. Similarly, Gileadite-Ammonite hostilities might date to the tenth century, when Israel's early kings allegedly vanquished the Ammonites and their allies. However, physical attestations to Ammonite expansion do not begin until the late ninth and escalate through the eighth century, favoring a later date. If battles in the twelfth to tenth centuries—for which we lack corroborating evidence—provided the template for our account, they took on renewed significance in later periods when Judg 11 was crafted.

By the late ninth or eighth century, Ammon succeeded Moab as Israel's Transjordanian adversary. For an audience that knew Ammon as the antagonist, an older story of battle with Sihon/Moab was cleverly adapted to justify war against Ammon. Several elements in the story facilitated the necessary alterations. First, formerly Moabite territory between the Arnon and the Jabbok now belonged to Ammon, giving the story a plausible Ammonite context. Second, eighth-century Israelites likely knew Ammonite Aroer, "which is close to Rabbah," rather than Aroer of Moab. This familiarity allowed the authors/editors to conclude with Israel's conquest of the Rabbat-Ammon vicinity, from Aroer to Abel-keramim (Judg 11:33), in spite of a justification tied to the Moabite plateau to the south. Third, the near homonyms "Amorite" and "Ammonite" perhaps facilitated the switch. Accordingly, this narrative conflates Moab and Ammon due to Ammon's supplanting Moab as Israel's Transjordanian enemy and ruler over the contested area. In a smooth transition effected by vv. 12–15 and 23–27, past warfare is invoked to explain current hostilities.

The version of events in Judg 11 was arguably crafted within memory of the Ammonite hostilities. Each of the adapted features, as well as the overall account, functions to explain and justify war against Ammon. The shrewd shift from Aroer of Moab to Aroer of Ammon demonstrates that those responsible for this iteration were familiar with Ammonite Aroer and exploited the coincidence. Additionally, the victorious outcome specifies settlements in the Rabbat-Ammon vicinity not elsewhere linked together and otherwise named only in Josh 13:25 (Aroer) and Ezek 27:17 (Minnith).

"Sihon king of the Amorites, the king of Heshbon" provides a clue to the date of the Judges version of Israel's Transjordanian conquest. Archaeology demonstrates that Dhiban, Mesha's capital according to the Mesha inscription, expanded and prospered from the mid- to late ninth through the mid-eighth centuries. Hesban, to the north, revived in the ninth century but flourished during the seventh and sixth centuries. Identifying Heshbon as Sihon's capital, rather than Dhiban, suggests a seventh- or sixth-century date either for this rendering of the story or for revisions to an earlier narrative. Just as seventh-century details including settlement names were woven into an earlier exodus story to lend familiarity,[60] the invocation of Heshbon rather than Dibon may indicate seventh- or sixth-century editorial updating. In contrast to the Heshbon Ballad (Num 21:27–30), our text shows no awareness of Heshbon's fiery demise, which probably occurred not before the sixth century. The fact that Judg 11 does not credit Jephthah with the destruction of Heshbon hints that this version predates the conflagration. Based on the archaeological evidence, the Jephthah narrative reflects multiple eras and literary stages: the early-ninth-century Israelite defeat of Sihon as surrogate for Moab; the late-ninth- or eighth-century Ammonite invasion of Gilead; and a seventh-century rendition of the Sihon episode.

Additional geographic and literary features of Judg 11 hint at Judahite, exilic, and perhaps postexilic crafting.[61] The possible or intentional conflation of Mizpah of Benjamin with Mizpah/Mizpeh of Gilead and the need to specify "Mizpeh of Gilead" suggest a Cisjordanian orientation and possibly limited familiarity with northern Transjordan. The narrative conflation of Moabite and Ammonite elements demands an explanation. Perhaps Israelites accepted the conflation as a literary device demonstrating that the narrative served theological and etiological rather than historical purposes. Alternatively, the average Israelite may not have known the distinctions, or the conflation may point to a late date when the distinctions were largely forgotten or irrelevant. In another literary argument, scholars including Richter, Becker, Böhler, and Groß consider Judg 11 to draw on the Deut 2 account, requiring a postexilic date.[62]

Why situate a seventh- or sixth-century version of ninth- and eighth-century battles in the premonarchic, tribal period? A number of explanations may be suggested. First, tribes may coexist with a monarchy (as in contemporary Jordan). Stories such as this might have afforded a vehicle for preserving the history and traditions of tribes within Israel's narrative without directly challenging the authority of the king. Second, according to the Bible, Gilead held a prominent place during the united monarchy. Thus, Judges may retroject later accounts describing Israel's acquisition and defense of the region into the premonarchic period. Third,

---

[60] Israel Finkelstein and Neil Asher Silberman, *The Bible Unearthed: Archaeology's New Vision of Ancient Israel and the Origin of Its Sacred Texts* (New York: Free Press, 2001), 65–68.

[61] Groß and Reinhard Achenbach represent the views of those who argue that Israelite claims to Transjordanian territory reflect the situation of postexilic Ammon and the claims of the returnees to Ammonite territory (Achenbach, *Die Vollendung der Tora: Studien zur Redaktionsgeschichte des Numeribuches im Kontext von Hexateuch und Pentateuch*, BZABR 3 [Wiesbaden: Harrassowitz, 2002], 11–12; Groß, *Richter*, 563, 567).

[62] Groß, *Richter*, 559–60.

invoking a precedent serves to promote popular acceptance for a current event such as battle for contested territory near the Jabbok, to legitimate by analogy, and to demonstrate continuity with the glorified past.[63]

Archaeology in conjunction with biblical and extrabiblical texts reveals the vicissitudes of Transjordanian Israelite, Moabite, and Ammonite hegemony and the rise and fall of prominent cities, notably Dhiban/Dibon and Hesban/Heshbon. These changing circumstances furnish historical contexts for events related in Judg 11:12–33 as well as other biblical texts that detail Israelite interaction with the neighbors to the east.

[63] Morris, "Use and Abuse of Homer," 129.

SBL PRESS New and Recent Titles

SOURCEBOOK FOR ANCIENT MESOPOTAMIAN MEDICINE
JoAnn Scurlock
Paper $84.95, 978-1-58983-969-4   786 pages, 2014   Code: 061536
Hardcover $104.95, 978-1-58983-970-0   E-book $84.95, 978-1-58983-971-7
Writings from the Ancient World 36

THE WITCHCRAFT SERIES MAQLÛ
Tzvi Abusch
Paper $29.95, 978-1-62837-081-2   216 pages, 2015   Code: 061537
Hardcover $44.95, 978-1-62837-082-9   E-book $29.95, 978-1-62837-085-0
Writings from the Ancient World 37

THE BURIED FOUNDATION OF THE GILGAMESH EPIC
The Akkadian Huwawa Narrative
Daniel E. Fleming and Sara J. Milstein
Paper $35.95   248 pages, 2014   Code: 069562
Cuneiform Monographs 39, Brill Reprints 62

DIVINATION, POLITICS, AND ANCIENT NEAR EASTERN EMPIRES
Alan Lenzi and Jonathan Stökl, editors
Digital open-access, 978-1-58983-998-4   220 pages, 2014   Code: 062807
http://www.sbl-site.org/publications/Books_ANEmonographs.aspx
Paper $29.95, 978-1-58983-996-0   Hardcover $44.95, 978-1-58983-997-7
Ancient Near East Monographs 7

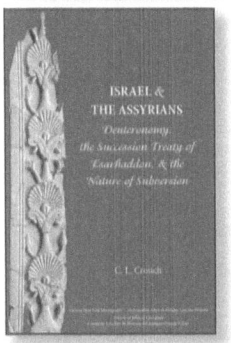

ISRAEL AND THE ASSYRIANS
Deuteronomy, the Succession Treaty of Esarhaddon, and the Nature of Subversion
C. L. Crouch
Digital open-access, 978-1-62837-026-3   234 pages, 2014   Code: 062808
http://www.sbl-site.org/publications/Books_ANEmonographs.aspx
Paper $32.95, 978-1-62837-025-6   Hardcover $47.95, 978-1-62837-027-0
Ancient Near East Monographs 8

SBL Press • P.O. Box 2243 • Williston, VT 05495-2243
Phone: 877-725-3334 (toll-free) or 802-864-6185 • Fax: 802-864-7626
Order online at www.sbl-site.org/publications

The Politics of Psalmody: Psalm 60 and the Rise and Fall of Judean Independence

CRAIG EVAN ANDERSON
craigevananderson@gmail.com
Azusa Pacific University, Azusa, CA 91702

Psalm 60 exhibits two conflicting literary structures. One of these structures is evident by the psalm's use of chiasmus; the other is evident by the psalm's use of meter. The identification of these two conflicting structures indicates a two-stage composition of Ps 60. Examination of the chiasmus within the psalm and a consideration of its two-stage composition elucidate the date of Ps 60. While most scholars date Ps 60 to sometime between the late eighth century and early sixth century BCE, careful observation of the psalm's structure and political references indicates that the two-stage composition of Ps 60 dates to the Hasmonean and Herodian periods. Building on a second- and first-century BCE date for the two-stage composition of the psalm, a text-critical analysis of the psalm indicates that the Greek version of the psalm reflects a Hebrew *Vorlage* that predates the MT version of the psalm. Consequently, proto-MT Ps 60 seems to date to the end of the first century CE.

Psalm 60 is one of the most politically oriented psalms in the Hebrew Bible.[1] In order to understand the psalm properly, therefore, it is crucial to identify effectively the psalm's historical context.[2] Despite ample scholarly investigation, however, the historical context of Ps 60 has remained elusive. For the past two centuries, scholars have proposed a range of dates for the psalm that spans nearly a millennium. In the nineteenth century and the early twentieth century, many scholars

---

I presented a shorter version of this paper under the same title at the Society of Biblical Literature Pacific Coast Regional Meeting in spring 2009.

[1] Unless otherwise indicated, this article follows the enumeration of the psalms of the MT (as it differs slightly from that of the LXX). This article also uses the Hebrew versification, which counts the psalm's superscription as vv. 1–2 and the psalm proper as vv. 3–14.

[2] See Frank-Lothar Hossfeld and Erich Zenger, *Psalms 2: A Commentary on Psalms 51–100*, trans. Linda Maloney, Hermeneia (Minneapolis: Fortress, 2005), 94.

argued for a date as late as the Hasmonean period.³ Yet other scholars have dated it to as early as the time of David or Solomon.⁴

Since the publication of an article on Ps 60 by Ulrich Kellermann in 1978 and, furthermore, since the publication of Hans-Joachim Kraus's commentary on the Psalms, which was instrumental in popularizing Kellermann's argument, scholars have formed a loose consensus dating the psalm to the last few years of Jerusalem before the Babylonian destruction of the city in 587 BCE.⁵ Kellermann's argument on behalf of this date rests largely on the confluence of two historical phenomena to which Kellermann believes Ps 60:6, 11 refer. Kellermann interprets קֶשֶׁט in v. 6 as a reference to archers representative of "die Gefahr aus dem Norden," and he understands v. 11 as indicative of a time of military conflict between Judah and Edom.⁶ On the basis of this observation, Kellermann notices that the one time that Judah faced invasion from a northern enemy while simultaneously standing in conflict with Edom was during the Babylonian invasion at the beginning of the sixth century BCE. Historically, it seems likely that Edom opportunistically capitalized on Judah's weakened state during the Babylonian invasion by launching incursions into Judean territory.⁷

Following the publication of Kellermann's article, commentaries on the Psalms and articles on Ps 60 have followed suit, routinely dating Ps 60 to the fall of Jerusalem at the beginning of the sixth century BCE.⁸ Most scholars see a two-stage composition for Ps 60.⁹ The first stage consists of a Josian oracle in

---

³See, e.g., Bernhard Duhm, *Die Psalmen*, KHC 14 (Tübingen: Mohr Siebeck, 1922), 236–39; Rudolf Kittel, *Die Psalmen, übersetzt und erklärt*, KAT 13 (Leipzig: Deichert, 1922), 208.

⁴Mitchell Dahood, *Psalms: Introduction, Translation, and Notes*, vol. 2, *Psalms 51–100*, AB 17 (Garden City, NY: Doubleday, 1968), 76; Moses Buttenwieser, *The Psalms: Chronologically Treated with a New Translation* (1938; repr., New York: Ktav, 1969), 67–82.

⁵Ulrich Kellermann, "Erwägungen zum historischen Ort von Psalm LX," *VT* 28 (1978): 56–65; Hans-Joachim Kraus, *Psalms 60–150: A Commentary*, trans. Hilton C. Oswald (Minneapolis: Augsburg, 1988), 3; Elmer A. Leslie is one of the few scholars prior to Kraus and Kellermann who dates Ps 60 to 587 BCE (*The Psalms: Translated and Interpreted in the Light of Hebrew Life and Worship* [New York: Abingdon, 1949], 232–34). Ironically, he reads Edom as an ally of Judah and a place of refuge in Ps 60:11.

⁶Kellermann makes this association between archers and "die Gefahr aus dem Norden" through his reading of Jer 4:29, 51:3 ("Erwägungen zum historischen Ort," 60–61).

⁷For a helpful overview of Edom's activity at this time, see John R. Bartlett, *Edom and the Edomites*, JSOTSup 77 (Sheffield: Sheffield Academic, 1989), 147–61. Such an act of opportunistic aggression may be the critical incident that provoked the wrath of the Judean prophets. See esp. Ezek 35:2–15; see also Isa 34:5–17, 63:1–6, Jer 49:7–22, Ezek 25:12–14, Obadiah, Mal 1:2–5.

⁸Marvin E. Tate, *Psalms 51–100*, WBC 20 (Dallas: Word, 1990), 104; Hossfeld and Zenger, *Psalms 2*, 95–96; Graham S. Ogden, "Psalm 60: Its Rhetoric, Form, and Function," *JSOT* 31 (1985): 83–94; Ernst Axel Knauf, "Psalm LX und Psalm CVIII," *VT* 50 (2000): 55–69.

⁹See, e.g., Leslie, *Psalms: Translated and Interpreted*, 232; W. O. E. Oesterley, *The Psalms: Translated with Text-critical and Exegetical Notes* (1939; repr., London: SPCK, 1953), 297; Artur Weiser, *The Psalms: A Commentary*, OTL (Philadelphia: Westminster, 1962), 438–39; A. A.

vv. 8–10.[10] The second stage consists of the early-sixth-century communal lament that was built around this oracle in vv. 3–7, 11–14.

Yet, despite the consensus that has formed around an early-sixth-century date for Ps 60, there are some major problems with this date, which, I believe, ultimately originate from a form-critical misreading of the psalm. Consequently, before I can directly address the problem of dating the psalm and propose an alternative to this date, a form-critical analysis of Ps 60 is in order.

I. Form-Critical Analysis of Psalm 60

Scholars almost unanimously affirm that Ps 60:3–14 features a tripartite structure. One of the clearest indications of this is the meter that the psalm employs: vv. 3–7 and 11–14 are arranged as bicola, while vv. 8–10 feature tricola. Most scholars' generic appraisal of the psalm follows this metric observation; they read vv. 3–7 and vv. 11–14 as two components of a communal complaint that flank an oracle (vv. 8–10) situated in the psalm's core.[11] However, the psalm stands structurally conflicted. Contrary to the psalm's metric arrangement, there are numerous indications that the oracle consists of vv. 8–11, not vv. 8–10. This single verse adjustment has substantial implications for how we must interpret the psalm.

Psalm 60:8aβ–11 exhibits a chiasmus that reveals the cohesion between v. 10 and v. 11. Psalm 60:8aβ–11 features a speech unit uttered by God comprised of three sections: two pairs of couplets (vv. 8aβ–9aα, vv. 10aβ–11) flanking a triplet (vv. 9aβ–10aα). Verses 8aβ and 8b constitute a couplet, as they both employ *piel* imperfect first person common singular verbs associated with a northern Israelite

---

Anderson, *Psalms 1–72*, vol. 1 of *The Book of Psalms*, NCB (Grand Rapids: Eerdmans, 1981), 441; Kraus, *Psalms 60–150*, 3; Ogden, "Psalm 60," 87; Erhard S. Gerstenberger, *Psalms: Part 1, with an Introduction to Cultic Poetry*, FOTL 14 (Grand Rapids: Eerdmans, 1988), 242; John Eaton, *The Psalms: A Historical and Spiritual Commentary with an Introduction and New Translation* (London: T&T Clark, 2003), 228.

[10] This observation that Ps 60 appears to exhibit a two-stage (or three-stage) composition, in which a psalmist utilized the preexisting oracle as the centerpiece of the psalm, furnishing the complaint in the introduction and conclusion of the psalm around this oracle, is well established in scholarship dating back to as early as the time of Heinrich Ewald (so Buttenwieser, *Psalms*, 68).

[11] Oesterley, *Psalms*, 297; Sigmund Mowinckel, *Real and Apparent Tricola in Hebrew Psalm Poetry*, Avhandlinger utgitt av Det Norske videnskaps-Akademi i Oslo 2.2 (Oslo: I Kommisjon hos Aschehoug, 1957), 16, 20–21; Kellermann, "Erwägungen zum historischen Ort," 58; Anderson, *Psalms 1–72*, 441; Kraus, *Psalms 60–150*, 3; Tate, *Psalms 51–100*, 103. Dahood also uses meter as a structural key. However, he sees a fourfold division (vv. 3–5, 6–7, 8–10, 11–14), blending metric and thematic criteria (*Psalms 51–100*, 76). Edward J. Kissane offers an unusual deviation from this scholarly trend by dividing the psalm into three strophes of four verses (vv. 3–6, 7–10, 11–14) (*The Book of Psalms: Translated from a Critically Revised Hebrew Text, with a Commentary* [Westminster, MD: Newman, 1953], 258).

city. Verses 9aα¹⁻² and 9aα³⁻⁴ stand as a couplet, as they both contain לִי ("to me"), expressing possession, and northern tribal territory, namely, Gilead and Manasseh. Furthermore, these two couplets form a chiasm as Shechem (v. 8aβ) is within Manasseh (v. 9aα³⁻⁴), and the Valley of Succoth (v. 8b) is within Gilead (v. 9aα¹⁻²).[12]

The last portion of God's speech in Ps 60:8aβ–11 consists of a pair of couplets as well. Verses 10aβ and 10b form a couplet, as they both feature the preposition עַל ("upon"), associated with a nation that immediately follows the preposition.[13] Verses 11a and 11b constitute a couplet by virtue of their striking similarity, as both v. 11a and v. 11b are questions beginning with מִי ("who?") followed by a verb meaning "to lead" (יבל in v. 11a and נחה in v. 11b) bearing a first person common singular suffix. Furthermore, these two couplets also form a chiasm.[14] The reference to Edom in vv. 10aβ and 11b is the clearest indication of this. On the interior of the chiasm, "Philistia" of v. 10b links to the "fortified city" (עִיר מָצוֹר) of v. 11a.[15]

The two chiasms consist of pairs of matching couplets (vv. 8aβ–9aα and vv. 10aβ–11) flanking a triplet in vv. 9aβ–10aα. Not only is this triplet signaled by the parameters designated by the two chiasms, but also the triplet is itself internally consistent.[16] Each of the three components within the triplet in vv. 9aβ–10aα consists of a political entity identified as a piece of personal equipment featuring a first person common singular suffix.[17]

---

[12] Kellermann, "Erwägungen zum historischen Ort," 62.

[13] Kellermann groups four pieces of equipment together: "Helm, Herrscherstab, Waschbecken und Schuh" ("Erwägungen zum historischen Ort," 62). This association obscures the structural division between v. 10aα and v. 10aβ. However, the text in no way links these four together. While the first three items undoubtedly constitute a unit, as will be argued below, the shoe stands in distinction from the former three. On the contrary, one should associate the shoe (נעל) in v. 10aβ with the shout (רוע) in v. 10b. Together, these terms express the completeness of God's victory over Edom and Philistia from head (i.e., "shout") to toe (i.e., "shoe").

[14] Although Kellermann recognizes the chiasm in vv. 8aβ–9aα and the triplet in vv. 9aβ–10aα ("Erwägungen zum historischen Ort," 62), surprisingly, he fails to notice the chiasm in vv. 10aβ–11, which balances the entire oracle.

[15] Contra Kellermann, "Erwägungen zum historischen Ort," 63; Kraus, *Psalms 60–150*, 5; Ogden, "Psalm 60," 87–88; Knauf, "Psalm LX und Psalm CVIII," 56. Although many scholars want to associate עִיר מָצוֹר of Ps 60:11a with an Edomite city (typically Bozrah), 2 Kgs 18:8 links Philistia with the phrase עִיר מִבְצָר, which is comparable to that in Ps 60:11a and matches the parallel line in Ps 108:11a exactly.

[16] Kellermann, "Erwägungen zum historischen Ort," 62.

[17] Some scholars allow their geographic presuppositions to distort their structural analyses of the psalm. Kraus discusses Ephraim and Judah together in terms of their roles as God's helmet and scepter respectively (*Psalms 60–150*, 5); however, he does not tie Moab to Ephraim and Judah as the psalm does. On the contrary, Kraus packages Moab within his discussion of "the fallen vassal states Edom, Moab, and Philistia." Similarly, Gerstenberger groups Moab not with Ephraim and Judah but in terms of the "three foreign territories" that "represent the fiercest neighbors, Moab, Edom, and the Philistines" (*Psalms: Part 1*, 240). Knauf also makes this error, noting a positive portrayal of Ephraim and Judah, yet two sentences later claiming, "eindeutig negativ werden Moab und Edom gesehen" ("Psalm LX und Psalm CVIII," 57).

Psalm 60

I	A	I will exult, I will divide Shechem	A	אֶעְלֹזָה אֲחַלְּקָה שְׁכֶם	8aβ
	B	And I will measure the Valley of Succoth	B	וְעֵמֶק סֻכּוֹת אֲמַדֵּד	8b
	B′	Gilead is mine	B′	לִי גִלְעָד	9aα$^{1-2}$
	A′	And Manasseh is mine	A′	וְלִי מְנַשֶּׁה	9aα$^{3-4}$
II	A	And Ephraim is my helmet	A	וְאֶפְרַיִם מָעוֹז רֹאשִׁי	9aβ
	B	Judah is my scepter	B	יְהוּדָה מְחֹקְקִי	9b
	A′	Moab is my washbasin	A′	מוֹאָב סִיר רַחְצִי	10aα
I′	A	Upon Edom I will throw my shoe	A	עַל־אֱדוֹם אַשְׁלִיךְ נַעֲלִי	10aβ
	B	Over Philistia I will shout	B	עָלַי פְּלֶשֶׁת הִתְרוֹעָעִי	10b
	B′	Who will lead me to the fortified city?	B′	מִי יֹבִלֵנִי עִיר מָצוֹר	11a
	A′	Who will lead me to Edom?	A′	מִי נָחַנִי עַד־אֱדוֹם	11b

It is also important to notice that the first political entity in the triplet, Ephraim (v. 9aβ), is closely associated with that which immediately precedes it, Manasseh (v. 9aα$^{3-4}$). At the same time, the third political entity in the triplet, Moab (v. 10aα), is associated with that which immediately follows it, Edom (v. 10aβ). Judah alone stands at the heart of the triplet and the entire poetic speech unit.

Consequently, while meter indicates that the tripartite arrangement of Ps 60 consists of vv. 3–7, vv. 8–10, and vv. 11–14, numerous other features indicate an alternative tripartite arrangement: vv. 3–7, vv. 8–11, and vv. 12–14.[18] First, we have already seen how vv. 8–11 exhibit a carefully orchestrated chiastic literary structure that is distinct from the rest of the psalm. Second, vv. 8–11 contain nine references to geographic locations, whereas vv. 3–7, 12–14 contain no explicit references to geographic locations. Third, vv. 8–11 feature God as the speaker, speaking in the first person singular. On the contrary, vv. 3–7, 12–14 feature the psalmist as the speaker, speaking in the first person plural.[19] Fourth, "God" (אֱלֹהִים) is consistently

---

Kraus advocates adding either "sea" (ים) or "waters" (מי) before "Moab" in v. 10 (*Psalms 60–150*, 2). However, this is unnecessary because (1) the verse is concerned with the *political entity* of Moab (like Ephraim and Judah in the preceding verse), not the waters of Moab; and (2) the verse claims that Moab is God's "basin" (סִיר), not the washing waters themselves.

[18] The few scholars who recognize the structural integrity of vv. 8–11 tend to be those who emphasize form-critical analysis in their examinations of the psalm. See Ogden, "Psalm 60," 83–84; Gerstenberger, *Psalms: Part 1*, 239–41.

[19] Remarkably, most scholars import a change of speaker between the first person voice of v. 10 and the first person voice of v. 11, despite the fact that the text gives no indication of such a change. Such interpreters typically claim that, in v. 11, the text abruptly shifts (without formal indication) from God as the speaker (vv. 8–10) to a military leader as the speaker (v. 11). See, e.g., Leslie, *Psalms: Translated and Interpreted*, 234; Weiser, *Psalms: A Commentary*, 438; Kellermann,

mentioned in the first line of each of these three sections (vv. 3, 8, 12) and is mentioned only once elsewhere in the psalm (v. 14). Similarly, the repetition of אֱלֹהִים זְנַחְתָּנוּ ("God has rejected us") in vv. 3 and 12 marks the beginning of both of these outer sections (vv. 3–7 and vv. 12–14).

II. Historical-Critical Analysis of the Oracle (Psalm 60:8–11)

The structural conflict within Ps 60 elucidates its composition history. A psalmist took a preexisting oracle (currently exhibited in vv. 8–11), which featured a chiastic arrangement, not a metric one. The psalmist composed a metrically oriented complaint around that oracle. Yet, in doing so, the psalmist tied his or her metric composition into the last line of the oracle (v. 11). In this way the psalmist granted some extra significance to v. 11 not only as the last line of the oracle but also as the first line of the concluding complaint (vv. 11–14).

This observation concerning v. 11 is crucial for an interpretation of the psalm, as most scholarly attempts to date the psalm rely primarily on this verse. Most scholars, however, tend to respect the mystery of this psalm, remaining cautiously undecided regarding its date of composition; those who argue for its date typically take v. 11 as the point of departure, label the psalm as "anti-Edomite," and search through the various times during which Judah and Edom were in conflict in order to try to find the one that is most suitable for the psalm. After anchoring the psalmist's complaint in vv. 11–14 (and typically vv. 3–7 as well) in an Edomite conflict based on v. 11, scholars routinely attempt to identify a historical context for vv. 8–10 in the decades that precede their date for v. 11.[20]

As I mentioned earlier, Kellermann's argument is essentially based on two points: (1) the reference to a "bow" in v. 6, and (2) the reference to Edom in v. 11. Both of these points are highly problematic. The problem with the first point is that, although Ps 59:6 LXX uses the word "bow" (τόξον) here, the Hebrew word "bow" (קֶשֶׁת) does not occur in Ps 60:6 MT. Instead, Ps 60:6 MT has the essentially Aramaic word קֹשֶׁט ("truth"), and there is no instance of the interchange of these words, קֶשֶׁת and קֹשֶׁט, before the Common Era.[21] The second point, regarding "Edom" in v. 11,

---

"Erwägungen zum historischen Ort," 58; Kraus, *Psalms 60–150*, 5; Anderson, *Psalms 1–72*, 445; Knauf, "Psalm LX und Psalm CVIII," 56; James Limburg, *Psalms* (WeBC; Louisville: Westminster John Knox, 2000), 200. Ogden ("Psalm 60," 83–84) and Gerstenberger (*Psalms: Part 1*, 241) stand as two of the few scholars who do not make this claim.

[20] See, e.g., Kellermann, "Erwägungen zum historischen Ort," 56–65; Ogden, "Psalm 60," 91; Knauf, "Psalm LX und Psalm CVIII," 55–58; Hossfeld and Zenger, *Psalms 2*, 94–96.

[21] Hoping to preserve a Davidic-Solomonic date for the psalm, Dahood discounts the Aramaic nature of קֹשֶׁט, claiming that the *tet* "resulted from the partial assimilation to emphatic *qoph*," appealing to Ugaritic texts to support his case (*Psalms 51–100*, 79). However, the fact that

is problematic for reasons I just discussed. That is, if we regard Edom as simply one of the four targets that the oracle in vv. 8–11 identifies, it takes on far less significance than if it were the one and only location about which the psalmist wrote in the complaint of vv. 3–7, 11–14. Of course, it is still meaningful that the psalmist tied v. 11 into his or her metric structure. Yet that significance is not as great as one would posit if the mention of Edom were the lamenting psalmist's own contribution.

If the arrangement that I have proposed is correct and the oracle extends until v. 11, then the dating technique of identifying a time of conflict between Edom and Judah and working backwards collapses. If the oracle consists of vv. 8–11, then it contains every geopolitical reference in the body of the psalm. Therefore, any attempt to date Ps 60 should begin with the oracle. In Ps 60:8–11, God equips himself with three political locations: Ephraim, Judah, and Moab. Among these, God stands centered on Judah. Ephraim and Moab serve as the two locations that, as part of God's equipment, God will use as launching platforms for exerting control over neighboring regions. From Moab (v. 10aα), God wishes to extend control over other southern foreign nations—Edom and Philistia (vv. 10aβ–11). Similarly, from Ephraim (v. 9aβ), God intends to establish authority over other northern Israelite tribes—Manasseh and Gilead (vv. 8aβ–9aα). The militant nuance is evident as the verbs חלק ("to divide"; see Gen 49:27, Isa 53:12, Mic 2:4) and מדד ("to measure"; see 2 Sam 8:2, Hab 3:6), used in reference to Shechem and the Valley of Succoth in v. 8aβ–b, express domination.[22]

As many scholars have already recognized, the fact that Ps 60 indicates a lack of control over northern Israel precludes any date for the oracle before the Assyrian invasion in 721 BCE.[23] Dating the oracle to a period during Hezekiah's rebellion against Sennacherib in 705–701 BCE is problematic. Hezekiah's foreign policy consisted primarily of diplomacy, not expansionistic aggression, as he committed himself to generating a network of alliances that were necessary to rebuff the military advances of Assyria.[24] We do not have evidence of Hezekiah gaining possession of

---

there are no instances of the term קֶשֶׁט meaning "bow" or "archery" in the Hebrew Bible greatly compromises his case. Furthermore, as many scholars have recognized, the fact that Judah does not seem to have control over the northern territories indicates a date for Ps 60 sometime after the Assyrian destruction in 721 BCE. Consequently, anchoring an argument in Ugaritic linguistics in order to try to explain a text that dates after 721 BCE is unpersuasive.

[22] Knauf, "Psalm LX und Psalm CVIII," 57.

[23] Kissane, *Book of Psalms*, 260; Kraus, *Psalms 60–150*, 3. For an extended rejection of a Davidic-Solomonic date for Ps 60, see Kellermann, "Erwägungen zum historischen Ort," 59.

[24] Hezekiah seems to have been in an alliance with Philistia. While the historical details are far from clear, there are some signs of political turbulence between Hezekiah's Judah and Edom. Hezekiah apparently engaged in diplomatic negotiations with Edom, although Edom evidently never committed to an alliance with Hezekiah. While 1 Chr 4:34–43 describes some territorial conflicts in the south during "the days of King Hezekiah of Judah" including a Simeonite incursion into Mount Seir, the target of that attack seems to have been Amalek (vv. 42–43). For helpful

Ephraim or Moab,[25] and neither do the rather aggressive claims of Ps 60:8:aβ–9aα concerning Manasseh and Gilead have historical support during Hezekiah's reign nor do they match the ostensibly conciliatory policy of Hezekiah toward northern Israel.

Moreover, dating the oracle to the time of Hezekiah either before 705 BCE or after 701 BCE simply cannot work. Before the death of Sargon II in 705 BCE, Hezekiah's Judah was an Assyrian vassal. Without the death of Sargon II, Hezekiah had no prompt to offer hope that aspirations of expansion would be credible. After 701 BCE, Judah was devastated. According to Sennacherib's records, during his tour of the Shephelah and Judah he ravaged forty-six cities and numerous villages, making it clear that, while Hezekiah may have retained control of Jerusalem, the countryside belonged to Assyria.[26] In such a context, a Judean-based claim of expansion would have been seen as nothing short of silly.

Many scholars have suggested a Josian date for the oracle of Ps 60, but this is highly questionable as well. Although Josiah certainly demonstrated expansionistic tendencies, such expansion was locally confined, essentially consisting of his attack on Bethel amid his religious reformation. Even if one were to claim that Ps 60 represented Josian expansionistic ideals, then we would expect Ps 60 to target Samaria, not Shechem or Succoth—much as we find in the idealized passages mentioning the extent of Josiah's reform such as 1 Kgs 23:19.

Furthermore, claims of Judean expansion into Philistia are out of place in a Josian context. Egypt seems to have been in control of the southern Levant throughout the reign of Josiah, especially the territory of Philistia, through which Egypt moved freely. The historical evidence points to the fact that Josiah was in an alliance with Egypt throughout almost the entirety of his reign until shortly before his death, and thus he would hardly have been in a position to make aggressive claims concerning Philistia.[27]

As the oracle must date to sometime after 721 BCE, and both Hezekian and Josian dates for the oracle are problematic—and an exilic date is obviously impossible for the oracle in Ps 60:8–11—we must consider a postexilic context for the oracle.[28] Once again, we are looking for a time period in which Judean leadership

---

reconstructions of the politics of Judah, Philistia, Edom, and their neighbors at the close of the eighth century BCE, see Bartlett, *Edom and the Edomites*, 131–32; Gösta W. Ahlström, *The History of Ancient Palestine* (Minneapolis: Fortress, 1993), 696–98; Alan Millard, "Assyrian Involvement in Edom," in *Early Edom and Moab: The Beginning of the Iron Age in Southern Jordan*, ed. Piotr Bienkowski, Sheffield Archaeological Monographs 7 (Sheffield: J. R. Collis, 1992), 36.

[25] Kellermann, "Erwägungen zum historischen Ort," 60.

[26] Daniel David Luckenbill, *The Annals of Sennacherib*, OIP 2 (Chicago: University of Chicago Press, 1924), 70.

[27] Ahlström, *History of Ancient Palestine*, 763–65.

[28] Regarding postexilic contexts for Psalm 60, Knauf persuasively discounts the plausibility of dating the psalm to the time of Nehemiah. The fact that early postexilic Judah had no army (v. 12) and was subservient to the central authority of Persia led Knauf to claim, "damit ist Ps lx

maintained control over Ephraim and Moab and sought to expand its control over northern Israel and southern neighboring foreign nations. This describes precisely the circumstances of the expansionistic military campaigns of John Hyrcanus I.[29] Consequently, I propose that a Hasmonean date for Ps 60, which had been popular among scholars about a century ago, deserves reconsideration.

According to Josephus, the death of Antiochus VII prompted Hyrcanus to embark on a series of military campaigns (Josephus, *J.W.* 1.62–63, *Ant.* 13.255). Hyrcanus first captured Medaba (Μήδαβαν) and Shechem (Σίκιμα).[30] By attacking Shechem, Hyrcanus demonstrated control over the region of Ephraim. By defeating Medaba, Hyrcanus gained control over a portion of Moabite (or Nabatean) Transjordan, thus granting him a strategic hold on the King's Highway.[31]

This may have been the time when Ps 60:8aβ–11 was written. On the basis of the scholarly opinion that Hyrcanus attacked Shechem in 128 BCE, I suggest a date of composition shortly thereafter—at some point early in the last quarter of the second century BCE.[32] Not only does Ps 60:8aβ–11 identify John Hyrcanus's control over Ephraim and Moab, but it also features his (or Hasmonean Judah's) interest in conquering the Shechem region, the Valley of Succoth, Edom, and Philistia. After his initial conquests over Ephraim (Shechem) and Moab (Medaba), Hyrcanus invaded Idumea (Edom), taking Adoreon (Ἀδωρεόν) and Marisa (Μάρισαν) (Josephus, *J.W.* 1.63, *Ant.* 13.257). Following this, Hyrcanus attacked Samaria (Josephus, *Ant.* 13.275).[33] Though he had already attacked Shechem, this victory did not grant him control of the region. Rather it would have given Hyrcanus

---

entweder vor 586 v. Chr. zu datieren oder nach 129 v. Chr." However, anticipating his argument concerning the compositional relationship between Ps 60 and Ps 108, Knauf continues, "wobei letzteres Datum hier aus redaktionsgeschichtlichen Gründen ausgeschlossen ist" ("Psalm LX und Psalm CVIII," 56).

[29] Regarding the vision of conquest detailed in the oracle of vv. 8–10, Weiser makes the incorrect assertion that "there has never been an historical situation in the history of Israel ... in which the aforementioned territories had been at one and the same time conquered and distributed" (*Psalms: A Commentary*, 441). In making this claim, Weiser clearly has neglected to consider a Hasmonean setting for this oracle.

[30] According to Joe D. Seger, Hyrcanus's initial attack on Shechem did not destroy the city but rather consisted of the destruction of the temple on Tell er-Ras ("Shechem," *OEANE* 5:23). Josephus reports (*Ant.* 13.255) that, along with these, Hyrcanus also captured Samoga (Σαμόγαν), a city that is unidentified to this day; see Joseph Sievers, *The Hasmoneans and Their Supporters: From Mattathias to the Death of John Hyrcanus I*, SFSHJ 6 (Altanta: Scholars Press, 1990), 142. Presumably Samoga is in the vicinity of Medaba; see Yohanan Aharoni and Michael Avi-Yonah, *The Macmillan Bible Atlas*, rev. 3rd ed. (New York: Macmillan, 1993), 155.

[31] Aharoni and Avi-Yonah, *Macmillan Bible Atlas*, 155.

[32] Edward F. Campbell dates Hyrcanus's attack on Shechem to 128 BCE ("Shechem," *NEAEHL* 4:1345–54). Seger dates the attack two years later in 126 BCE (*OEANE* 5:23).

[33] Campbell cites numismatic evidence to argue that Hyrcanus's final destruction of Shechem did not occur until 107 BCE—the same time that Josephus claims that Hyrcanus besieged Samaria (*NEAEHL* 4:1354).

control of everything up to Shechem, which is situated on the border between Ephraim and Manasseh. Thus, his initial raid of Shechem indicates his domination of the region *between* Judea and Shechem—that is, the region of Ephraim, *not* the region of Manasseh. However, after he conquered the Idumean cities of Adoreon and Marisa, Hyrcanus overcame Samaria, which gave him control over the region of Manasseh as far northeast as Scythopolis (Σκυθοπόλεως) and northwest as they "laid waste the whole country south of Mount Carmel" (τὴν ἐντὸς Καρμήλου τοῦ ὄρους χώραν ἅπασαν κατενείμαντο) (Josephus, *J.W.* 1.65–66).

Though Hyrcanus was not able to overcome the other two regions mentioned in Ps 60:8–11, Gilead and Philistia, the Hasmonean interest in these regions remains apparent, as Alexander Jannaeus conquered these regions shortly after the death of Hyrcanus. Josephus catalogued Jannaeus's dominion, which included (1) nine "seacoast" cities that encompassed the traditional Philistine region stretching from Straton's Tower (Στράτωνος πύργον; in the vicinity of Dor) as far south as Rhinocorura ('Ρινοκορούραν; southwest of Raphia); (2) the "Idumean" (i.e., Edomite) cities of Adora, Marisa, and "the whole of Idumea" (ὅλην Ἰδουμαίαν); (3) the territory of Manasseh (i.e., the region of Shechem), featuring "Samaria, Mount Carmel, Mount Tabor, Scythopolis, and Gamala" (Σαμάρειαν Καρμήλιον ὄρος καὶ τὸ Ἰταβύριον ὄρος Σκυθόπολιν Γάδαρα); and (4) the entire Transjordan from Seleucia (Σελεύκειαν; northeast of the Sea of Chinnereth) to Zoara (Ζόαρα; biblical Zoar, southeast of the Dead Sea) (Josephus, *Ant.* 13.395–397).

Jannaeus's conquests are an indicator of Hyrcanus's desire to overcome Gilead and Philistia, some of Hyrcanus's own moves attest to this desire as well. We know that Hyrcanus was interested in controlling the Transjordan (which includes Gilead) because the first place that he attacked was Medaba (Josephus, *J.W.* 1.62–63; *Ant.* 13.255). Furthermore, before he was even leading Judea, he made incursions into "Philistine" territory, successfully attacking the "fields of Azotus" (τοῖς ἀγροῖς Ἀζώτου; biblical Ashdod) under the leadership of his father, Simon (1 Macc 16:4–10).

III. Historical-Critical Analysis of the Complaint (Psalm 60:3–7, 12–14)

Unfortunately for the first-century BCE Judeans, the political success of the Hasmoneans did not last. By 67 BCE, Judea faced civil war due to the leadership conflict between Hyrcanus II and Aristobulus II. In 63 BCE, Pompey eventually resolved the conflict by taking control of Judea on behalf of Rome. Part of the resolution of Roman governance of Palestine entailed the restoration of lands that the Hasmoneans had won from their neighbors. Pompey reestablished the independence of the seacoast ("Philistine") cities. He restored the independence of the Samaritans. He unified the major cities of the Transjordan into a "League of Ten

Cities"—the Decapolis. More importantly, Pompey placed Judea under Idumean administration. I propose that this is the context in which a psalmist wrote the complaint (Ps 60:3–7, 12–14) that couches the oracle (vv. 8–11). This psalmist laments Judea's present political misfortune, citing God's claim of Judean dominion over neighboring regions in the light of its loss of precisely those same regions.

The complaint utilizes prophetic imagery, derived chiefly from the book of Isaiah. Graham Ogden has claimed that Isa 63:1–6 constitutes a response to Ps 60.[34] However, this claim is problematic. Ogden does not develop formal arguments for the dating of these texts; he essentially assumes a ca. 600 BCE date for Ps 60 and a postexilic date for Isa 63:1–6. Thereafter, he points to semantic similarities between these two texts, thinking that such similarities indicate that Isa 63 borrowed from Ps 60.

Against Ogden's claim, I argue that Isa 63:1–6 is a response not to Ps 60, but rather to Isa 34:5–8. Both Isaiah texts refer to Edom in conjunction with its capital city, Bozrah (Isa 34:6, 63:1). Both Isaiah texts graphically describe the abundant volume of blood flow resulting from YHWH's wrath (34:6–7, 63:2–3). Both Isaiah texts specifically mention the blood soaking into the earth (34:7, 63:6). Both Isaiah texts claim that YHWH's destruction of Edom will occur on יוֹם נָקָם, "the day of vengeance" (34:8, 63:4). The only differences between these two texts pertain to the fact that 34:5–8 utilizes a metaphor of YHWH slaughtering livestock while 63:1–6 depicts YHWH treading grapes in a press.

Contrary to Ogden's theory, the semantic correspondence between Isa 63:1–6 and Ps 60 reflects Ps 60's dependence on Isa 63:1–6 and other passages in the book of Isaiah. First, Ogden claims that the question of Isa 63:1, "Who is this that comes from Edom?" responds to Ps 60:11.[35] However, as I have already indicated, the aforementioned question in Isa 63:1 refers to the fulfillment of YHWH's attack on Edom, as was announced in Isa 34:5–8. Furthermore, as my form-critical analysis of Ps 60 has already attempted to demonstrate, the questions of Ps 60:11 were part of the original oracle, which does not necessarily show any overt connection with the book of Isaiah. Nevertheless, by hitching the last section of the oracle (v. 11) to his or her metric scheme, the psalmist cleverly links v. 11 to the rest of the Isaianic complaint (Ps 60:3–7, 12–14). In doing so, the psalmist may indicate a reinterpretation of Isa 34:5–8 and 63:1–6, applying the prophecies to the psalmist's historical circumstance.

Second, Ogden claims that the metaphor of YHWH treading the winepress in Isa 63:1–6 responds to the reference to the people staggering due to strong wine in Ps 60:5 and the image of YHWH treading down enemies in Ps 60:14.[36] However, Isa 63:1–6 is a highly cohesive pericope, in which the metaphor of treading the grape press permeates almost every verse. Yet the allusions to drunkenness in

---

[34] Ogden, "Psalm 60," 91–93.
[35] Ibid., 91–92.
[36] Ibid., 92.

Ps 60:5 and treading in Ps 60:14 bear no internal relationship to each other. It is unlikely that the author of Isa 63:1–6 drew upon two disparate verses in Ps 60 to craft such a cohesive metaphor in Isa 63:1–6, which, once again, seems to couple with Isa 34:5–8, both of which revolve around food preparation. It is far more likely that the psalmist who wrote Ps 60:3–7, 12–14 drew upon a loose array of prophetic material, which included Isa 63:1–6. The fact that both Isa 63:6 and Ps 60:14 have the word "tread" (בוס) may indicate such a correspondence. However, a far more reasonable association between the drunkenness in Ps 60:5 and treading in Ps 60:14 would be through the possibility that Ps 60 is dependent on Isa 51:17–23, which indicates that the people of Jerusalem who are staggering from the drunkenness of the cup of YHWH's wrath will find relief, as YHWH will pass that cup to Jerusalem's enemies who have trampled upon the people of Jerusalem.

Third, as Ogden observes, the semantic correspondence of the terms "help" (עזר) and "salvation" (ישע) in Ps 60:13 and Isa 63:5, and the concept of divine "anger" (אף) in Ps 60:3 and Isa 63:3, 6, certainly may bolster the case for a direct relationship between Ps 60 and Isa 63:1–6. However, they give no indication of the direction of the relationship.

The psalmist composed the complaint in vv. 3–7, 12–14 in the light of Judea's military defeat in Pompey's recent siege of Jerusalem in 63 BCE and in a context of frustration with Judea's necessary submission Idumean governance represented by Antipater (and later by Herod). The psalmist begins the complaint (v. 3) by mentioning God's rejection of his people, referring to the recent loss of Judean independence. The earthquake imagery of v. 4, which is common stock in prophetic and apocalyptic literature reflecting political turbulence,[37] and the reference to retreating from the bow in v. 6 both refer to Judea's recent military conflict.[38] As was discussed earlier, v. 5 provides an Isaianic metaphor of the suffering of God's people. Although v. 7 calls for God's answer, contrary to the opinion of most scholars, the citation of the oracle in vv. 8–11 does not provide that answer.[39] Rather, the psalmist incorporates the oracle as evidence of how God had been sponsoring Judean expansion under Hasmonean leadership not long ago. The citation of the oracle (vv. 8–11) provides the basis for the psalmist to challenge God by juxtaposing the psalmist's depiction of Judea's state of misfortune (vv. 3–6) with this oracle, in which God promises military success (vv. 8–11).[40] Upon citing the oracle,

---

[37] Kellermann, "Erwägungen zum historischen Ort," 59. For earthquakes in prophetic and apocalyptic literature, see Isa 24:18–20; 29:6; Ezek 38:19; Amos 1:1; Matt 27:51–54; Rev 6:12; 8:5; 11:13, 19; 16:18.

[38] See the text-critical discussion of the "bow" later in this article.

[39] For those who identify vv. 8–10 as God's comforting answer to the psalmists complaint in vv. 3–7, see, e.g., Weiser, *Psalms: A Commentary*, 438; Kellermann, "Erwägungen zum historischen Ort," 61.

[40] Ogden is one of the few scholars to recognize the ambiguity of the oracle in its present context, stating, "The question we face here is whether it is God who addresses Israel directly, or

the psalmist returns to his or her original claim and presents it once again in v. 12a in question format, "Have you not rejected us, O God?" (הֲלֹא־אַתָּה אֱלֹהִים זְנַחְתָּנוּ) revealing the psalmist's confidence that he or she has laid out an effective indictment of God and immediately linking this to Judea's depleted military (v. 12b).

There are three ways in which the psalmist cleverly ties the last line of the oracle (v. 11) into the psalmist's own work (vv. 3–7, 12–14). The first, as I have already discussed, is the psalmist's technique of writing in bicola, thereby matching the meter of the psalmist's own composition (vv. 3–7, 12–14) with that of v. 11. The second consists of the parallelism between the twin interrogatives of v. 11 and the double reference to אֱלֹהִים in v. 12.[41] The third way is through semantic selection in v. 13. The psalmist matches the last feet of the bicolon in v. 13 with the last feet of the bicolon in v. 11. Thus, the semantic similarity between מְצָר of v. 13a and עִיר מָצוֹר of v. 11a along with the similarly between עַד־אֱדוֹם of v. 13b and אָדָם of v. 11b draws a parallel between these two bicola, thereby strengthening the association between v. 11 and vv. 12–14. The psalm concludes with a standard expression of hope in v. 14.

IV. Psalm 108

Any discussion of the composition of Ps 60 ought to address the composition of Ps 108 as well. As scholars well know, Ps 108 is a composite of Pss 57:8–12 and 60:7–14.[42] Because of the dependence of Ps 108 on Ps 60, one's dating of Ps 108 sets a *terminus ante quem* for the composition of Ps 60.

Recently, Ernst Axel Knauf wrote an important article on these psalms in which he argued for a preexilic date for Ps 60 and a Hasmonean date for Ps 108.[43] I have already provided several counters to his argument for a preexilic date for Ps 60, and therefore I will no longer address the first half of his article. In the second half of his article, Knauf states that Ps 108 serves as the first part of the Davidic composition of Pss 108–110, as Ps 108 and Ps 110 are two kingly psalms that frame

---

whether it is reported speech, that is to say, Israel or some spokesperson reporting what God has uttered on some other occasion" ("Psalm 60," 87). I argue for the latter, as I believe that the psalmist is using the oracle as a key piece in his or her indictment of God in the light of Judah's present political calamity.

[41] Ogden, "Psalm 60," 84.

[42] Michael D. Goulder offers two observations explaining the rationale for Ps 108 to blend Ps 57 and Ps 60. First, the compiler who assembled Ps 108 viewed the later portion of Ps 60 (vv. 7–14) as hopeful but the earlier portion of the psalm (vv. 1–6) as negative. Given the optimistic outlook of the compiler of Ps 108, he or she simply replaced the "depressing introduction" of Ps 60 with the much more positive material from Ps 57. Second, by utilizing Ps 57:9, the compiler was able to establish a tie between Ps 107:1 and Ps 108:4 (*The Psalms of the Return [Book V, Psalms 107–150]: Studies in the Psalter, IV*, JSOTSup 258 [Sheffield: Sheffield Academic, 1998], 129).

[43] Knauf, "Psalm LX und Psalm CVIII."

the revenge psalm, Ps 109. Based on Herbert Donner's argument, which claims that Ps 110 is written about Simon Thassi, Knauf claims that this three-part collection, Pss 108–110, was compiled during the reign of John Hyrcanus.[44] For Knauf, Pss 108–110 collectively function to present John Hyrcanus as *David redivivus*. As such, Knauf argues that Ps 108 portrays the alignment between the preexilic Ps 60 and the military exploits of Hyrcanus, demonstrating his fulfillment of Davidic expectations.

While Donner certainly asserts that Ps 110 pertains directly to Simon Thassi, the real thrust of his argument is that Ps 110 must have a late date.[45] He especially ties this claim to the reference to Melchizedek in Ps 110:4. However, the fact that 1 Macc 14:41–49 portrays Simon as both king and high priest in no way necessitates a link between him and Melchizedek. David and Solomon both exhibited priestly qualities as well (see, e.g., 2 Sam 6:13–14, 17–19; 8:18; 1 Kg 3:4). Yet Donner is right to recognize that the reference to Melchizedek in Ps 110 indicates a very late date for this psalm. I would amend Donner's argument in that the era of Simon Thassi is not the only time to date Ps 110, but rather it is perhaps the *earliest* time that one should date Ps 110. The rise of the Maccabees was a tremendous catalyst promoting messianic hope among the Judeans in the second century BCE. Yet such messianic hope certainly did not die with the Hasmonean line but rather consistently continued until the failure of Simon Bar Kokhba in 135 CE. The fact that numerous NT texts cite Ps 110 in reference to Jesus of Nazareth dictates that Ps 110 must have been widely known by the end of the first century CE. However, that is two hundred years after the death of Simon Thassi.

Even if Ps 110 dates as early as the time of Simon (ca. 140 BCE), this by no means indicates that we should date the entire Davidic composition of Pss 108–110 to just a couple of decades later. Once again, the messianic movement in Judea spanned almost three hundred years, from the middle of the second century BCE to the middle of the second century CE. Therefore, the blending of Ps 57 and Ps 60 to form Ps 108 along with the canonical arrangement of this psalm with Pss 109–110 to form a Davidic composition could have occurred at any point within this window of time. Based on my argument for a mid-first century BCE date for Ps 60, I contend that Ps 108 is a product of either the late first century BCE or perhaps the early first century CE.

V. Text-Critical Analysis of Psalm 60 MT//Psalm 59 LXX

Finally, I must address the text-critical aspects of Ps 60. The manuscript evidence from the Judean Desert can be reviewed quickly due to the paucity of data.

---

[44] Herbert Donner, "Der verlässliche Prophet: Betrachtungen zu I Makk 14,41 ff und zu Ps 110," in *Prophetie und geschichtliche Wirklichkeit im alten Israel: Festschrift für Siegfried Herrmann zum 65. Geburtstag* (Stuttgart: Kohlhammer, 1991), 89–98.

[45] Ibid., 91–95.

Manuscript evidence accommodates the theory for the composition of Ps 60 that I have argued. No trace of Ps 108 has been recovered. 4QpPs^a (4Q171) frag. 13 includes a portion of commentary of Ps 60:8–9. It preserves אלו[הים דבר of v. 8aα¹⁻², סכ[ות אמדדה לי of v. 8b²⁻³–9aα¹, and a reference to מנשה] גלע[ד וחצי שבט and the verb ונקבצו in the commentary.⁴⁶

11QPs^d (11Q8) frag. 17 might also be an excerpt from Ps 60 although only four letters are legible. It reads גלע[ד ולי], which, if it is from Ps 60, represents v. 9aα²⁻³.⁴⁷ Paleographically, 11QPs^d features a writing style "of a developed to late formal Herodian, indicating a date from the middle of the 1st century C.E."⁴⁸

It is important to note that the verses present in both 4QpPs^a frag. 13 (vv. 8–9) and 11QPs^d frag. 17 (v. 9) are part of the earlier section of the psalm. This may be (but is not necessarily) reinforced by the fact that 4QpPs^a frag. 13 has a space larger than a simple line space above v. 8.⁴⁹ It seems that Ps 60:8aβ–11 not only was written in the last quarter of the second century BCE but also would have most likely been popularized due to its political relevance of restoring the land of Israel to Judean control through the agency of John Hyrcanus. Consequently, this oracle may have received broad circulation.

The evidence from the LXX requires much more attention. Psalm 60 MT and its LXX equivalent, Ps 59, differ at several points. The most important difference between the two is in v. 9b: While Ps 60:9b MT (and Ps 108:9b MT) reads יְהוּדָה מְחֹקְקִי, "Judah is my scepter," Ps 59:9 LXX (and Ps 107:9 LXX) reads Ιουδας βασιλεύς μου, "Judah is my king." Although unfortunately few commentators address the LXX in their analyses of this psalm, those who do, recognize that Ps 59:9 LXX reflects a Maccabean agenda. This recognition is undoubtedly correct. This single datum, paired with the fact that the LXX seems to exhibit a highly consistent translation of the proto-MT Psalms, has led many scholars to posit that the LXX Psalm originates from the height of Maccabean success (i.e., the late second century BCE), and, consequently, the proto-MT Psalms originated some time before that. If this were true, then it would indicate a pre-Hasmonean origin of the proto-MT Psalms, which would obviously dismiss the possibility of a Hasmonean date for (the core of) Ps 60. However as I will argue, the logic of such a supposition is flawed and does not necessarily hold.

On the basis of metric analysis, it is clear that Ps 60 was written in Hebrew and later translated into Greek. This does not mean, however, that proto-MT Ps 60 served as the *Vorlage* for Ps 59 LXX. On the contrary, Ps 59 LXX bears evidence of a Hebrew version of the psalm that served as the *Vorlage* for both Ps 59 LXX and proto-MT Ps 60. In order to illustrate this, I will provide an analysis of the three

---

⁴⁶ John M. Allegro, *Qumran Cave 4.I (4Q158–4Q186)*, DJD V (Oxford: Clarendon, 1968), 49 and pl. xvii frag. 13.

⁴⁷ Florentino García Martinez et al., *Qumran Cave 11.II (11Q2–18, 11Q20–31)*, DJD XXIII (Oxford: Clarendon, 1998), 76 and pl. viii frag. 17.

⁴⁸ Ibid., 64.

⁴⁹ Allegro, *Qumran Cave 4.I*, pl. xvii frag. 13.

most significant differences between Ps 59 LXX and Ps 60 MT. The analysis will attempt to show that, while Ps 59 LXX preserves this Hebrew *Vorlage* rather faithfully, proto-MT Ps 60 does not. Consequently, for this psalm, the LXX reflects an earlier version of the psalm than the MT does. While Ps 59 LXX retains the politico-militant character of the psalm, Ps 60 MT reveals some slight yet distinct changes in order to demilitarize and depoliticize the psalm.

First, Ps 59:6b LXX has the phrase ἀπὸ προσώπου τόξου ("from before the bow"). We may easily reconstruct the Hebrew *Vorlage* of this phrase as מִפְּנֵי קֶשֶׁת. However, Ps 60:6b MT renders the phrase as מִפְּנֵי קֹשֶׁט ("from before the truth"). Commentators routinely accept קשט as an alternative spelling for קשת, despite the fact that there are no other instances of this in the Hebrew Bible. Aside from its occurrence in Ps 60:6b MT, קשט occurs three times in the Hebrew Bible: Prov 22:21, Dan 2:47, 4:34. In each instance, it expresses "truth." Certainly the words קשת ("bow") and קשט ("truth") are interrelated, as they both pertain to straightness in direction, and the Aramaic term קשט, was occasionally used in reference to a bow or an archer.[50] However, it should immediately be noted as a problem for anyone trying to assert a preexilic date for Ps 60 MT that (1) the term קשט is essentially Aramaic; (2) all three aforementioned Hebrew Bible texts in which קשט occurs, aside from Ps 60 MT, are widely recognized as very late texts; and (3) aside from its occurrence in Ps 60, we see the conflation of קשט and קשת only in texts dating to the Common Era.[51] Given that the Old Greek translates all three other occurrences of קשט as some form of the word "truth" (ἀληθῆ in Prov 22:21; ἀληθείας in Dan 2:47; ἀληθινά in Dan 4:37 Theodotion [cf. Dan 4:34 MT]), if the psalm's Hebrew *Vorlage* contained the term קשט, we should most likely expect a similar translation in Ps 59:6 LXX. Instead, Ps 59:6 LXX has the term τόξον, which is almost exclusively used to translate קשת. Consequently, by the witness of the Greek, we should acknowledge that the Hebrew *Vorlage* of v. 6 originally read מִפְּנֵי קֶשֶׁת. Once again, it is completely appropriate that we find the psalmist referring to fleeing "from the bow," as he or she writes in the aftermath of the Judean loss of independence in the middle of the first century BCE. However, the scribes of the proto-MT who inherited this psalm slightly nudged the nuance of this word by changing one letter so that the verse could carry the broad and timeless notion of rallying before truth while still expressing a hint of its original meaning.[52]

Second, those who address Ps 59 LXX are quick to flag the phrase Ιουδας βασιλεύς μου ("Judah is my king") in v. 9 as a Maccabean "update," presuming that the Ps 60 MT phrase יְהוּדָה מְחֹקְקִי ("Judah is my scepter") represents the original text.[53] However, if Ps 60 MT existed before the Hasmonean period, what did the

---

[50] Marcus Jastrow, *A Dictionary of the Targumim, the Talmud Babli and Yerushalmi, and the Midrashic Literature* (1950; repr., New York: Judaica, 1971), 1429–30, s.v. קשט.

[51] Ibid., 1429–30, s.v. קשט; 1433, s.v. קשת.

[52] Tate acknowledges the possibility of a pun with the use of this term (*Psalms 51–100*, 102).

[53] Hossfeld and Zenger, *Psalms 2*, 103.

Hasmoneans think that the oracle lacked to merit such an overt alteration of the text? This leads to one of the main points on which a non-Hasmonean date for Ps 60 falls apart: the targets that the oracle identifies (vv. 8–11) match the Hasmonean map simply too perfectly to date Ps 60 to any other time period. It is by this same reasoning that scholars date the book of Isaiah to the postexilic period rather than the eighth century BCE and the book of Daniel to the second century BCE rather than the sixth century BCE. Isaiah mentions sixth-century BCE events, and Daniel mentions second-century BCE events with greater precision than would be possible at an earlier date. According to the same logic, it would be a striking coincidence for the Hasmoneans to inherit a preexisting psalm designating numerous military targets that just happened to match precisely their own agenda. If this were the case, there would hardly be any need for an "update," since the psalm already corresponded more closely to the agenda of the people inheriting the text than those who supposedly wrote it. Furthermore, an examination of the manner in which the term מְחֹקְקִי is used in the Hebrew Bible indicates that it lacks nothing in its capacity to indicate royalty.

Moreover, we can recognize that the phrase Ιουδας βασιλεύς μου of Ps 59:9b LXX is a better reading than the phrase יְהוּדָה מְחֹקְקִי in Ps 60:9b MT, as Ιουδας βασιλεύς μου provides the *lectio difficilior*. As we saw earlier, the three lines in Ps 60:9aβ–10aα constitute a triplet, as each line consists of a political entity identified as a piece of personal equipment featuring a first person common singular suffix. However, this is true only of Ps 60 MT, not Ps 59 LXX, due to the fact that Ιουδας βασιλεύς μου is, of course, not a piece of equipment. It seems unlikely that Hasmonean scribes broke up a balanced triplet that already existed in their text so that they could use the title βασιλεύς μου, when מְחֹקְקִי already carries this connotation. It is far more reasonable to think that the original oracle had יְהוּדָה מַלְכִּי as the Hebrew *Vorlage* of Ps 59:9b LXX at its core.[54] While this does not flow quite as easily as the Ps 60 MT version of the oracle, the oracle of this Hebrew *Vorlage* still featured a symmetrical text in which Judah, as king, stood centered in the arrangement, flanked by the two key points of expanded Hasmonean occupation, the territories of Ephraim and Moab. Like Ps 60 MT, the Hebrew *Vorlage* exhibited some sense of the triplet, as Ps 59:9aβ–10aα LXX retains the threefold repetition of μου ("my") in this section.

It seems that the scribes of proto-MT Ps 60 replaced the phrase יְהוּדָה מַלְכִּי ("Judah is my king") with יְהוּדָה מְחֹקְקִי ("Judah is my scepter")," as the latter phrase still carries the royal connotation of the former; however, the latter provides a broader range of meaning than the former. While יְהוּדָה מַלְכִּי ("Judah is my king") is somewhat limited due to its applicability to a specific political setting, the phrase יְהוּדָה מְחֹקְקִי ("Judah is my scepter") takes on a more timeless notion of Judean

---

[54] This datum may indicate that the core oracle of Ps 60 was originally written during the reign of Aristobulus I (104–103 BCE), as he was the first Hasmonean to bear the title "king"; see Lester L. Grabbe, *Judaism from Cyrus to Hadrian*, 2 vols. (Minneapolis: Fortress, 1992), 1:302.

leadership regardless of any particular political system. Moreover, the verb חָקַק, the root of מְחֹקְקִי, and its noun counterpart, חֹק, bear a legal connotation, as חָקַק pertains to prescribing a law or decree and חֹק pertains to the legal statute prescribed. Thus, proto-MT Ps 60 maintains the notion of leadership in Ps 59:9b LXX, but it converts it from military leadership to legal (i.e., theocratic) leadership.

Third, Ps 59:10aα LXX has the phrase Μωαβ λέβης τῆς ἐλπίδος μου ("Moab is a basin of my hope"). While the first two words of the Hebrew *Vorlage* would have been identical to that of Ps 60:10aα MT, מוֹאָב סִיר, there are numerous possibilities for the third word of this line, which Ps 59:10aα LXX translates as τῆς ἐλπίδος μου. I tentatively suggest that perhaps the Hebrew *Vorlage* of Ps 59:10aα LXX originally read מוֹאָב סִיר תִּקְוָתִי. As was the case with v. 9b, once again the LXX reading of Μωαβ λέβης τῆς ἐλπίδος μου should be preferred over the MT reading of מוֹאָב סִיר רַחְצִי, as the LXX offers the *lectio difficilior* both in terms of the honor it ascribes to Moab and in terms of the basic sensibility of the phrase. Psalm 60:10aα grants Moab the surprising honor of standing side by side with Judah and Ephraim as pieces of God's equipment. Although Ps 60:10aα MT at least tries to minimize that honor by relegating Moab to a mere סִיר רַחְצִי ("washbasin"), Ps 59:10aα LXX preserves the more difficult reading, lacking any negative connotation whatsoever. Furthermore, Ps 59:10aα LXX is a more difficult reading on a level of basic sensibility: What exactly is a "basin of hope"? Psalm 60:10aα MT improves on the strangeness of this phrase by converting the word to a common utensil—a washbasin.

Despite the fact that it constitutes the *lectio difficilior*, the phrase Μωαβ λέβης τῆς ἐλπίδος μου, probably translating מוֹאָב סִיר תִּקְוָתִי, makes complete sense in the Hasmonean setting in which the phrase originally occurred in the Hebrew *Vorlage*. Joachim Schaper has indicated the importance of Moab, claiming, "Moab was of central significance in the 'system' of Jewish eschatology in Hasmonean times."[55] Schaper notes that part of John Hyrcanus's rationale for attacking the Moabite city of Medaba was to fulfill the messianic expectation of the Davidic king as expressed by the prophecies in Isa 15–16, 25:9–12, and Jer 48. Thus, as Schaper explains, "Moab was the λέβης τῆς ἐλπίδος μου because it was considered the first-fruit of the eschatological harvest."[56] However, once the Romans had quashed Judean independence, the territory of Moab lost its role as a symbol of Judean hope. In this context, the proto-MT scribes cleverly altered the reading of מוֹאָב סִיר תִּקְוָתִי in the Hebrew *Vorlage* to מוֹאָב סִיר רַחְצִי, which Ps 60:10aα MT retains. The brilliance of these scribes' alteration of the Hebrew *Vorlage* of proto-MT Ps 60:10aα was that it simultaneously accomplished two goals. On the one hand, by exchanging the term תִּקְוָתִי for רַחְצִי, the proto-MT scribes, uncomfortable with the lack of ethnic distinction between Jew and gentile evident in the positive portrayal of Moab alongside Judah

---

[55] Joachim Schaper, *Eschatology in the Greek Psalter*, WUNT 2/76 (Tübingen: Mohr Siebeck, 1995), 44.

[56] Ibid., 44–45.

and Ephraim in the *Vorlage*, remedied this problem by relegating Moab to a utensil as debased as a "washbasin," according to the Hebrew meaning of רחץ. Yet, on the other hand, as the Aramaic sense of the term רחץ means "hope," the proto-MT scribes preserved some sense of the original reading of the *Vorlage*.

In each of these three instances, the scribes of the proto-MT Ps 60 made slight adjustments to the Hebrew *Vorlage* that (1) downplayed the martial aspects of the text and (2) featured a double meaning that preserved the original sense of the Hebrew *Vorlage* yet also broadened it, granting it more of a timeless ideological veneer. Thus, once again Ps 60:6b MT utilizes the ideological Aramaic word "truth" (קֹשֶׁט), preserving the meaning of "bow" (קֶשֶׁת) in the Hebrew *Vorlage*; Ps 60:9b MT uses the theocratic term "scepter" (מְחֹקְקִי), retaining the royal authority of "king" (מֶלֶךְ) in the Hebrew *Vorlage*; Ps 60:10aα MT describes Moab with the derogatory term "washbasin" (רַחְצִי), while yet, through its Aramaic meaning, still maintaining the sense of "hope" (probably קוה) in the Hebrew *Vorlage*. Furthermore, proto-MT Ps 60 improved the artistry of the Hebrew *Vorlage* by changing מַלְכִּי to מְחֹקְקִי and by changing the ambiguous סִיר תִּקְוָתִי to סִיר רַחְצִי, so that now Ps 60:9aβ–10aα MT features a balanced triplet in which each location is described as a piece of a military leader's equipment. These adjustments were most likely made at some point in the late first century CE by scribes who were part of a Jewish faction that saw the futility of placing their hope in attempts to challenge Roman supremacy militarily, possibly in the wake of the catastrophic Jewish War of 66–73 CE, and, therefore, transformed the psalm into a slightly more abstract expression that promoted Judean religious ideals instead of military aspirations.

VI. Summary and Concluding Implications

The foregoing analysis suggests the following compositional process. In the last quarter of the second century BCE, scribes of John Hyrcanus wrote the chiastic oracle found in the Hebrew *Vorlage* of Ps 59:8–11 LXX as a gesture of divine endorsement celebrating Hyrcanus's expansionistic campaigns. In the mid-first century BCE, a psalmist who was theologically concerned about Judah's subjugation to Rome integrated the oracle, as an indictment of God's unfulfilled promise, into a metrically arranged complaint (the Hebrew *Vorlage* of Ps 59:3–7, 12–14 LXX) that was highly influenced by passages from the book of Isaiah. At the end of the first century BCE or the beginning of the first century CE, a psalmist blended Ps 57 and the Hebrew *Vorlage* of Ps 59 LXX to create the Hebrew *Vorlage* of Ps 107 LXX, which either that psalmist or a subsequent compiler utilized as the first component of the messianic Davidic composition of Pss 108–110. Finally, at the end of the first century CE, scribes reworked the Hebrew *Vorlagen* of Ps 59 LXX and Ps 107 LXX, downplaying the militaristic nuances and abstracting some of the concepts in the psalms, yielding proto-MT Ps 60 and proto-MT Ps 108.

Perhaps the most important implication of this theory is the potential impact that it has on the dating of LXX Psalms. Fascinatingly, scholars have anchored their chronology for the Greek translation of the book of Psalms largely on a single datum: Ps 59:9 LXX. Tyler F. Williams writes,

> There is only one potential piece of internal evidence to which one may appeal in order to date the LXX Psalms. This is the rendering of יְהוּדָה מְחֹקְקִי "Judah is my staff" by Ιουδας βασιλεύς μου in Ps. 59(60).9 and its parallel 107(108).9. This translation may constitute an allusion to Judas Maccabaeus (166–61 BCE), the leader of the Jewish revolt against Antiochus IV Epiphanes, as has been proposed recently by Schaper. If this is the case, then it provides a *terminus a quo* for the translation of the Psalter.[57]

If the theory for the composition of Ps 60 that I have advanced is correct, then the most prominent piece of internal evidence for the dating of LXX Psalms is disrupted, as this datum now points to a contribution of the Hebrew *Vorlage* of Ps 59 LXX rather than the work of the Greek translator. In such a case, scholars will not only need to give much greater consideration to the possibility that many other Hebrew Bible texts may date as late as this one, but we may also need to reevaluate our entire time line pertaining to the relationship of the textual witnesses of the book of Psalms.

---

[57] Tyler F. Williams, "Towards a Date for the Old Greek Psalter," in *The Old Greek Psalter: Studies in Honour of Albert Pietersma*, ed. Robert J. V. Hiebert, Claude E. Cox, and Peter J. Gentry, JSOTSup 332 (Sheffield: Sheffield Academic, 2001), 261.

Love Conquers All: Song of Songs 8:6b–7a as a Reflex of the Northwest Semitic Combat Myth

AREN M. WILSON-WRIGHT
wilsonwright@utexas.edu
Waggener 14a, 2210 Speedway C3400, Austin, TX 78712

Scholars have often noted YHWH's apparent absence from the Song of Songs. At best, he appears under the name Yah in the difficult and morphologically frozen term שלהבתיה in Song 8:6. In this article, I go beyond שלהבתיה to suggest that love plays the role of YHWH in the Song. Using Calvert Watkins's work on inherited formulae, I argue that Song 8:6b–7a draws on the Northwest Semitic combat myth to identify love with YHWH, the victorious divine warrior. As part of this argument, I identify three inherited formulae in the Hebrew Bible, the Baal Cycle, and later Christian and Jewish literature: "Leviathan, the fleeing serpent, the twisting serpent," "rebuke Sea," and "strong as Death." Within the Song, the phrase "strong as Death" connects this passage with the Baal Cycle, while the references to מים רבים and נהרות evoke scenes of mythic combat from the rest of the Hebrew Bible. This interpretation, I argue, also has mythic resonances in the adjuration refrain in Song 2:7, 3:5, and 8:4 and the phrase "sick with love" in Song 2:5 and 5:8.

כי־עזה כמות אהבה קשה כשאול קנאה
רשפיה רשפי אש שלהבתיה
מים רבים לא יוכלו לכבות את־האהבה

For love is as strong as Death, jealousy harsh as Sheol.
Its flashes are flashes of fire, the flame of Yah.
Many waters cannot quench love, neither can rivers drown it.[1] (Song 8:6b–7a)

This article had its genesis in a doctoral seminar on Song of Songs taught by Dr. Jonathan Kaplan. I would like to thank the members of the seminar for their comments on this paper. In particular, I would like to thank M. L. Case, Geoffrey D. McElroy, Thomas Sowards, Saralyn McKinnon-Crowley, and Jonathan Kaplan. I would also like to thank the two anonymous *JBL* reviewers for their comments and critiques. Any remaining errors are my own.

[1] All translations from Hebrew and Ugaritic are my own.

The Song of Songs does not explicitly refer to the God of Israel under the name YHWH or any other epithet. The noun שלהבתיה in Song 8:6 may contain a shortened form of the Tetragrammaton, but scholars debate the interpretation of this difficult term.² In this article, I go beyond שלהבתיה to suggest that YHWH is present in the Song in the form of love. Drawing on Calvert Watkins's work on inherited formulae, I argue that Song 8:6b–7a utilizes language and imagery from the Northwest Semitic combat myth to identify love with YHWH as the victorious divine warrior. As part of this argument, I identify three inherited formulae in the Hebrew Bible, the Baal Cycle, and later Christian and Jewish literature: "Leviathan, the fleeing serpent, the twisting serpent," "rebuke Sea," and "strong as Death." Within the Song, the phrase "strong as Death" connects this passage with the Baal Cycle, while the references to מים רבים and נהרות evoke scenes of mythic combat from the rest of the Hebrew Bible. By way of conclusion, I demonstrate the importance of this reading for interpreting the adjuration refrain in Song 2:7, 3:5, and 8:4 and the phrase "sick with love" in Song 2:5 and 5:8.

I. The Northwest Semitic Combat Myth

As many commentators have noted, Song 8:6b–7a employs a rich array of cosmic language to highlight the power of love (אהבה). In these verses, love is set against death (מות), Sheol (שאול), mighty waters (מים רבים), and rivers (נהרות), and likened to fire (רשפי אש) and flame (שלהבתיה). Most commentators, however, downplay the mythic significance of these verses, preferring to treat them as a theological or philosophical statement about the nature of love. Othmar Keel, for example, claims that "the statement about love being as strong as death cannot have a mythical sense in the context of the Song, but to a large degree it owes its strength and intensity to the several myths about the struggle between the powers of life or love and those of death." Meanwhile, J. Cheryl Exum calls these verses "a succinct credo on the subject of love."³ Yet all of these terms and concepts are part of a cross-cultural tradition of combat myths, as will be shown now.

Many of the myths from the ancient Near East focus on divine combat. In the Enuma Elish, Marduk defeats Ti'āmat (the Deep) and her serpentine allies; in the

---

²David R. Blumenthal, "Where God Is Not: The Book of Esther and Song of Songs," *Judaism* 44 (1995): 81–82.

³Othmar Keel, *The Song of Songs: A Continental Commentary*, trans. Frederick J. Gaiser (Minneapolis: Fortress, 1994), 276. See also idem, *Deine Blicke sind Tauben: Zur Metaphorik des Hohen Liedes*, SBS 114–115 (Stuttgart: Katholisches Bibelwerk, 1984), 119; J. Cheryl Exum, *Song of Songs: A Commentary*, OTL (Louisville: Westminster John Knox, 2005), 249. See further Roland E. Murphy, *The Song of Songs: A Commentary on the Book of Canticles or the Song of Songs*, Hermeneia (Minneapolis: Fortress, 1990), 196–98; and Marvin H. Pope, *Song of Songs: A New Translation with Introduction and Commentary*, AB 7C (Garden City, NY: Doubleday, 1977), 673.

Baal Cycle, Baal challenges Yamm (Sea) and Môt (Death) for the kingship of the gods; and in several passages in the Hebrew Bible, YHWH battles a variety of aqueous foes, including Yām (Sea), Těhôm (the Deep), and Leviathan.[4] Traditionally, scholars have explained the similarities between these myths in terms of narrative typology and cultural contact. The Enuma Elish, the Baal Cycle, and the passages from the Hebrew Bible are all versions of a single "combat myth" archetype.[5] In the first act, the divine warrior—usually a storm god—confronts and defeats the turbulent powers of the Sea and/or its serpentine allies using a lightning bolt. His victory allows him to claim kingship over the gods in the second act and, as an encore, create the world using the body of the slain Sea. The cast of characters may change, but the plot remains the same. The dispersal of this motif is the result of cultural contact: the combat myth originated in either the Levant or Mesopotamia and spread to other societies through trade, conquest, and migration.[6]

This line of reasoning for the dispersal of the combat myth is difficult to apply to the Song of Songs because its historical context is poorly understood. True, Song 8:6b–7a shares typological similarities with many versions of the combat myth—water, fire, and death all make an appearance—but typological similarities alone prove insufficient for demonstrating concrete connections between two myths since divine combat is a common motif in the world's narratives.[7] The similarities may be accidental. Likewise, the possibility of cultural contact or literary influence of an earlier myth on Song 8:6b–7a proves hard to substantiate because Song of Songs in general, and ch. 8 in particular, is short on historical detail that would permit the identification of relevant source material. Even if the Song of Songs did contain a sufficient level of historical detail, it is unlikely that a source myth could

---

[4] Other examples from the ancient world include the Akkadian Anzu myth, Hesiod's *Theogony*, the Hittite Illuyankas myth, the Egyptian Repulsing of the Dragon, and Revelation 12.

[5] Beginning with Hermann Gunkel, some scholars have referred to the "combat myth" as *Chaoskampf* and have identified the divine warrior's opponents with the forces of chaos. I prefer the term "combat myth," since the modern term "chaos" does not have a direct equivalent in the languages of the ancient Near East.

[6] Hermann Gunkel, for example, argued that the references to divine combat in the Hebrew Bible were an adaptation of Enuma Elish (*Creation and Chaos in the Primeval Era and the Eschaton: A Religio-Historical Study of Genesis 1 and Revelation 12*, trans. K. William Whitney Jr., Biblical Resource Series [Grand Rapids: Eerdmans, 2006], 78–111; German original, *Schöpfung und Chaos in Urzeit und Endzeit: Eine religionsgeschichtliche Untersuchung über Gen 1 und Ap Joh 12* [Göttingen: Vandenhoeck & Ruprecht, 1895], 114–17). Thorkild Jacobsen, by contrast, suggested that the combat myth originated in a West Semitic environment where the ocean was more culturally relevant ("The Battle between Marduk and Tiamat," *JAOS* 88 [1968]: 104–8). John Day traces this quest for origins in *God's Conflict with the Dragon and the Sea: Echoes of a Canaanite Myth in the Old Testament*, UCOP 35 (Cambridge: Cambridge University Press, 1985), 10–13.

[7] For myths of "combat between god of light and dragon of ocean," see Stith Thompson, *Motif-Index of Folk-Literature: A Classification of Narrative Elements in Folktales, Ballads, Myths, Fables, Mediaeval Romances, Exempla, Fabliaux, Jest-Books, and Local Legends*, rev. and enl. ed. (Bloomington: Indiana University Press, 1966), motif A162.

be found. Each surviving version of the combat myth represents a single link in an ongoing process of oral and literary transmission. Hundreds of miles and hundreds of retellings separate even the most closely related versions. As a result, it is often impossible to determine the direct influence of one myth upon another.

The comparative method from historical linguistics offers another way to demonstrate a concrete relationship between classes of myth that relies on an analogy between language and myth. Just as genetically related languages share cognate words—words originating from a common ancestor, like English "foot" and German "*Fuß*"—genetically related myths share cognate formulae.[8] As Calvert Watkins has shown in his study of Indo-European poetics, certain formulae can persist unchanged for millennia even as languages split and diversify, leaving their traces in related languages. He attributes this longevity to a combination of enduring cultural saliency—formulae, for Watkins, convey important themes—and mutability. Because of this mutability, inherited formulae need not contain exact cognates or preserve the same word order. Lexical replacement and syntactic alternation can occur as long as semantic equivalence is preserved.[9]

Before turning to Song 8:6b–7a, I will apply Watkins's insights to the Northwest Semitic languages, the subset of the Semitic family including Hebrew, Aramaic, and Ugaritic.[10] I will demonstrate the existence of a specifically Northwest Semitic combat myth defined by three inherited formulae preserved in the Ugaritic material, the Hebrew Bible, and Christian and Jewish literature such as the NT and Midrash Rabbah.[11] These formulae are "Leviathan, the twisting serpent, the fleeing serpent," "rebuke Sea," and "strong as Death." The presence of other inherited formulae in the Hebrew Bible increases the chances that the phrase "strong as death" in the Song is an inherited formula.

---

[8] Calvert Watkins cites Greek *kleos aphthiton* and Sanskrit *ákṣiti śrávaḥ*, both meaning "imperishable fame," as examples of an inherited Indo-European formula (*How to Kill a Dragon: Aspects of Indo-European Poetics* [Oxford: Oxford University Press, 1995], 13).

[9] Ibid., 9–10.

[10] For the linguistic subgrouping of these languages within Semitic and the features that distinguish them, see John Huehnergard, "Remarks on the Classification of the Northwest Semitic Languages," in *The Balaam Text from Deir ʿAlla Re-evaluated: Proceedings of the International Symposium Held at Leiden 21–24 August 1989*, ed. J. Hoftijzer and G. van der Kooij (Leiden: Brill, 1991), 282–93.

[11] I choose to focus on the Northwest Semitic languages to the exclusion of Akkadian because they are closely related linguistically. Ultimately, the Northwest Semitic combat myth and Akkadian myths like the Enuma Elish and Anzu may originate from a Proto-Semitic combat myth dating perhaps to the fourth millennium BCE. Cultural contact between Mesopotamia and the Levant and between speakers of Akkadian and West Semitic languages complicates the recovery of this mythic complex. Although a reconstruction of the Proto-Semitic combat myth is beyond the scope of this paper, Mesopotamian and Northwest Semitic versions of the combat myth do share at least one inherited formula. In the Enuma Elish, Hab 3:15, and later Jewish literature, the victorious divine warrior tramples the Sea. Both the Enuma Elish and Jewish literature use the verb *kbs* ("to trample"), which does not occur in Biblical Hebrew or Ugaritic with this meaning.

The Hebrew Bible preserves several inherited Northwest Semitic formulae related to the Northwest Semitic combat myth. The phrase "Leviathan, the fleeing serpent ... Leviathan, the twisting serpent" (*liwyātān nāḥāš bāriaḥ ... liwyātān nāḥāš ʿăqallātôn*) found in Isa 27:1, for example, offers a close parallel to the phrase "Lītan the fleeing serpent ... the twisting serpent"(*ltn bṯn brḥ ... bṯn ʿqltn*) in the Baal Cyle *KTU* 1.5.1.1–2. The only difference between the two phrases is the alternation of *bṯn* and *nāḥāš*, both meaning "snake." Most likely, the Hebrew formula has undergone lexical replacement. *Bešen*, the expected reflex of Proto-Semitic **baṯn-* ("snake") does not occur in Hebrew due perhaps to taboo avoidance, which suggests that the original formula was **lawiy(a)tanu baṯnu bariḥu baṯnu ʿaqallatānu*.[12] Both the Ugaritic and Hebrew reflexes of this formula appear in the context of divine combat. In Isa 27:1, YHWH's victory over Leviathan is projected into the eschatological era, while in the Baal Cycle, Môt includes Lītan in a list of enemies that Baal has defeated.

Another inherited Northwest Semitic formula describes the storm god's use of effective language against Sea. In Nah 1:4, YHWH "rebukes Sea so that it dries up" (*gôʿēr bayyām wayyabašēhû*). Other descriptions of YHWH's mastery over the Sea employ a nominal form of the root *gʿr*. In Isa 50:2, YHWH declares, "by my rebuke I dry up Sea, I make the rivers a desert" (*bəgaʿărātî ʾaḥărîb yām ʾāśîm nəhārôt midbār*), and in 2 Sam 22:16 and Ps 18:16 the poet asserts that "the channels of Sea were seen, the foundations of the world were laid bare at YHWH's rebuke [*bəgaʿărat yhwh*], at the blast of the breath of his nostrils."[13] In the Baal Cycle *KTU* 1.2.4.28-29, ʿAthartu aids Baal in his fight against Yamm using incantations: "By name ʿAthartu rebuked [Yamm], 'Dry up [Yamm], O Mighty Baal! Dry up [Yamm] O Rider on the clouds!'" (*bšm tgʿrm ʿtrt bṯ ʾalîyn bʿ[l] bṯ l rkb ʿrpt*).[14] All of these examples reflect the inherited Northwest Semitic formula **gaʿara yamma* ("he rebuked the Sea"), which could appear in collocation with the verb *yabiṯa* ("to dry up").[15]

---

[12] The names of dangerous animals are often subject to lexical replacement or taboo deformation. The English word "bear," for example, comes from the Germanic word for brown, not Proto-Indo-European **r̥kto-*. See Calvert Watkins, *The American Heritage Dictionary of Indo-European Roots*, 2nd ed. (Boston: Houghton Mifflin, 2000), 72. Within Semitic, *ʾaryēh* and *ʾărî*, two of the Hebrew words for "lion," come from Proto-Semitic **ʾary-* ("wild animal") and provide a further example of lexical replacement. See Joshua Fox, *Semitic Noun Patterns*, HSS 52 (Winona Lake, IN: Eisenbrauns, 2003), 74.

[13] Mark and Luke alter this tradition slightly when they depict Jesus rebuking both the storm and the sea (Mark 4:39, Luke 8:24).

[14] Yamm is mentioned two lines earlier and is therefore the implicit object of these imperatives.

[15] Theodore Lewis drew attention to these verbal parallels in his study of *KTU* 1.2.4.28, but he did not treat them as reflexes of an inherited Northwest Semitic formula ("ʿAthartu's Incantations and the Use of Divine Names as Weapons," *JNES* 70 [2011]: 212).

The final inherited formula, *ᶜazzu mawtu ("Death is strong") with the variant *ᶜazzu ka-mawti ("strong like Death"), highlights the power of Death. In Baal's second confrontation with Môt, the recurring refrain "Môt is strong, Baal is strong" (mt ᶜz bᶜl ᶜz) (KTU 1.6.6.17, 19, 20) indicates the parity of the two combatants. The comparative aspect of this phrase is implicit. A similar phrase appears in a Ugaritic letter describing the effects of a plague (KTU 2.10.11–13), in which the sender laments that "the hand of god is exceedingly strong here, like Death" (yd . ilm . p . kmtm ᶜz . mid).[16] As this letter shows, the formula "strong like Death" was not limited to descriptions of mythic combat but had achieved proverbial status. The Hebrew personal name ᶜazmāwet ("Death is strong"), attested in 2 Sam 23:31, Ezra 2:24, Neh 7:28, 1 Chr 8:36, 9:42, 11:33, 12:3, and 27:5, represents a further refraction of the formula—the transformation of an inherited formula into a personal name.[17] The formula "Death is strong" was well suited to this transformation, since Northwest Semitic personal names often consist of pithy "theological" statements describing the attributes of a divinity. Strength is one of Death's distinguishing characteristics. He is a pugnacious deity who can be overcome only by an equally strong opponent.[18]

II. The Northwest Semitic Combat Myth in Song of Songs

Song 8:6b uses the inherited Northwest Semitic formula עזה כמות as well in order to qualify the power of love.[19] At first glance, it is unclear whether death in

[16] Dennis Pardee prefers to treat k as the subordinating conjunction kī since ᶜz does not agree in gender with yd. As a result, he translates this sentence as "the hand of god is here for Death is exceedingly strong (here)" ("As Strong as Death," in *Love and Death in the Ancient Near East: Essays in Honor of Marvin H. Pope*, ed. John H. Marks and Robert M. Good [Guilford, CT: Four Quarters, 1987], 68). Doing so, however, confuses cause and effect. The power of Death does not explain the presence of plague in the land, but rather qualifies the strength of the plague. Furthermore, yd can be construed as masculine in Ugaritic (KTU 23:33–35), as Pardee admits. See also Pope, *Song of Songs*, 668.

[17] Jeffery H. Tigay regards this name as "a plausibly pagan theophoric name" and compares it to Song 8:6 (*You Shall Have No Other Gods: Israelite Religion in the Light of Hebrew Inscriptions*, HSS 31 [Atlanta: Scholars Press, 1986], 66–67 n. 12).

[18] Inherited Northwest Semitic formulae persist even beyond the biblical period, appearing in later Jewish literature. In their interpretations of Job 26:12, b. B. Bat. 75a, Tanḥ., Ḥuqqat I, and Num. Rab. 18:1 all refer to a recalcitrant figure known as the "Prince of the Sea" (śar šel yām). This title parallels zbl ym ("Prince Sea"), a common epithet of Yamm in the Baal Cycle. Irving Jacobs provides a detailed overview of these lexical parallels ("Elements of Near Eastern Mythology in Rabbinic Aggadah," JJS 28 [1977]: 2–3). Michael Fishbane also treats these passages in his work on rabbinic mythmaking (*Biblical Myth and Rabbinic Mythmaking* [Oxford: Oxford University Press, 2003], 118).

[19] The date of Song 8:6b–7a is unimportant for my argument because the Northwest Semitic combat myth survived and evolved well into the Common Era. As shown in n. 18, inherited formulae persist in later Christian and Jewish material, dated to the first century CE and beyond,

this verse refers to a deity or an abstract concept. Several other passages in the Hebrew Bible, however, portray מות as an active force in the world and draw on inherited Northwest Semitic material to describe the conflict between YHWH and Death. According to Isa 25:8, YHWH "will swallow Death forever" (בלע המות לנצח) during the eschatological era.[20] This verse inverts the events of the Baal Cycle, in which Môt swallows Baal whole, and foreshadows YHWH's ultimate victory over Death.[21] In Isa 28:14–18, the rulers of Jerusalem are said to make a covenant with death, and here death must refer to a deity. Deities, after all, were natural covenant partners in the religious practice of ancient Israel; abstract concepts were not. מות also appears in the Israelite onomasticon, suggesting his continuing status as a deity at the level of personal piety.[22] In addition to עזמות, two other Israelite personal names contain the element מות: אחימות ("Brother of Death" or "My Brother is Death"; 1 Chr 6:10) and ירימות ("May Death See!" 1 Chr 24:30, 25:4, 27:19, 2 Chr 11:18, 31:13).[23] Taken together, these diverse pieces of evidence suggest that Song 8:6b does refer to a mythic battle between love and Death reminiscent of the Baal Cycle.

The second half of Song 8:6b shares its grammatical structure with the first: a predicate adjective precedes both a comparative clause and the subject. The purpose of this clause, however, is not to pit Sheol against jealousy but to equate love with jealousy (קנאה), one of YHWH's more ferocious attributes, through strict parallelism. Unlike Môt, Sheol never spars with the divine warrior directly in either the Hebrew Bible or the Baal Cycle. It does, however, occur in parallel to death seven times in the Hebrew Bible as part of a stereotyped pairing (2 Sam 22:6; Isa 28:15, 18; 38:18; Hos 13:14; Hab 2:5; Psa 6:5; 18:5). Likewise, עז and קשתה appear in parallel in Gen 49:7, leaving love and jealousy as parallel terms in Song 8:6b.

The noun קנאה, usually translated "jealousy," occurs forty three times in the Hebrew Bible. Twenty-one times it is associated with YHWH, often in the context

---

well after 4QCant[a] (4Q106), the earliest manuscripts of Song of Songs from Qumran, which dates to the end of the first century BCE (Emanuel Tov, "Canticles," in *Qumran Cave 4.XI: Psalms to Chronicles*, ed. E. Ulrich et al., DJD XVI (Oxford: Clarendon, 2000], 195; idem, "Three Manuscripts [Abbreviated Texts?] of Canticles from Qumran Cave 4," *JJS* 46 [1995]: 88).

[20] As noted above, the Isaiah Apocalypse already shares the inherited Northwest Semitic formula "Leviathan, the fleeing serpent ... the twisting serpent" with the Baal Cycle. This parallel increases the probability that Isa 25:8 also draws on inherited material.

[21] I am tempted to classify *DN billaʿa mawt- ("Death swallowed DN" or "DN swallowed Death") as what Watkins calls a reciprocal formula, a formula in which the subject and object can switch depending on the desired meaning. As an example of a reciprocal formula, Watkins cites the Indo-European formula "hero slays [*gʷhen-] serpent" and "serpent slays [*gʷhen-] hero" (*How to Kill a Dragon*, 325). For a refraction of the formula *DN billaʿa mawt- in an early Christian context, see 1 Cor 15:54, where Paul quotes Isa 25:8 and Hos 13:14 to show that believers, both living and dead, will experience bodily transformation at the eschaton.

[22] Tigay, *You Shall Have No Other Gods*, 66–67.

[23] It is interesting that many of the Israelite names containing *māwet* occur in Persian-period sources, since some scholars date the Song of Songs to the Persian period.

of divine anger or combat.²⁴ In the redemptive vision of Isa 42:13, "YHWH goes forth like a warrior, like a man of war he stirs up his קנאה. He shouts and prevails against his enemies," while in Zeph 1:18, "neither their silver nor their gold will be able to deliver them on the day of YHWH's wrath. The whole earth will be consumed in the fire of his jealousy [באש קנאתו]." Elsewhere קנאה refers to the jealousy provoked by an adulterous wife or rival suitor (e.g., Num 5). These two usages are integrally related, since many prophetic texts portray YHWH as the jealous husband of adulterous Israel (e.g., Hos 2).²⁵ The pairing of love and jealousy also recalls biblical law: YHWH is a jealous (קנא) god (Exod 20:5, 34:14, Deut 4:24, 5:9, 6:15) whose love the Israelites are supposed to reciprocate (Exod 20:6, Deut 5:10, 6:4–5). Failure to do so tempts YHWH's wrath. Thus, the reciprocal parallelism between love and jealousy in Song 8:6b identifies love with YHWH in his role as divine warrior and fierce defender of his commitments.

Love, like YHWH's jealousy, runs hot: "Its flashes are flashes of fire, the flame of Yah" (רשפיה רשפי אש שלהבתיה; Song 8:6b). This phrase likens the power of love to the divine warrior's lightning bolts and the fiery force of his jealousy. W. F. Albright and Marvin Pope treat רשפיה רשפי אש as a reference to Reshep, the West Semitic god of plague and war, which would provide an additional reference to the divine realm in an already dense constellation of cosmic language.²⁶ But I disagree with their assessment for three reasons. First, the Jewish Aramaic cognate of רשפי, *rišpā*, simply means "flame," which fits the earlier reference to קנאה better than a sudden invocation of Reshep. Second, the vocalization of the verse does not support a reference to Reshep: רשפי comes from earlier *rišp-, while the divine name Reshep comes from earlier *rašp-. They are separate nouns from the same root.²⁷ Third, a reference to Reshep does not make sense in the context of the verse. "Its Resheps are Resheps of fire" is a non sequitur. Instead, this colon highlights love's fiery qualities leading up to the equation of love's power with שלהבתיה, which I translate as "Yah's flame."

The final word of v. 6, שלהבתיה, is a well-known interpretational crux. It could be the plural of שלהבת with a third feminine singular possessive suffix, an intensive form of שלהבת ("flame") utilizing the divine name, or a construct phrase meaning "Yah's flame."²⁸ I argue that a construct phrase makes the most sense and serves to

---

²⁴ In a few cases, קנאה refers to zeal *for* YHWH as in 2 Kgs 10:16, Pss 69:10, 119:139.

²⁵ On the connection of these texts, see Gershon Cohen, "The Song of Songs and the Jewish Religious Mentality," in *The Samuel Friedland Lectures, 1960–1966*, ed. L. Finkelstein (New York: Jewish Theological Seminary of America, 1966), 5–8; and David M. Carr, "Gender and the Shaping of Desire in the Song of Songs and Its Interpretations," *JBL* 119 (2000): 238–39.

²⁶ W. F. Albright, "Archaic Survivals in the Text of Canticles," in *Hebrew and Semitic Studies Presented to Godfrey Rolles Driver in Celebration of His Seventieth Birthday, 20 August 1962*, ed. D. Winton Thomas and W. D. McHardy (Oxford: Clarendon, 1963), 7; Pope, *Song of Songs*, 670.

²⁷ Compare Amorite *rašap* and Ugaritic *rašpu* for the earlier vocalization of the divine name.

²⁸ The Vulgate and the Peshitta do not offer much help in deciding between the different options. The Vulgate treats שלהבתיה as a second *nomen rectum* in construct with רשפי—which is grammatically impossible in Hebrew—and translates *lampades eius lampades ignis atque*

further identify love with the divine warrior. The other two interpretations prove difficult on linguistic grounds and receive little help from the versions, as I will show below.

The LXX reads φλόγες αὐτῆς ("its flames") here, which reflects Hebrew *šălhābōtêhā but lacks a predicate with which to form a second clause. This absence poses a general problem for the suffix theory and has led some commentators to restore additional material at the end of v. 6 in parallel with רשפי אש, but there is no evidence for doing so.[29] Therefore, it is unlikely that שלהבתיה represents the plural of שלהבת with a third feminine singular possessive suffix.

As vocalized in the Ben Asher tradition, שלהבתיה shares its morphological form with מאפליה ("deep shadow") in Jer 2:31. This similarity has led some scholars to suggest that שלהבתיה and מאפליה are intensive forms that originally contained the divine name יה but were later revocalized.[30] Such an explanation proves unnecessary for שלהבתיה. The connection with YHWH was never lost, as the following evidence shows, and even if it were, the "intensive theory" assumes that שלהבתיה originally contained יה.

The divine reading receives support from the Ben Naphtali vocalization of the MT, Ibn Ezra, and the Targum of Canticles. The Ben Naphtali tradition points שלהבתיה as two separate words, שלהבת יה. Ibn Ezra follows a similar tradition by translating שלהבתיה as "God's flame," while the Targum turns this verse into an extended discourse on the relationship between God, Israel, and the nations:

> For strong as death is the love of your divinity, and powerful as Gehinnom is the jealousy which the peoples harbor toward us. The enmity which they nurture toward us is like the coals of the fires of Gehinnom [גומרין דאישתא דגיהנם] which YHWH created on the second day of the creation of the world to burn therewith the devotees of foreign worship.

At first glance, it is difficult to determine what became of the word שלהבתיה in this highly expansionistic rendering. A closer inspection, however, suggests that the Targum based its interpretation on a *Vorlage* containing שלהבת יה ("flame of Yah"). YHWH creates the "coals of the fires of Gehinnom," so in that sense they are "Yah's fires."

The phrase שלהבת יה ("flame of Yah") does not occur elsewhere in the Hebrew Bible. But several verses depict YHWH brandishing lightning bolts as part of his theophany in the storm cloud. In Ps 29:7, "YHWH's voice [i.e., thunder] flashes forth flames of fire [להבות אש]," while in Isa 30:30 YHWH "causes the majesty of his voice to be heard and the descent of his arm to be seen in raging fury and a

---

flammarum, "its lamps are lamps of fire and also flames." The Peshitta interprets שלהבתיה as a misspelling for the related noun *šalhebītā* ("flame").

[29] Pope summarizes the different restorations that have been proposed (*Song of Songs*, 670).

[30] Gillis Gerleman, *Ruth. Das Hohelied*, BKAT 18 (Neukirchen-Vluyn: Neukirchener Verlag, 1965), 216–17, followed by Ariel Bloch and Chana Bloch, *The Song of Songs: A New Translation* (Berkeley: University of California Press, 2000), 213. See also Blumenthal, "Where God Is Not," 81.

flame of devouring fire [להב אש אוכלה] with a cloudburst, a rainstorm, and hailstones."³¹ The word for flame used in these verses, להב, is etymologically related to שלהבת.³² Thus, Song 8:6b equates the flashes of love with YHWH's lightning bolt. Not only does love take on Death, one of YHWH's enemies; it also wields YHWH's signature weapon.

In Song 8:7a, additional forces arise to challenge love but prove unfit for the task. "Many waters cannot quench love," the female lover declares, "neither can the rivers drown it." The phrase "many waters" is hard to interpret. In his study of the phrase, Herbert G. May recognized the multivalent meanings of מים רבים but did not provide criteria for distinguishing cosmic and common usage. In the end, he concedes that the reference to מים רבים in Song 8:7 "perhaps too temptingly suggests the storm-God who was in conflict with the waters."³³ There is evidence, however, that מים רבים in this verse does refer to the cosmic waters that YHWH must master.

The phrase מים רבים ("many waters") occurs twenty-eight times in the Hebrew Bible and describes a variety of aquatic phenomena, ranging from the mundane to the mythic.³⁴ On the mundane level, מים רבים can refer to everyday water features like the pools of Gibeon (Jer 41:12) and the watercourses around Jerusalem (2 Chr 33:4). It can also refer to the ocean (Isa 23:3), the Euphrates (Jer 51:13), the Nile (Ezek 32:13), and the abundant waters suitable for irrigation (Ezek 17:5, 8). On the mythic level, מים רבים appears in descriptions of the divine warrior's theophany and battle against aqueous foes. In 2 Sam 22 and Ps 18, for example, the poet praises YHWH for coming to his aid in the guise of the divine warrior and identifies his human enemies with the divine warrior's aquatic foes: "The channels of Sea were seen, the foundations of the world were laid bare at YHWH's rebuke, at the blast of the breath of his nostrils. He reached out from on high and took me and drew me from mighty waters" (vv. 15–16). Psalm 77:16–20 casts the Red Sea crossing in terms of mythic combat:

> When the waters saw you, O God, when the waters saw you, they trembled. Indeed, the depths shook. The clouds poured water, the sky gave its voice. Indeed your arrows flew about. The sound of your thunder was in the whirlwind. Lightning lit the world. The earth trembled and shook. Your road was in the Sea and your path in the mighty waters, but your footsteps were not seen. You led your people like a flock by the hand of Moses and Aaron.

---

³¹ See further Isa 66:15.

³² Both להב and שלהבת contain the root *lhb*, related to Arabic *lahiba* ("to blaze") and Ethiopic *lahaba* ("to burn"). The *ša-* prefix of שלהבת is most likely the prefix of the causative stem found occasionally in Aramaic and ultimately borrowed from Akkadian.

³³ Herbert G. May, "Some Cosmic Connotations of Mayim Rabbîm, 'Many Waters,'" *JBL* 74 (1955): 18.

³⁴ Northwest Semitic parallels to *mayim rabbîm* are lacking. In *KTU* 1.3.3.39, ʿAnat brags about "finishing off River, the great god" (*lklt.nhr.il.rbm*), which could be an elliptical reference to *mym rbm*, the Ugaritic cognate of *mayim rabbîm*. This verse makes sense as it is, however.

Here, YHWH facilitates Israel's deliverance by fighting the Red Sea and forcing it to part.

By itself מים רבים has both mythic and mundane connotations. But the collocation of "many waters" and "rivers" (נהרים/נהרות) is restricted to the context of divine combat and control over aqueous forces. In Hab 3:2–15, for example, מים רבים appears in an extended theophany scene in which YHWH rages against the rivers (נהרים) and the Sea (ים) (3:8) and tramples the mighty waters with his horses (3:15).[35] Likewise, in Ps 93, the clamor of "rivers" and "mighty waters" imagined as personal forces serves as a foil to the glory of the enthroned Lord: "The rivers have lifted up, O YHWH, the rivers have lifted up their voice, the rivers their roaring. More majestic than the sound of mighty waters, more majestic than the breakers of Sea, majestic on high is YHWH" (Ps 93:3–4). In Ezek 31:15, YHWH uses the Deep (תהום), mighty waters, and rivers to shutter Tyre in Sheol: "On the day it went down to Sheol, with a heavy heart I closed the Deep over it and I withheld its rivers and the mighty waters were restrained." As in the Priestly creation account, YHWH exercises control over the subterranean waters as if he had subdued them earlier. Most likely, the collocation of "many waters" and "rivers" in Song 8:7 evokes images of divine combat as well.

Through the use of an inherited Northwest Semitic formula and mythic language, Song 8:6b–7a identifies love with the victorious divine warrior. Like YHWH and Baal, love tangles with Death and Sea and proves an equal match for both opponents. Like Baal in *KTU* 1.6.6.17, 19, 20, "love is as strong as Death," and, like YHWH, love confronts both many waters (מים רבים) and rivers (נהרות). Love uses fiery projectiles (רשפיה רשפי אש), including YHWH's own thunderbolt (שלהבתיה), to overcome its enemies and is identified with YHWH's jealousy (קנאה) through poetic parallelism.[36]

III. Mythic Resonances

Song of Songs contains the densest concentration of love language of any book of the Hebrew Bible. The root אהב occurs eighteen times in 117 verses, and the word "love" (אהבה) itself occurs ten times. Because of this, the identification of love with the divine warrior in Song 8:6b–7a reverberates throughout the final version

---

[35] The word נהר usually takes the feminine plural marker ות- in Hebrew and most other Semitic languages. For this reason, W. F. Albright treats נהרים here as singular with an enclitic mem ("The Psalm of Habakkuk," in *Studies in Old Testament Prophecy: Presented to Professor Theodore H. Robinson by the Society for Old Testament Study on His Sixty-Fifth Birthday, August 9th, 1946*, ed. H. H. Rowley [Edinburgh: T&T Clark, 1950], 15 note y).

[36] In light of this identification, it is significant that the earliest identifiable allusions to the Song occur in Revelation and 4 Ezra, both of which draw heavily on combat-myth imagery to describe the eschaton. See Jonathan Kaplan, "The Song of Songs from the Bible to the Mishnah," *HUCA* 81 (2010): 54–65.

of Song of Songs as a whole.[37] As Exum recognizes, "The affirmation that love is as strong as death in vv. 6–7 is the climax of the poem and its raison d'être."[38] It provides an orienting simile that affects other sections of the Song. In particular, it nuances the adjuration refrain "Do not awaken or stir up love until it pleases" (אם־תעירו ואם־תעוררו את־האהבה עד שתחפץ) in Song 2:7, 3:5, and 8:4 and the phrase "love sick" (חולת אהבה) in Song 2:5 and 5:8 by affirming the supreme power of love.

The mythic imagery of Song 8:6b–7a motivates and informs the adjuration refrain on both a linguistic and a thematic level. On the linguistic level, the root עור occurs primarily in military contexts, where it refers to the muster of armies for battle (e.g., Isa 13:17, 45:13, Jer 6:22, Joel 4:9, Zech 9:13) and the prowess of individual warriors (e.g., 2 Sam 23:18, Hab 3:9; see also Isa 42:13 above). It can also occur in contexts of divine combat, most likely as an extension of its mundane usage, and thus furnishes another point of contact between love and YHWH as the divine warrior. In Isa 51:9–10, for example, the prophet entreats YHWH to awake (עורי) and recapitulate his past victories over Rahab, the dragon, Sea, and the waters of the great Deep. Elsewhere in the Hebrew Bible, עור takes Leviathan as its direct object, providing another link to the Northwest Semitic combat myth. In Job 3:8, Job invokes "those who are ready to rouse Leviathan" (העתידים ערר לויתן) to curse the day of his birth, while in Job 41:2 YHWH counters that "no one is so fierce that he stirs it [Leviathan] up [לא־אכזר כי יעורנו]. Who could stand before it?" According to Job, Leviathan, like YHWH, must be roused for battle. But once roused it can only be confronted by the divine warrior. In the Song, love proves similarly implacable. Because love battles cosmic forces in Song 8:6b–7a, human agency has little hope of controlling it. It is no accident, then, that the final adjuration in Song 8:4 closely precedes Song 8:6b–7a.

The phrase "love sick" (חולת אהבה) in Song 2:5 and 5:8 also takes on new meaning in light of the mythic context of Song 8:6b–7a. If, as Song 8:6b–7a suggests, love is a warrior, then it fights on the battlefield of the human heart and mind. Naturally, this experience proves both draining and exhilarating for those in its grip and can, if left unchecked, lead to bodily harm.[39] I suggest, therefore, that the root metaphor in these verses is both martial and medical; the woman is not "lovesick" but rather "lovestruck." She has sustained a "wound" in the course of romance and must recuperate.[40] This interpretation correlates well with the military imagery applied to the woman throughout the Song (4:4; 6:4, 10) and is borne out by

---

[37] I leave open the question of whether Song of Songs is an anthology of separate poems or a unified composition.

[38] Exum, *Song of Songs*, 245.

[39] Another area of study that deserves further inquiry is the issue of love, as identified with the divine warrior, becoming too violent and militaristic. Unfortunately, such an analysis is beyond the scope of this article.

[40] In this regard, love in Song 2:5 and 5:8 resembles Eros/Cupid from Greco-Roman myth.

linguistic evidence.⁴¹ Although the root חלה typically refers to what modern individuals would call disease, it can designate any bodily infirmity, including wounds sustained in battle (e.g., 1 Kgs 22:34, 2 Kgs 8:29, 2 Chr 35:23).⁴² Furthermore, the LXX translates חולת אהבה as τετρωμένη ἀγάπης ("wounded by love"). Most likely, the potential dangers of love invoked in 2:5 motivate the first adjuration two verses later.

At the same time, love, like YHWH, invigorates its adherents. If, as I have argued, Song 8:6b–7a identifies love with the divine warrior, then to be in love is to be empowered by the divine spirit. In the mythic realm of Song 8:6b–7a, love takes on Death, many waters, and rivers using the power of the thunderstorm. This confrontation is couched in the language of the Northwest Semitic combat myth and invokes the inherited formula "as strong as Death." In the rest of the Song, love lends strength to the lovers—particularly the woman—in their pursuit of each other. The woman wanders the street alone at night in search of her lover (3:2–4, 5:6–7), endures abuse at the hands of the guards (5:7), and dwells, even if metaphorically, with lions and leopards (4:8).⁴³ All of this is possible because the Song identifies love with the most powerful force in the Israelite imagination—YHWH, the divine warrior.

---

⁴¹ For this imagery, see Carol Meyers, "Gender Imagery in the Song of Songs," *HAR* 10 (1986): 215.

⁴² The *niphal* participle of חלה also modifies מכה ("wound") in Jer 10:19, 14:17, 30:12, and Nah 3:19.

⁴³ The Deuteronomistic History may offer several parallels to the Song in this regard. In the Deuteronomistic History, the spirit of YHWH (רוח־יהוה) impels warriors, kings, and prophets to perform superhuman feats, often in a military context. In Judg 14:6, for example, Samson tears apart a young lion under the influence of YHWH's spirit (see further Judg 3:10, 6:34, 11:29, 14:19, 15:14, 1 Sam 10:6, 16:13).

Textbook eSources
from BAKER ACADEMIC

Textbook eSources are Baker Academic's supplementary resources for our ever-expanding selection of textbooks. To make teaching as seamless as possible, we provide quality ancillary content for professors and students on select textbooks. These resources include PowerPoint slides, tests and quizzes, instructor's manuals, flashcards, study questions, videos, and much more.

Select titles also have learning management cartridge test banks that can be imported directly into your school's learning management system. These cartridges are available in numerous LMS formats, including Blackboard and Moodle.

To learn more visit www.bakeracademic.com/professors

eSources are currently available for 15 textbooks, including

   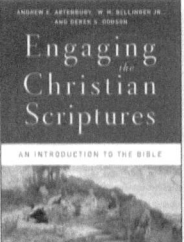

bakeracademic.com
Available in bookstores or by calling 800.877.2665
Visit our blog: blog.bakeracademic.com

The Poetry of the Lord's Prayer: A Study in Poetic Device

MICHAEL WADE MARTIN
Michael.Martin@lcu.edu
Lubbock Christian University, Lubbock, TX 79407

This study argues the Lord's Prayer (Matt 6:9–13) belongs to the tradition of ancient Jewish religious poetry, as evidenced by its use in every sentence of multiple, coordinated poetic figures that were characteristic of the tradition and determinative of its strophic form. The study defines each device using the terms and conceptual categories of the ancient world and identifies examples from poetic texts in both the Hebrew Bible and the Septuagint. The study then shows the concentrated use of these same devices in every line of the prayer, as well as the strophic form that emerges from this usage. The devices identified are homoeoteleuton, homoeokatarkton, antistrophe, epanaphora, anadiplosis, polyptoton, antithesis, parisosis, and paronomasia. These devices work together to shape the prayer into two stanzas, each a tripartite petition expressed in tricolon form. The study concludes with English translations that attempt to capture both the devices and their resultant stichometry.

Scholarship has given some attention in the past to the poetic dimensions of the Lord's Prayer (Matt 6:9–13). Several scholars have argued for a poetic original in Aramaic or Hebrew.[1] Some have interpreted the prayer in translation as a

[1] In Aramaic, Charles C. Torrey, "A Possible Metrical Original of the Lord's Prayer," *ZA* 28 (1914): 312–17; Enno Littman, "Torreys Buch über die vier Evangelien," *ZNW* 34 (1935): 20–34; C. F. Burney, *The Poetry of Our Lord: An Examination of the Formal Elements of Hebrew Poetry in the Discourses of Jesus Christ* (Oxford: Clarendon, 1925), 112–13, 160–62; Ernst Lohmeyer, *The Lord's Prayer*, trans. John Bowden (London: Collins, 1965), 25–31; K. G. Kuhn, *Achtzehngebet und Vaterunser und der Reim*, WUNT 1 (Göttingen: Vandenhoeck & Ruprecht, 1961), 30–40; Joachim Jeremias, *The Prayers of Jesus*, trans. John Bowden and Christoph Burchard (Philadelphia: Fortress, 1967), 85–94; G. Schwarz, "Matthäus vi.9–13/Lukas xi.2–4: Emendation und Rückübersetzung," *NTS* 15 (1968–69): 233–47, http://dx.doi.org/10.1017/S0028688500019068; Johannes C. de Moor, "The Reconstruction of the Aramaic Original of the Lord's Prayer," in *The Structural Analysis of Biblical and Canaanite Poetry*, ed. Willem van der Meer and Johannes C. de Moor, JSOTSup 74 (Sheffield: JSOT Press, 1988), 397–422. In Hebrew, Jean Carmignac, *Recherches sur le "Nôtre Père"* (Paris: Letouzey & Ané, 1969), 383–86. These scholars generally assume that the

poem.² A few have argued that the final, Matthean form should be considered poetry.³ Generally, however, commentators make no mention of the prayer as a poem,⁴ and translators ignore or efface its poetic qualities.⁵

This study argues that the Lord's Prayer employs in every line a number of coordinated poetic devices characteristic of poetry in both the Hebrew Bible and the Septuagint. These devices, through their symmetries of sound, sense, and structure, lend the prayer a discernible strophic form. Given the thematic and liturgical ties that the prayer obviously shares with ancient Jewish poetry, this form suggests that the prayer is a poem belonging to the Jewish religious literary tradition.⁶

---

poetry of the prayer has largely been lost in translation; see, e.g., Lohmeyer, who calls the final form a "faded reflection" of the Aramaic (*Lord's Prayer*, 27).

²Denis Wortman, "The Inspirational Rhythm of Our English Bible," *Christian Advocate* 81 (8 March 1906): 326; Josiah Harmar Penniman, *A Book about the English Bible* (New York: Macmillan, 1919), 76–77.

³C. F. Burney, though primarily concerned with reconstruction of an Aramaic original, nonetheless considers the Matthean version "a little poem or hymn consisting of two four-beat tristichs" (*Poetry of Our Lord*, 112–13). The Church of England Liturgical Commission observantly identifies multiple poetic devices—parallelism, antithesis, assonance, and rhyme (*Modern Liturgical Texts* [London: SPCK, 1968], 1–3). William R. Farmer notes that the prayer "has a certain poetic character" that, typical of Hebrew poetry, is based not "so much on rhyme" as on "a balance of ideas" (*The Gospel of Jesus: The Pastoral Relevance of the Synoptic Problem* [Louisville: Westminster John Knox, 1994], 44). H. Benedict Green, whose analysis is the most thorough to date, argues that the "whole composition has a recognizable verse structure": the first half is organized concentrically with some "rhyming correspondence" among the three petitions, and the second half, by three distichs, each containing a single petition (*Matthew, Poet of the Beatitudes*, JSNTSup 203 [Sheffield: Sheffield Academic, 2001], 79–81).

⁴See, e.g., W. D. Davies and Dale C. Allison Jr., *A Critical and Exegetical Commentary on the Gospel according to Saint Matthew*, 3 vols., ICC (Edinburgh: T&T Clark, 1988–1997), 1:590–617; Ulrich Luz, *Matthew 1–7: A Commentary*, trans. Wilhelm C. Linss (Minneapolis: Augsburg, 1989), 369–89. See, too, the literary-critical commentaries, e.g., Robert H. Gundry, *Matthew: A Commentary on His Literary and Theological Art* (Grand Rapids: Eerdmans, 1982), 104–9; Charles H. Talbert, *Matthew*, Paideia (Grand Rapids: Baker, 2010), 88–89. At best, one generally finds discussion of the thesis of Kuhn et al. of a poetic Aramaic original behind the prayer (e.g., Luz, *Matthew 1–7*, 371–72), or passing mention of a poetic quality or two (e.g., Luz, 371: "a continuing rhythmic quality").

⁵Several translations represent the prayer as prose: KJV, LSG (Bible Segond 1910), NET, SG21 (Segond 21), LUO (Luther Bibel 1545), NGÜ (Neue Genfer Übersetzung), SCL (Schlachter Bibel 1951; 2000), ELB (Elberfelder), HOF (Hoffnung für Alle); see, too, the *SBL Greek New Testament*. Others attempt a strophic arrangement, though generally without clarifying whether a poetic or merely liturgical (i.e., periodic prose) form is intended. In any case, these reflect ambiguous and conflicting judgments concerning the form and generally efface the figures identified in this study.

⁶Alternative theories that potentially account for the use of the devices on the basis of other literary traditions are problematic by comparison. Greek poetry employed these same devices but took its strophic form primarily from hexameter, pentameter, and the like. Such metrical form is altogether lacking in the Lord's Prayer, just as it is in the poetry if the Hebrew Bible and the

I. The Devices in Ancient Jewish Poetry

To illustrate the use of these devices in the Lord's Prayer, I first examine their use in ancient Jewish poetry. In the survey that follows, I define each device using the terms and conceptual categories of ancient Hellenistic literary theory,[7] and I highlight examples of each device from poetic texts in both the Hebrew Bible and the Septuagint.[8] I limit my survey to texts identified in previous scholarship as poetry[9] and to those devices that appear in the Lord's Prayer: homoeoteleuton, homoeokatarkton, antistrophe, epanaphora, anadiplosis, polyptoton, antithesis, parisosis, and paronomasia.

1. *Homoeoteleuton*

Homoeoteleuton is similarity of sound at the conclusion of affiliated cola, usually in the concluding syllable(s) of the concluding word(s).[10]

Septuagint. Similarly, Greek prose oratory used the devices for occasional poetic flourish, but not in the same concentration seen in the Lord's Prayer or other ancient Jewish (or Greek) poetry. Indeed, the kind of concentrated usage I will show in the Lord's Prayer—usage that spans the full length of the composition and entails multiple devices in every line—is precisely the kind of usage textbooks discourage for oratory because it is overly "poetic" (see Aristotle, *Rhet.* 3.1.8–10 [1404a], 3.3.4 [1407a]; Demetrius, *Eloc.* 12–15; Cicero, *Or. Brut.* 174–176; cf., too, Dionysius of Halicarnassus, *Lys.* 2–3, *Is.* 19, *Dem.* 25; Diodorus Siculus 12.53.4). Moreover, while it is true the Lord's Prayer is set in a speech in both Matthew and Luke, these speeches are prose in form and do not display across their length a concentration of devices similar to that seen in the prayer itself—a fact discouraging the attribution of the prayer's form to a poetic oratorical style of the Matthean or Lukan Jesus.

[7] I take as my sources the handbooks of rhetoric (esp. Aristotle, *Rhetorica*, *Rhetorica ad Alexandrinum*; Demetrius, *De elocutione*; Rhetorica ad Herennium; Quintilian, *Institutio oratoria*), which taught the devices as "figures of speech and thought" in their discussions of style. Though these accounts have prose declamation primarily in view, they acknowledge the poetic origin and quality of the devices, cite valuable examples of the devices not only from oratory but also from poetry, and, most important, provide ancient terminology and definitions of the devices. These textbooks are thus an invaluable (and our only) resource for ancient theory, and their perspective can help us guard against using anachronistic literary categories in our description of ancient discourse.

[8] Translations of the MT were made in consultation with the NRSV, and translations of the LXX were made in consultation with the translation of Sir Lancelot Charles Lee Brenton, *The Septuagint Version of the Old Testament: With an English Translation, and with Various Readings and Critical Notes* (London: Samuel Bagster & Sons, 1851). In many cases the translations offered here are revisions of those translations.

[9] I follow esp. Wilfred G. E. Watson, *Classical Hebrew Poetry: A Guide to Its Techniques* (London: T&T Clark, 2001); for Watson's methodology, see ch. 3.

[10] See Aristotle, *Rhet.* 3.9.9 (1410a); Rhet. Her. 4.28; Quintilian, *Inst.* 9.3.77; Heinrich Lausberg, *Handbook of Literary Rhetoric: A Foundation for Literary Study*, trans. Matthew T. Bliss,

kî yhwh (ʾădōnāy) šōpəṭēnû
yhwh (ʾădōnāy) məḥōqəqēnû
yhwh (ʾădōnāy) malkēnû
hûʾ yôšîʿēnû

For the Lord is our judge,
the Lord is our ruler,
the Lord is our king;
he will save us. (Isa 33:22)

hôy ʾaššûr šēbeṭ ʾappî
ûmaṭṭeh-hûʾ bəyādām zaʿmî

Ah, Assyria, the rod of my anger—
The club in their hands is my fury. (Isa 10:5)

kî-bēn hāyîtî ləʾābî
rak wəyāḥîd lipnê ʾimmî

When I was a son with my father,
tender, and my mother's favorite. (Prov 4:3)

See also Job 10:8b–12; 21:14–15a; 31:25; Pss 15:1; 18:3, 15; 123:3ab, 4bc; Prov 4:5, 6, 8; Nah 1:2; 2:1.[11]

δικαιοσύνη καὶ κρίμα ἑτοιμασία τοῦ θρόνου σου
ἔλεος καὶ ἀλήθεια προπορεύσεται πρὸ προσώπου σου

Justice and judgment are the establishment of your throne:
mercy and truth shall go before your face. (LXX Ps 88:15)

ἀναβαίνουσιν ἕως τῶν οὐρανῶν
καὶ καταβαίνουσιν ἕως τῶν ἀβύσσων
ἡ ψυχὴ αὐτῶν ἐν κακοῖς ἐτήκετο

They go up to the heavens,
and go down to the depths;
their soul melts because of troubles. (LXX 106:26)

Annemiek Jansen, and David E. Orton (Leiden: Brill, 1998), §§725–31. Homoeoteleuton is broader than modern rhyme, in that it includes parallelism of sound limited even to a single, unstressed concluding syllable (Aristotle, *Rhet.* 3.9.9 [1410a]). For examples of the device in Greek poetry and Greek and Roman oratory, see Aristotle, *Rhet.* 3.9.9 (1410a–b), *Rhet. Alex.* 28 (1436a); Demetrius, *Eloc.* 25, 28; Rhet. Her. 4.28; Quintilian, *Inst.* 9.3.77.

[11] Homoeoteleuton occurs frequently in Hebrew poetry. Watson refers to it as "end-rhyme" or "end-assonance" (*Classical Hebrew Poetry*, 222–25, 229–35). Examples identified in biblical scholarship have generally fit the more narrow strictures of modern English rhyme. If, however, the ancient Greek definition of homoeoteleuton (which includes assonance even among single unstressed syllables at the close of parallel cola) is followed, the number of occurrences in Hebrew poetry is even greater.

υἱὸς γὰρ ἐγενόμην κἀγὼ πατρὶ ὑπήκο<u>ος</u>
καὶ ἀγαπώμενος ἐν προσώπῳ μητρ<u>ός</u>

For I also was a son obedient to *my* father,
and loved in the sight of *my* mother. (LXX Prov 4:3)

See also LXX Job 40:8, 14; Pss 1:2; 2:11; 35:1; 77:4; 150:2; Prov 4:2; Eccl 10:9; Isa 40:4, 12; Nah 1:10; 2:10; 3:2.[12]

2. Homoeokatarkton

Homoeokatarkton is similarity of sound at the beginning of affiliated cola, usually in the concluding syllable(s) of the opening word(s).[13]

<u>dām</u>îtî liqʾat midbār
<u>hāy</u>îtî kəkôs ḥŏrābôt

I am like an owl of the wilderness,
like a little owl of the waste places. (Ps 102:7)

hă<u>yig</u>ʾeh-gōmeʾ bəlōʾ biṣṣâ
yi<u>śgeh</u>-ʾāḥû bəlî-māyim

Can papyrus grow where there is no marshy land?
Can reeds flourish where there is no water? (Job 8:11)

<u>ṣāp</u>ôn wəyāmîn ʾattâ bərāʾtām
<u>tāb</u>ôr wəḥermôn bəšimkā yərannēnû

The north and the south—you created them;
Tabor and Hermon joyously praise your name. (Ps 89:13)

<u>qošrēm</u> ʿal-libbəkā tāmîd
<u>ʿondēm</u> ʿal-gargərōtekā

Bind them upon your heart always;
tie them around your neck. (Prov 6:21)

See also Pss 9:5; 89:15; 107:26; Cant 6:2b; Jer 12:2cd, 7; Lam 1:1; Nah 1:2.[14]

---

[12] Homoeoteleuton is commonly attested also in the LXX. Occurrences original to the Hebrew, however, are often replaced in translation by other devices with similar poetic effect (e.g., polyptoton in Job 31:25; antistrophe in Isa 33:22bcd, Nah 2:1).

[13] Cf. Aristotle, *Rhet.* 3.9.9 (1410a); Demetrius, *Eloc.* 25; John C. Robertson, *The Gorgianic Figures in Early Greek Prose* (Baltimore: Friedenwald, 1893), 18. The theorists who mention the device do not assign it a name but instead account for it as paramoeosis (assonance) at the beginning of the sentence. I follow Robertson's anachronistic "homoeokatarkton" for convenience's sake. For Greek examples, see Aristotle, *Rhet.* 3.9.9 (1410a); *Rhet. Alex.* 28 (1436a); Demetrius, *Eloc.* 25, 28.

[14] Watson identifies the device as "colon-initial assonance" (*Classical Hebrew Poetry*, 223–25).

ἄφαψαι δὲ αὐτοὺς ἐπὶ σῇ ψυχῇ διὰ παντὸς
καὶ ἐγκλοίωσαι ἐπὶ σῷ τραχήλῳ

But bind them upon your soul continually,
and hang them as a chain about your neck. (LXX Prov 6:21)

ὡμοιώθην πελεκᾶνι ἐρημικῷ
ἐγενήθην ὡσεὶ νυκτικόραξ ἐν οἰκοπέδῳ

I have become like a pelican of the wilderness;
I have become like an owl in a ruined house. (LXX Ps 101:7)

περιχαράκωσον αὐτήν καὶ ὑψώσει σε
τίμησον αὐτήν ἵνα σε περιλάβῃ

Secure it, and it shall exalt you,
honor it, that it may embrace you. (LXX Prov 4:8)

See also LXX Job 3:5; Pss 1:3; 2:3; 3:5; 37:22; 106:26; Prov 4:3, 18–19, 25; Eccl 10:13; Isa 40:2, 3, 5.[15]

3. Antistrophe

Antistrophe (also, epiphora) is the repetition of precisely the same word(s) at the conclusion of affiliated cola.[16]

wəzāraḥ haššemeš
ûbāʾ haššāmeš

And the sun rises
And the sun goes down. (Eccl 1:5)

kî ṣaw lāṣāw
ṣaw lāṣāw
qaw lāqāw
qaw lāqāw
zəʿêr šām
zəʿêr šām

For it is precept upon precept,
precept upon precept,
line upon line,

---

[15] Homoeokatarkton is regularly employed in the poetic texts of the LXX. Occurrences original to the Hebrew, however, are often rendered by other devices, for example, epanaphora (LXX Cant 6:2bc) or antistrophe (LXX Ps 88:15).

[16] Cf. Alexander, *Fig.* 3.29; *Rhet. Her.* 4.19; Quintilian, *Inst.* 9.3.30; Lausberg, *Handbook of Literary Rhetoric*, §§631–32. See also Demetrius, *Eloc.* 26, who treats this figure as a form of homoeoteleuton. For Greek and Roman examples, see Aristotle, *Rhet.* 3.9.9 (1410a); Demetrius, *Eloc.* 26–29; *Rhet. Her.* 4.19; Quintilian, *Inst.* 9.3.30–31.

line upon line,
here a little,
there a little. (Isa 28:10)[17]

δικαιοσύνη καὶ κρίμα ἑτοιμασία τοῦ θρόνου <u>σου</u>
ἔλεος καὶ ἀλήθεια προπορεύσεται πρὸ προσώπου <u>σου</u>

Justice and judgment are the establishment of your throne:
mercy and truth shall go before your face. (LXX Ps 88:15)

καὶ ἀνατέλλει <u>ὁ ἥλιος</u>
καὶ δύνει <u>ὁ ἥλιος</u>

And the sun rises
And the sun goes down. (LXX Eccl 1:5)

καὶ ἐξολεθρεύσω τὰ γλυπτά <u>σου</u>
καὶ τὰς στήλας σου ἐκ μέσου <u>σου</u>
καὶ οὐκέτι μὴ προσκυνήσῃς τοῖς ἔργοις τῶν χειρῶν <u>σου</u>

And I will utterly destroy your graven images,
and your statues out of your midst;
and you shall never again worship the works of your hands. (LXX Mic 5:12)

See also LXX Pss 2:3, 4, 6; 3:4; 14:1; 17:3, 15; 135:21–22; 150:1–2; Isa 33:22bcd; 40:19; Mic 5:9–14; 7:11–12.[18]

4. Epanaphora

Epanaphora (also, anaphora) is the repetition of precisely the same word(s) at the beginning of affiliated cola.[19]

<u>qārôb</u> yôm-yhwh (ʾădōnāy) haggādôl
<u>qārôb</u> ûmahēr məʾōd

Near is the great day of the LORD,
near and hastening fast. (Zeph 1:14ab)

<u>kî mî</u>-yaḥmōl ʿālayik yərûšālaim
<u>ûmî</u> yānûd lāk
<u>ûmî</u> yāsûr lišʾōl ləšālōm lāk

---

[17] Watson identifies the device as "end repetition" and "epistrophe" (*Classical Hebrew Poetry*, 276). It is rarely used in the poetry of the Hebrew Bible.

[18] In the poetry of the LXX, the device occurs much more frequently, since the most common form of homoeoteleuton in the Hebrew Bible, that involving pronominal suffixes, is usually rendered in Greek as antistrophe (e.g., LXX Mic 5:9, 10, 12).

[19] Cf. Alexander, *Fig.* 3.20.30; Rhet. Her. 4.19; Quintilian, *Inst.* 9.3.30; Lausberg, *Handbook of Literary Rhetoric*, §629. For Greek and Roman examples, see Demetrius, *Eloc.* 26–27; Rhet. Her. 4.19; Quintilian, *Inst.* 9.3.30.

> For who will have pity on you, O Jerusalem,
> or who will bemoan you,
> or who will turn aside to ask about your welfare? (Jer 15:5)

See also Job 19:23; Pss 15:1; 40:1, 6; Prov 30:4, 11–14; Eccl 1:4, 8; Isa 3:24; Jer 23:10; 51:20–23; Lam 2:5; Obad 18; Mic 1:9; 5:9–13; 7:11–12; Nah 2:10; 3:2; Zeph 1:15–16.[20] See also examples of "staircase parallelism" belong to this device.[21] See, e.g., Num 24:3 (= 24:15), Pss 29:1–2, 96:7–9, Prov 31:4.

> ὅτι ἐγγὺς ἡ ἡμέρα κυρίου ἡ μεγάλη
> ἐγγὺς καὶ ταχεῖα σφόδρα
> For near is the great day of the Lord,
> Near and speedy. (LXX Zeph 1:14ab)

> τίς φείσεται ἐπὶ σοί Ιερουσαλημ
> καὶ τίς δειλιάσει ἐπὶ σοί
> ἢ τίς ἀνακάμψει εἰς εἰρήνην σοι
> Who will spare you, O Jerusalem?
> And who will fear for you?
> Or who will turn back for your welfare? (LXX Jer 15:5)

See also LXX Pss 1:1, 2, 4; 14:1; 37:4; 40:1, 12–13, 18, 21; 113:20; 150:1–5; Prov 30:4, 11–14; 40:12; Eccl 1:4, 8; Isa 3:24; Jer 28:20–23; Joel 1:4; Obad 18; Mic 5:9–13; 7:11–12; Nah 2:10; 3:2; Zeph 1:15–16. For "staircase parallelism," see LXX Num 24:3 (= 24:15), Pss 28:1–2, 95:7–9.

5. Anadiplosis

Anadiplosis (also, palillogia, epanadiplosis) is the repetition of a preceding colon's concluding word(s) at or near the beginning of a subsequent colon.[22]

> ʾāmartî lōʾ-ʾerʾeh yāh
> yāh bəʾereṣ haḥayyîm
> I said, I shall not see the LORD,
> the LORD in the land of the living. (Isa 38:11)

> ʾānnâ yhwh (ʾădōnāy) kî-ʾănî ʿabdekā
> ʾănî-ʿabdekā ben-ʾămātekā

---

[20] Watson refers to the device as "repetition-initial" or "anaphora" (*Classical Hebrew Poetry*, 276).

[21] Ibid., 152.

[22] Cf. Zonae, *Fig.* 3.165.24; Tiberius, *Fig.* 3.70.12; Quintilian, *Inst.* 9.3.44; Lausberg, *Handbook of Literary Rhetoric*, §§619–22. Various relaxations of form, including polyptoton, may occur when the repeated word is used as a different part of speech. For Greek and Roman examples of the device, see Quintilian, *Inst.* 9.3.44, 57.

O Lord, I am your servant;
I am your servant, the child of your serving girl. (Ps 116:16)

wəhāyâ hannās miqqôl happaḥad yippōl ʾel-happaḥat
wəhāʿôleh mittôk happaḥat yillākēd bappaḥ
Whoever flees at the sound of the terror shall fall into the pit;
and whoever climbs out of the pit shall be caught in the snare. (Isa 24:18)

See also Judg 5:23; Pss 115:12, 14; 116:16; 135:12; 136:21–22; Isa 29:17; 38:11; Ezek 22:2; Hos 2:23–24; Joel 1:3–4; Amos 4:7; Nah 1:2.[23]

ὦ κύριε ἐγὼ δοῦλος σός
ὁ δὲ ἐκβαίνων ἐκ τοῦ βοθύνου ἁλώσεται ὑπὸ τῆς παγίδος ὅτι θυρίδες ἐκ τοῦ οὐρανοῦ ἠνεῴχθησαν καὶ σεισθήσεται τὰ θεμέλια τῆς γῆς
And it shall come to pass, *that* he that flees from the fear shall fall into the pit; and he that comes up out of the pit shall be caught by the snare. (LXX Isa 24:18)

ὦ κύριε ἐγὼ δοῦλος σός
ἐγὼ δοῦλος σός
καὶ υἱὸς τῆς παιδίσκης σου
O Lord, I am you servant;
I am your servant,
and the son of your handmaid. (LXX Ps 115:7)

See also LXX Judg 5:23; Pss 113:12, 22; 115:7; 134:12; 135:21–22; Isa 29:17; Hos 2:23–24; Joel 1:3–4; Amos 4:7; Nah 1:2.[24]

6. Polyptoton

Polyptoton is the repetition in affiliated cola of the same noun or pronoun in different inflections, including case, gender, and number alterations.[25]

---

[23] Watson refers to the device as "anadiplosis" or "the terrace pattern" (*Classical Hebrew Poetry*, 208–12).

[24] Though the device is frequently retained in the LXX, a change is case is often required (polyptotonic anadiplosis).

[25] Cf. Aristotle, *Rhet.* 3.9.9 (1410a); Aquila, 37; *Rhet. Her.* 4.30–31; Quintilian, *Inst.* 9.3.36–37; Lausberg, *Handbook of Literary Rhetoric*, §641. Lausberg notes that "verbal alterations" are not included in this device but belong to paronomasia—which for some theorists is a broader category that includes polyptoton while for others it is a category distinct from polyptoton. For Greek and Roman examples, see Aristotle, *Rhet.* 3.9.9 (1410a); *Rhet. Her.* 4.31; Quintilian, *Inst.* 9.3.36–38, 66. The theorists' examples usually entail epanaphoric repetition, but the device "is found empirically in all types of word repetition" (Lausberg, *Handbook of Literary Rhetoric*, §642). The theorists show a special fondness for comprehensive inflection, for example, "*Alexander* Macedo summo labore animum ad virtutem a pueritia confirmavit. *Alexandri* virtutes per orbem terrae cum laude et gloria vulgatae sunt. *Alexandrum* omnes maxime metuerunt, idem plurimum

> *hôy hămôn ʿammîm rabbîm kahămôt yammîm yehĕmāyûn*
> *ûšəʾôn ləʾummîm kišʾôn mayim kabbîrîm yiššāʾûn*
> Ah, the thunder of many peoples, they thunder like the thundering of the sea!
> Ah, the roar of nations, they roar like the roaring of mighty waters! (Isa 17:12)

> *šûbû bānîm šôbābîm ʾerpâ məšûbōtêkem*
> *hinənû ʾātānû lāk kî ʾattâ yhwh (ʾădōnāy) ʾĕlōhênû*
> Return, O faithless children, I will heal your faithlessness.
> "Here we come to you; for you are the Lord our God." (Jer 3:22)

See also Prov 7:14, 35:1, Isa 24:16, 32:19.[26]

> καὶ ἔσται ὁ φεύγων τὸν φόβον ἐμπεσεῖται εἰς τὸν βόθυνον
> ὁ δὲ ἐκβαίνων ἐκ τοῦ βοθύνου ἁλώσεται ὑπὸ τῆς παγίδος ὅτι θυρίδες ἐκ τοῦ
> οὐρανοῦ ἠνεῴχθησαν καὶ σεισθήσεται τὰ θεμέλια τῆς γῆς
> And it shall come to pass, *that* he that flees from the fear shall fall into the pit;
> and he that comes up out of the pit shall be caught by the snare. (LXX Isa 24:18)

> ὦ κύριε ἐγὼ δοῦλος σός
> ἐγὼ δοῦλος σὸς
> καὶ υἱὸς τῆς παιδίσκης σου
>
> O Lord, I am your servant;
> I am your servant,
> and the son of your handmaid. (LXX Ps 115:7)

> μηδὲ ἐγκαταλίπῃς αὐτήν
>   καὶ ἀνθέξεταί σου
> ἐράσθητι αὐτῆς
>   καὶ τηρήσει σε
>
> Do not forsake her,
> and she will hold fast to you.
> Love her,
> and she will keep you. (LXX Prov 4:6)

---

dilexerunt. *Alexandro* si vita data longior esset, trans Oceanum Macedonum transvolassent sarisae" ("Alexander of Macedon with consummate toil from boyhood trained his mind to virtue. Alexander's virtues have been broadcast with fame and glory throughout the world. All men greatly feared Alexander, yet deeply loved him. Had long life been granted Alexander, the Macedonian lances have blown across the ocean" [Rhet. Her. 4.31; Caplan, LCL]).

[26] Though the Hebrew language does not have case endings, ancient Hebrew poetry does employ a figure that has some overlap with the Greek polyptoton. Watson identifies a form of "wordplay" he calls the "turn" (or "figura etymologica"), which features the repetition of a root in different forms (*Classical Hebrew Poetry*, 239). In instances where the repetition involves a noun or pronoun root and a change in number or gender (e.g., Jer 3:22), the device corresponds to the Greek polyptoton (though in Hebrew, there is no reason as in Greek to distinguish this kind of root play from others). All other occurrences of the "figura etymologica" belong to the broader paronomasia.

See also LXX Job 31:25; 40:7; Pss 1:6; 2:7; 3:3; 4:1; 16:2; 37:22; Prov 4:6; Isa 40:4, 6; Hos 2:23–24; Joel 1:3, 4; Mic 5:11.[27]

7. Antithesis

Antithesis is the juxtaposing of opposite terms, opposite meanings, or (most commonly) both in two affiliated cola.[28]

Opposition of Both Terms and Meaning

> *yaʿălû šāmayim*
> *yērədû təhômôt*
> They mounted up to heaven,
> they went down to the depths. (Ps 107:26)

Opposition Strictly of Terms

> *ʾĕmet mēʾereṣ tiṣmāḥ*
> *wəṣedeq miššāmayim nišqāp*
> Faithfulness will spring up from the ground,
> and righteousness will look down from the sky. (Ps 85:12)

Opposition Strictly of Meaning

> *ʿênê yhwh (ʾădōnāy) nāṣərû dāʿat*
> *wayəsallēp dibrê bōgēd*
> The eyes of the LORD keep watch over knowledge,
> but he overthrows the words of the faithless. (Prov 22:12)

See also Isa 3:24a; Pss 1:6; 37:22; Prov 10:3, 4, 12; 11:14; 12:20; 13:8, 24; 14:3, 4, 5, 6, 8, 9, 10, 11, 12, 13, 15, etc.; 15:6; 20:9; Hos 13:11.[29]

Opposition of Both Terms and Meaning

> ἀναβαίνουσιν ἕως τῶν οὐρανῶν
> καὶ καταβαίνουσιν ἕως τῶν ἀβύσσων
> They go up to the heavens,
> and go down to the depths. (LXX Ps 106:26)

---

[27] Poetry in the LXX naturally employs polyptoton more frequently than Hebrew poetry.

[28] The threefold division is the theorists'; cf. Aristotle, *Rhet.* 3.9.7 (1410a); *Rhet. Alex.* 26 (1435b); Demetrius, *Eloc.* 22–23; Robertson, *Gorgianic Figures in Early Greek Prose*, 18. For Greek examples of all three kinds, see Aristotle, *Rhet.* 3.9.7 (1410a); *Rhet. Alex.* 26 (1435b); Demetrius, *Eloc.* 22, 23, 27.

[29] The device is commonly referred to as "antithetical parallelism" in biblical scholarship.

Opposition Strictly of Terms

> ὅτι αἱ ψύαι μου ἐπλήσθησαν ἐμπαιγμῶν
> καὶ οὐκ ἔστιν ἴασις ἐν τῇ σαρκί μου
>
> For my soul is filled with mockings;
> and there is no health in my flesh. (LXX Ps 37:8)

Opposition Strictly of Meaning

> οἱ δὲ ὀφθαλμοὶ κυρίου διατηροῦσιν αἴσθησιν
> φαυλίζει δὲ λόγους παράνομος
>
> The eyes of the Lord preserve discretion;
> but the transgressor despises wise words. (LXX Prov 22:12)

See also LXX Isa 3:24a; Pss 1:6; 36:22; 118:50; Prov 10:3, 4a, 12; 11:14; 12.20; 13:8, 24; 14:4, 5, 6, 8, 9, 10, 11, 12, 13, 15, etc.; 15:6; 20:9; Hos 13:11.

8. Parisosis

Parisosis (also, parison, isocolon) is a parallelism of structure across affiliated cola and consisting minimally of a roughly equal number of syllables[30]*—but preferably of additional parallel features (semantic parallels, grammatical parallels, parallelisms of sound and sense).*[31]

> *šəʾû-nēs bāʾāreṣ*
> *tiqʿû šôpār baggôyīm*
> *qaddəšû ʿālêhā gôyīm*
> *hašmîʿû ʿālêhā mamləkôt*
>
> Raise a standard in the land,
> blow the trumpet among the nations;
> prepare the nations for war against her,
> summon against her the kingdoms. (Jer 51:27)[32]

> *kî-šibbar daltôt nəḥōšet*
> *ûbərîḥê barzal giddēaʿ*
>
> For he shatters the doors of bronze,
> and the bars of iron he cuts in two. (Ps 107:16)[33]

---

[30] So Demetrius, *Eloc.* 25; Rhet. Her. 4.28.

[31] So *Rhet. Alex.* 27 (1436a); Lausberg, *Handbook of Literary Rhetoric*, §§719–54. Aristotle's vague definition may be to blame for the disparity of views: "Equality of clauses is parisosis" (*Rhet.* 3.9.9 [1410a; LCL, Freese]). For Greek and Roman examples of both kinds, see *Rhet. Alex.* 27 (1436a); Demetrius, *Eloc.* 23; Rhet. Her. 4.27; Quintilian, *Inst.* 9.3.80.

[32] Cited by Watson as an example of "parallelism proper" (*Classical Hebrew Poetry*, 118).

[33] Cited by Watson as an example of "chiasmus" or "mirror symmetry" (*Classical Hebrew Poetry*, 118).

ʾĕmet mēʾereṣ tiṣmāḥ
wəṣedeq miššāmayim nišqāp

Faithfulness will spring up from the ground,
and righteousness will look down from the sky. (Ps 85:12)[34]

pî-ṣaddîq yehgeh ḥokmâ
ûləšônô tədabbēr mišpāṭ

The mouths of the righteous utter wisdom,
and their tongues speak justice. (Ps 37:30)[35]

See also Pss 1:1; 7:17; 8:4; 15:1; 37:30; 54:9; 57:5–11; 66:8; 107:26; Prov 4:6, 8, 9, 10; 26:1; Isa 2:4; 41:2; Jer 48:37.[36]

ἄρατε σημεῖον ἐπὶ τῆς γῆς
σαλπίσατε ἐν ἔθνεσιν σάλπιγγι
ἁγιάσατε ἐπ' αὐτὴν ἔθνη
παραγγείλατε ἐπ' αὐτὴν βασιλείαις

Lift up a standard in the land,
sound the trumpet among the nations,
consecrate the nations against her,
raise up kings against her by me. (LXX Jer 28:27)

ὅτι συνέτριψεν πύλας χαλκᾶς
καὶ μοχλοὺς σιδηροῦς συνέκλασεν

For he broke to pieces the brazen gates,
the iron bars he crushed. (LXX Ps 106:16)

ἀλήθεια ἐκ τῆς γῆς ἀνέτειλεν
καὶ δικαιοσύνη ἐκ τοῦ οὐρανοῦ διέκυψεν

Truth has sprung out of the earth;
and righteousness has looked down from heaven. (LXX Ps 84:12)

---

[34] Cited by Watson as an example of "proper anti-congruence" (with parallel reversals, both gender and semantic) (*Classical Hebrew Poetry*, 118).

[35] Cited by Watson as an example of "reflexive" or "chiastic anti-congruence" (with gender reversals introduced chiastically) (*Classical Hebrew Poetry*, 119).

[36] In the poetry of the Hebrew Bible, the use of "parallelism" is well documented. Watson distinguishes "parallelism" proper ("proper congruence": $a_1, a_2, a_3,\ldots // a_1, a_2, a_3,\ldots$) from three other theoretical forms: "chiasmus or mirror symmetry" ("reflexive congruence": $a_1, a_2, a_3,\ldots // a_3, a_2, a_1,\ldots$), "proper anti-congruence" ($a_1, a_2, a_3,\ldots // -a_1, -a_2, -a_3,\ldots$), and "reflexive anti-congruence" ("chiastic": $a_1, a_2, a_3,\ldots // -a_3, -a_2, -a_1,\ldots$) (*Classical Hebrew Poetry*, 114–22). Viewed from the perspective of ancient Greek theory, all four forms would be considered parisosis (with the latter two also being antithesis). Moreover, many couplets in Hebrew poetry *not* classified as parallelism in biblical scholarship would still, by virtue of their constituent cola's similar length, fit the Greek theorists' minimalist definitions of parisosis. The examples cited, however, are drawn from Watson's analysis and fit the Greek theorists' maximalist definitions of parisosis (i.e., those requiring semantic or grammatical mirroring).

στόμα δικαίου μελετήσει σοφίαν
καὶ ἡ γλῶσσα αὐτοῦ λαλήσει κρίσιν
The mouth of the righteous will meditate wisdom,
and his tongue will speak of judgment. (LXX Ps 36:30])

See also LXX Pss 1:1; 7:17; 8:4; 14:1; 36:30; 53:9; 56:5–11; 65:8; 106:26; Prov 4:6, 8, 9, 10; 26:1; Isa 2:4; 41:2; Jer 48:37.[37]

9. Paronomasia

Paronomasia (also, parachesis) is a play on words seen either in the intentional juxtaposition of two words separated by slight phonetic modification, or in double entendre.[38] *The modification may be organic or inorganic.*[39]

Organic Paronomasia

wāʾōmar rāzî-lî rāzî-lî ʾôy lî
bōgədîm bāgādû ûbeged bōgədîm bāgādû
But I say, I pine away, I pine away. Woe is me!
For the treacherous deal treacherously, the treacherous deal very treacherously.
(Isa 24:16b)

lədāwīd rîbâ yhwh (ʾădōnāy) ʾet-yərîbay ləḥam ʾet-lōḥămāy
Contend, O LORD, with those who contend with me;
fight against those who fight against me! (Ps 35:1)

šûbû bānîm šôbābîm ʾerpâ məšûbōtêkem
Return, O faithless children, I will heal your faithlessness. (Jer 3:22)

---

[37] In the poetry of the LXX, the same range of parallelism Watson identifies in Hebrew poetry is represented. That is, element order is repeated both in the same sequence (proper parallelism) and chiastically, and elements within the repeated sequence are reflected both congruently (with semantic parallels) or anticongruently (with semantic opposites). Gender anticongruence, however, while possible in Greek, rarely occurs in the LXX because is it nearly impossible to retain in translation.

[38] Cf. Rhet. Her. 4.29; Quintilian, *Inst.* 9.3.66; Lausberg, *Handbook of Literary Rhetoric*, §637. For Greek and Roman examples, see Aristotle, *Rhet.* 3.9.9 (1410a); *Rhet. Alex.* 28 (1436a); Demetrius, *Eloc.* 27; Rhet. Her. 4.29–30; Quintilian, *Inst.* 9.3.66, 69. Paronomasia may occur in parallel positions in affiliated cola, thereby contributing to the demarcation of cola as parallel within a period. In these cases, paronomasia can subsume other devices such as homoeoteleuton, homoeokatarkton, and so on. Parallel positioning, however, is not a requirement, and in this regard, paronomasia is exceptional among the devices we have surveyed.

[39] See Robertson, *Gorgianic Figures in Early Greek Prose*, 22; cf. Lausberg, *Handbook of Literary Rhetoric*, §638.

Inorganic Paronomasia

> *ûbārad bəredet hayyāʿar*
> *ûbaššiplâ tišpal hāʿîr*
>
> The forest will disappear completely,
> and the city will be utterly laid low. (Isa 32:19)

> *kî ʿad-sîrîm səbūkîm*
> *ûkəsobʾām səbûʾîm*
> *ʾukkəlû kəqaš yābēš mālēʾ*
>
> Like thorns they are entangled,
> like drunkards they are drunk;
> they are consumed like dry straw. (Nah 1:10)

> *maddûaʿ ʾādōm lilbûšekā*
> *ûbəgādêkā kədōrēk bəgat*
>
> "Why are your robes red,
> and your garments like theirs who tread the wine press?" (Isa 63:2)

See also Job 29:16a, Pss 15:3, 35:1, Prov 7:14, 28:3, Isa 9:10, 17:12, 29:4, 33:4, 40:4.[40]

Organic Paronomasia

> ἐπιστράφητε υἱοὶ ἐπιστρέφοντες καὶ ἰάσομαι τὰ συντρίμματα ὑμῶν
> ἰδοὺ δοῦλοι ἡμεῖς ἐσόμεθά σοι ὅτι σὺ κύριος ὁ θεὸς ἡμῶν εἶ
>
> Turn, you children who are given to turning, and I will heal your bruises. Behold, we will be your servants; for you are the Lord our God. (LXX Jer 3:22)

> καὶ ἐροῦσιν οὐαὶ τοῖς ἀθετοῦσιν οἱ ἀθετοῦντες τὸν νόμον
>
> But they shall say, "Woe to the despisers, that despise the law." (Isa 24:16)

> καὶ ἔσται ὁ φεύγων τὸν φόβον ἐμπεσεῖται εἰς τὸν βόθυνον
> ὁ δὲ ἐκβαίνων ἐκ τοῦ βοθύνου ἁλώσεται ὑπὸ τῆς παγίδος ὅτι θυρίδες ἐκ τοῦ οὐρανοῦ ἠνεῴχθησαν καὶ σεισθήσεται τὰ θεμέλια τῆς γῆς
>
> And it shall come to pass, *that* he that flees from the fear shall fall into the pit; and he that comes up out of the pit shall be caught by the snare. (LXX Isa 24:18)

---

[40] Watson identifies five kinds of wordplay in Hebrew poetry, all of which correspond to the Greek paronomasia: (1) the "turn," or "figura etymologica," defined as a wordplay involving repetition of the same root (though some nominal and pronominal forms correspond to polyptoton—see above); (2) "root play," a common and specific kind of wordplay involving two roots separated by a transposition of consonants; (3) the polysemantic pun, wherein a word is used once in a double entendre; (4) punning repetition, wherein a word is used twice with two different meanings in view; (5) (what Watson calls) "paronomasia," defined narrowly as "the deliberate choice of two (or more) different words which sound nearly alike"; and (6) wordplay on names. Types 1, 3, and 4 are forms of organic paronomasia, while types 2 and 5 are forms of inorganic paronomasia. Type 6 may be organic or inorganic (*Classical Hebrew Poety*, 237–50).

Inorganic Paronomasia

ὅτι ἕως θεμελίου αὐτῶν χερσωθήσεται
καὶ ὡς σμῖλαξ περιπλεκομένη βρωθήσεται
καὶ ὡς καλάμη ξηρασίας μεστή

For *the enemy* shall be laid bare even to the foundation,
and shall be devoured as twisted yew,
and as stubble fully dry. (LXX Nah 1:10)

οὐκ ἔγνω ὁ ἄνθρωπος
τί τὸ γενόμενον
καὶ τί τὸ ἐσόμενον

man knows not
what has been,
nor what will be (LXX Eccl 10:14bcd)

See also LXX Ps 3:2; 34:1; Isa 3:24; 24:18; 33:4; 40:6; Lam 2:5; Hos 2:23–24.[41]

II. The Devices Employed in the Lord's Prayer

The same devices that characterize ancient Jewish poetry and order its stichometry are used throughout the Lord's Prayer. These I identify in the order of their appearance in the prayer, and by the poetic clusters in which they appear. There are seven such groupings, each a strophe comprised of two or three cola (i.e., a bi- or tricolon[42]) made parallel by multiple, constituent devices.

1. ἁγιασθήτω τὸ ὄνομά σου
   ἐλθέτω ἡ βασιλεία σου
   γενηθήτω τὸ θέλημά σου

This tri-colon is formed by:
  1. parisosis, or parallelism of structure across the length of the cola, seen in the similar number of words, syllables, and grammatical structure;

---

[41] In the poetry of the LXX, both puns and inorganic wordplays are usually lost in translation, while the remaining organic wordplays are only sometimes retained. Inorganic paronomasia, however, does still occur, as verb and noun endings in Greek allow for the formation of resemblances even among words not etymologically related. The translators of the LXX, too, show an awareness of wordplays in Hebrew and, where possible, a desire to retain them in translation. On the translation of punning repetition and double entendre, see Scott B. Noegel, "Wordplay and Translation Technique in the Septuagint of Job," *AuOr* 14 (1995): 33–44; Hans Ausloos, "Judges 3.12–30: An Analysis of the Greek Rendering of Hebrew Wordplay," in *Text-Critical and Hermeneutical Studies in the Septuagint*, ed. Johann Cook and Hermann-Josef Stipp, VTSup 157 (Leiden: Brill, 2012), 53–68.

[42] A common strophic structure in Jewish poetry; see Watson, *Classical Hebrew Poetry*, 114–59, 174–84.

Martin: The Poetry of the Lord's Prayer   363

2. homoeokatarkton: ἁγια<u>σθήτω</u>...; ἐλ<u>θέτω</u>...; γενη<u>θήτω</u>...;
3. homoeoteleuton: ...τὸ ὄνο<u>μά σου</u>; ...ἡ βασιλεί<u>α σου</u>; ...τὸ θέλη<u>μά σου</u>;
4. antistrophe: the threefold repetition of <u>σου</u> at the conclusion of each colon.[43]

    2. <u>ὁ ἐν</u> τοῖς <u>οὐρανοῖς</u>
       ἁγιασθήτω τὸ ὄνομά σου
       ἐλθέτω ἡ βασιλεία σου
       γενηθήτω τὸ θέλημά σου
       <u>ὡς ἐν</u> <u>οὐρανῷ</u>

Bracketing the tricolon above is a couplet formed by two devices:
1. homoeokatarkton: ὁ ἐν ...; ὡς ἐν ...;[44]
2. polyptoton: ...οὐρανοῖς; ...οὐρανῷ.[45]

Alternatively, the *inclusio* may be represented as follows:

      Πάτερ ἡμῶν <u>ὁ ἐν τοῖς οὐρανοῖς</u>
        ἁγιασθήτω τὸ ὄνομά σου
        ἐλθέτω ἡ βασιλεία σου
        γενηθήτω τὸ θέλημά σου
          <u>ὡς ἐν οὐρανῷ</u> καὶ ἐπὶ γῆς[46]

In this understanding of arrangement, the bracketing bicolon would be formed by:

---

[43] Of the seven groupings identified here, this tricolon is most commonly recognized in the commentaries (though the full number of devices comprising it is usually overlooked). See, e.g., Davies and Allison, *Gospel according to Saint Matthew*, 603; Church of England Liturgical Commission, *Modern Liturgical Texts*, 1–3; Green, *Poet of the Beatitudes*, 79–81.

[44] The historical pronunciations of the short *omicron* and the long *ōmega* are likely closer to each other than the Erasmian pronunciations of the same, so that the resemblance is even closer than may seem to many modern readers.

[45] The change to the singular is thus best explained on formal grounds, contra those who see a distinction in meaning. On numeric polyptoton, see the definition and example (grata ... gratum...) in Aquila 37; cf. Lausberg, *Handbook of Literary Rhetoric*, §641. The Middle Egyptian version and the Didache attest the "correction" of the polyptoton (... τοῖς οὐρανοῖς; ... οὐρανῷ) to antistrophe (... τῷ οὐρανῷ; ... οὐρανῷ).

[46] Green, *Poet of the Beatitudes*, 79: "The line ὡς ἐν οὐρανῷ καὶ ἐπὶ γῆς forms an inclusion with the opening address Πάτερ ἡμῶν ὁ ἐν τοῖς οὐρανοῖς"; so too several commentators, e.g., Davies and Allison, *Gospel according to Saint Matthew*, 606. On *inclusio* as a structuring principle in Jewish poetry, see Watson, *Classical Hebrew Poetry*, 285–86; see, too, Lausberg, *Handbook of Literary Rhetoric*, §§625–27. Watson writes, "In most cases the framewords are not identical ... but either synonymous or from the same root" (p. 285). Correspondingly in this bicolon the framewords involve a polyptotonic variation on the same root.

1. anadiplosis: ... ὁ ἐν τοῖς οὐρανοῖς; ... ὡς ἐν οὐρανῷ...;[47]
2. polyptoton: ... οὐρανοῖς; ... οὐρανῷ.[48]

3. ὡς <u>ἐν οὐρανῷ</u>
   καὶ <u>ἐπὶ γῆς</u>

This couplet is formed by:
  1. antithesis: ... ἐν οὐρανῷ; ... ἐπὶ γῆς;
  2. parisosis, consisting in the same number of words in each clause and a similar grammatical structure and number of syllables.

4. τὸν ἄρτον <u>ἡμῶν</u>
   τὸν ἐπιούσιον
   δὸς <u>ἡμῖν</u>
   σήμερον
   καὶ ἄφες <u>ἡμῖν</u>
   τὰ ὀφειλήματα ἡμῶν
   ὡς καὶ <u>ἡμεῖς</u> ἀφήκαμεν
   τοῖς ὀφειλέταις ἡμῶν
   καὶ μὴ εἰσενέγκῃς <u>ἡμᾶς</u>
   εἰς πειρασμόν
   ἀλλὰ ῥῦσαι <u>ἡμᾶς</u>
   ἀπὸ τοῦ πονηροῦ

This unit is held together by polyptoton, seen in the sixfold inflection of ἡμεῖς at or near the conclusion of every half clause.[49] The inflection occurs through all four Greek cases and so is a strong polyptoton.[50] The device ties the unit's three constituent couplets, described below, together as a single tricolon.

5. τὸν ἄρτον <u>ἡμῶν</u>
   <u>τὸν ἐπιούσιον</u>
   δὸς <u>ἡμῖν</u>
   <u>σήμερον</u>

---

[47] Several witnesses (D* a b c k bo^mss; Tert Cyp) eliminate ὡς with the result that the anadiplosis is closer but consists of one fewer word: ... ἐν τοῖς οὐρανοῖς; ... ἐν οὐρανῷ.

[48] On polyptotonic anadiplosis, see Lausberg, *Handbook of Literary Rhetoric*, §648.4.

[49] The twofold repetition of ἡμῶν comes at the end of whole clauses, not half clauses, and so is treated separately as an epiphoric repetition below. On half-verse polyptoton, see Lausberg, *Handbook of Literary Rhetoric*, §633 n. 1; §648 nn. 3, 4; cf. §§629, 631.

[50] See, e.g., the examples in Rhet. Her. 4.31, which advance through the same four cases (see Caplan [LCL], 306 note c).

This bicolon is formed by:
1. polyptoton (as part of the larger sixfold inflection through four cases): τὸν ἄρτον ἡμῶν …; δὸς ἡμῖν …;
2. homoeoteleuton: … τὸν ἐπιούσιον; … σήμερον;
3. possible antithesis, if the much-debated ἐπιούσιον has the sense of "tomorrow" (as in, "the bread for tomorrow, give us today"): … τὸν ἐπιούσιον; … σήμερον.[51]

6. καὶ ἄφες ἡμῖν
   τὰ ὀφειλήματα ἡμῶν
   ὡς καὶ ἡμεῖς ἀφήκαμεν
   τοῖς ὀφειλέταις ἡμῶν

Multiple coordinated devices form this couplet:
1. epanaphora (if ὡς is taken strictly in a coordinating function): καὶ …; καὶ …; but cf. ὡς in item 3 above;
2. paronomasia (organic), the play on words evident from the petitioners' shift from object to subject of forgiveness: καὶ ἄφες ἡμῖν …; καὶ ἡμεῖς ἀφήκαμεν …; this is technically a double occurrence (ἄφες/ἀφήκαμεν; ἡμῖν/ἡμεῖς);
3. polyptoton (as part of the larger sixfold inflection through four cases): … ἡμῖν; … ἡμεῖς …;
4. possible homoeoteleuton, seen in a similarity of sound at the end of the half clauses: … ἄφες ἡμῖν; … ἀφήκαμεν;[52]
5. paronomasia (organic), the play on words evident in the shift from "our debts" to "our debtors" as the object of forgiveness: … τὰ ὀφειλήματα; … τοῖς ὀφειλέταις …;[53]
6. antistrophe: … ἡμῶν; … ἡμῶν;
7. antithesis spanning the length of the entire parallelism, and as a consequence of the reversals of both instances of paronomasia: "forgive us our debts, as we forgive our debtors";
8. parisosis, fairly strong, spanning the length of the entire parallelism, and seen in the similar number of words and syllables and the similar grammatical structure.

---

[51] Favoring this view is the fact that every other petition in the prayer ends in antithesis. Therefore, formal considerations support the current majority view on the meaning of the word. On this debate, see Jeremias, *Prayers of Jesus*, 85–94; Davies and Allison, *Gospel according to Saint Matthew*, 607–8; Luz, *Matthew 1–7*, 380–83.

[52] This parallelism may account for the penultimate positioning of ἡμεῖς in its half clause, when all five other inflections occur at the conclusion of the half clause.

[53] This, the most prominent device of the petition, is commonly effaced through the rendering of the second colon with a relative clause: "Forgive us our trespasses as we forgive those who trespass against us."

7. καὶ μὴ εἰσενέγκῃς ἡμᾶς
   εἰς πειρασμόν
   ἀλλὰ ῥῦσαι ἡμᾶς
   ἀπὸ τοῦ πονηροῦ.

The final couplet of the prayer is formed by:
1. antistrophe: … ἡμᾶς; … ἡμᾶς;[54]
2. possible paronamasia (inorganic; πειρασμόν/πονηροῦ),[55] the interesting range of meaning seen in the juxtaposition of two new exodus motifs (testing/deliverance);[56]
3. antithesis of meaning spanning the length of the entire parallelism, seen in the directional contrast of both petitions (not into/but away from) and in the aforementioned juxtaposition of good and bad new exodus motifs (led into testing/delivered from evil);
4. parisosis, fairly strong, seen in the similar number of words and in similar grammatical structure.

The recognition of these devices and the strophes formed by them has important implications for a number of interpretive issues facing the prayer. I mention only a few examples in illustration of the range of issues affected. Space does not allow an exhaustive examination presently.

Translation

Versions frequently efface the symmetrical form of the figures in various ways unnecessarily. For example, the tricolon of vv. 9–10 has been traditionally rendered with the subject and verb transposed after the first petition:

---

[54] Though within the bicolon the twofold repetition of ἡμᾶς is epiphanic, in the larger unit it climactically completes the sixfold, polyptotonic repetition of ἡμεῖς by supplying the anticipated final case, the accusative, and repeating it for emphasis.

[55] The alliteration is noted also by Green, *Poet of the Beatitudes*, 81. On the phonetic distance that may exist between two words linked by paronomasia, Robertson writes: "The precise amount of similarity in sound is not fixed; it is greater in μέλλει … μέλει (Timer. III 71) than in προσήκει πρόθυμος (Hermog. II 335)" (*Georgianic Figures in Early Greek Prose*, 21). The latter example suggests that πειρασμόν/πονηροῦ falls within the range of acceptable similarity for the device. Interestingly, in the various Aramaic reconstructions that have been proposed, the assonance underlying πειρασμόν/πονηροῦ is stronger and, as in other lines of the prayer, in the form of homoeoteleuton; e.g.: *lᵉnisyōnā/min bīšā* (Lohmeyer, *Lord's Prayer*, 28).

[56] On the new exodus background of the prayer, see N. T. Wright, "The Lord's Prayer as a Paradigm for Christian Prayer," in *Into God's Presence: Prayer in the New Testament*, ed. Richard N. Longenecker, McMaster New Testament Studies (Grand Rapids: Eerdmans, 2001), 132–54; Brant Pitre, "The Lord's Prayer and the New Exodus," *Letter and Spirit* 2 (2006): 69–96.

> Hallowed be thy name.
> Thy kingdom come,
> Thy will be done (KJV)[57]

By preserving the parallel structure (parisosis) of the original, however, and by restoring only one of its many symmetries of sound (homoeoteleuton), the aesthetically appealing form of the tricolon as a single, tripartite petition may also be restored:

> hallowed be your name,
> come be your reign,
> done be your aim,[58]

In some cases, the devices are not as readily translated. The sixfold polyptotonic repetition of ἡμεῖς in the second half of the prayer, for example, is impossible to render in languages that lack case inflection. At best, all one can do is employ in place of the polyptoton half-verse antistrophe, a starker repetition that requires substituting subjects for objects or possessives and that, consequently, shifts meaning in subtle ways:

> Grant that we
>   may receive this day,
> the bread that we
>   have the coming day,
> and grant that we
>   be forgiven our debts,
> as even we
>   have forgiven our debtors,
> and grant that we
>   be seen not into trial,
> but rather that we
>   be freed from Evil.

The better route, perhaps, is to forgo the attempt to render the sixfold repetition of sound and yet still honor its effect on stichometry and structure.

---

[57] The transposition is common; see, e.g., the ASV, NAB, NRSV, ESV, TNIV, CEB (after second petition), LSG, BDS (La Bible du Semeur); MB (Menge-Bibel), SCL; ELB; also *Catechism of the Catholic Church*/Anglican *Book of Common Prayer* (1928); English Language Liturgical Consultation (1988); Ökumenische Übersetzung der Arbeitsgemeinschaft für liturgische Texte (1970).

[58] I am thankful to my colleague Brandon Fredenburg for suggesting the word "aim" to complete the repetition of sound.

Stichometry

Translators and interpreters alike frequently efface the stichometry of the prayer by dismembering the bi- and tricola formed by the figures and reconfiguring their constituent stichoi in ways unoriginal to the prayer. For example, in the first tricolon mentioned above, the first petition is often separated from the second and third with a hard break and is grouped instead with the opening address:

> Our Father which art in heaven,
> Hallowed be thy name.
> Thy kingdom come,
> Thy will be done (KJV)[59]

Similarly, the third petition is often separated from the first two and is tied more closely through punctuation to the colon that follows:

> Dein Name werde geheiligt.
> Dein Reich komme.
> Dein Wille geschehe auf Erden wie im Himmel. (LUO)[60]

If, however, the original stichometry of the prayer is to be preserved, then the tricolon must be retained—either through punctuation or arrangement or both—as a single, poetic unit:

> Our Father in the heavens,
>   hallowed be your name,
>   come be your reign,
>   done be your aim,
>   as in heaven so too on earth.

In the second half of the prayer, stichometry is commonly effaced in two important ways. First, the petition for bread is commonly rendered as a monocolon: "Give us this day our daily bread" (KJV).[61] As we have seen, however, polyptoton, homoeoteleuton, and (probably) antithesis form the petition as a bicolon.

---

[59] So, too, the NRSV, ESV, TNIV, NET, CEB, ELB; also *Catechism of the Catholic Church*/Anglican *Book of Common Prayer* (1928); Ökumenische Übersetzung der Arbeitsgemeinschaft für liturgische Texte (1970).

[60] So, too, the NRSV, NASB, ESV, TNIV, NET, CEB, LSG, NEG (Nouvelle Edition de Genève), BDJ (Bible de Jérusalem), FRC (Bible en français courant), SG21, MB, EÜ (Einheitsübersetzung), SCL, ELB, ZUR (Zürcher Bibel), NGÜ, HOF; also *Catechism of the Catholic Church*/Anglican *Book of Common Prayer* (1928); Traduction œcuménique (Église catholique, Conseil œcuménique des Églises, 1966); Ökumenische Übersetzung der Arbeitsgemeinschaft für liturgische Texte (1970).

[61] So, too, the ASV, NAB, NRSV, NAU, ESV, TNIV, NET, CEB, LSG, NEG, BDJ, FRC, BDS, SG21; LUO, MB, SCL, ELB, NGÜ; also, *Catechism of the Catholic Church*/Anglican *Book of Common Prayer* (1928); English Language Liturgical Consultation (1988); Traduction œcuménique (Église catholique, Conseil œcuménique des Églises, 1966); Ökumenische Übersetzung der Arbeitsgemeinschaft für liturgische Texte (1970).

By retaining only the latter two devices, we may retain the two-part structure of the couplet: "Our bread for the coming day, give us today." This, in turn, preserves symmetries evident in the original among the three final petitions, namely, their common bicolonic form and (if σήμερον indeed means "tomorrow" or "the coming day" instead of "today" or "daily"[62]) antithetical resolution.

Second, the final three bicolonic petitions, though bound together as a unit poetically by the aforementioned sixfold, polyptotonic repetition of ἡμεῖς and grammatically by connecting καί's, are often divided by the same hard breaks used earlier in the prayer:

> Our Father which art in heaven, Hallowed be thy name.
> Thy kingdom come. Thy will be done in earth, as *it is* in heaven.
> Give us this day our daily bread.
> And forgive us our debts, as we forgive our debtors.
> And lead us not into temptation, but deliver us from evil. (KJV)[63]

As a consequence, the petitions for bread, debt forgiveness, and deliverance appear to continue a series of uninterupted petitions and to bear no unique relationship to one another distinct from the first three petitions (which, as I have said, are also uniquely related to one another). Even if we forgo the attempt to render polyptoton somehow in English, we may nonetheless retain its effect on stichometry by setting the final three petitions apart through punctuation and arrangement as a single period, distinct from the first, and comprised of three closely bound, parallel, antithetical couplets:[64]

> Our bread for the coming day,
>   give us today,
> and forgive us our debts,
>   as we forgive our debtors,
> and see us not into trial,
>   but free us from Evil.

Structure

The stichometry derived from the figures has important implications, too, for debated questions concerning the prayer's structural organization. In the first half

---

[62] See n. 51 above.

[63] So, too, the ASV, NRSV, NAU, ESV, TNIV, NET, CEB, BDJ, FRC, BDS, LUO, MB, EÜ, SCL, ZUR, NGÜ, HOF; also English Language Liturgical Consultation (1988); Ökumenische Übersetzung der Arbeitsgemeinschaft für liturgische Texte (1970).

[64] That is, with regard to punctuation, I use a hard break (a period) at the end of v. 10 to set the unit apart from what precedes it, but softer breaks (commas, or perhaps semicolons) in coordination with the twofold use of the conjunction "and" to represent the unit as a single, tripartite period or sentence. With regard to arrangement, I retain the sixfold structure established across the unit through polyptoton and reinforced in every line by additional devices.

of the prayer, for example, interpreters have long debated whether the phrase "as in heaven so too on earth" modifies the third petition only or all three opening petitions as a set.[65] When the three petitions are preserved as a symmetrical tricolon, however, it is most natural to take the phrase as a modifier of all three[66]—an interpretation strengthened by the fact that the phrase completes an *inclusio* bracketing the tricolon (the effect of polyptotonic anadiplosis).

In the second half of the prayer, interpreters have debated whether the final petition, "and lead us not into trial, but deliver us from evil," should be viewed structurally as a single petition (the sixth) or as two distinct petitions (the sixth and seventh). At stake in this question is the larger and centuries-old debate concerning whether the prayer should be viewed as having six or seven parts in its structure.[67] Clearly, the figure-determined stichometry detailed above in the second half of the prayer—a tricolon petition comprised of three couplets, held together as a single unit by polyptoton, and mirroring the tricolon petition in the first half of the prayer—commends the six-part thesis.[68]

Content

Observations concerning poetic form inevitably affect (constructions of) meaning. For example, if the observation above is correct that "as in heaven so too on earth" modifies the tricolon as a unit, then the entire first half of the prayer, and not just the third petition, must be viewed as a prayer for the earth—that is, for the Father's name, kingdom, and will to be respectively hallowed, come, and done on earth.[69] Further encouraging this reading, the petitions in the second half of the prayer for bread, debt forgiveness, and deliverance also appear to concern the earth—and all the more so in view of formal considerations. That is, when the three petitions are viewed as a single unit bound together by sixfold, four-case polyptoton (like stars bound together in a constellation) rather than three independent and unrelated requests (like stars bearing no relationship to one another)—they can

---

[65] So, respectively, Luz, *Matthew 1–7*, 380; and R. T. France, *The Gospel according to Matthew: An Introduction and Commentary*, TNTC (Grand Rapids: Eerdmans, 1985), 135.

[66] The minority view among modern commentators, but the view expressed by Origen, *Or.* 16.

[67] The six-part thesis prevailed historically in the East; the seven-part, in the West (Calvin and Barth being important exceptions). See Kenneth W. Stevenson, *The Lord's Prayer: A Text in Tradition* (Minneapolis: Fortress, 2004), 15, and passim.

[68] Both theses in my judgment, however, protect different truths. Whereas the prayer is certainly six-part in its poetic form or structure (insofar as it consists of two tricola stanzas), it is seven-part in its poetic content (insofar as the final couplet consists climactically of two petitions, bringing the total number of petitions to the symbolically important sum of seven).

[69] This perspective lends further support to the view increasingly held in scholarship that the first three petitions reflect parallel *eschatological* hopes. See Raymond Brown, "The Pater Noster as an Eschatological Prayer," *TS* 22 (1961): 175–208.

only evoke what for Israel was an abiding hope: jubilee.[70] In this reading, the second stanza of the prayer may thus be seen as the complement, both formally and thematically, to the first. If the prayer opens with a tripartite depiction of the Father's coming reign on earth, then it closes with a tripartite depiction of what that reign effects on earth, "the year of the Lord's favor."

III. Conclusion

It is clear that Lord's Prayer displays a highly poetic form characterized by the recurring use throughout of multiple coordinated figures of speech and thought. This usage, together with the prayer's religious and liturgical themes and historical origins, suggests that the prayer belongs to the tradition of ancient Jewish liturgical poetry.

We may represent the prayer in two stanzas, each a tripartite petition expressed in tricolon form:

> Πάτερ ἡμῶν ὁ ἐν τοῖς οὐρανοῖς
> ἁγιασθήτω τὸ ὄνομά σου
> ἐλθέτω ἡ βασιλεία σου
> γενηθήτω τὸ θέλημά σου
> ὡς ἐν οὐρανῷ καὶ ἐπὶ γῆς
>
> τὸν ἄρτον ἡμῶν
> τὸν ἐπιούσιον
> δὸς ἡμῖν
> σήμερον
> καὶ ἄφες ἡμῖν
> τὰ ὀφειλήματα ἡμῶν
> ὡς καὶ ἡμεῖς ἀφήκαμεν
> τοῖς ὀφειλέταις ἡμῶν
> καὶ μὴ εἰσενέγκῃς ἡμᾶς
> εἰς πειρασμόν
> ἀλλὰ ῥῦσαι ἡμᾶς
> ἀπὸ τοῦ πονηροῦ

Translation ideally should reflect this same form and capture the symmetries of sound and thought native to each figure or, shy of that, should render related symmetries with similar formal effect. The possibilities are boundless. I offer in conclusion two translations, a minimalist version more closely aligned with

---

[70] Given the eschatological orientation of the first half of the prayer, the second half likely has in view the eschatological jubilee proclaimed by Isaiah (61:1–4) and Jesus (Luke 4:17–19).

traditional English liturgy and a maximalist version that reflects more fully the range of devices employed in the prayer:[71]

Minimalist Version

Our Father in the heavens,
   hallowed be your name,
   come be your reign,
   done be your aim,
      as in heaven, so too on earth.
Give us this day,
   our bread for the coming day,
and forgive us our debts,
   as we forgive our debtors,
and see us not into trial,
   but free us from Evil.

Maximalist Version

Our Father in the heavens,
   holy-sung, be the name that is yours,
   come, be the reign that is yours,
   done, be the aim that is yours,
      as in heaven, so too on earth.

Grant that we
   may receive this day,
the bread that we
   have the coming day,
and grant that we
   be forgiven our debts,
as even we
   have forgiven our debtors,
and grant that we
   be seen not into trial,
but rather that we
   be freed from Evil.

---

[71] The latter takes greater poetic license in attempting to render all symmetries of sound original to the prayer, especially the sixfold polyptoton of the second stanza.

"The Thoughts of Many Hearts Shall Be Revealed": Listening in on Lukan Interior Monologues

MICHAL BETH DINKLER
mb.dinkler@yale.edu
Yale Divinity School, New Haven, CT 06511

A constant refrain in contemporary NT studies is that ancient people were "anti-introspective." I contend that this view has caused us to overlook a significant aspect of the early Christian witness, namely, the importance of what one says to one's soul. Several times in Luke's Gospel, characters' thoughts are revealed through the literary device of interior monologue, yet these inner speeches remain underexplored. In this article, I begin by describing the view that ancient societies eschewed interiority; the subsequent section discusses interior speech in Hellenistic and ancient Jewish literature. I then read six Lukan interior monologues from the parables in light of these comparanda. As in ancient Hellenistic narratives, Luke's interior monologues depict the thinker's inner turmoil in a crisis moment; they also provide narrative articulations of Jewish warnings against foolish self-talk. Rhetorically, the interior monologues in the first four parables foster readerly identification with the thinker; readers who accept this invitation will experience the corrections implied by the narrative rhetoric. In the latter two parables, however, narratorial guidance indicates that the audience is not meant to identify with the thinking characters. In these cases, inner speech introduces dramatic irony, privileging the reader over the thinker. Overall, I aim to show that Luke's interior monologues challenge the dominant paradigm of the "anti-introspective" Mediterranean self. Our focus should be on the kinds, degrees, and functions of interiority and introspection in ancient texts, rather than on a generic portrait of ancient societies as "anti-introspective."

In an article titled, "The Soul's Comeback: Immortality and Resurrection in Early Christianity" (2010), François Bovon pushes back against a current trend in

I offer this article in celebration of Professor François Bovon's life and work, as an extension of ideas he and I discussed before he passed away on 1 November 2013. I would also like to thank Jerry Camery-Hoggatt, Benjamin Lappenga, Aaron Engler, John Darr, and the *JBL* reviewer for their helpful feedback on this piece.

studies of early Christianity: the tendency to emphasize the external, corporeal aspect of the ancient self—the "body" (σῶμα)—*at the expense of* the inner, immaterial dimension of the ancient self—the "soul" (ψυχή).[1] Bovon implores scholars to avoid letting the pendulum swing too far to either side of the *psychē/sōma* divide, lest we miss a crucial component of the early Christian witness.[2] The scope of this article is more modest than Bovon's,[3] but it similarly pushes back against a current consensus in which the scholarly pendulum has again swung too far toward an unhelpful extreme: in this case, not between the poles of "soul" and "body" but between the poles of so-called introspective individualistic societies and anti-introspective collectivistic societies.[4]

A constant refrain in contemporary NT studies is that ancient people lacked a concept of the interior life; they were "anti-introspective."[5] I contend that this view has caused us to overlook a significant aspect of the early Christian witness, namely, the importance of *what one says to one's soul or in one's heart*.[6] The Third Gospel in particular demonstrates interest in an individual's inner life, in four respects:

---

[1] François Bovon, "The Soul's Comeback: Immortality and Resurrection in Early Christianity," *HTR* 103 (2010): 387–406, http://dx.doi.org/10.1017/S0017816010000787. Recognizing the valuable contributions of theorists like Maurice Merleau-Ponty, Michel Foucault, Hannah Arendt, Pierre Hadot, and Peter Brown, Bovon argues that the "rediscovery of the body" eclipsed the "soul" in academic discourse (p. 388).

[2] The literature on selfhood and individuality in antiquity is extensive; see Bovon, "Soul's Comeback," 405 n. 72. More recent contributions include Karen L. King, "Willing to Die for God: Individualization and Instrumental Agency in Ancient Christian Martyr Literature," in *The Individual in the Religions of the Ancient Mediterranean*, ed. Jörg Rüpke (Oxford: Oxford University Press, 2013), 342–84 (esp. 342–44 on the nuanced distinctions between concepts of individuality and agency today and in antiquity); Dorothea Frede and Burkhard Reis, eds., *Body and Soul in Ancient Philosophy* (Berlin: de Gruyter, 2010); Pauliina Remes and Juha Sihvola, eds., *Ancient Philosophy of the Self*, New Synthese Historical Library 64 (Dordrecht: Springer, 2008); Joel B. Green, *Body, Soul, and Human Life: The Nature of Humanity in the Bible*, STI (Grand Rapids: Baker Academic, 2008); Pauliina Remes, "Ownness of Conscious Experience in Ancient Philosophy," in *Consciousness: From Perception to Relection in the History of Philosophy*, ed. Sara Heinämaa, Vili Lähteenmäki, Pauliina Remes, Studies in the History of Philosophy of Mind 4 (Dordrecht: Springer, 2007), 67–94.

[3] Bovon surveyed a wide range of early Christian authors from the NT through late antiquity.

[4] Though Bovon never published on exactly this topic, he often told me he believed the dichotomy had been too starkly drawn in current scholarship.

[5] Bruce J. Malina, *Timothy: Paul's Closest Associate*, Paul's Social Network (Collegeville, MN: Liturgical Press, 2008), xv.

[6] On a terminological note, I wish to echo Bovon's caveat from his Ingersoll lecture: "I do not wish to define the soul, as Aristotle or Tertullian did. I do not wish to speculate, as Descartes did. I do not dare to explain the relationship between the body and the soul or embodiment, as Merleau-Ponty does. My only purpose is to avoid attributing a disappointing limitation to the body and to draw attention to the danger of academic skepticism with respect to the afterlife" ("Soul's Comeback," 404). Like Bovon, I do not wish to define anthropological categories like ψυχή, καρδία, πνεῦμα, σάρξ, or σῶμα; Luke's Gospel is unconcerned with such distinctions.

1. In the importance of "paying attention" (βλέπω) to "how" (πῶς) one "hears" (ἀκούω) God's word (8:18).[7] For Luke, this "'hearing' is ... an *inner, consensual* attitude."[8]
2. In Jesus' attention to what is on the "inside" (τὸ ἔσωθεν, 11:40). Contrary to Bruce Malina's assertion that "what counted [in ancient society] was what went on the *outside* of a person,"[9] Jesus teaches that those who focus on the outside alone are "fools" (ἄφρονες, 11:39–40),[10] and that good and evil come from the heart (καρδία, 6:45).
3. In the fulfillment of Simeon's early prophecy that, as a result of Jesus, "the thoughts of many hearts will be revealed" (ἀποκαλυφθῶσιν ἐκ πολλῶν καρδιῶν διαλογισμοί, 2:35). Due to the "primacy effect," Luke's implied reader[11] is prompted to expect the "thoughts" of people's "hearts" to play a role in the ensuing narrative.[12]

Regarding the most relevant terms in this article, καρδία and ψυχή, we can affirm that (1) for Luke, καρδία refers to a comprehensive realm of one's intentions, thoughts, feelings, desires, and/or processing and remembering what one sees and hears (see Luke 2:19, 35, 51; 10:27; 12:34; 16:15; 21:34; F. Baumgärtel and J. Behm, "καρδία," *TDNT* 3:605–13); and (2) ψυχή refers to the essential self, or one's inner life, though Luke's uses of the word differ slightly in various contexts (see Luke 1:46; 2:35; 6:9; 9:24; 10:27; 12:19, 20, 22, 23; 14:26; 17:33; 21:19; Edmund Jacob, "ψυχή," *TDNT* 9:611).

[7] See John Darr, "'Watch How You Listen' (Lk. 8:18): Jesus and the Rhetoric of Perception in Luke-Acts," in *The New Literary Criticism and the New Testament*, ed. Elizabeth Struthers Malbon and Edgar V. McKnight, JSOTSup 109 (Sheffield: Sheffield Academic, 1994), 87–107.

[8] Bovon writes that Luke works "to avoid the juxtaposition between 'outer' and 'inner'" (*Luke 1: A Commentary on the Gospel of Luke [1:1–9:50]*, Hermeneia [Minneapolis: Fortress, 2002], 314).

[9] Malina, *Timothy: Paul's Closest Associate*, xv (emphasis added).

[10] God cares for both "the outside and the inside" (τὸ ἔξωθεν καὶ τὸ ἔσωθεν, 11:40). Jesus also teaches that ethical behavior originates in the καρδία (6:45), and not to be anxious about one's ψυχή (12:22–23). See John Darr, "Narrative Therapy: Treating Audience Anxiety through Psychagogy in Luke," *PRSt* 39 (2012): 335–48.

[11] The "implied readers" are the intended recipients of the narrative, who cooperate with and share the "implied author's" assumptions (i.e., Luke's earliest readers). See Wayne C. Booth, *The Rhetoric of Fiction*, 2nd ed. (Chicago: University of Chicago Press, 1983); Wolfgang Iser, *The Implied Reader: Patterns of Communication in Prose Fiction from Bunyan to Beckett* (Baltimore: Johns Hopkins University Press, 1974); Umberto Eco, *The Role of the Reader: Explorations in the Semiotics of Texts*, Advances in Semiotics (Bloomington: Indiana University Press, 1979). Of course, Luke's "implied readers" likely were not readers at all, but *hearers*. Still, readers and hearers share common meaning-making strategies: they assume that events in a story are causally connected, and they draw upon extratextual knowledge and conventions to make sense of what they read/hear. My observations regarding Lukan "implied readers" apply to "hearers" as well.

[12] The "primacy effect" describes how early details shape a reader's experience of subsequent events. See Mark Coleridge, *The Birth of the Lukan Narrative: Narrative as Christology in Luke 1–2*, JSNTSup 88 (Sheffield: Sheffield Academic, 1993), 28; Robert Tannehill, "Beginning to Study

4. In the emphasis on aligning what one says internally with the divine perspective (as expressed by the Lukan narrator).[13]

Throughout Luke's Gospel, characters think, consider, ponder, wonder (συμβάλλω, δοκέω, κατανοέω, διαλογίζομαι), or marvel (θαυμάζω, ἐκπλήσσω, γίνομαι θάμβος).[14] Several times the narrator explicitly reveals characters' thoughts through the literary device of interior monologue: "the direct, immediate presentation of the unspoken thoughts of a character without any intervening narrator."[15] Yet the Lukan interior monologues remain underexplored.[16]

The Lukan text shows real concern with what we today call "self-talk," what Plato described as "a talk which the soul has with itself about the objects under its consideration" (*Theaet.* 189e).[17] In the pages that follow, I suggest that attention to Luke's depictions of interiority can lead to more nuanced understandings of the Lukan narrative landscape.[18] Furthermore, placing Luke's[19] interior monologues

---

'How Gospels Begin,'" *Semeia* 52 (1991): 188; Shlomith Rimmon-Kenan, *Narrative Fiction: Contemporary Poetics* (London: Methuen, 1983), 121.

[13] For more developed treatments of the ways in which Luke attends to interiority, see my own discussions in Michal Beth Dinkler, *Silent Statements: Narrative Representations of Speech and Silence in the Gospel of Luke*, BZNW 191 (Berlin: de Gruyter, 2013).

[14] See, e.g., Luke 1:21, 29, 63; 2:19, 33; 3:15; 5:21–22; 6:8; 9:47; 11:17; 12:17; 20:14, 23; 24:12, 38. The narrator typically mentions *that* a character is thinking (without citing the thoughts), as when Mary ponders "in her heart" (ἐν τῇ καρδίᾳ αὐτῆς, 2:19).

[15] Robert Scholes and Robert Kellogg, *The Nature of Narrative* (New York: Oxford University Press, 1966), 177. Contemporary literary theory generally treats *internal/interior/inner monologue* and *soliloquy* as synonyms. Cf. Gérard Genette's more restrictive definition in *Narrative Discourse: An Essay in Method*, trans. Jane Lewin (Ithaca, NY: Cornell University Press, 1983), 173.

[16] To my knowledge, prior to my own work, only Bernhard Heininger and Philip Sellew have given sustained attention to this feature of Lukan storytelling. See Heininger, *Metaphorik, Erzählstruktur und szenisch-dramatische Gestaltung in den Sondergutgleichnissen bei Lukas*, NTAbh 24 (Münster: Aschendorff, 1991); Sellew, "Interior Monologue as a Narrative Device in the Parables of Luke," *JBL* 111 (1992): 239–53. I presuppose Heininger's and Sellew's insights in order to reopen the conversations regarding Lukan interior monologue that began—but ended prematurely—over a decade ago.

[17] Plato, *Theaetetus*, ed. Bernard Williams, trans. M. J. Levett (Indianapolis: Hackett, 1992), 65.

[18] For example, Lukan interior monologues suggest that one's internal response to God is critically important; this challenges traditional theological assessments that, as Ernst Haenchen famously put it, Luke's human responses are "very nearly the twitching of human puppets" (*The Acts of the Apostles*, trans. Bernard Noble et al. [Philadelphia: Westminster, 1971], 362). John T. Squires outlines previous scholarship in *The Plan of God in Luke-Acts*, SNTSMS 76 (Cambridge: Cambridge University Press, 1993), 3–14, 27–32. See also Siegfried Schulz, "Gottes Vorsehung bei Lukas," ZNW 54 (1963): 104–16, http://dx.doi.org/10.1515/zntw.1963.54.1-2.104; François Bovon, *Luke the Theologian: Fifty-Five Years of Research (1950–2005)* (Waco, TX: Baylor University Press, 2006), 21.

[19] "Luke" refers to the implied author/final redactor of the Third Gospel. I also assume that the Lukan narrator and implied author are indistinguishable and thus use "narrator" and "Luke"

alongside the writings of other ancient thinkers—both theorists and actual storytellers—demonstrates that Luke was not the only ancient writer to care deeply (if differently than we do) about introspection and interiority.[20]

Let me be clear: our options are not either/or—soul or body, individualistic or communalistic, introspective or anti-introspective. Like human interactions more generally, ancient narrative depictions of the self are complex and often ambiguous. Characterizing all ancient Mediterranean people as "anti-introspective" does not do justice to the "diversity of opinion" on such matters found in the ancient texts themselves.[21]

I begin by describing the increasingly common view that ancient societies eschewed interiority, and then I discuss uses of inner speech in Hellenistic and ancient Jewish literature. The final section reads the Lukan interior monologues in light of these comparanda and suggests that Luke's depictions of self-talk have important rhetorical effects. In the end, I aim to show that an individual's interior life was a significant topic of discussion in the ancient world and thus merits more careful, contextualized attention in NT studies.

I. Interpreting Interiority in Antiquity: the "Anti-Introspective" Ancient Self

The most frequently cited view of ancient selfhood in NT studies is that ancient people were *allocentric* (defined by their relations to others), while today's Western person is *idiocentric* (defined as an autonomous, individual self).[22]

---

interchangeably. Cf. James Dawsey, *The Lukan Voice: Confusion and Irony in the Gospel of Luke* (Macon, GA: Mercer University Press, 1988).

[20] I use these terms interchangeably, recognizing that they are not exactly synonymous in studies of later Christian spirituality and theology. On the distinction between them in medieval theology, see Kenneth L. Schmitz, "The Geography of the Human Person," *Communio* 13 (1986): 27–48.

[21] Bovon, "Soul's Comeback," 394. Karen King's distinction between ancient and modern conceptions of identity is appropriately nuanced: ancient identity is "not about individual characteristics or development, *seen as those of an I-centered, interiorized consciousness acting from solely self-selected motives and world view*, but of a person fundamentally embedded in and embodying the (normative) life and beliefs of a social group" (King, "Willing to Die for God," 9; emphasis added).

[22] For a useful overview of distinctions between ancient and modern conceptions of individuality/personhood, see Christopher Gill, *Personality in Greek Epic, Tragedy, and Philosophy: The Self in Dialogue* (Oxford: Clarendon, 1996), 11–12. More recent discussions include, e.g., the contributions in *Ancient Models of Mind: Studies in Human and Divine Rationality*, ed. David Sedley and Andrea Nightingale (Cambridge: Cambridge University Press, 2010); Christopher Gill, *The Structured Self in Hellenistic and Roman Thought* (Oxford: Oxford University Press, 2006).

Drawing on anthropology and the social sciences, scholars also depict "ancient culture" as *agonistic*, which is then understood in an allocentric form: the conflicts are all external—between people or people groups. Many scholars take as "givens" that ancient people were defined by their roles within "in-groups," or clans,[23] and that ancient "personhood" was determined by *social* variables like socioeconomic status or legal rights, forms of honor gained or lost in agonistic combat (such as challenge–riposte scenarios).[24] A common corollary to such claims is that "persons in antiquity were *anti-introspective* and not psychologically minded *at all*."[25]

For years, Bruce Malina has been the most vocal proponent of the view that collectivistic societies are uninterested in interiority. In his highly influential book *The New Testament World: Insights from Cultural Anthropology*, he asserts that ancient people "*avoid introspection* as uninteresting."[26] This continues as a repeated refrain: in Malina's biography of Timothy, he insists that ancient people "neither knew nor cared about psychological development; they were *not introspective*";[27] and later, "People in collectivistic societies are *not introspective*."[28] Ancient people "rarely if ever [had] an experience of an autonomous self,"[29] since as "dyadic personalities," they were defined by group loyalty, honor and shame, and reciprocal patron–client obligation.[30]

The popularity of this perspective has grown as the Context Group and others have picked up Malina's models.[31] What matters here is that depictions of the

---

[23] E.g., Marcel Mauss's *personnage* ("role-player") contrasted with the *personne morale* ("moral subject"). See Mauss, "A Category of the Human Mind: The Notion of Person; the Notion of Self," in *The Category of the Person: Anthropology, Philosophy, History*, ed. Michael Carrithers, Steven Collins, and Steven Lukes (Cambridge: Cambridge University Press, 1985), 1–25.

[24] See, e.g., Bruce J. Malina and Jerome H. Neyrey, "Honor and Shame in Luke-Acts: Pivotal Values of the Mediterranean World," in *The Social World of Luke-Acts: Models of Interpretation*, ed. Jerome H. Neyrey (Peabody, MA: Hendrickson, 1991), 25–65.

[25] Malina, *Timothy: Paul's Closest Associate*, xv (emphasis added).

[26] Bruce J. Malina, *The New Testament World: Insights from Cultural Anthropology*, 3rd ed. (Louisville: Westminster John Knox, 2001), 68 (emphasis added).

[27] Malina, *Timothy: Paul's Closest Associate*, 5 (emphasis added).

[28] Ibid., 20 (emphasis added). Louise Joy Lawrence suggests that "Malina does not deny the *existence* of introspection but rather assumes that it is culturally *unimportant*" (*An Ethnography of the Gospel of Matthew: A Critical Assessment of the Use of the Honour and Shame Model in New Testament Studies*, WUNT 2/165 [Tübingen: Mohr Siebeck, 2003], 117). This précis softens Malina's own language. Even so, my objection stands: Luke's Gospel and other ancient writings attest to the *significance* of introspection.

[29] Bruce J. Malina, *Portraits of Paul: An Archaeology of Ancient Personality* (Louisville: Westminster John Knox, 1996), 169, 229.

[30] Bruce J. Malina and Jerome H. Neyrey, "First Century Personality: Dyadic, Not Individualistic," in Neyrey, *Social World of Luke-Acts*, 67–96.

[31] For a description, see www.contextgroup.org. See also Dietmar Neufeld and Richard E. DeMaris, eds., *Understanding the Social World of the New Testament* (New York: Routledge, 2010); John Pilch, ed., *Social Scientific Models for Interpreting the Bible: Essays by the Context Group in*

ancient Mediterranean self as "anti-introspective" have led most NT scholars to overlook moments of interiority in the NT texts themselves. In the *Social-Scientific Commentary on the Synoptic Gospels*, for example, none of the Lukan interior monologues is recognized as such.[32]

Let me be clear here also: there is much to be gained from the social sciences. Scholars like Malina and Neyrey helpfully challenge the common tendency to ascribe modern conceptions of selfhood and abstract inner thought to ancient people.[33] I do not wish to disparage these valuable contributions. Indeed, I fully agree that, in Bovon's words, "As interpreters, we should not project our culturally specific conception of reality into the first century."[34] Scholarly opinion, however, has now swung too far in the opposite direction: many have simply replaced one overly simplistic view (ancient people are introspective in the same way we are) with another (ancient people cared nothing for the interior life). The result is a general disregard for interiority in NT texts and a widespread perception that ancient people lacked self-awareness. The time has come to situate social-scientific insights within a more nuanced framework, one that recognizes characters as narrative constructions, and their thoughts as rhetorically significant.

Social-scientific approaches aim to unearth the biblical writers' historical assumptions about the self. A narratological approach shifts the focus by foregrounding the fact that character thoughts occur *within a narrative*.[35] An individual in a text is a character, constructed to perform certain rhetorical functions;[36]

Honor of Bruce J. Malina, BibInt 53 (Leiden: Brill, 2001); Neyrey, *Social World of Luke-Acts*. Richard Bauckham critiques "Malina's school" in *Jesus and the Eyewitnesses: The Gospels as Eyewitness Testimony* (Grand Rapids: Eerdmans, 2006), 173.

[32] Bruce J. Malina and Richard L. Rohrbaugh, *Social-Science Commentary on the Synoptic Gospels*, 2nd ed. (Minneapolis: Fortress, 2003).

[33] Similarly, in Pauline studies, scholars now largely reject the twentieth-century profile of Paul as a "hero of the introspective conscience." See Krister Stendahl, "The Apostle Paul and the Introspective Conscience of the West," *HTR* 56 (1963): 199–215, http://dx.doi.org/10.1017/S0017816000024779; Markus Barth, "The Social Character of Justification," *JES* 5 (1968): 241–61; Nils A. Dahl, "The Doctrine of Justification: Its Social Function and Implications," in *Studies in Paul: Theology for the Early Christian Mission* (Minneapolis: Augsburg, 1977), 95–120; Luther H. Martin, "The Anti-Individualistic Ideology of Hellenistic Culture," *Numen* 41 (1994): 117–40; cf. Troels Engberg-Pedersen, "Philosophy of the Self in the Apostle Paul," in Remes and Sihvola, *Ancient Philosophy of the Self*, esp. 178; Gary W. Burnett, *Paul and the Salvation of the Individual*, BibInt 57 (Leiden: Brill, 2001); Valérie Nicolet-Anderson, *Constructing the Self: Thinking with Paul and Michel Foucault*, WUNT 2/324 (Tübingen: Mohr Siebeck, 2012).

[34] Bovon, *Luke 1*, 388.

[35] It is important to emphasize that these are not competing or mutually exclusive concerns; ideally, they will inform one another in analyses of particular texts.

[36] Characters are semiotic representations, "fabricated creatures … paper people, without flesh and blood" (Mieke Bal, *Narratology: Introduction to the Theory of Narrative*, 2nd ed. [Toronto: University of Toronto Press, 1997], 115). Still, as John Darr writes, "Characters are not *just* words … or textual functions, but rather, affective and realistic personal images generated by text and

as such, his internal monologue is a literary device used to do particular kinds of rhetorical work in dialogical relationship with the implied reader.

II. Internal Monologues in Ancient Literature

It can be easy to overlook "the important but sparing"[37] uses of interior monologue in ancient narratives because stream-of-consciousness narration is so common in modern literature.[38] Nevertheless, interior monologue as quoted inner thought is quite ancient.[39] We find self-address in such esteemed ancient writers as Homer, Plato, Vergil, Ovid, Apollonius, Longus, and Xenophon of Ephesus.[40] In contrast to many NT scholars, classicists generally embrace a more complex view of ancient selfhood:[41] acknowledging that ancient "self-knowledge" (σωφροσύνη) differs from modern notions, classicists identify different modes and degrees of interest in interiority in ancient narratives.[42]

---

reader" (*On Character Building: The Reader and the Rhetoric of Characterization in Luke-Acts*, Literary Currents in Biblical Interpretation [Louisville: Westminster John Knox, 1992], 147; emphasis added). Exploring the rhetorical functions of "paper people's" interior monologues is not the same as anachronistically projecting post-Freudian concepts of individuality upon literary constructions. Rather, it is a recognition that, in practice, readers intuitively relate to characters as though they were human. Unless directed otherwise, readers typically trust that characters' self-talk reliably reflects their inner nature. See Robert Alter, *The Art of Biblical Narrative* (New York: Basic Books, 1981), 117.

[37] Mary Ann Tolbert, *Sowing the Gospel: Mark's World in Literary-Historical Perspective* (Minneapolis: Fortress, 1989), 214.

[38] "Stream-of-consciousness" narration, popularized by James Joyce, is marked by fragmentation and discontinuity. The classic discussion of interiority in modern literature is Dorrit Cohn, *Transparent Minds: Narrative Modes for Presenting Consciousness in Fiction* (Princeton: Princeton University Press, 1978).

[39] I situate Lukan interior monologues within a wider literary context *not* to argue along source-critical lines but to demonstrate that Luke is not alone in using this method of dramatizing a character's inner life, and to highlight rhetorical functions of this narrative device in ancient literature.

[40] See, e.g., Vergil, *Aen.* 4.534–552; Ovid, *Metam.* 10.319–333; Homer, *Il.* 18.5–15; Xenophon of Ephesus, *An Ephesian Tale* 1.4.1–7; Longus, *Daph.* 1.14, 18. Scholes and Kellogg (*Nature of Narrative*, 178–88 and appendix, 283–99) assert that Apollonius Rhodius "invented" interior monologue (see Apollonius, *Argon.* 3.463–471, 772–801), though they also posit that Homer modeled the device for other ancient writers.

[41] Here I am focusing on narratives specifically, though discussions of selfhood in ancient philosophical and medical literature would be relevant as well.

[42] Examples include Silvia Montiglio, "'My Soul, Consider What You Should Do': Psychological Conflicts and Moral Goodness in the Greek Novels," *Ancient Narrative* 8 (2010): 25–58; Massimo Fusillo, "Apollonius as 'Inventor' of the Interior Monologue," in *A Companion to Apollonius Rhodius*, ed. Theodore D. Papanghelis and Antonios Rengakos, Mnemosyne 217 (Leiden: Brill, 2001), 127–46; Ulrike Auhagen, *Der Monolog bei Ovid*, ScriptOralia 119 (Tübingen:

Contrary to the generalization noted above that, in ancient cultures, conflicts were external (between people or people groups), interior monologues in ancient Greek literature typically were used in high-stakes moments of internal crisis, when the hero must negotiate an inner conflict.[43] Through inner speech, the hero's inner turmoil mirrors the struggles engendered by external circumstances. Several famous monologues from the *Odyssey* typify this tendency. Twice, Odysseus wrestles internally (ὁρμαίνω) over how he should respond to Poseidon's fury; both instances occur in intensely dramatic moments, with Odysseus nearly drowning in Poseidon's thunderous waves (*Od.* 5.365-367, 424-425). Later, as he "debates a great deal in mind and heart" (πολλὰ δὲ μερμήριζε κατὰ φρένα καὶ κατὰ θυμόν) over how to handle Penelope's suitors, Odysseus chides himself, addressing his heart in the vocative: "Endure, my heart" (τέτλαθι δή, καρδίη) (*Od.* 20.18-21).

The device is not limited to tragedies; Bernhard Heininger identifies the following tripartite formula employed in ancient Greek comedies: (1) the speech introduction (*Redeeinleitung*); (2) the identification of the problem (*Bestandsaufnahme*); (3) the chosen solution (*Problemlösung*).[44] This progression sets the character's dilemma right at the heart of interior monologue, highlighting the thinker's plight and amplifying the scene's emotional intensity.

Like his Hellenistic predecessors, Luke tends to incorporate interior monologue into crisis situations in which the thinking character must make an important decision. Each parable employs Heininger's formula: a dilemma is introduced; the thinker takes stock of the problem; and he chooses a solution (Luke 12:17, 45; 15:17-19; 16:4-7; 18:4-5; 20:13). In three of the parables, the thinking character explicitly asks the telltale question for such moments of crisis: "What should I do?" (τί ποιήσω; 12:17; 16:3; 20:13)[45] Structurally, Luke's interior monologues in these scenes resemble those we find in ancient Greek literature: faced with a dilemma, a character's self-talk increases the dramatic tension in pivotal moments of decision making.[46]

In their treatments of Lukan interior monologue, both Heininger and Philip

---

Narr, 1999); Stephen Halliwell, "Traditional Greek Conceptions of Character," in *Characterization and Individuality in Greek Literature*, ed. Christopher Pelling (Oxford: Clarendon, 1990), 53-55; George Walsh, "Surprised by Self: Audible Thought in Hellenistic Poetry," *CP* 85 (1990): 1-21, http://dx.doi.org/10.1086/367171; Bernard C. Fenik, "Stylization and Variety: Four Monologues in the Iliad," in *Homer: Tradition and Invention*, ed. Bernard C. Fenik, Cincinnati Classical Studies NS 2 (Leiden: Brill, 1978), 68-90; Gerhard Petersmann, "Die Entscheidungsmonologe in den Homerischen Epen," *Grazer Beiträge* 2 (1974): 147-69.

[43] The crisis often is prompted by, or concerns, interpersonal predicaments, but the point remains that the struggle occurs internally, within the individual thinker.

[44] Heininger, *Metaphorik, Erzählstruktur*, 34.

[45] The question itself is common (see also 3:10, 14; 10:25; 18:18), but these are the only places in the NT where a character asks the question *of himself*. In Acts 22:10, this question is directed toward God; cf. Exod 17:4, 1 Sam 10:2.

[46] Bovon recognized this, noting, "Dieser literarische Kniff ermöglicht dem Verfasser, die

Sellew refer almost exclusively to interior speech in Hellenistic narratives,⁴⁷ and their results proffer helpful insights. There is an important difference, however, between Luke's thinkers and those in most ancient Greek narratives: in stories like the Homeric epics, the thinkers are archetypal Hellenistic heroes, marked by larger-than-life ἀριστεία ("bravery") and superior μῆτις ("intelligence").⁴⁸ Luke's thinkers, on the other hand, tend to be *un*-heroic, requiring correction.⁴⁹ Too readily equating Luke's thinkers with Hellenistic heroes obscures a key rhetorical function of the Lukan internal monologues: quoted self-talk effectively characterizes a person as wise or foolish.⁵⁰

Indeed, this is a prominent theme in ancient Jewish literature: what one says in/to one's soul conditions and reflects one's relationship with God, especially indicating wisdom or foolishness. Inner speech in the Hebrew Bible commonly appears in wisdom literature, where self-talk often characterizes the wicked.⁵¹ The fool says "in his heart" (בלבו) that there is no God (Ps 14:1).⁵² The one who turns away from

---

innere Entwicklung seiner Figuren darzustellen und der Erzählung eine neue Richtung zu geben" (*Das Evangelium nach Lukas [Lk 15,1–19,27]*, EKKNT 3.3 [Düsseldorf: Benziger, 2001], 48).

⁴⁷ Sellew does note Saul's self-address in 1 Sam 18 ("Interior Monologue," 241).

⁴⁸ See, e.g., Jeffrey Barnouw, *Odysseus, Hero of Practical Intelligence: Deliberation and Signs in Homer's Odyssey* (Lanham, MD: University Press of America, 2004). In this, the apocryphal Acts of the Apostles are quite similar. See Bovon's discussion of an "apostolic *normative psychology*" (emphasis original), marked by the apostle's individual fortitude, lack of cowardice, modesty, and self-sacrifice ("Jesus' Missionary Speech," in Bovon, *Studies in Early Christianity*, WUNT 161 [Tübingen: Mohr Siebeck, 2003], 202–3). Cf. Montiglio's insightful analysis of interior monologue in Xenophon's *Ephesian Tale*, where the only two characters to experience inner conflict are "morally weak" ("'My Soul, Consider What You Should Do,'" 35).

⁴⁹ To be fair, Sellew underscores the point that Luke's thinkers tend to be negative characters, calling them "immoral [characters] looking out for their own interests above all" ("Interior Monologue," 242). Sellew, however, does not consider the Jewish thematic concerns I discuss below.

⁵⁰ Characterization, the depiction of agents in a literary work, is a highly contested theoretical issue. Key works include Pierre Létourneau and Michel Talbot, eds., *Et vous, qui dites-vous que je suis? La gestion des personnages dans les récits bibliques*, Sciences bibliques 16 (Paris: Médiaspaul, 2006); David Rhoads and Kari Syreeni, eds., *Characterization in the Gospels: Reconceiving Narrative Criticism*, JSNTSup 184 (Sheffield: Sheffield Academic, 1999); David R. Beck, *The Discipleship Paradigm: Readers and Anonymous Characters in the Fourth Gospel*, BibInt 27 (Leiden: Brill, 1997); Darr, *On Character Building*; Elizabeth Struthers Malbon and Adele Berlin, eds., *Characterization in Biblical Literature*, Semeia 63 (Atlanta: Scholars Press, 1993); Mary Ann Tolbert, "How the Gospel of Mark Builds Character," *Int* 47 (1993): 347–57; Fred Burnett, "Characterization and Reader Construction of Characters in the Gospels," *Semeia* 63 (1993): 3–23.

⁵¹ Unlike in Greek, Hebrew markers of direct discourse can be fairly fluid (Cynthia L. Miller, *The Representation of Speech in Biblical Hebrew Narrative: A Linguistic Analysis*, HSM 55 [Atlanta: Scholars Press, 1996]). Often, context is the sole indicating factor (e.g., Gen 3:22, 18:17, Judg 15:2). In the LXX, the Greek formulation used most often is ἐν καρδίᾳ αὐτοῦ (as in Luke 5:22, 12:45).

⁵² LXX Ps 13:1: ἐν καρδίᾳ αὐτοῦ. See also Ps 10:6, 11 (LXX 9:27, 32).

God blesses himself "in his heart" (בלבבו, Deut 29:18).⁵³ Hebrew Bible passages like these highlight the importance of what one says in/to one's own heart, especially emphasizing the folly of wicked self-address.⁵⁴

The Hebrew Bible also contains grammatically marked interior monologues in *narrative* settings;⁵⁵ in fact, as Maren Niehoff declares, "The biblical narrator presents a surprisingly large number of figures in self-reflection."⁵⁶ To note a few here, in Gen 27:41, Esau plans "in his heart" (בלבו) to kill his brother.⁵⁷ Interior monologue is indicated twice in the story of Abraham and Sarah (Gen 17–18), though these instances have been variously interpreted.⁵⁸ First, Abraham questions "in his heart" (בלבו, Gen 17:17)⁵⁹ whether he and Sarah can truly have a baby, despite their old age. Later, when Sarah overhears this news, she laughs "to/in herself" (בקרבה, Gen 18:12).⁶⁰ In Esth 6:6, Haman speaks self-servingly "in his heart" (בלבו).⁶¹

Noncanonical Jewish literature also highlights the dangers of negative self-talk. In Pseudo-Philo's Liber antiquitatum biblicarum, Saul is disappointed at no longer being recognizable, a detail that is missing from the biblical version: "And Saul said within himself (*intra se*), 'When I was king in Israel … they knew that I was Saul'" (64:4). In Pseudo-Philo, Saul is a villain;⁶² interior monologue exposes his moral failures, underscoring his self-centeredness and his ultimate fall from grace.

Philo of Alexandria uses inner speech in diverse ways.⁶³ Within narratives, he

---

⁵³ LXX Deut 29:18: ἐν τῇ καρδίᾳ αὐτοῦ. On the sources of sin in Jewish thought, see Miryam T. Brand, *Evil Within and Without: The Source of Sin and Its Nature as Portrayed in Second Temple Literature*, JAJSup 9 (Göttingen· Vandenhoeck & Ruprecht, 2013).

⁵⁴ E.g., Eccl 1:16; 2:1, 3, 15; 3:17, 18; Zeph 2:15; 1 Sam 18:17, 21, 27:1; 1 Kgs 12;26. Trevor Donald, "The Semantic Field of 'Folly' in Proverbs, Job, Psalms, and Ecclesiastes," *VT* 13 (1963): 285–92.

⁵⁵ Not all self-talk in the Hebrew Bible is negative; in Gen 8:21, for example, God speaks "in his heart" (אל־לבו [LXX: διανοηθείς]).

⁵⁶ Maren Niehoff, "Do Biblical Characters Talk to Themselves? Narrative Modes of Representing Inner Speech in Early Biblical Fiction," *JBL* 111 (1992): 577–95, here 579.

⁵⁷ Though logically, someone must have overheard, as his mother learns of his plan (Gen 27:42).

⁵⁸ Abraham's and Sarah's reactions have been read negatively as their lack of faith, or positively, as their amazement at a miracle.

⁵⁹ LXX Gen 17:17: ἐν τῇ διανοίᾳ αὐτοῦ.

⁶⁰ LXX Gen 18:12: ἐν ἑαυτῇ. Note that the divine visitor perceives Sarah's private response (18:13). Cf. 2 Sam 14:1, where Joab perceives the king's internal (though unquoted) meditations about Absalom.

⁶¹ LXX Esth 6:6: ἐν ἑαυτῷ.

⁶² Abram Spiro, "Pseudo-Philo's Saul and the Rabbis' Messiah ben Ephraim," *PAAJR* 22 (1953): 119–37.

⁶³ Allegorically, Philo draws upon the Stoic distinction (e.g., Sextus Empiricus, *Math*. 8.275–276) between internal speech (*logos endiathetos*) and speech uttered aloud (*logos prophorikos*) to

uses internal monologue to depict both positive and negative ways of thinking. A godly ruler is one who thinks to himself about the laws he writes, "in order that … I might at once proceed to impress them on my heart, and that I might stamp upon my intellect their divine and indelible characters" (*Spec.* 4.163).[64] Flaccus's despairing soliloquys in Philo's *In Flaccum* (e.g., 172) resemble those found in Hellenistic narratives, as they depict him in exile, lamenting his circumstances.[65]

These instances of interior monologue demonstrate how, for many ancient Jews, an individual's thoughts were a reliable indicator of her or his posture toward God.[66] Usually, in the contexts of these writings, the thinker is *not* wise but foolish.[67] Though Lukan interior monologues resemble Hellenistic inner speech structurally by heightening the dramatic tension of a character's inner conflict, they are more similar to Jewish literature insofar as the thinking characters exhibit foolish self-talk. The evidence for these claims lies in the text itself, to which I turn next.

III. Lukan Interior Monologues

Of the seven times inner speech is explicitly quoted in Luke's Gospel, six are found in Jesus's parables.[68] I have discussed the one clear instance that occurs

---

describe Moses and Aaron (Philo, *Mos.* 2.12.65); Max Mühl, "Der *logos endiathetos* und *prophorikos* von der älteren Stoa bis zur Synode von Sirmium 351," *Archiv für Begriffsgeschichte* 7 (1962): 7–56.

[64] Ellen Muehlberger takes *Legat.* 67–70 as an ironic internal monologue ("The Representation of Theatricality in Philo's *Embassy to Gaius*," *JSJ* 39 (2008): 64, http://dx.doi.org/10.1163/157006308X246017.

[65] The narrative implies that Flaccus expresses inner thoughts.

[66] In Pauline scholarship, G. Burnett (*Paul and the Salvation of the Individual*, 87) and Nicolet-Anderson (*Constructing the Self*, 9) make similar observations.

[67] This is an interesting twist on the common ancient connection between the heart and verbalized speech (Luke 6:45). See Prov 6:12; 10:18–19; 14:3; 15:2; 16:27; 17:7; 18:6–7; 19:1; Sir 20:7, 19–20; 37:17–18; Euripides, *Iph. aul.*, 475; Longinus, [*Subl.*] 9.2. This can be distinguished from another prevailing ancient view, namely, that behavior (including uses of speech) can change one's inner character. See Plato, *Resp.* 3.395D.

[68] The foolish farmer (12:16–20); the unfaithful servant (12:42–46); the prodigal son (15:11–32); the crafty steward (16:1–8); the unjust judge (18:2–5); and the owner of the vineyard (20:9–16). In the following discussion, I draw upon (among others) Joachim Jeremias, *The Parables of Jesus*, trans. S. H. Hooke, 2nd rev. ed. (New York: Scribner's Sons, 1972); Paul Ricoeur, "Listening to the Parables of Jesus," *Criterion* 13 (1974): 18–22; Kenneth E. Bailey, *Poet and Peasant: A Literary Cultural Approach to the Parables in Luke* (Grand Rapids: Eerdmans, 1976); Norman Perrin, *Jesus and the Language of the Kingdom: Symbol and Metaphor in New Testament Interpretation* (Philadelphia: Fortress, 1976); John R. Donahue, *The Gospel in Parable: Metaphor, Narrative, and Theology in the Synoptic Gospels* (Philadelphia: Fortress, 1988); Bernard Brandon Scott, *Hear Then the Parable: A Commentary on the Parables of Jesus* (Minneapolis: Fortress, 1989); François Bovon, "Parabel des Evangeliums—Parabel des Gottesreiches," in *Die Sprache der Bilder: Gleichnis und Metapher in Literatur und Theologie*, ed. Hans Weder, Zeitzeichen 4 (Gütersloh: Mohn, 1989), 11–21; Jean Delorme, ed., *Les paraboles évangéliques: Perspectives nouvelles. XIIe congrés de*

outside a parable elsewhere (Luke 7:36–50),[69] so here I will focus on the six Lukan parables that include this literary technique. The following chart summarizes the basic relevant details.

INSTANCES OF INTERNAL MONOLOGUE IN THE LUKAN PARABLES

Passage	Parable	Thinking Character	Other Characters	Mention of internal monologue
12:16–20	foolish farmer	farmer	God	17 καὶ διελογίζετο ἐν ἑαυτῷ λέγων, Τί ποιήσω; ... 19 καὶ ἐρῶ τῇ ψυχῇ μου ...
12:42–46	unfaithful servant	servant	master; other servants	45 ... εἴπῃ ἐν τῇ καρδίᾳ αὐτοῦ ...
15:11–32	prodigal son	prodigal son	father; servants; elder son	17 εἰς ἑαυτὸν δὲ ἐλθὼν ἔφη ...
16:1–8	crafty steward	steward	master; master's debtors	3 εἶπεν δὲ ἐν ἑαυτῷ ὁ οἰκονόμος, Τί ποιήσω;
18:2–5	unjust judge	judge	widow	4 εἶπεν ἐν ἑαυτῷ ...
20:9–16	owner of the vineyard	vineyard owner	tenants	13 εἶπεν δὲ ὁ κύριος τοῦ ἀμπελῶνος, Τί ποιήσω;

The Foolish Farmer (Luke 12:16–20)

In Luke 12:16–20, a successful farmer "thinks to himself" (διελογίζετο ἐν ἑαυτῷ, v. 17) about what to do with his abundant harvest. Accurately identifying

---

l'ACFEB, Lyon (1987), LD 135 (Paris: Cerf, 1989); Charles W. Hedrick, *Parables as Poetic Fictions: The Creative Voice of Jesus* (Peabody, MA: Hendrickson, 1994); William Herzog, *Parables as Subversive Speech: Jesus as Pedagogue of the Oppressed* (Louisville: Westminster John Knox, 1994); David B. Gowler, *What Are They Saying about the Parables?* (New York: Paulist, 2000); Bovon, *Das Evangelium nach Lukas (Lk 15,1–19,27)*; Klyne Snodgrass, *Stories with Intent: A Comprehensive Guide to the Parables of Jesus* (Grand Rapids: Eerdmans, 2008).

[69] In 7:39, Luke depicts inner speech where his canonical counterparts do not (cf. Mark 14:3–9, Matt 26:6–13, and John 12:1–11) (Dinkler, *Silent Statements*, 121–30). A case could be made that Jesus's prayer in Luke 22:42 is interior monologue, though that would take more space than I have here. On controversies over this prayer, see Kevin Madigan, "Ancient and High-Medieval Interpretations of Jesus in Gethsemane: Some Reflections on Tradition and Continuity in Christian Thought," *HTR* 88 (1995): 157–73, http://dx.doi.org/10.1017/S001781600003042X.

the problem—he has nowhere to store his crops—he asks himself, "What should I do?" (Τί ποιήσω; v. 17). The farmer decides to build bigger barns, so that he might, as he puts it, "say to my soul, 'Soul [ἐρῶ τῇ ψυχῇ μου, Ψυχή], you have plenty of goods stored up for many years. Relax, eat, drink, be merry'" (v. 19).⁷⁰ God (ὁ θεός)⁷¹ then says he is a "fool" (ἄφρων, v. 19),⁷² who will die that very night.

God's declaration clearly casts the farmer in a negative light. Jesus corroborates this with the note that one who thinks like the farmer is "not rich toward God" (μὴ εἰς θεὸν πλουτῶν, v. 21). Further, the farmer's solution to his conundrum exemplifies the covetousness about which Jesus has just warned his listeners, "Watch out and guard yourself from all types of greed, because one's life does not consist in the abundance of his possessions" (v. 15). Debates continue over what precisely makes the man a "fool,"⁷³ but he is clearly *not* a heroic character. The narrative rhetoric suggests that he has read his situation too myopically; the interior monologue demonstrates his foolish thinking.

The Unfaithful Servant (12:42–46)

Later in ch. 12, we encounter a servant whose master is delayed in returning home; the servant thinks to himself about how to respond to his master's delay: he can carry on service as usual, or he can disobediently take on the master's role for himself. Jesus clarifies which decision would be best with a classic if–then scenario: *if* the servant "should say . . . in his heart" (εἴπῃ . . . ἐν τῇ καρδίᾳ αὐτοῦ, v. 45) that his master is delayed, and respond by beating the other slaves, eating, and getting drunk, *then* the master will "cut him in two" (διχοτομήσει αὐτόν) and banish him to a place "with the unbelieving ones" (μετὰ τῶν ἀπίστων, v. 46). This harsh punishment, juxtaposed with the positive assessment of the faithful servant who continues working despite his master's delay (vv. 42–43), clearly demonstrates that the unfaithful servant's thinking and his response to the problem are unacceptable to the master—and, concomitantly, to the narrator.

---

⁷⁰ In the similar story in Sir 11:14–20, he says to himself (LXX: ἐν τῷ εἰπεῖν αὐτόν), "I have found rest, and now I shall feast on my goods!"

⁷¹ Only here does Luke name God (ὁ θεός) as the speaker. Luke 3:22 and 9:35 are more ambiguous, and in 11:49, "the wisdom of God" (ἡ σοφία τοῦ θεοῦ εἶπεν) is the speaker.

⁷² The word ἄφρων occurs in Luke here and in 11:40–41 (which also connects interiority with generous giving).

⁷³ For example, individualistic decision making (Joel B. Green, *The Theology of the Gospel of Luke*, New Testament Theology [Cambridge: Cambridge University Press, 1995], 131); "sinful arrogance" (Egbert Seng, "Der Reiche Tor: Eine Untersuchung von Lk. xii 16–21 unter besonderer Berücksichtigung form- und motivgeschichtlicher Aspekte," *NovT* 20 [1978]: 144–45); selfishness (Arthur T. Cadoux, *The Parables of Jesus: Their Art and Use* [London: James Clarke, 1931], 205); or that he has forgotten God (Snodgrass, *Stories with Intent*, 399).

The Prodigal Son (15:11–32)

In the parable of the prodigal son (15:11–32), a father's younger son leaves home and squanders his inheritance in reckless living (ζῶν ἀσώτως, 15:13). The moment of crisis occurs when he becomes so destitute that he desperately longs to eat the pigs' slop (15:17). The narrative implies, rather than explicitly states, that the son thinks to himself:

> I will get up and go to my father and say to him, "Father, I have sinned against heaven and against you. I am no longer worthy to be called your son; treat me like one of your hired workers." (vv. 18–19)

Despite the absence of an explicit marker of inner speech, the scene is related through the son's point of view; the reader's attention is directed to the son's internal state by the fact that no hearer is indicated and by the idiomatic expression for coming to his senses (εἰς ἑαυτὸν δὲ ἐλθών, v. 17).[74] When the son returns, the father rejoices and throws a party, to the elder son's chagrin (vv. 22–32).

Whereas the farmer and the servant both unmistakably demonstrate erroneous thinking, this parable is more ambiguous. The younger son quite obviously *begins* as a negative figure: commentators have long agreed that he exemplifies self-indulgent, wasteful behavior.[75] Many interpreters also assert that, when the son plans to return home, he shifts into a positive role: his thinking is now in line with the father's (and hence, the narrator's) views.[76] Despite the son's apparently humble interior monologue, however, several clues suggest that he may not be truly repentant. As Bernard Brandon Scott wryly observes, it was not a change of heart but rather "his stomach [that] induced his return."[77] Sellew agrees, pointing out that the two prior parables in Luke 15 mention the character's repentance (vv. 7, 10), but no such note appears here.[78] Not only this, but the son's attempt to solve matters himself never comes to fruition. Upon returning, he does not finish his prepared speech; rather, his father unexpectedly throws a party (vv. 20–22). Although the son's self-talk is not overtly negative, as in the prior interior monologues, narrative

---

[74] Sellew ("Interior Monologue," 246) and Charles H. Talbert (*Reading Acts: A Literary and Theological Commentary on the Acts of the Apostles*, Reading the New Testament [New York: Crossroad, 1997], 108) both consider the similar expression in Acts 12:11 (ἐν ἑαυτῷ γενόμενος) to indicate interior monologue, not repentance.

[75] David A. Holgate and others connect the son's behavior with the Greco-Roman topos of covetousness. See Holgate, *Prodigality, Liberality and Meanness in the Parable of the Prodigal Son: A Greco-Roman Perspective on Luke 15:11–32*, JSNTSup 187 (Sheffield: Sheffield Academic, 1999), 16.

[76] E.g., Gerhard Lohfink, "'Ich habe gesündigt gegen den Himmel und gegen dich': Eine Exegese von Lk 15,18–21," *TQ* 155 (1975): 51–52; Joel B. Green believes that "shades of repentance are clearly evident" (*The Gospel of Luke*, NICNT [Grand Rapids: Eerdmans, 1997], 581).

[77] Scott, *Hear Then the Parable*, 116.

[78] Sellew, "Interior Monologue," 246.

details converge to indicate that he misreads the situation and misunderstands his father; his thinking is incongruent with his father's will.[79]

The Crafty Steward (16:1–8)

The parable of the crafty steward (16:1–8) tells of a rich man's steward who is accused of mismanaging the master's funds and told he will lose his job. The steward speaks "to himself" (ἐν ἑαυτῷ, v. 3), asking the same question the farmer asks in 12:17: "What should I do?" (Τί ποιήσω;). About to be unemployed, he solves his problem by forgiving his master's debtors (vv. 4–7), and the master praises (ἐπῄνεσεν) him for this shrewdness (v. 8).

Some might take the master's praise as evidence that the steward's thinking is commendable. Dan O. Via and Scott, for example, both suggest that the master is the antagonist while the steward is a positive "successful rogue."[80] The steward, however, is described consistently in negative terms. He is a "manager of unrighteousness" (τὸν οἰκονόμον τῆς ἀδικίας, v. 8) who, like the wayward son in ch. 15, has reportedly "squandered" (διασκορπίζω, v. 1) his master's resources. In the end, Jesus likens him to the "sons of this world" (οἱ υἱοὶ τοῦ αἰῶνος τούτου, v. 8), who are unrighteous (ἄδικος, v. 10) and untrustworthy (πιστοὶ οὐκ, vv. 11, 12), *unlike* the "sons of light" (τοὺς υἱοὺς τοῦ φωτός, v. 8), who are faithful/trustworthy (πιστός, v. 10). Additionally, following the parable, Jesus declares that the Pharisees justify themselves (οἱ δικαιοῦντες ἑαυτούς, v. 14) but God "knows their hearts" (γινώσκει τὰς καρδίας, v. 15). This comparison solidifies the point that the steward is to be judged negatively because the Pharisees have already been established as antagonists in the narrative.[81]

The Unjust Judge (18:2–5)

In Luke 18:2–5, Jesus begins by describing a judge who "neither feared God nor respected people" (τὸν θεὸν μὴ φοβούμενος καὶ ἄνθρωπον μὴ ἐντρεπόμενος, v. 2). Just two verses later, the judge repeats the very same phrase about himself (τὸν θεὸν οὐ φοβοῦμαι οὐδὲ ἄνθρωπον ἐντρέπομαι, v. 4). A widow asks this unrighteous judge repeatedly[82] for justice against her adversary (v. 3), which prompts the judge to

---

[79] See similarly Bailey, *Poet and Peasant*, 173–80; and George W. Ramsey, "Plots, Gaps, Repetitions, and Ambiguity in Luke 15," *PRSt* 17 (1990): 38–40.

[80] Dan O. Via, *The Parables: Their Literary and Existential Dimension* (Philadelphia: Fortress, 1974), 159; Scott, *Hear Then the Parable*, 264.

[81] The Pharisees challenge Jesus in conversational combat in 5:21, 30, 33; 6:2, 11; 7:36–50 and have already "attack[ed] him with hostile questions" (ἀποστοματίζω, 11:53) and begun "plotting against [ἐνεδρεύω] him" (11:54). On the vexed issue of the Pharisees' characterization in Luke, I follow John Darr, "Observers Observed: The Pharisees," in idem, *On Character Building*, 85–126.

[82] The iterative imperfect form of ἤρχετο (18:3) indicates that she "keeps coming."

speak "to himself" (ἐν ἑαυτῷ) about what he should do. After some delay, he finally decides to grant the widow's request in order to avoid being "worn out" (ὑπωπιάζω) by her continual pleas for justice (v. 5).

The repeated description of the judge directly contrasts with injunctions in the Hebrew Bible for all people to fear God[83] and for judges to be righteous and honor God.[84] Readers familiar with this tradition would immediately recognize his failure to perform his duties, which casts him in a negative light. In fact, history is replete with vivid denunciations of the judge. Hippolytus and Irenaeus equated him with the antichrist;[85] John Calvin called him "ungodly and cruel";[86] and Alexander B. Bruce described him as "an unprincipled, lawless tyrant, devoid of the sense of responsibility and of every sentiment of humanity and justice."[87] More recently, Joachim Jeremias has called the judge "brutal," and Robert Farrar Capon discusses him as an "anti-hero."[88]

The shock occurs in v. 7, where Jesus compares this "judge of injustice" (ὁ κριτὴς τῆς ἀδικίας, v. 6) to God, who "brings justice" (ποιήσῃ τὴν ἐκδίκησιν, v. 7). If the judge is truly unjust, then this raises a theodical challenge: is Jesus really comparing God to a judge whose thoughts and behaviors directly contrast with the two-pronged Great Commandment of Luke 10:27—to love God and love neighbor?[89] The comparison is "bewildering in its near-blasphemous overtones, which is grimly at odds with conventional, pious, received opinion" about God.[90] Is William Herzog right to conclude that the judge represents, "a darker and more sinister God, whose callous delay fails to alleviate the suffering of the elect"?[91]

---

[83] E.g., Prov 1:7, 9:10, 10:27, 15:33, 16:6, 19:23, Pss 15:4, 22:23, 25:12, 33:18.

[84] E.g., Deut 1.16-17, 2 Chr 19:5-11. On ancient judicial systems, see Herzog, *Parables as Subversive Speech*, 220–28.

[85] Hippolytus, *Christ and Anti-Christ*, trans. S. D. F. Salmond, in *Hippolytus, Bishop of Rome*, vol. 2, Ante-Nicene Christian Library 9, ed. A. Roberts and J. Donaldson (Edinburgh: T&T Clark, 1869), 33. Irenaeus, *Against Heresies*, in ibid., 124.

[86] John Calvin, *A Harmony of the Gospels Matthew, Mark, and Luke* 11 (Edinburgh: Saint Andrew Press, 1972), 125.

[87] Alexander B. Bruce, *The Parabolic Teaching of Christ: A Systematic and Critical Study of the Parables of Our Lord* (New York: George Doran, 1886), 158.

[88] Jeremias, *Parables of Jesus*, 156; Robert Farrar Capon, *Kingdom, Grace, Judgment: Paradox, Outrage, and Vindication in the Parables of Jesus* (Grand Rapids: Eerdmans, 2002), 330.

[89] Some counter that in the original, pre-Lukan parable, the widow, not the judge, represents God. See, e.g., Herman Hendrickx, *The Third Gospel for the Third World*, 4 vols. (Quezon City, Philippines: Claretian Publications, 2001), 3:77; Barbara E. Reid, *Choosing the Better Part? Women in the Gospel of Luke* (Collegeville, MN: Liturgical Press, 1996), 294.

[90] Roger White, "MacKinnon and the Parables," in *Christ, Ethics, and Tragedy: Essays in Honour of Donald MacKinnon*, ed. Kenneth Surin (Cambridge: Cambridge University Press, 1989), 49–70, http://dx.doi.org/10.1017/CBO9780511659515.006.

[91] Herzog, *Parables as Subversive Speech*, 217. Most commentators label this a lesser-to-greater argument (*qal wahomer*; Lat: *a minore ad maius*). See Simon J. Kistemaker, *The Parables of Jesus* (Grand Rapids: Baker, 1980), 252; Bailey, *Poet and Peasant*, 136; Joseph A. Fitzmyer, *The*

Perhaps the bafflements engendered by this comparison are why some scholars downplay or reinterpret the judge's "negative" characteristics.[92] John Dominic Crossan views both the judge and the widow as ethically neutral.[93] Scott suggests that, in light of depictions of God as a just judge in the Hebrew Bible (e.g., Sir 35:12–18, Deut 24:17), Luke's audience might expect the judge to "return to honor."[94] This is plausible, but Scott's suggestion ignores the importance of literary sequence.[95] Jesus does not compare the judge to God until v. 7; implied readers more likely would view the judge as just another corrupt magistrate. Furthermore, the previous instances of internal monologue have set no precedent for the reader to expect that the judge will "return to honor."

Along with other narrative elements, the internal monologue establishes that the judge is not neutral or positive. Speaking "to himself" (ἐν ἑαυτῷ, vv. 4–5), the judge repeats his true nature (he does not fear God or respect people), and then reveals to the reader that he grants the widow's request only out of selfish motives; she is "bothering" (παρέχειν ... κόπον)[96] him and he wants to avoid being "given a black eye/worn out/slandered" (ὑπωπιάζω).[97]

Gospel According to Luke: A New Translation with Introduction and Commentary, 2 vols., AB 28, 28A (Garden City, NY: Doubleday, 1981–1985), 2:1180; Wolfgang Wiefel, *Das Evangelium nach Lukas*, THKNT 3 (Berlin: Evangelische Verlagsanstalt, 1988), 315; Darrell L. Bock, *Luke*, 2 vols., BECNT 3 (Grand Rapids: Baker, 1994–1996), 2:1450; Arland J. Hultgren, *The Parables of Jesus: A Commentary*, Bible in Its World (Grand Rapids: Eerdmans, 2000), 258; Mary Ann Tolbert, *Perspectives on the Parables: An Approach to Multiple Interpretations* (Philadelphia: Fortress, 1979), 53; Malina and Rohrbaugh, *Social-Science Commentary*, 299; Daniel J. Harrington, *The Synoptic Gospels Set Free: Preaching without Anti-Judaism*, Studies in Judaism and Christianity (Mahwah, NJ: Paulist, 2009), 193. Too quickly affixing a *qal waḥomer* label, however, obscures the oddity of Jesus's comparison and neutralizes the parable's rhetorical force. See also Luke 11:13.

[92] J. Duncan M. Derrett, "Law in the New Testament: The Parable of the Unjust Judge," *NTS* 18 (1972): 178–91, esp. 180–86; Annette Merz, "How a Woman Who Fought Back and Demanded Her Rights Became an Importunate Widow: The Transformations of a Parable of Jesus," in *Jesus from Judaism to Christianity: Continuum Approaches to the Historical Jesus*, ed. Tom Holmén, LNTS 352 (New York: T&T Clark, 2007), 49–86. Such readings make the judge neutral/positive based on extratextual conjecture, not literary details.

[93] John Dominic Crossan, "Parable, Allegory and Paradox," in *Semiology and Parables: Exploration of the Possibilities Offered by Structuralism for Exegesis. Papers of the Conference Sponsored by the Vanderbilt Interdisciplinary Project, "Semiology and Exegesis," and Supported by a Grant from the National Endowment for the Humanities, Held at Vanderbilt University, Nashville, Tennessee, May 15–17, 1975*, ed. Daniel Patte, PTMS 9 (Pittsburgh: Pickwick, 1976), 247–81, esp. 255.

[94] Scott, *Hear Then the Parable*, 185.

[95] A classic text is Menakhem Perry, "Literary Dynamics: How the Order of a Text Creates Its Meanings (With an Analysis of Faulkner's 'A Rose for Emily')," *Poetics Today* 1 (1979): 35–64, 311–61, http://dx.doi.org/10.2307/1772040.

[96] Elsewhere in Luke this Greek construction appears only in 11:7.

[97] The translation of ὑπωπιάζω (used elsewhere in the NT only in 1 Cor 9:27) is a matter of debate. Most commentators take this boxing term ("to give someone a black eye") metaphorically,

Presumably, the widow believes that the judge will vindicate her. Ironically,[98] the reader and narrator know what the widow does not: the judge cares nothing for justice (v. 2). Hedrick's suggestion that the judge is "impartial and objective" cannot stand in light of the judge's own implied admission that he has thus far failed to "give her justice" (ἐκδικήσω αὐτήν, v. 5).[99] The internal monologue stands as a reliable indicator of the judge's negative inner nature.

The Owner of the Vineyard (20:9–16)

The parable of the owner of the vineyard (20:9–16) describes a man who leases his vineyard to some tenant farmers; three times the vineyard owner sends slaves to collect his portion of the harvest, and three times the tenants beat the slave, sending him away empty-handed. The owner asks himself what he should do, deciding to send his son as his emissary (v. 13). Though not marked as internal monologue, his question ("What should I do?" Τί ποιήσω;)[100] and the evident lack of an interlocutor imply that he is speaking to himself. The parable ends tragically, as the tenants kill the son in order to gain the inheritance for themselves (vv. 14–15), clearly mirroring the larger Gospel narrative.[101]

Unlike in the previous parable, in this story, the thinking character is not the one who fails to "respect" (ἐντρέπω) others—the tenants are (vv. 13–14; cf. 18:2, 4). Typically, commentators assert that the vineyard owner embodies God's selfless μακροθυμία (putting anger far away from oneself).[102] The father's use of the phrase "my one beloved son" (τὸν υἱόν μου τὸν ἀγαπητόν, v. 13) echoes God's description

---

as a way of saying "to beat," "to annoy," or "to wear out" (BDAG, 848), though many cite Derrett's view that ὑπωπιάζω is "to slander/shame" ("Law in the New Testament," 190–91). Either way, the judge is concerned with himself.

[98] Barbara Reid insists that translating ὑπωπιάζω as "wear me out" (see previous note) "dilutes the irony of the literal 'strike,' which is part of the twist of the story" ("The Power of the Widows and How to Suppress It (Acts 6:1–7)," in *A Feminist Companion to the Acts of the Apostles*, ed. Amy-Jill Levine [London: T&T Clark, 2004], 77). Indeed, the picture of a judge who fears physical violence from a widow is quite comical.

[99] Hedrick, *Parables as Poetic Fictions*, 112–13.

[100] The parallel versions in Mark 12:1–9, Matt 21:33–46, and Gos. Thom. 65 do not include this question. Most commentators point to Isa 5:1–7 as the source text for this parable; Isa 5:4 LXX also reads Τί ποιήσω;

[101] This is an instance of *mise en abyme*, a term coined by André Gide that refers to "an internal reduplication of a literary work or part of a work" (*The Oxford Dictionary of Literary Terms*, ed. Chris Baldick, 3rd ed. [Oxford: Oxford University Press, 2008], 211). See also Lucien Dällenbach, *Le récit spéculaire: Contribution à l'étude de mise en abyme*, Collection Poétique (Paris: Seuil, 1977). For a multileveled analysis of the parable of the vineyard owner as *mise en abyme*, see Robert L. Brawley, *Text to Text Pours Forth Speech: Voices of Scripture in Luke-Acts*, ISBL (Bloomington: Indiana University Press, 1995), esp. 27–41.

[102] Kenneth E. Bailey, *Jesus through Middle Eastern Eyes: Cultural Studies in the Gospels* (Downers Grove, IL: IVP Academic, 2008), 410.

of Jesus (Luke 3:22, 9:35); this and Jesus's allusion to Ps 118:22–23 (Luke 20:17) make it clear that the parable represents God sending his son Jesus into the world. These narrative elements lead almost universally to a positive assessment of the owner; indeed, of all the thinking characters in Luke, the vineyard owner is most commonly read in positive terms.

The above readings, however, deflect attention from the disconcerting detail that the vineyard owner is an absentee landlord (v. 9). Neither do they grapple with the "bizarre, even absurd"[103] fact that the father, fully aware of the previous beatings, ultimately becomes complicit in his own son's death (vv. 10–12). Craig A. Evans asks starkly, "How could the owner have been so foolish and so reckless with the lives of his servants? How could he have been so stupid as to send his son to the vineyard after his servants had been maltreated?"[104]

Whereas most commentators contrast the owner's/God's selfless love with the tenants' greedy desire to collect an inheritance that is not theirs,[105] a few point out that the father, too, wants his goods so much that he puts three servants and his son in harm's way. Perhaps Sellew is correct that the owner makes this "chilling" decision because he is "too intent on getting that rent to perceive the danger."[106] In Herzog's estimation, as well, this "elite" landowner "continually sought to expand [his] holdings and add to [his] wealth at the expense of the peasants."[107] These suggestions are mere conjecture; what we can say for certain is that he struggles internally, wondering what to do. Whether he is greedy, oppressive, or merely naïve, the window into his thoughts demonstrates for the reader that these are "not the calculation[s] of a wise man."[108] His decision making ends tragically for everyone. This is why Crossan compares the landowner to the foolish farmer of Luke 12:16–20, and Neyrey concludes, "He is foolish beyond measure."[109]

To varying degrees, the farmer, servant, son, steward, judge, and vineyard owner exhibit foolish thinking. None of these characters is "heroic" in any traditional Hellenistic sense. None has a wise or honorable interior disposition, as Jewish teachings would commend. Indeed, Evans calls them "remarkably foolish and

---

[103] Hultgren explains this as perfectly plausible in an ancient setting (*Parables of Jesus*, 362).

[104] Craig A. Evans, "Parables in Early Judaism," in *The Challenge of Jesus' Parables*, ed. Richard N. Longenecker, McMaster New Testament Studies (Grand Rapids: Eerdmans, 2000), 70.

[105] Matthew S. Rindge helpfully situates this parable in the context of other Second Temple (mostly sapiential) warnings about the dangers of scheming to acquire an inheritance (*Jesus' Parable of the Rich Fool: Luke 12:13–14 among Ancient Conversations on Death and Possessions*, ECL [Atlanta: Society of Biblical Literature, 2011], 184–85). See also Herzog's discussion of the parable as a "codification" of a "conflict of interpretations over the meanings of owner, heir, and inheritance" (*Parables as Subversive Speech*, 112).

[106] Sellew, "Interior Monologue," 248.

[107] Herzog, *Parables as Subversive Speech*, 108.

[108] Jerome H. Neyrey, *Render to God: New Testament Understandings of the Divine* (Minneapolis: Fortress, 2004), 75.

[109] John Dominic Crossan, "Structuralist Analysis and the Parables of Jesus," *Semeia* 1 (1974): 208; Neyrey, *Render to God*, 75.

incautious" characters who "lack common sense."[110] How might these characters' interior lives affect Luke's implied readers rhetorically? The following section makes several suggestions.

IV. Rhetorical Effects of the Lukan Interior Monologues

Without a mediating narratorial voice, interior monologue can create the impression that the reader is encountering the character's immediate and exact thoughts;[111] as such, quoted inner speech can enhance what social psychologist Melanie Green calls "narrative transportation" (the natural tendency for readers to become absorbed in a story).[112] In narratological terms, cited self-talk is "directly related to mimesis and inversely related to diegesis."[113] The first person pronoun further prompts the reader to identify with the thinking character by metaphorically placing the character's words into the reader's mouth/mind; the reader "voices" the character's unmediated thoughts.

Access to a character's private inner experience can cause readers to empathize with the thinker, identifying with his or her plight. As Heininger writes, "Der Leser erkennt in den Gefühlsausbrüchen der handelnden Personen seine eigenen Stimmungen wieder, und das umso mehr, als die äußeren Ereignisse, denen die Reaktionen im Selbstgespräch gelten, seinen eigenen Lebenserfahrungen gleichen."[114] This gives rise to what literary critic Leona Toker calls "parallel experience": "By placing us in an intellectual predicament analogous to that of the characters, parallel experience can turn into a direct means of conveying to us the specific emotional climate of the [story's] world."[115] Quoted self-talk facilitates "parallel experience" if readers accept the parable's implicit invitation and identify with the thinker.[116]

---

[110] Evans traces parallels between the foolish characters in Jesus' parables and those in rabbinic parables ("Parables in Early Judaism," 70).

[111] Thus, Genette calls this "immediate speech" (*Narrative Discourse*, 173–74).

[112] Melanie C. Green, "The Role of Transportation in the Persuasiveness of Public Narratives," *Journal of Personality and Social Psychology* 79 (2000): 701–21, http://dx.doi.org/10.1037/0022-3514.79.5.701. Green argues that a reader's level of narrative transportation corresponds to the degree of influence that story has on his or her later beliefs and behaviors. As long as the narrative is coherent, plausible, and adheres to genre expectations, the reader's processing of the story will be both more intense and less critical. In short, a reader in a state of "high transportation" is less likely to develop rational counterarguments and more likely to become involved with the characters and experience subsequent transformation.

[113] Michael S. Kearns, *Rhetorical Narratology*, Stages 16 (Lincoln: University of Nebraska Press, 1999), 158.

[114] Heininger, *Metaphorik, Erzählstruktur*, 62.

[115] Leona Toker, *Eloquent Reticence: Withholding Information in Fictional Narrative* (Lexington: University Press of Kentucky, 1993), 4.

[116] As C. H. Dodd asserts, a parable "leav[es] the mind in sufficient doubt about its precise

The soliloquies invite readerly identification, and this invitation has an evaluative dimension to it. The narrator constructs the story so as to elicit particular readerly judgments with respect to the characters; these judgments, in turn, prompt readers to consider whether their own views align with the narrator's perspective, thereby encouraging the μετάνοια—"change in thinking"—that is so prominent in Luke's Gospel.[117]

Luke's interior monologues can prompt readers to consider what they would say in their own hearts if they faced a similar dilemma and to assess whether their self-talk would align with the divine will (as constructed by the narrator): the farmer's "What should I do?" (12:17) becomes the reader's *"What would I do?"*[118] In a case of ironic reversal, a reader who sympathizes with a thinking character's incorrect perspective will also experience the narratorial judgment that follows. If, for example, the reader agrees with the farmer that saving up one's surplus goods is the best course of action, she or he will then also undergo the stinging "parallel experience" of God calling her a "fool" (12:20).

Of course, not all readers will relate to specific characters in the same way. While some identify with a character,[119] others will distance themselves from him or her.[120] Either way, Luke's internal monologues encourage readers to evaluate the

---

application to tease it into active thought" (*The Parables of the Kingdom*, rev. ed. [New York: Scribner's Sons, 1961], 5). Though commentators often (unwittingly) dismiss surprising elements, parabolic power inheres precisely in the fact that a parable "invites and surprises a participant into an experience" (Sallie McFague, *Speaking in Parables: A Study in Metaphor and Theology* [Philadelphia: Fortress, 1975], 69).

[117] The word μετάνοια, usually translated "repentance/to repent," literally means "afterthought," or "change in thinking," though the concept is not restricted to cognitive change. Luke uses this terminology more than any other NT author (see Luke 3:3, 8; 5:32; 10:13; 11:32; 13:3, 5; 15:7, 10; 16:30; 17:3, 4; 24:7). On Luke's uses of the term and its cognates, see Guy D. Nave, *The Role and Function of Repentance in Luke-Acts,* AcBib (Atlanta: Society of Biblical Literature, 2002).

[118] The parallel version in Gos. Thom. 63 contains no reference to the man speaking "to himself," nor does he ask himself "what to do." Rindge rightly notes that this makes the Lukan version more amenable to readerly identification (*Jesus' Parable of the Rich Fool*, 235).

[119] Hans Robert Jauss identifies five different types of readerly identification vis-à-vis a protagonist: associative, admiring, sympathetic, cathartic, and ironic ("Levels of Identification of Hero and Audience," *New Literary History* 5 [1974]: 283–317, http://dx.doi.org/10.2307/468397). Joanna Dewey extends Jauss's typology to include narrative sequence, which gives rise to "sequential identification" ("The Gospel of Mark as an Oral-Aural Event: Implications for Interpretation," in Malbon and McKnight, *New Literary Criticism*, 148–57).

[120] Many readers actively maintain a critical distance in order to resist the goals, values, and views of objectionable narratives; Adele Reinhartz and others have discussed such "resistant readers," who read with a "hermeneutics of suspicion" (a phrase coined by Paul Ricoeur in the 1970s). See Reinhartz, "The New Testament and Anti-Judaism: A Literary Critical Approach," *JES* 25 (1988): 524–37. Strategies of reading "against the grain" obviously differ from that of the "implied reader" in view here (see n. 11 above).

thinker's views with respect to their own; in so doing, they contribute to the parables' transformative power.

The last two parables containing internal monologue (the unjust judge [18:2–5] and the owner of the vineyard [20:9–16]) raise an intriguing question with respect to readerly identification. Each of these parables compares the thinker to God. Are Luke's readers invited to identify with—and evaluate the foolish thoughts of—these God-characters?[121] Sellew implies that the answer to these questions is yes. He writes:

> We see ourselves reflected in [Jesus's] little people caught in awkward places. The frantic thoughts and calculations, the desperate attempts to claw out of trouble, these defining moments of the Farmer, the Lost Son, the Judge or the Steward, could just as well be our own.[122]

Yet, in the parables of the unjust judge and the owner of the vineyard, the text does not warrant readerly identification with the thinking character; the quoted inner speech functions differently in these parables.[123]

Most readers recognize that in the story of the widow and the judge (Luke 18:2–5), Luke emphasizes the importance of prayer. The surrounding literary framework clearly establishes this focus.[124] For example, this is one of the few Lukan parables that the narrator prefaces with interpretive guidance: he says explicitly that Jesus tells this parable "to show them they should always pray and not lose heart" (18:1), which means that from the outset the audience should know that the character with whom they are invited to identify is not the judge but the prayerful widow. Jesus's explanatory addendum underscores the importance of "calling out" (βοάω) to God "day and night" (ἡμέρας καὶ νυκτός, 18:7). Not only this, but the parable directly following this one explicitly concerns prayer (18:9–14). All

---

[121] Herein lies an intriguing theological dilemma that Sellew mentions but does not explore: if the unjust judge and vineyard owner represent God but exhibit foolish thinking, what does this mean for "the theology implicit in the parables that Jesus tells in this Gospel: theology in the strict sense"? ("Interior Monologue," 248–49). This important question deserves fuller treatment than I can offer here. Still, I would suggest that the conundrum itself is part of the power of these parables.

[122] Sellew, "Interior Monologue," 253.

[123] As Sellew writes, Luke "is not always consistent in his use of inner speech, nor does he always employ the device even when it might have been expected" ("Interior Monologue," 249).

[124] Herzog takes scholars like Jeremias, Perrin, Bailey, and Fitzmyer to task for analyzing the parable of the unjust judge "in continuity with the Lukan reading of the parable," rather than "separating the parable from its Lukan context" in order to discern its original meaning (*Parables as Subversive Speech*, 220). Like all stories, however, parables function rhetorically within some transactional discursive situation. Contra Seymour Chatman (*Coming to Terms: Rhetoric of Narrative Fiction and Film* [Ithaca, NY: Cornell University Press, 1990], 144), no *story* can be ontologically separated from its *discourse* (Thomas M. Leitch, *What Stories Are: Narrative Theory and Interpretation* [University Park: Pennsylvania State University Press, 1986], 201). Therefore, I consider the parables within the Lukan discourse.

of these textual details support the view that this parable is not aimed at fostering readerly identification with the judge; rather, the "entire point of the story" is to compare the woman's supplications with the disciples' prayers.[125]

In the parable of the owner of the vineyard, the audience is again compared *not* to the thinking character (the owner) but rather to those who respond to him (the tenants).[126] And again, the surrounding literary framework clarifies the point. Just prior to the parable, Luke describes the religious authorities reasoning "to themselves" (πρὸς ἑαυτούς) about how they should respond to Jesus's question (20:5); this directly parallels the tenants' discussion "with one another" (πρὸς ἀλλήλους) regarding how they ought to respond to the owner's son (20:14). Jesus pronounces judgment on the tenants, focusing attention on their reprehensible behavior (20:16). The narrator's clarification about audience identification comes after the parable, with the note that the experts in the law and chief priests "understood he had told this parable against them" (20:19).[127] This narratorial statement and the people's response ("May this never happen!" μὴ γένοιτο, 20:16) together imply that Jesus's hearers understand that the father is God, and that *they* are being compared to the tenants who behave so badly.[128]

If these inner speeches are not meant to elicit readerly identification, how might they be functioning? Notice that in the parable of the unjust judge, the judge does not reveal to the woman the reason he decides to help her. This means that his interior monologue deepens the dramatic irony of the situation (when characters in the story know less than the audience knows).[129] The judge's privately disclosed reasoning reveals to the reader what the woman cannot know: the judge fears her. He is afraid that the widow will best him with her "unending pleas," a fear that subtly attests to the effectiveness of the woman's unconventional means of attaining justice. By offering what Meir Sternberg calls a "telescoped view" of the

---

[125] Tolbert, *Perspectives on the Parables*, 53.

[126] Perhaps this is why most English Bibles label this the "parable of the (wicked) tenants/vinedressers/husbandmen" (e.g., ESV, NET, NIV, NKJV, NRSV, RSV).

[127] François Bovon notes that πρός followed by an accusative can contain the idea of hostility, as is the case here (*Luke 3: A Commentary on the Gospel of Luke [19:28–24:53]*, Hermeneia [Minneapolis: Fortress, 2012], 44).

[128] Scholars disagree about whether the parable invites an identification that would have been natural for Jesus's hearers, "who may have been tenant farmers or landless peasants" (James Hester, "Socio-Rhetorical Criticism and the Parable of the Tenants," *JSNT* 45 [1992]: 55), or whether it "blocks the identification that corresponds to their social location as landowners and offers instead an identification they reject, the identification with rebellious tenant peasants" (Edward H. Horne, "The Parable of the Tenants as Indictment," *JSNT* 71 [1998]: 113). Nevertheless, most concur that the tenants are the characters with whom the audience ought to identify.

[129] A commonly cited example of dramatic irony is Sophocles's *Oedipus the King*, in which the audience knows what Oedipus does not: he has unwittingly murdered his father and married his mother. An ancient audience would have thought of this in terms of Oedipus fulfilling his fate, rather than as an instance of "dramatic irony."

judge's inner life[130] to which the widow is not privy,[131] internal monologue invites the reader to draw the correct conclusions and judge the various characters' (mis)perceptions accordingly.

The irony runs even deeper when one considers the social power dynamics operative in the complex systemic hierarchies of the ancient world.[132] By revealing the judge's inner concerns, the interior monologue allows the reader to see how "a judge who neither fears God nor respects man comes to fear a widow, the weakest member of society."[133] True to the common Lukan emphasis on reversals, the apparently powerless figure receives vindication by exerting her power over the one who supposedly has external authority but fails to use it wisely. As Barbara Reid writes, "Her persistence is *an exercise of power* that finally accomplishes its end."[134]

Similarly, the vineyard owner's self-talk deepens the dramatic irony of that scene: his wondering what to do (Τί ποιήσω; 20:13) and his use of the word "perhaps" (ἴσως, 20:13) suggest that he does not know that his "beloved" (ἀγαπητός, 20:13) son will be killed. By this point in the Gospel narrative, however, implied readers should sense that this is the outcome of the story, since Jesus has predicted his death repeatedly (9:22, 44; 7:25; 18:31–34).[135] The interior monologue thus elevates the reader above the father, subtly inviting the reader "to collude with the narrator behind his back."[136] Like the judge, the vineyard owner occupies a place of prestige in relation to the workers in his employ. Again the tables are turned as the apparently subordinate characters ironically best the person of privilege. The privileged vineyard owner's interior monologue creates a community of a different kind of privilege: a privilege of knowing. The narrator and reader—sharing a secret—stand "in the know" above the vineyard owner, who appears the fool.

Of course, in the end, the father has the last laugh. Jesus tells us that the

---

[130] See Meir Sternberg, "Between the Truth and the Whole Truth in Biblical Narrative: The Rendering of Inner Life by Telescoped Inside View and Interior Monologue," *Hasifrut* 29 (1979): 110–46.

[131] The fact that characters cannot normally "hear" others' thoughts is important for Jesus's characterization, since often in Luke, Jesus discerns others' thoughts and engages them in public conversation. Verbs that describe Jesus knowing others' thoughts are consistently connected with verbs that depict him speaking directly to them: 5:22, 6:8–9, 7:40, 9:47–48, 11:17, 20:23, 24:37–38. Luke 7:40 and 24:38 are the only cases in which Jesus is not the subject of a verb of knowing, but they imply that he knows the others' thoughts.

[132] See, e.g., Malina, "The Perception of Limited Good: Maintaining One's Social Status," in idem, *New Testament World*, 81–105.

[133] Scott, *Hear Then the Parable*, 186. See also Ceslas Spicq, "La parabole de la veuve obstinée et du juge inerte, aux décisions impromptues," *RB* 68 (1961): 68–90, esp. 75. Cf. the kind of irony proposed by W. Harnisch in "Die Ironie als Stilmittel in Gleichnissen Jesu," *EvT* 32 (1972): 421–36.

[134] Reid, "Power of the Widows," 77.

[135] The reader discerns what Jesus's audience does not: the one telling them the parable is God's beloved son, and, like the vineyard owner's son, he will soon be killed.

[136] Kearns, *Rhetorical Narratology*, 156.

vineyard owner eventually wrests power back from the tenants, coming to "destroy those tenants and give the vineyard to others" (20:16). In Bovon's words, "Having been seen as powerless to this point, [the father] suddenly awakens, self-confident and master of his decisions."[137] As the setting then shifts from the parable itself to the surrounding Gospel narrative, the import of the parable becomes clear. Together, "the narrator and his hearers are navigating here in allegorical water. Each reader understands that the story is about God and God's judgments."[138] The reader's privileged knowing remains intact, even as the character in view shifts from the father in Jesus's parable to the Jewish leaders who hear it (20:19).

V. Concluding Thoughts

As tools in the Lukan narrator's toolbelt, the interior monologues can function in diverse ways. The above discussion of the parables can be summarized as follows: Luke's moments of interiority are a kind of fusion between Hellenistic literature's structural uses of inner speech and Hebrew tropes about the danger of foolish self-talk. As we find in ancient Hellenistic narratives, Luke's internal monologues depict the inner turmoil his characters experience in moments of crisis. Interior monologue also creates the illusion that the reader is encountering the character's true nature, apart from the biased mediating influence of the narrator. In this way, these internal monologues indicate that, unlike in most ancient Greek narratives, Luke's thinking characters are far from heroic; they demonstrate foolish perspectives. In this, Luke's interior monologues more closely resemble those found in ancient Jewish literature, providing narrative articulations of the common Jewish emphasis on the importance of what one says in one's heart vis-à-vis God.

Rhetorically, the internal monologues in the first four parables foster readerly identification with the thinking character. If the reader accepts this invitation, she also will experience the corrections implied by the narrative rhetoric. In the parables of the unjust judge and the owner of the vineyard, however, narratorial guidance indicates that the audience is meant to relate to the characters without inner monologues (the widow and tenants), not the thinkers (the judge and the vineyard owner). In these latter parables, inner speech introduces dramatic irony, privileging the reader over the thinking characters in the story. In each case, internal monologue functions rhetorically to invite readerly transformation.

To return to the point with which I began, I hope to have shown how the presence of interior monologues in the Gospel of Luke challenges the dominant paradigm of the "anti-introspective" Mediterranean self. My reading of the Lukan interior monologues supports Louise Joy Lawrence's claim that, even in collectivist

---

[137] Bovon, *Luke 3*, 41.
[138] Ibid.

societies, "interior thought and self-consciousness is morally significant.... Honour is formed in the nexus of not only what others think of a person, but also that person's 'introspective' view of the self."[139] Our focus should be on the kinds, degrees, and functions of interiority and introspection in ancient texts, rather than on a generic portrait of ancient societies as "*anti*-introspective"; though ancient people would not have undergone psychoanalysis on Freud's couch, many were concerned with the inner thoughts, values, beliefs, and emotions of the individual.[140]

[139] Lawrence, *Ethnography of the Gospel of Matthew*, 140; see esp. 113–41.

[140] Richard Rohrbaugh is right: it is "important to recognize that no society is one way or the other, either completely individualistic or collectivist," though he goes on to emphasize Jesus's "in group" self ("Ethnocentrism and Historical Questions about Jesus," in *The Social Setting of Jesus and the Gospels*, ed. Wolfgang Stegemann, Bruce Malina, and Gerd Theissen [Minneapolis: Fortress, 2002], 32).

Annual Meetings 2015
Atlanta, GA • November 21–24

Don't Miss It

Annual Meetings 2015, hosted by AAR and SBL, will take place in Atlanta, GA. This meeting showcases the latest in biblical research, fosters collegial contacts, advances research, and focuses on issues of the profession.

Register Now at sbl-site.org and Save!

The Afterlives of New Testament Apocrypha

ANNETTE YOSHIKO REED
reedanne@sas.upenn.edu
University of Pennsylvania, Philadelphia, PA 19104

This essay explores the place of parabiblical literature in biblical studies through a focus on New Testament apocrypha. Countering the assumption that the significance of this literature pivots on its value for understanding the origins of Christianity, this essay calls for fresh attention to the afterlives of these writings. The first section traces the genealogy of the notion of the NT apocrypha as countercanon, as well as the history of the debate over whether "apocrypha" preserve secret or suppressed truths about Jesus and his earliest followers. It points to the influence of post-Reformation anthological efforts and new concerns for forgery and censorship in the wake of the advent of printing, especially for popularizing a disjunctive model whereby "apocrypha" are imagined to have been systematically suppressed by ecclesiarchs during the Christianization of the Roman Empire. The second section surveys evidence for the elasticity of such writings and for their reception in contexts as far-flung as medieval Christian art and contemporary Japanese anime. This evidence points to the value of alternate approaches to NT apocrypha, reread as an integral part of the making of the memory of the biblical past from late antiquity to the present.

Why should scholars of biblical studies care about parabiblical literature? In the case of those parabiblical writings associated with patriarchs and prophets in the Tanak, recent research has emphasized their potential both to shed light on the origins of Christianity and to add to our knowledge of the history of biblical interpretation. Fragments discovered among the Dead Sea Scrolls confirmed the antiquity of some of these writings, affirming their utility for filling the gaps in our knowledge of Judaism before and during the time of Jesus. In addition, many

This essay is a companion piece to "The Modern Invention of 'Old Testament Pseudepigrapha,'" *JTS* 20 (2009): 403–36, http://dx.doi.org/10.1093/jts/flp033. An earlier form was presented at the York Christian Apocrypha Symposium in 2013; it owes much to feedback in that forum as well as to the students in my 2013 Stouffer College House seminar "From Apocalypse to Anime" at the University of Pennsylvania.

so-called Old Testament pseudepigrapha preserve early attestations of motifs that later became common in rabbinic midrash and Christian biblical interpretation.[1] Consequently, parabiblical writings of this sort have attracted scholarly and popular attention as resources for reconstructing the dynamic complex of exegetical, narrative, and other related traditions through which premodern Jews, Christians, and Muslims encountered the biblical past—what James Kugel calls the "Bible as It Was."[2]

But what about those parabiblical writings associated with Jesus and the apostles—those works conventionally studied under the rubric of "New Testament apocrypha"? For these works too, modern manuscript finds have expanded our data. Papyri recovered from Oxyrhynchus included ancient Greek copies of texts such as the Gospel of Thomas and the Gospel of Mary, for instance, and the discovery of the Nag Hammadi codices yielded full Coptic versions of these and other long-lost books mentioned by early Christian authors. Whereas the Dead Sea Scrolls brought new attention to OT pseudepigrapha as part of the continued creativity surrounding the biblical past in Judaism, Christianity, and Islam, popular and scholarly curiosity about NT apocrypha has remained largely tied to perceptions of their value for reconstructing Christian origins.[3]

The varied writings studied under this rubric include narratives about Jesus and his mother Mary in their childhood such as the Protevangelium of James and the Infancy Gospel of Thomas; writings related to Jesus's teachings and death such as the Gospel of Thomas, Gospel of Peter, and Gospel of Nicodemus; pseudepigraphical epistles associated with Jesus, Paul, and others; visionary texts such as the Apocalypse of Paul; and apocryphal acts associated with Andrew, John, Peter, Paul, Philip, Thecla, and Thomas.[4] Among specialists, they are prized for their

---

[1] On this corpus and category, see further Reed, "Modern Invention"; Jean-Claude Picard, *Le continent apocryphe: Essai sur les littératures apocryphes juives et chrétienne*, Instrumenta patristica 36 (Turnhout: Brepols, 1999), 13–51; Eibert J. C. Tigchelaar, "Old Testament Pseudepigrapha and the Scriptures," Presidential Address, Colloquium Biblicum Lovaniense, 26 July 2012.

[2] James L. Kugel, *The Bible as It Was* (Cambridge: Belknap Press of Harvard University Press, 1999). See further John C. Reeves, ed., *Tracing the Threads: Studies in the Vitality of Jewish Pseudepigrapha*, EJL 6 (Atlanta: Scholars Press, 1994); Michael E. Stone and Theodore A. Bergren, eds., *Biblical Figures outside the Bible* (Harrisburg, PA: Trinity Press International, 1998).

[3] I use the term "NT apocrypha" since it exemplifies the specific problem here discussed. On the adoption of alternate terminology of "Christian apocrypha," see further below.

[4] For English translations of a basic core of these materials, see M. R. James, *The Apocryphal New Testament* (Oxford: Clarendon, 1924), especially as revised by J. K. Elliot (Oxford: Clarendon, 1993). For the most up-to-date translations and broadest set of relevant writings, see François Bovon and Pierre Geoltrain, eds., *Écrits apocryphes chrétiens I* (Paris: Gallimard, 1997); Pierre Geoltrain and Jean-Daniel Kaestli, eds., *Écrits apocryphes chrétiens II* (Paris: Gallimard, 2005). Compare Edgar Hennecke and Wilhelm Schneemelcher, eds., *Neutestamentlichen Apokryphen in deutscher Übersetzung*, 3rd rev. ed., 2 vols. (Tübingen: Mohr Siebeck, 1959–1964)—the first

preservation of a rich literary deposit of continued reflection about Jesus, his family, and his first followers, attesting the diversity of early Christianity as well as the continued dynamism surrounding the apostolic past in late antique and medieval cultural memory.[5] Outside of specialist circles, however, their significance has been construed quite differently: particularly in North America, it has been reduced to *one* possible feature of *some* of these texts—namely, their potential to shed light on the beliefs of Jesus and his earliest followers.

This possibility loomed large in some of the most prominent and popular attempts to integrate NT apocrypha into biblical studies. In the late 1960s, for instance, Helmut Koester broached the question of whether "apocryphal and 'heretical' Gospels have their origin in very early layers of the Gospel tradition—perhaps even in certain aspects of the words and works of the historical Jesus himself,"[6] and he answered in the affirmative, proclaiming that "the *Gospel of Thomas* appears to be a direct continuation of the eschatological sayings of Jesus."[7] No less prominent—and even more popular—were the possibilities raised by Elaine Pagels in her 1979 *Gnostic Gospels*. Pagels, too, raised questions about Jesus on the basis of the Gospel of Thomas: "Did Jesus have a twin brother, as this text implies? Could the text be an authentic record of Jesus' sayings?"[8] Furthermore, she argued for the significance of such writings by positing their preservation of "early forms of Christian teaching," reflecting the diversity of Christianity in the time before "their suppression as banned documents" by the ecclesiarchs who remade the church as "an institution headed by a three-rank hierarchy of bishops, priests, and deacons, who understood themselves to be the guardians of the only 'true faith.'"[9]

---

edition of which was edited by Hennecke and published in 1904, and the third and sixth German editions of which have been translated into English and published under the title *The New Testament Apocrypha*, Eng. trans. ed. R. McL. Wilson, 2 vols. (Philadelphia: Westminster, 1963; rev. ed., 1991). On the seventh edition in relation to more recent trends in German scholarship, see further below.

[5] Stephen Shoemaker, "Early Christian Apocryphal Literature," in *The Oxford Handbook of Early Christian Studies*, ed. Susan Ashbrook Harvey and David G. Hunter (Oxford: Oxford University Press, 2008), 521–48.

[6] Helmut H. Koester, "One Jesus and Four Primitive Gospels," *HTR* 61 (1968): 211; also, even more programmatically, idem, "Apocryphal and Canonical Gospels," *HTR* 73 (1980): 105–30, http://dx.doi.org/10.1017/S0017816000002066.

[7] Koester, "One Jesus and Four Primitive Gospels," 175.

[8] Elaine Pagels, *The Gnostic Gospels* (New York: Vintage, 1979), xv. Notably, she leaves these questions unanswered.

[9] Ibid., xvii. This emphasis resonates with the concern for diversity in research on those centuries since Walter Bauer's *Rechtgläubigkeit und ketzerei im ältesten Christentum*, BHT 10 (Tübingen: Mohr, 1934)—and especially since its English translation by the Philadelphia Seminar on Christian Origins: *Orthodoxy and Heresy in Earliest Christianity*, ed. Robert A. Kraft and Gerhard Krodel (Philadelphia: Fortress, 1971).

Among specialists, such theories have been debated for decades and attenuated accordingly. Their sway on the popular imagination, however, still remains. When parabiblical writings attract the attention of North American journalists, for instance, it is virtually always as a potential source of information about Jesus himself.[10] This is the valuation voiced in the wake of each new discovery, as the popular press frames their importance in terms of the likelihood that this or that manuscript might reveal Jesus's secret life or family, or the "real story" about his betrayal by Judas, or the like.[11] In response, even specialists sometimes seem pressed to backdate the materials at hand—or, at the very least, to broach the possibility that a late antique fragment or medieval compilation might preserve some fossil of the first or second century; it is this possibility, after all, that makes the translation of a Coptic manuscript into a matter to be reported in the *New York Times*.[12] Just as positive presentations of such writings in the popular press pivot on their potential to expose what church fathers supposedly suppressed, so their critics commonly counter such claims by dismissing the book in question as "late."[13]

---

[10] Note the appeal to the Infancy Gospel of Thomas, Pseudo-Matthew, Gospel of Peter, Gospel of Mary, and Gospel of Philip in the National Geographic documentary *The Secret Lives of Jesus* (2006) as well as the place of the Protevangelium of James in the nativity episode of their *Science of the Bible* series (2005). Some of the same materials appear in the History Channel's *Time Machine: Banned from the Bible* (2003) and *Banned from the Bible II* (2007).

[11] E.g., John Noble Wilford and Laurie Goodstein, "Gospel of Judas Surfaces after 1,700 Years," *New York Times*, 6 April 2006, A1; Laurie Goodstein, "Document Is Genuine, but Is Its Story True?" *New York Times*, 7 April 2006, A20—the latter stresses explicitly that "the *real* debate is whether the text says anything *historically* legitimate about Jesus and Judas" (italics mine). Likewise, even while quoting Marvin Meyer and Elaine Pagels asserting the importance of this find for illumining the diversity of early Christianity, the Associated Press headline proclaimed "Ancient manuscript suggests new relationship between Jesus and Judas" (6 April 2006).

[12] That is, as most recently the case with the "Gospel of Jesus' Wife." See, e.g., Laurie Goodstein, "A Faded Piece of Papyrus Refers to Jesus' Wife," *New York Times*, 18 September 2012, National Desk, p. 1—there stressing that Karen King "repeatedly cautioned that this fragment should not be taken as proof that Jesus, the historical person, was actually married," but nevertheless opining that "the discovery could reignite the debate over whether Jesus was married, whether Mary Magdalene was his wife and whether he had a female disciple." Other news sources were less cautious, proclaiming, "Ancient Papyrus Could Be Evidence That Jesus Had a Wife" (*Telegraph*, 19 September 2012); "Jesus 'Was Married,' Papyrus Scrap Reveals" (James Bone, *The Times* [London], 20 September 2012); and "Did Jesus Have a Wife?" (Jeremy Hsu, FoxNews.com, published 17 October 2012).

[13] For example, an article published about a month prior to the release of the Gospel of Judas and the 2006 National Geographic documentary on it reported James T. Robinson's caution that "there are a lot of second-, third- and fourth-century gospels attributed to various apostles.... We don't really assume they give us any first century information" (Richard N. Ostling, "The mysterious Gospel of Judas won't tell us anything about Jesus' infamous disciple, an expert predicts," Associated Press, 2 March 2006). Even though the original article stressed that "the text is valuable to scholars of the second century," others soon interpreted this assertion as a dismissal

What is reinscribed, in both cases, is the assumption that the value of such works is proportional to their antiquity.

To be sure, there are very few specialists in NT apocrypha who would frame their significance in quite this fashion. But there are also very few who have not experienced some version of the bias whereby "early" texts of this sort are presumed to be more important than "late" ones and whereby parabiblical writings are treated as sources of *either* hidden truth *or* forged falsehood. It is not just that scholars are faced with the minor industry of sensationalizing such works as "secret," "lost," "forbidden," or "suppressed" in popular print, television, and documentary journalism, and the counterindustry of answering such claims in Christian confessional contexts. Many of the same assumptions are structurally embedded within modern scholarship. Consistent with the marginalization implied by the term "apocrypha" (lit., hidden things), their study has not been fully integrated into biblical studies. Even in the accounts of Koester and Pagels, parabiblical literature is relegated to the realm of the ancient, secret, and suppressed. More recent introductory works—such as Bart Ehrman's 2003 *Lost Scriptures: Books That Did Not Make It into the New Testament* and Tony Burke's 2013 *Secret Scriptures Revealed*—dispel this esotericism but still bear titles that evoke it.[14] Others who have sought to debunk such tropes for a popular audience, moreover, have typically done so in a manner geared specifically to Christian readers, asserting the authenticity of NT literature by denigrating its apocryphal counterparts as inauthentic, inferior, and "late."[15]

This essay is an experiment in reversing the arrow of valuation to focus instead on the afterlives of NT apocrypha. To do so, I first historicize the assumption that the significance of apostolically aligned parabiblical writings rises or falls with their value for the recovery of a secret history of Christian origins. Tracing the genealogy of this idea from late antiquity to the present, I show how it came to predominate in the early modern period, particularly at the public interface of specialist and popular perspectives in Anglophone milieux. I then turn to suggest, however, that this is only one of many trajectories in the reception of such works. It is certainly possible to draw a line connecting late antique denunciations of "apocrypha" to

---

of the work as completely irrelevant: "Scholar: Gospel of Judas will be flop" (*Commercial Appeal*, 3 March 2006); "Scholar predicts *Judas* will be dud" (*Deseret News*, 3 March 2006); "Judas text unlikely to say much: Document is not old enough" (*Washington Times*, 7 March 2006).

[14] Bart Ehrman, *Lost Scriptures: Books That Did Not Make It into the New Testament* (Oxford: Oxford University Press, 2003); Tony Burke, *Secret Scriptures Revealed: A New Introduction to the Christian Apocrypha* (Grand Rapids: Eerdmans, 2013).

[15] E.g., N. T. Wright, *Judas and the Gospel of Judas: Have We Missed the Truth about Christianity?* (Grand Rapids: Baker, 2006); Ben Witherington III, *What Have They Done with Jesus? Beyond Strange Theories and Bad History—Why We Can Trust the Bible* (San Francisco: HarperCollins, 2006); Craig A. Evans, *Fabricating Jesus: How Modern Scholars Distort the Gospels* (Downers Grove, IL: InterVarsity Press, 2006).

early modern collections of NT apocrypha to the popularization of conspiracy theories about lost Gospels preserving suppressed secrets about the life of Jesus. Yet the afterlives of "apocrypha" also include much information that does not fit along this one thin line. Examples from late antique and medieval art and literature highlight the dazzlingly diverse range of forms and contexts in which parabiblical writings were received and repurposed, and they push us to expand our purview for their reception in the present as well. Just as the historical significance of these parabiblical writings goes well beyond debates about the bounds of biblical canons, so their influence today is not limited to Christian believers or even to the West, even encompassing unexpected genres like East Asian manga and anime.

In specialist research on Infancy Gospels and Marian apocrypha, attention has already begun to shift away from the reconstruction of their *Ur*-texts and the pinpointing of origins for their constituent motifs and toward the multivalent mapping of their *Nachleben*.[16] Likewise, some of the most productive areas of recent research on apocryphal acts are not in biblical studies at all but among scholars of late antiquity and the Middle Ages.[17] In what follows, I take these trends as an invitation to rethink the dominant narratives about the significance of NT apocrypha noted above and to engage a broader array of perspectives on the memory and meanings of the biblical past. In the process, attention to some of the more surprising paths in the afterlives of NT apocrypha may prove useful not just to counterbalance the privileging of origins pervasive within biblical studies but also to historicize and contextualize this very tendency, pushing us to assess the value and limits of older approaches even as we chart new paths and possibilities ahead.

---

[16] E.g., Mary Dzon and Theresa M. Kenney, eds., *The Christ Child in Medieval Culture: Alpha es et O!* (Toronto: University of Toronto Press, 2012); Stephen J. Davis, *Christ Child: Cultural Memories of a Young Jesus*, Synkrisis (New Haven: Yale University Press, 2014), http://dx.doi.org/10.12987/yale/9780300149456.001.0001; Cornelia Horn, "Mary between Bible and Qurʾān," *Islam and Muslim-Christian Relations* 18 (2007): 509–38, http://dx.doi.org/10.1080/09596410701577332; Stephen Shoemaker, "Between Scripture and Tradition: The Marian Apocrypha of Early Christianity," in *The Reception and Interpretation of the Bible in Late Antiquity: Proceedings of the Montréal Colloquium in Honour of Charles Kannengiesser, 11–13 October 2006*, ed. Lorenzo DiTommaso and Lucian Turcescu, Bible in Ancient Christianity 6 (Leiden: Brill, 2008), 491–510; idem, "The Virgin Mary's Hidden Past: From Ancient Marian Apocrypha to the Medieval *vitae Virginis*," *Marian Studies* 60 (2009): 1–30.

[17] E.g., Scott Fitzgerald Johnson, "Apocrypha and the Literary Past in Late Antiquity," in *From Rome to Constantinople: Studies in Honour of Averil Cameron*, ed. Hagit Amirav and Bas ter Haar Romeny, Late Antique History and Religion 1 (Leuven: Peeters, 2007), 47–66; idem, "Reviving the Memory of the Apostles: Apocryphal Tradition and Travel Literature in Late Antiquity," in *Revival and Resurgence in Christian History: Papers Read at the 2006 Summer Meeting and the 2007 Winter Meeting of the Ecclesiastical History Society*, ed. Kate Cooper and Jeremy Gregory, SCH 44 (Woodbridge, UK: Boydell, 2008), 1–26; Els Rose, *Ritual Memory: The Apocryphal Acts and Liturgical Commemoration in the Early Medieval West (c. 500–1215)*, Mittellateinische Studien und Texte 40 (Leiden: Brill, 2009).

I. Toward a Genealogy of New Testament Apocrypha as Countercanon

The notion that NT apocrypha preserve secret teachings and lost histories is rooted, to some degree, in the rhetoric of some of the ancient texts now categorized under this rubric. The Apocalypse of Paul, for instance, is prefaced by an account of its own loss and rediscovery, and parts of the Pseudo-Clementine corpus claim to preserve the real teachings of Jesus, James, and Peter, as misrepresented by Paul and Luke.[18] One need only read the first lines of the Gospel of Thomas or the Apocryphon of James to find examples of secrecy construed as an emblem of apostolic truth in the Nag Hammadi codices as well.[19] The generalization of this idea into a textual category of "apocrypha," however, awaited the period of Christian canon formation in late antiquity, while the modern sense of NT apocrypha as corpus or countercanon did not take form until well after the Protestant Reformation.

In the NT, the Greek adjective ἀπόκρυφος is used either neutrally or positively (Mark 4:22, Luke 8:17, Col 2:3). The term came to take on negative connotations, especially when applied to texts within the heresiological discourse of early Christianity.[20] In the second century, Irenaeus accused the Valentinians of "gather[ing] their views from other sources than the Scriptures" (*Haer.* 1.4.1; also 3.11.9), and he claimed that the Marcosians deliberately created "apocryphal and spurious writings" [ἀποκρύφων καὶ νόθων γραφῶν] to deceive the ignorant (1.20.1). In this, he appears to answer claims about hidden knowledge akin to those expressed in the texts noted above, reversing the valence of secrecy and interpreting the trope of

---

[18] Pierluigi Piovanelli, "The Miraculous Discovery of the Hidden Manuscript, or the Paratextual Function of the Prologue to the *Apocalypse of Paul*," in *The Visio Pauli and the Gnostic Apocalypse of Paul*, ed. Jan N. Bremmer and István Czachesz, Studies on Early Christian Apocrypha 9 (Leuven: Peeters, 2007), 23–49; Annette Yoshiko Reed, "'Jewish Christianity' as Counterhistory? The Apostolic Past in Eusebius' *Ecclesiastical History* and the Pseudo-Clementine *Homilies*," in *Antiquity in Antiquity: Jewish and Christian Pasts in the Greco-Roman World*, ed. Gregg Gardner and Kevin L. Osterloh, TSAJ 123 (Tübingen: Mohr Siebeck, 2008), 173–216.

[19] Antti Marjanen, "Sethian Books of the Nag Hammadi Library as Secret Books," in *Mystery and Secrecy in the Nag Hammadi Collection and Other Ancient Literature: Ideas and Practices. Studies for Einar Thomassen*, ed. Christian H. Bull, Liv Ingeborg Lied, and John D. Turner, NHMS 76 (Leiden: Brill, 2012), 87–106.

[20] The textualization of the term could also have positive connotations, as when the neuter form of ἀπόκρυφον and its Coptic counterpart were "used as a noun with the connotation of a 'secret book'" in book titles such as Apocryphon of John and Apocryphon of James (Marjanen, "Sethian Books," 90). Note also Origen's neutral use of ἀπόκρυφα, as discussed by William Adler, "The Pseudepigrapha in the Early Church," in *The Canon Debate*, ed. Lee M. McDonald and James A. Sanders (Peabody, MA: Hendriksen, 2002), 211–28.

hidden truth as merely a ruse to invent an ancient lineage for new ideas.[21] Although often cited, however, these passages remain somewhat exceptional: even as Irenaeus makes an early and influential association of "apocrypha" with "heresy,"[22] he himself remains far more concerned to answer those who "abuse the Scriptures by endeavoring to support their own system out of them" (1.9.1).[23] Furthermore, like other second- and third-century Christians, he exhibits some interest in delimiting the bounds of Scripture while not yet assuming or promoting a closed canon per se.[24]

Irenaeus's approach to "apocryphal and spurious writings" was picked up and extended in the fourth and fifth centuries, concurrent with the rise of more systematic attempts to list the contents of Christian Scripture, to define its bounds, and to promote it as a norm for all Christian communities within the Roman Empire. Most influential in this regard was Athanasius's Thirty-Ninth Festal Letter (367 CE), well known as the earliest source to apply the term "canonized" to a group of texts.[25] It is also here that we find the term "apocrypha" deployed in the categorical sense determinative for later canon lists. Athanasius enumerated OT and NT Scriptures, and he set works like the Didache in an intermediate category of books to be "read." Others, however, were dismissed as "so-called apocrypha," which should not be read even if they might appear to contain some value. Not only did he depict

---

[21] André Benoit, "Écriture et tradition chez Saint Irénée," *RHPR* 40 (1960): 41–43; Guy G. Stroumsa, *Hidden Wisdom: Esoteric Traditions and the Roots of Christian Mysticism*, SHR 70 (Leiden: Brill, 1996), 30, 38, 85–86; Annette Yoshiko Reed, "ΕΥΑΓΓΕΛΙΟΝ: Orality, Textuality, and the Christian Truth in Irenaeus' *Adversus Haereses*," *VC* 56 (2002): 22.

[22] Compare the comments attributed to Hegesippus in Eusebius, *Hist. eccl.* 4.22.9. One finds a similar use of the term in Clement, *Strom.* 3.4.29.1—although note also 1.15.69.6, where βίβλοι ἀπόκρυφοι refers to writings associated with Zoroaster. The Latin equivalent is used by Tertullian of the Shepherd of Hermas in *Pud.* 10.6.

[23] Irenaeus, *Haer.* 1.1.3; 1.3.4–6; 1.8–9; 1.18–19; 1.29.11; 2.praef.1, 10.1, 27.3; 3.12.12, 21.3; 4.26.1; 5.13.5; Frances M. Young, *Biblical Exegesis and the Formation of Christian Culture* (Cambridge: Cambridge University Press, 1997), 18–21, http://dx.doi.org/10.1017/CBO9780511583216; Elaine Pagels, "Irenaeus, the Canon of Truth, and the Gospel of John," *VC* 56 (2002): 339–71.

[24] Reed, "ΕΥΑΓΓΕΛΙΟΝ," 11–46; Lee M. McDonald, *The Formation of the Christian Biblical Canon*, rev. and expanded ed. (Peabody, MA: Hendrickson, 1995), 170–72. Contrast Irenaeus's much-cited comments about the "fourfold Gospel" in *Haer.* 3.11.8, for instance, with his concept of the "κανών of truth" as an extratextual measure of proper belief and biblical exegesis in 1.praef.1–2, 3.6, 8.1, 9.1–5; 2.praef.1, etc.

[25] McDonald, *Formation of the Christian Biblical Canon*, 13–18; David Brakke, "Canon Formation and Social Conflict in Fourth-Century Egypt," *HTR* 87 (1994): 395–419, http://dx.doi.org/10.1017/S0017816000030200; Brakke, "A New Fragment of Athanasius's Thirty-Ninth Festal Letter: Heresy, Apocrypha, and the Canon," *HTR* 103 (2010): 47–66, http://dx.doi.org/10.1017/S0017816009990307; Pierluigi Piovanelli, "Rewriting: The Path from Apocryphal to Heretical," in *Religious Conflict from Early Christianity to the Rise of Islam*, ed. Wendy Mayer and Bronwen Neil, Arbeiten zur Kirchengeschichte 121 (Berlin: de Gruyter, 2013), 87–108.

"apocrypha" and "heresy" as coterminous, but he generalized this assessment into a taxonomic principle within a system of textual categorization wherein "canonized" Scriptures become elevated as unique sources of "orthodoxy."[26] As with Irenaeus, Athanasius's own arguments pivoted more on epistemology and exegesis than on the problem of parabiblical literary production per se.[27] In the process, however, he reframed the range of disagreements as if a dichotomy, thus providing a powerful precedent for the appeal to "apocrypha" as a rhetorical foil to argue for the uniqueness of "canonized Scriptures" (e.g., as "orthodox" as opposed to "heretical," authentic as opposed to spurious, public as opposed to secret, inspired as opposed to invented).

That Athanasius's notion of "apocrypha" differed from modern senses, however, is clear from the scope of his category. When he cited specific examples, for instance, what he adduced were writings of the sort that scholars now call "OT pseudepigrapha"—works that claim authorship by figures like Enoch, Moses, or Isaiah. This pattern departed from Irenaeus but had some precedent in Origen.[28] The articulations of the category of "apocrypha" with a focus on the OT, moreover, also finds some parallel in Jerome, who famously used the same term to question the canonicity of works like Judith, Tobit, Wisdom of Solomon, Wisdom of Ben Sira, and 1–2 Maccabees.[29]

Throughout late antiquity and the Middle Ages, the category of "apocrypha" remained fluid, encompassing a shifting set of writings associated with figures from both OT and NT, as well as other writings deemed either forbidden for Christian use or acceptable only for nonliturgical or learned consultation. The Apostolic Constitutions, for instance, has the apostles caution (pseudepigraphically) against "those books which obtain in our name but are written by the ungodly" but also warn that "among the ancients too, some have written apocryphal books [βιβλία ἀπόκρυφα] of Moses, Enoch, Adam, Isaiah, David, Elijah, and of the three patriarchs—pernicious and repugnant to the truth" (6.16). Likewise, texts listed as "apocrypha" in the Gelasian Decree include Testament of Job, Shepherd of Hermas,

---

[26] Compare the rabbinic category of "outside books": m. Sanh. 10:1; y. Sanh. 10:1; b. Sanh. 100b; m. Yad. 4:6; t. Yad. 2:13; Num. Rab. 14:4; Pesiq. Rab. 3:9.

[27] Brakke, "New Fragment of Athanasius's Thirty-Ninth Festal Letter," 56.

[28] Adler, "Pseudepigrapha in the Early Church," 212–24. See also Augustine, *Civ.* 15.23, 18.38, on the problem of the citation of "apocrypha" such as the books of Enoch by NT writers like Jude, as well as the argument in favor of "apocrypha" on this basis made by Priscillian and others (Andrew Jacobs, "The Disorder of Books," *HTR* 93 [2000]: 135–59).

[29] Bonifatius Fischer et al., eds., *Biblia Sacra iuxta Vulgatam Versionem*, 4th ed. (Stuttgart: Deutsche Bibelgesellschaft, 1994), 365, 957. Jerome seems to be the first to use "apocrypha" to refer to some Jewish-authored books in Christian Old Testaments but not in the Tanak. Although common among Protestants today, his proposal did not find much acceptance in its own time. On the reactions by Rufinus and Augustine, and the effects on the discourse about canonicity in the Latin West, see Thomas O'Loughlin, "Inventing the Apocrypha," *ITQ* 74 (2009): 59–65.

and writings of Tertullian, Eusebius, and Lactantius, alongside apocalypses associated with Paul and Thomas, acts attributed to Andrew, Thomas, Peter, and Philip, and gospels associated with Matthias, Barnabas, James, Peter, Thomas, Bartholomaeus, Andrew, Lucian, and Hesychius.

William Adler has shown how anxieties about apocrypha clustered in the period of canon formation, after which Christians tended to be more open to their use.[30] Yet even in late antiquity, as Stephen Shoemaker notes, "the anti-apocryphal rhetoric of certain church fathers did not always correspond with the real status of apocrypha in Christian churches."[31] Below, I will survey some of the ample evidence for the continued use of such writings, both during and after the eras in which theologians and canon lists denounce them. For now, it suffices to note that the discursive practice of denouncing apocrypha is one distinctive trajectory in the afterlives of parabiblical writings—important in its own right but not necessarily determinative for the rest.

Isidore of Seville, for instance, attests the ongoing appeal to apocrypha as a contrastive category to elevate canonical Scriptures as inerrant, inspired, and authentic.[32] Furthermore, as Thomas O'Loughlin has shown, Isidore's approach is but one of many medieval examples of the "logical device of assuming that there was a contradictory opposition between the category 'scripture' and the category 'apocrypha,' namely that they opposed each other in all respects without overlaps."[33] Just as medieval denunciations of apocrypha often function more to theorize Scripture than to police the actual usage of parabiblical writings, so too with the continued compilation of canon lists: the lists may tell us more about theories of textual authority than about actual reading practices in the Middle Ages.

It is in one of these lists—the ninth-century *Stichometry of Nicephorus*—that we first find a systematic distinction between apocrypha associated with the OT and those associated with the NT.[34] The former include works that modern scholars now call OT pseudepigrapha, such as the books of Enoch and the Testaments of the Twelve Patriarchs. The latter include works associated with apostles, such as the Gospel of Thomas and "circuits" of Paul, Peter, John, and Thomas, listed alongside works like the Didache and the writings of Clement, Ignatius, and Polycarp. In the Middle Ages, this distinction seems to have been more theory than practice. Centuries later, however, it would provide an important precedent for the modern

---

[30] So Adler, "Pseudepigrapha in the Early Church," 227–28, citing Jacob of Edessa, *Epistle* 13.15 and other evidence for use of what we now call OT Pseudepigrapha; for examples pertaining to NT apocrypha, see below.

[31] Shoemaker, "Early Christian Apocryphal Literature," 526.

[32] O'Loughlin, "Inventing the Apocrypha," 53–55; Rose, *Ritual Memory*, 42–78.

[33] O'Loughlin, "Inventing the Apocrypha," 55.

[34] The former are introduced by Καὶ ὅσα ἀπόκρυφα τῆς παλαιᾶς [sc. διαθήκης], and the latter by Καὶ ὅσα τῆς νέας εἰσὶν ἀπόκρυφα; *Nicephori archiepiscopi Constantinopolitani opuscula historica*, ed. Carolus de Boor, BSGRT (Leipzig: Teubner, 1880), 134–35.

systemization of such taxonomic distinctions and their practical application to the collection and transmission of texts.³⁵

Regardless of whether the rise of the codex was one impetus for the late antique interest in creating lists of "canonical" and "apocryphal" Scriptures, it is clear that the advent of printing played an important part in the renewed concern for textual taxonomies during and after the Reformation. As is well known, this era saw a shifting of textual taxonomies whereby some Jewish works that had long been interspersed in Christian Old Testaments came to be collected together and distinguished by Protestants as "Old Testament Apocrypha."³⁶ It was in the wake of this shift, in turn, that "Old Testament Pseudepigrapha" was invented as a new category to contain parabiblical works associated with biblical patriarchs and prophets—as now newly distinguished from their apostolically aligned counterparts in the NT apocrypha.³⁷

Both of these new categories were produced and popularized through the influential anthologies of the German bibliographer Johann Albert Fabricius (1668–1736). Fabricius published the first systematic printed anthology of NT apocrypha in 1703 and a second expanded edition beginning in 1719—both distinguished from his anthology of OT Pseudepigrapha, the first volume of which was published in 1713.³⁸ For his collection of NT apocrypha, Fabricius had some precedents.³⁹ Nevertheless, as Irena Backus has stressed, "not only did he assemble

---

³⁵ As Paul Foster stresses, "no systematic attempt to create a collection of non-canonical gospels is known in antiquity or the pre-Modern period" (*The Non-Canonical Gospels* [London: T&T Clark, 2008], vii).

³⁶ Daniel J. Harrington, "The Old Testament Apocrypha in the Early Church and Today," in McDonald and Sanders, *Canon Debate*, 196–210.

³⁷ J. A. Fabricius, *Codex pseudepigraphus Veteris Testamenti* (Hamburg: Felginer, 1713); idem, *Codicis pseudepigraphi Veteris Testamenti, volumen alterum accedit Josephi veteris Christiani auctoria Hypomnesticon* (Hamburg: Felginer, 1723)—on which see further Reed, "Modern Invention," 414–24.

³⁸ J. A. Fabricius, *Codex apocryphus Novi Testamenti* (Hamburg: Schiller, 1703; 2nd rev. ed., 1719). Part 1 of the first edition included the Gospel of the Nativity of Mary (pp. 1–39), Protevangelium of James (pp. 40–128), Infancy Gospel of Thomas and related materials (pp. 159–212), Gospel of Nicodemus and materials related to Pilate (pp. 238–300), Jesus's Letter to Abgar and related materials (pp. 301–20), as well as materials less often included in modern collections like the Epistola Lentuli. Part 2 focused more on apocryphal acts (pp. 743–833) and pseudepigraphical epistles such as Paul's Epistle to the Laodiceans and Correspondence with Seneca (pp. 853–906) and the Epistle of Peter to James (pp. 907–22).

³⁹ For the various precedents—including Michael Neander's *Apocrypha* (Basel, 1564)—see Edgar Hennecke, "Geschichte der Erforschung," in *Neutestamentliche Apokryphen* (Tübingen: Mohr, 1904), 1:22–24; Irena Backus, "Christoph Scheurl and His Anthology of 'New Testament Apocrypha' (1506, 1513, 1515)," *Apocrypha* 9 (1998): 133–56, http://dx.doi.org/10.2307/2901964; Backus, *Historical Method and Confessional Identity in the Era of the Reformation (1378–1615)*, SMRT 94 (Leiden: Brill, 2003), 253–325.

the hitherto dispersed writings into a corpus, but he was also the first to give them an extracanonical status" in a categorical fashion.[40] Fabricius's efforts were thus critical for the creation, popularization, and naturalization of the notion of the NT apocrypha as a countercanon, defined in contrast to the NT.[41]

It was with Fabricius that the term "NT apocrypha" became repurposed as an anthological rubric, naturalizing the long-standing contrast with "canonical Scriptures" but also newly isolating these particular parabiblical writings *both* from OT pseudepigrapha *and* from patristic literature. What had previously formed part of Christian literature was now cordoned off as a separate corpus, defined specifically in contrast to the NT. As for Athanasius in the fourth century and Isidore in the seventh, so too for Fabricius in the eighteenth: the circulation of numerous writings in the names of apostles endangered the integrity of what he considered to be Scripture. The early modern bibliographer, however, exhibits an unprecedented confidence that this danger could be neutralized by the collection, categorization, and publication of all known apocrypha. Even as his taxonomic and anthological practices were oriented toward ordering knowledge about the past, his practices—and their products—were thus shaped by the new technologies of memory within print culture as well as by attendant anxieties about forgery and false attribution.[42]

Fabricius's anthologies were widely used, serving as major reference works for scholars well into the twentieth century. Significantly, for our purposes, his *Codex apocryphus Novi Testamenti* also shaped the ways in which NT apocrypha were first read and studied *as such* in the English language. Around the same time that Fabricius was publishing his collections, William Whiston (1667–1752) was defending the apostolicity of works like the Apostolic Constitutions and the Pseudo-Clementine Recognitions. Not only did Whiston posit that these texts preserved elements of "Primitive Christianity" allegedly suppressed by Athanasius, but he argued for them "to be reckoned among the sacred authentick books of the New Testament; as also ... the Acts of Paul, [and] the Revelation, Preaching, Gospel, and Acts of Peter."[43]

---

[40] Irena Backus, "Renaissance Attitudes towards New Testament Apocryphal Writings: Jacques Lefèvre d'Étaples and His Epigones," *Renaissance Quarterly* 51 (1998): 1169.

[41] Before Fabricius, such materials were typically printed in whole or in part alongside works like the Testaments of the Twelve Patriarchs and patristic literature for the purposes of pious edification; see Irena Backus, "Praetorius' Anthology of New Testament Apocrypha (1595)," *Apocrypha* 12 (2001): 211–36 with n. 40.

[42] That is, extending Fabricius's participation in the compilation of lists of falsely attributed writings to bring order to the proliferating chaos of books in the wake of the advent of printing. See further Reed, "Modern Invention," 424–30; Martin Muslow, "Practices of Unmasking: Polyhistors, Correspondence, and the Birth of Dictionaries of Pseudonymity in 17th Century Germany," *Journal for the History of Ideas* 67 (2006): 219–50, http://dx.doi.org/10.1353/jhi.2006.0015.

[43] William Whiston, *Primitive Christianity Reviv'd*, 5 vols. (London, 1711–1712), e.g., 1:ii,

Whiston's theologically motivated efforts formed part of a broader continuum of interest in apocrypha in eighteenth-century England, encompassing the antiquarian pursuits of scholars but also their deployment by Deists as ammunition against established religion.[44] Most extensive were the interventions of the Irish freethinker John Toland (1670–1722). Appropriating and inverting the *Listenwissenschaft* of premodern canon formation, Toland compiled an extensive "Catalogue of Books attributed in the Primitive Times to Jesus Christ, his Apostles and other eminent Persons."[45] Here and elsewhere, Toland relativized the NT by pointing to the quantity of related sources known to ancient readers since Luke (1:1–2) and by reading these works with a skepticism about antiquity and authorship earlier reserved for apocrypha. Not only did he suggest that "there is not one single Book in the New Testament, which was not refus'd by som of the Ancients as unjustly fathr'd upon the Apostles," but he redescribed the Christian biblical canon as a product of acts of suppression and censorship in fourth-century ecumenical councils, wherein "the prevailing Party did strictly order all those Books which offended them to be burnt, or otherwise suppress."[46] In *Nazarenus*, he went even further, claiming to have discovered relics of the authentic but suppressed Christianity preserved in the Gospel of Barnabas.[47]

Here as elsewhere, Whiston and Toland were idiosyncratic. Yet the reactions that they sparked were influential—and included the catalyst for the first translation of Fabricius's *Codex apocryphus Novi Testamenti* into English. The Welsh minister Jeremiah Jones bemoaned that "the Canon has been judged imperfect, and it

---

defending Arius; and see further idem, *A collection of authentick records belonging to the Old and New Testament* (London, 1728); idem, *Athanasian forgeries, impositions, and interpolations* (London, 1736). Quotation from Whiston, "Essay on the Const.," 4, after Jeremiah Jones, *A New and Full Method of Settling the Canonical Authority of the New Testament* (Oxford: Clarendon, 1798), 6.

[44] Jonathan Sheehan, *The Enlightenment Bible: Translation, Scholarship, Culture* (Princeton: Princeton University Press, 2005), 39–44; Justin Champion, "Apocrypha, Canon and Criticism from Samuel Fisher to John Toland, 1650–1718," in *Judaeo-Christian Intellectual Culture in the Seventeenth Century: A Celebration of the Library of Narcissus Marsh (1638–1713)*, ed. Allison P. Coudert et al., Archives internationales d'histoire des idées 163 (Dordrecht: Kluwer, 1999), 91–117; Francis Schmidt, "John Toland, critique déiste de la littérature apocryphe," *Apocryphe* 1 (1990): 119–45.

[45] John Toland, *Amyntor, or, A defence of Milton's life* (London, 1699), 20–41, later expanded into *A Catalogue of Books Mentioned by the Fathers and Other Ancient Writers, as Truly or Falsely ascrib'd to Jesus Christ, his Apostles, and other eminent persons* (London, 1726).

[46] Toland, *Amyntor*, 56; idem, *Life of John Milton* (London, 1699), 92. See further Pierre Lurbe, "'Those Fabulous Dragons Teeth': Invented beginnings, lost causes and new beginnings in John Toland's *Amyntor* (1699)," *Études anglaises* 66 (2013): 134–46—although there taking such suppression at face value.

[47] John Toland, *Nazarenus, or, Jewish, Gentile, and Mahometan Christianity*, 2nd rev. ed. (London, 1718).

has been thought necessary by several learned men, that some other books which are in being, and the remaining fragments of those which are lost, should be received"—citing, in particular, "How much Mr. Whiston has enlarged the Canon of the New Testament."[48] To answer this assault on the canon, Jones included translations of the apocrypha collected by Fabricius as part of his 1798 treatise *A New and Full Method of Settling the Canonical Authority of the New Testament*, which would be widely consulted by churchmen and scholars alike.[49]

The debate became even more widely disseminated when Jones's translations were reprinted for broader public consumption in 1820 by the controversial bookseller William Hone (1780–1842). Hone chose the catchier title *The Apocryphal New Testament*, and in his subtitle, he claimed to collect in one affordable volume *All the Gospels, Epistles and Other Pieces Now Extant, Attributed in The First Four Centuries to Jesus Christ, His Apostles, and Their Companions and Not Included in the New Testament By Its Compilers*. The very first line of its first page placed these translations in a context very different from that intended by Jones: "After the writings contained in the New Testament were selected from the numerous Gospels and Epistles then in existence, what became of the Books that were rejected by the compilers?"[50] Hone claimed to publish what had been omitted, such that "he who possesses this and the New Testament has, in the two volumes, a collection of all the historical records relative to Christ and his Apostles, now in existence, and considered sacred by Christians during the first four centuries after his birth."[51] Hone's edition was cobbled together from Jones's *New and Full Method* and William Wake's 1693 *The Genuine Epistles of the Apostolic Fathers*—but with one important difference, as J. W. Robinson notes: "Neither Jones' nor Wake's book looks like a New Testament; but Hone subdivided their chapters into verses, provided summaries at the head of each chapter, and printed two columns to a page, so that the results ... look rather aggressively like an edition of the Authorized Version."[52]

Much like Toland, Hone interpreted the fourth-century closing of the biblical canon as akin to an act of censorship.[53] This notion resonated with concerns about clerical power in his own time but also with his particular personal situation: when Hone published these apocrypha, he was already famous for having suffered three governmental prosecutions for blasphemous libel and for having successfully

---

[48] Jones, *New and Full Method*, 5–6, also 20–21, 316, 334, 357, 373, 442.

[49] Bruce M. Metzger, *The Canon of the New Testament: Its Origin, Development, and Significance* (Oxford: Clarendon, 1987), 14.

[50] William Hone, *Apocryphal New Testament* (London, 1820), iii.

[51] Ibid., vi–viii. This approach has some precedent in Toland's notion that "the true Writings of Apostles us'd to be bound up in a one Volum with the Apocryphal" (*Amyntor*, 71–72)—an interesting example of the retrojection of early modern print culture into pre-Nicene Christianity.

[52] J. W. Robinson, "Regency Radicalism and Antiquarianism: William Hone's *Ancient Mysteries Described* (1823)," *Leeds Studies in English* 10 (1978): 127.

[53] Hone, *Apocryphal New Testament*, iii–vi.

defended his right to parody political and religious authorities.[54] Although Hone was no stranger to controversy, even he was surprised at the wrath aroused by his *Apocryphal New Testament*, and he eventually regretted having published it.[55] Nevertheless, it would become his most widely read publication—reprinted to this day, both under his original title and also under an even catchier alternate title since 1926, *The Lost Books of the Bible*.

Inasmuch as the eighteenth and early nineteenth centuries were determinative for the emergence of the category of NT apocrypha, it proves significant that scholarly, religious, and popular interest in this literature centered on debates over the integrity of the NT—as defended by thinkers like Fabricius and Jones, and questioned and relativized by thinkers like Whiston, Toland, and Hone. Despite their many differences, they all operated under the shared assumption that such parabiblical writings are *either* "late" forgeries that serve only to highlight the antiquity, apostolicity, and historicity of the NT *or* potential sources for exposing the suppressed truth, which undermine ecclesiastical claims about the canon and, hence, the church's authority to censor diversity of opinion. In their notions of NT apocrypha, we see how the early modern transition from manuscript culture to print culture also shifted the discourse surrounding parabiblical writings away from the ancient evocation of secrecy and textual loss and toward more modern concerns with forgery and censorship.[56]

Hone's collection remained the dominant resource for NT apocrypha in English until the collection of M. R. James in 1924. James was attuned to the danger that the very collections of translations that make these writings more accessible can also reinscribe the misleading notion that they function together as a countercanon to the NT. He thus expressed some concern that the title *Apocryphal New Testament* implied a set corpus, even as he nevertheless retained the title as conventional, as did J. K. Elliot after him.[57] When James's collection was superseded

---

[54] William Hone, *The Three Trials of William Hone for Publishing Three Parodies* (London, 1818); Marcus Wood, *Radical Satire and Print Culture, 1790-1822*, Oxford English Monographs (Oxford: Clarendon, 1994); Joss Marsh, *Word Crimes: Blasphemy, Culture and Literature in Nineteenth-Century England* (Chicago: University of Chicago Press, 1998), 18–60.

[55] William Hone, *Aspersions Answered: An Explanatory Statement, Addressed to the Public at Large, and to Every Reader of the Quarterly Review in Particular* (London, 1824). In the wake of the controversy, he also published a collection of medieval plays to underline the widespread diffusion of NT apocrypha: *Ancient Mysteries Described, especially the English Miracle Plays, founded on Apocryphal New Testament Story* (London, 1823).

[56] In addition, printing enabled the concretization of canon lists into physical anthologies, which could be widely diffused among a variety of readers, thus potentially collapsing the earlier gap between the theory and practice surrounding apocrypha. Yet it also facilitated the potential presentation and reception of NT apocrypha as if they formed a countercanon of temptingly forbidden texts.

[57] Elliot, *Apocryphal New Testament*, xi.

in 1963 by the English translation of the third edition of Edgar Hennecke and Wilhelm Schneemelcher's *Neutestamentliche Apokryphen*, this sense of counter-canon arose again—in part because of Schneemelcher's provisional definition of the term as denoting "writings which have not been received into the canon, and which from the point of view of Form Criticism further develop and mould the kinds of style created and received in the NT."[58]

French-language scholarship has long modeled a different approach—from Éric Junod's critiques of Schneemelcher since the 1980s to the much broader scope of *Écrits apocryphes chrétiens* (1997, 2005).[59] Today, specialists working in English and German are increasingly following suit, not least by adopting the alternate terminology of "Christian apocrypha" and the broader scope that it enables.[60] This shift of terminology, as Shoemaker notes, embodies recent efforts "to remove [these texts] from the shadow of the New Testament writings and to free them from the biblical concepts and categories that have heretofore dominated their study and interpretation."[61]

Nevertheless, the notion of NT apocrypha as countercanon continues to have powerful cultural effects on contemporary popular discourse. Particularly in North America, older ideas about "Lost Books of the Bible" have dovetailed with the renewed curiosity about apocrypha in the wake of the discovery of the Nag Hammadi codices in the middle of the twentieth century, thereby reigniting

---

[58] Schneemelcher, "Canonical and Apocryphal," in *New Testament Apocrypha*, 1:27. Shoemaker thus points to Schneemelcher as the proximate cause for the widespread view of NT apocrypha as "failed scriptures" and especially for its establishment in the twentieth century as "a doctrine of early Christian studies" (Shoemaker, "Apocrypha and Liturgy in the Fourth Century," in *Jewish and Christian Scriptures: The Function of "Canonical" and "Non-canonical" Religious Texts*, ed. James H. Charlesworth and Lee Martin McDonald, Jewish and Christian Texts in Contexts and Related Studies 7 [London: T&T Clark, 2010], 153–54).

[59] Beginning with Éric Junod, "Apocryphes du Nouveau Testament ou apocryphes chrétiens anciens?" *ETR* 59 (1983): 409–21, and leading to some attenuation of the above claims in later editions of *Neutestamentliche Apokryphen*.

[60] Consistent with the embrace of the broader category, *Écrits apocryphes chrétiens* is much more expansive than its English and German counterparts, including Christian-authored texts associated with biblical patriarchs and prophets that have been more often studied under the rubric of OT pseudepigrapha (e.g., Ascension of Isaiah, Apocalypse of Sedrach, Odes of Solomon, and various Ezran works in Bovon and Geoltrain, *Écrits apocryphes chrétiens I*, 499–670) but also medieval works that extend earlier apocrypha. *Antike christliche Apokryphen in deutscher Übersetzung*, vol. 1, ed. Christoph Markschies and Jens Schröter (Tübingen: Mohr Siebeck, 2012) moves in the same direction, as does Tony Burke and Brent Landau's forthcoming *More Christian Apocrypha*. See further Christophe Markschies, "Neutestamentliche Apokryphen: Bemerkungen zu Geschichte und Zukunft einer von Edgar Hennecke im Jahr 1904 begründeten Quellensammlung," *Apocryphe* 9 (1998): 97–132; Tobias Nicklas, "*Écrits apocryphes chrétiens*: Ein Sammelband als Spiegel eines Weitreichenden Paradigmenwechsels in der Apokryphenforschung," *VC* 61 (2007): 70–95.

[61] Shoemaker, "Early Christian Apocryphal Literature," 521.

popular optimism in the power of parabiblical writings to restore what church fathers supposedly suppressed.[62] It is in this context, for instance, that texts such as the Gospel of Philip and the Gospel of Mary have become fodder for novels like Dan Brown's *Da Vinci Code*, and it is also in this context that their fictional worlds can feed the fires of sensationalist journalism—as peddled in part, for profit, by the modern-day heirs of controversialists like Hone. As in the age of Whiston, we find popular interest in parabiblical literature alongside religious efforts to experiment with expanding the bounds of Christian Scripture, such as most recently in Hal Taussig's *New New Testament*.[63] And, as in the age of Jones, positive interest has been countered by polemics that defend the received canon of the NT by attempting to unmask "apocryphal" counterparts as forged, fanciful, or "late."[64]

Tony Burke has analyzed the denigration of NT apocrypha by theologians and scholars like Ben Witherington III and Craig Evans, suggesting that their rhetoric echoes that of heresiologists like Irenaeus.[65] More pressing, for our purposes, are the assumptions that they share with Taussig—and with Fabricius, Whiston, Toland, Jones, and Hone before them. Arguments on both sides of the current debate function to reduce the question of the value of NT apocrypha to what these texts may or may not tell us about the origins of Christianity, and whether they can (or should) contribute to the encounter with Scripture among Christians in particular. Both the popularizing promoters of these texts and their critics treat their significance as predicated on their antiquity; by this logic, to reveal such works as "late" is also to unmask them as irrelevant.

II. Apocryphal Afterlives from Medieval Art to Modern Anime

Today, there is a potent intersection between popular, Christian, and scholarly conversations about NT apocrypha that resonates with late antique and medieval

---

[62] Maia Kotrosits, "Romance and Danger at Nag Hammadi," *Bible and Critical Theory* 8 (2012): 39–52; Emily McAvan, *The Postmodern Sacred: Popular Culture Spirituality in the Science Fiction, Fantasy and Urban Fantasy Genres* (Jefferson, NC: McFarland, 2012), 98–107.

[63] Hal Taussig, ed., *A New New Testament: A Bible for Twenty-first Century, Combining Traditional and Newly Discovered Texts* (Boston: Houghton Mifflin Harcourt, 2013). Aside from the Odes of Solomon and Acts of Paul and Thecla, most of the "added" works here are writings popularized by Pagels's *Gnostic Gospels*, particularly in relation to the possible preservation of perspectives on gender and knowledge suppressed by later ecclesiarchs (e.g., Gospel of Thomas, Thunder: Perfect Mind, Gospel of Mary, Gospel of Truth, Apocryphon of John).

[64] E.g., Witherington, *What Have They Done*; Evans, *Fabricating Jesus*; Darrell L. Bock, *The Missing Gospels: Unearthing the Truth behind Alternative Christianities* (Nashville: Nelson, 2006); Darrell L. Bock and Daniel B. Wallace, *Dethroning Jesus: Exposing Popular Culture's Quest to Unseat the Biblical Christ* (Nashville: Nelson, 2007).

[65] Tony Burke, "Heresy Hunting in the New Millennium," *SR* 39 (2010): 405–20.

theorization of apocrypha as the opposite of canonical Scriptures as well as with its early modern concretization into printed collections. Yet this is only one piece of the story of the contemporary reception of these materials. Perhaps much more diffuse—both demographically and geographically—is the remarkable creativity sparked by these writings, especially now with the widespread availability of older anthologies both in reprints and online. Attending to this creativity, in turn, may aid us in uncoupling the judgment of the significance of NT apocrypha from the question of their antiquity.

To be sure, some of this creativity resonates with the trajectories traced above. The appeal to the Gospel of Mary, Gospel of Philip, and Acts of Thomas in Brown's *Da Vinci Code* and the reuse of themes from the Infancy Gospel of Thomas by Anne Rice, for instance, activate much the same allure as Whiston's evocation of apocrypha as lost sources for ancient truths.[66] Likewise, the playful docetism of Philip Pullman's *The Good Man Jesus and the Scoundrel Christ* has an ancestor in Toland's rationalistic appeal to alternate Christianities to parody organized religion.[67] It is perhaps not accidental, in turn, that novels of this sort have inspired responses by Christian authors attuned to the broader cultural resonance of even fictional worlds.[68]

Yet creative engagement with these texts is not limited to concern with Christianity. Some of the most vibrant trajectories in their contemporary afterlives, in fact, can be found in non-Western and secular contexts—most notably, in the Japanese illustrative genres of manga and anime.[69] In some cases the debt to specific ancient texts is clear, as in the reuse of names and ideas from the Apocryphon of John in Hiroki Endo's *Eden*.[70] In other cases, influence is less direct, with names, terms, and motifs mediated by the mining of parabiblical literature by earlier authors and artists working within the same tradition. Some of the first prominent

---

[66] Dan Brown, *The Da Vinci Code: A Novel* (New York: Doubleday, 2003); Anne Rice, *Christ the Lord: Out of Egypt* (New York: Knopf, 2005).

[67] Philip Pullman, *The Good Man Jesus and the Scoundrel Christ* (Edinburgh: Canongate, 2010).

[68] E.g., Darrell L. Bock, *Breaking The Da Vinci Code: Answers to the Questions Everyone's Asking* (Nashville: Nelson, 2004); Ben Witherington III, *The Gospel Code: Novel Claims about Jesus, Mary Magdalene, and Da Vinci* (Downers Grove, IL: InterVarsity Press, 2004); Hugh Rayment-Pickard, *The Devil's Account: Philip Pullman and Christianity* (London: Darton, Longman & Todd, 2004). Interestingly, Rayment-Pickard cites a *Daily Telegraph* article from 7 April 2010, in which Pullman mentions James's *Apocryphal New Testament* (pp. 16–17, 23–29).

[69] For an introduction that focuses on religious themes, see Jolyon Baraka Thomas, *Drawing on Tradition: Manga, Anime, and Religion in Contemporary Japan* (Honolulu: University of Hawai'i Press, 2012). The key question, as Thomas there notes (p. viii), is "Why—in light of Japan's evident and often fervent secularism—were manga and anime with apparently religious themes so numerous and so popular?"

[70] Published serially in 月刊アフタヌーン from 1998 to 2008, and now partially accessible in graphic novel form in English (4 vols.; Milwaukie, OR: Dark Horse, 2005–2006).

manga and anime to use Western religious themes—such as Kaori Yuki's manga *Angel Sanctuary* (天使禁猟区)[71] and Anno Hideaki's anime *Neon Genesis Evangelion* (新世紀エヴァンゲリオン)[72]—were influential enough that others followed their lead. Names of angels, demons, and otherworldly realms have been culled from NT apocrypha and OT pseudepigrapha for reuse in and across story lines about imagined futures and cosmic realities—sometimes alongside fresh twists on Japanese folklore about foxes, forest spirits, and hungry ghosts, and sometimes entwined with modern mythologies of robots and aliens.[73] For this, apocryphal apocalypses have proved particularly rich reservoirs, and perhaps partly as a result, subgenres common therein, such as heavenly ascents and tours of hell, now have counterparts in manga, anime, and video games as well.[74]

The phenomenon, moreover, is not merely a local curiosity. Within the last decade, manga and anime have become one of the major East Asian cultural exports to the West, particularly to North America.[75] Specialists in religious studies have

---

[71] Published serially in 花とゆめ from 1994 to 2000 and reissued as stand-alone volumes as 天使禁猟区, 20 vols. (Tokyo: Hakusensha, 1995–2001) and in English as *Angel Sanctuary*, 20 vols. (San Francisco: Viz Media, 2004–2007).

[72] Initially televised as twenty-six episodes from 1995 to 1996. Accessible English versions include *Neon Genesis Evangelion: Perfect Collection*, six-DVD box set (ADV Films, 2005); *End of Evangelion*, dir. Anno Hideaki (1997), DVD (Manga Entertainment, 2002); and the new rebuilds (Studio Khara, 2008–2012; DVD releases 2010–2014).

[73] On apocryphal, gnostic, and kabbalistic motifs in *Neon Genesis Evangelion*, see Mariana Ortega, "My Father, He Killed Me; My Mother, She Ate Me: Self, Desire, Engendering, and the Mother in *Neon Genesis Evangelion*," *Mechademia* 2 (2007): 216–32, http://dx.doi.org/10.1353/mec.0.0010; and for preliminary reflections on its Christian themes, Christophe Thouny, "Waiting for the Messiah: The Becoming-Myth of *Evangelion* and *Densha otoko*," *Mechademia* 4.1 (2009): 111–29, http://dx.doi.org/10.1353/mec.0.0066.

[74] *Angel Sanctuary*, for instance, set a precedent for harvesting angelological, demonological, and cosmological motifs from works like First, Second, and Third Enoch as well as for innovating variations on narratives about ascent to heaven and tours of hell more along the lines of the Apocalypse of Paul. Apocalyptic eschatology is also widespread in manga and anime, although often owing more to *Akira* (dir. Katsuhi Otomo, 1988) than to any distinctively Christian doctrine. See further Susan J. Napier, *Anime from Akira to Howl's Moving Castle*, rev. ed. (New York: Macmillan, 2005), 249–74; Napier, "When the Machines Stop: Fantasy, Reality, and Terminal Identity in Neon Genesis Evangelion and Serial Experiments Lain," *Science Fiction Studies* 29.3 (2002): 418–35; Mick Broderick, "Anime's Apocalypse," *Intersections* 7 (2002): 1–11; Dennis Owen Frohlich, "Evil Must Be Punished: Apocalyptic Religion in the Television Series Death Note," *Journal of Media and Religion* 11.3 (2012): 141–55, http://dx.doi.org/10.1080/15348423.2012.706158. Notably, some of the scholarship on apocalyptic anime misses connections with relevant apocrypha by virtue of framing Christian influence only in terms of the NT or modern Protestantism.

[75] Wendy Siuyi Wong, "Globalizing Manga," *Mechademia* 1 (2006): 23–45, http://dx.doi.org/10.1353/mec.0.0060; Susan Napier, "The World of Anime Fandom in America," *Mechademia* 1 (2006): 47–63, http://dx.doi.org/10.1353/mec.0.0072.

just begun to analyze these genres as a crucible for the making of modern mythologies.[76] What is already clear, however, is that Christian materials here play a part in the evocation of a transnational vocabulary of mythic motifs but are drawn almost wholly from noncanonical sources[77]—perhaps in part because of their redeployment apart from any confessional claims or contexts.[78] Although still understudied, manga and anime exemplify the surprisingly diverse afterlives of "apocrypha" in contemporary contexts, while also serving as a poignant reminder that engagement with such literature need not be rooted in any commitment or connection to Christianity (or even Western culture per se).

Such dynamics have not yet been surveyed or studied. For our purposes, this material remains useful to mention, even if in passing, insofar as it challenges us to reconsider the resonance and reception of NT apocrypha as far more varied in form and scope than is typically assumed. At the very least, this evidence offers a humbling reminder of what scholars can miss when we assume that the reception of ancient writings can be traced in any single or simple line from the past to *one particular* present. It is certainly possible to reduce the story of the formation and reception of NT apocrypha to a series of footnotes to the story of the formation of the Christian biblical canon and its study in present-day biblical studies. It is also possible to tell the tales of these texts in counterpoint to the tale of the power and limits of the process of canonization, and it is possible to correlate their modern reception to inner-Christian religious concerns and debates. As much as we learn from such approaches, however, we might also miss a bigger picture, which may be

---

[76] Thomas, *Drawing on Tradition*; Adam Barkman, "Anime, Manga and Christianity," *Journal for the Study of Religions and Ideologies* 27 (2010): 25–45.

[77] One partial exception to this pattern is the common culling of the book of Revelation for eschatological and postapocalyptic imagery, e.g., in Clamp's *X* (serially published in *Monthly Asuka* from 1992 to 2003).

[78] Assistant director Kazuya Tsurumaki explained in an interview: "There are a lot of giant robot shows in Japan, and we did want our story to have a religious theme to help distinguish us. Because Christianity is an uncommon religion in Japan we thought it would be mysterious. None of the staff who worked on *EVA* are Christians. There is no actual Christian meaning to the show, we just thought the visual symbols of Christianity look cool. If we had known the show would get distributed in the US and Europe we might have rethought that choice" (Owen Thomas, "Amusing Himself to Death: Kazuya Tsurumaki speaks about the logic and illogic that went into creating FLCL," www.akadot.com, archived at http://wiki.evageeks.org/StatementsbyEvangelionStaff). Despite the lack of religious motives for such works, some Christian groups have answered by producing manga-like comics of their own, countering these newly globalized and hybridized creations with narratives governed by the canonical constraints of the NT; see Zondervan's *Manga Bible* series, e.g., Young Shin Lee, J. S. Earls, Brett Burner, and Bud Rogers, *Manga Bible*, vol. 6, *Parables, Miracles, and the Prince of Peace* (Grand Rapids: Zondervan, 2009); NEXT and Tyndale's parallel series, e.g., Hidenori Kumai et al., *Manga Messiah* (Wheaton, IL: Tyndale, 2007); Matthew Salisbury, Gabrielle Gniewek, and Sean Lam, *Paul: Tarsus to Redemption* (San Rafael, CA: Manga Hero, 2012). Such volumes are marketed to Christian youth rather than manga fans.

far more diffuse and diverse in its scope, shaped by a greater variety of local settings, historical paths, and acts of creative agency.

Contemporary examples also caution against reducing the afterlives of these and other ancient texts to evidence for direct citation. When we listen for the contemporary echoes of NT apocrypha and follow the traces of their afterlives, what we find is more often a fluid continuum from direct engagement or interpretation, to indirect inspiration or emulation, to atomized absorption into a reservoir of cultural materials ripe for use in creative bricolage—as marked, moreover, by some specific moments of intensively intentional repurposing. We find something akin, in other words, to what Lorenzo DiTommaso has observed with respect to the contemporary reception and repurposing of ancient apocalypses and apocalypticism in science fiction—which (perhaps not coincidentally) is yet another of the distinctively modern discourses in which motifs and materials from NT apocrypha have been creatively redeployed.[79]

Although these genres are uniquely modern, the dynamics therein are not wholly unprecedented. Indeed, if anything, contemporary examples provide poignant confirmation of one of the features that Averil Cameron has deemed characteristic of NT apocrypha already in late antiquity—namely, "elasticity."[80] Following Cameron, Scott Fitzgerald Johnson shows how evidence from late antiquity runs counter to the "fashionable 'disjunctive' model of early Christian and late antique literature" noted above, which holds that "a variety of literature available in the earliest Christian period … was subsequently suppressed and destroyed under the authoritative regime of the Constantinian and post-Constantinian Christian empire."[81] This model, as we have seen, makes sense in a modern world of print culture and censorship, and it also resonates with the drama of twentieth-century manuscript discoveries. Yet it remains, as Johnson stresses, that "Christian apocrypha of the second and third centuries are extremely well attested in

---

[79] Lorenzo DiTommaso, "At the Edge of Tomorrow: Apocalypticism and Science Fiction," in *End of Days: Essays on the Apocalypse from Antiquity to Modernity*, ed. Karolyn Kinane and Michael A. Ryan (Jefferson, NC: McFarland, 2009), 221–41.

[80] Averil Cameron, *Christianity and the Rhetoric of Empire: The Development of Christian Discourse*, Sather Classical Lectures 55 (Berkeley: University of California Press, 1991), 114–15. A similar parallel is noted by Mark MacWilliams in his review of Thomas, *Drawing on Tradition*, in *Monumenta Nipponica* 68.1 (2013): 156–58, with appeal to the late antique cult of the saints: "The religious experience of watching anime and reading manga can move beyond traditional views to new notions of the sacred. Like saints' festivals, manga and anime, while greatly entertaining, thereby provide meaningful religious content for their audiences."

[81] Johnson, "Apocrypha and the Literary Past," 50, extending Cameron, *Christianity and the Rhetoric of Empire*, 89–119. Contrast Foster's generalized characterization of apocryphal Gospels as "marginal documents read by liminal communities in the face of a progressively more assertive and authoritarian Orthodox Church in the late antique and medieval periods" (*Non-Canonical Gospels*, viii, although with attenuation on pp. ix–x).

Byzantine manuscripts," and the fourth and following centuries were marked not by the loss of these materials but rather by their persistence and vitality. Not only did they aid in "filling in the gaps of the Gospel narratives with regard to the lives and experiences of biblical figures," but they also contributed to creating a "symbolic universe" forged in remembrance and emulation of the apostolic past.[82] Glen Most has gone so far as to suggest that "without what later came to be termed the Apocrypha there would not have been a canon of the New Testament *as such* in the first place."[83] It is clear, in any case, that the two were interdependent in practice, and, as Johnson notes, "circulated side-by-side and mutually established reading and writing practices."[84] The interpenetration of NT apocrypha with liturgy and hagiography further suggests that such parabiblical writings often functioned in late antiquity and the Middle Ages in a manner akin more to a constituent component of the "Bible as It Was" than to a separate, secret, or suppressed countercanon.[85]

So too with Christian art. It is impossible—as art historians have long known—to understand medieval European monumental art, sculpture, and manuscript illumination, or even Renaissance painting, without some sense of the apocrypha that often provide the first or main literary witness to scenes enshrined in the Christian iconographical tradition. David Cartlidge and J. Keith Elliot have gone so far as to contend that "virtually every cycle of Christian art exhibits its parallels with Christian Apocrypha."[86] Even if such a claim risks homogenizing diverse data, the base insight is borne out even by a glance at Cartlidge's online ApocIcon database or by a skim through the catalogue of motifs in the Princeton Index of Christian Art.

In some cases, the development of iconographical motifs may root in the production of illustrated manuscripts of NT apocrypha or parts thereof, which came to be used as models for other pictorial work.[87] Most, however, seem to be more akin in their dynamics to the sprawling creativity that we see in play in contemporary manga, anime, and fiction, wherein the seeds of inspiration sown by parabiblical writings spring up from a fertile complex of reflection in multiple genres and settings—and, in turn, are developed through cross-fertilization across different media, locales, and languages. For instance, some texts that we now categorize as NT apocrypha, such as the Protevangelium of James, can be deemed the "source" of this or that iconographical motif only inasmuch as they are also the

---

[82] Johnson, "Apocrypha and the Literary Past," 48.
[83] Glenn W. Most, *Doubting Thomas* (Cambridge: Harvard University Press, 2005), 85.
[84] Johnson, "Apocrypha and the Literary Past," 59.
[85] See now Rose, *Ritual Memory*, and ample bibliography there.
[86] David R. Cartlidge and J. Keith Elliott, *Art and the Christian Apocrypha* (London: Routledge, 2001), xv.
[87] Examples of apocrypha illustrated in medieval manuscripts include the Apocalypse of Paul in Bibliothèque Municipale of Toulouse MS 815; the Arabic Gospel of the Infancy in MS Laurenziano orientale 387; and Pseudo-Matthew in Milan Ambrosian MS L.58.

fountainhead (or one early font) of a much broader array of traditions—in this case, traditions about Mary, the mother of Jesus, which circulated in multiple written forms but also in multiple oral, spatial, and visual contexts linked variously to liturgy, ritual, pilgrimage, and devotional reflection.[88]

Just as the textual traditions of different NT apocrypha were shifting and myriad in late antiquity and the Middle Ages, so they intersected with artistic traditions in different ways and times. This interplay has been examined perhaps most intensively in relation to Infancy Gospels, both by art historians like Kathryn Smith and by scholars of medieval literature like Mary Dzon. Approaching the issue from the perspective of illuminated Books of Hours such as that of Neville of Hornby (BL Egerton MS 2781), for instance, Smith points to the prominence of childhood images of Jesus corresponding to traditions not found in the NT Gospels but featured in the Infancy Gospel of Thomas, Pseudo-Matthew, and even the Arabic Infancy Gospel.[89] She explains their inclusion against the background of growing "interest in the Infancy miracles ... registered in the composition beginning c. 1200 of new genres of Latin and particularly vernacular literature—Gospel harmonies, biographies of the Virgin and Christ, world chronicles, and comprehensive sacred histories—which incorporate Infancy miracles into their narrative schemes," as well as the concurrent rise of poetry dedicated specifically to the topic, such as in *Evangile de l'Enfance* (ca. 1250) and its derivatives.[90] Approaching the issue from the other direction, Dzon elucidates the concurrent use of motifs from older apocrypha in Middle English poems about the Jesus's birth and childhood in part by looking to their intersections with the illustrations in manuscripts such as the Holkham Picture Book and the interplay between text and art.[91] Taken together, their findings suggest that apocrypha of this sort were hardly received as "marginal," "forbidden," or "esoteric" by medieval readers. The Gelasian Decree may

---

[88] Common iconographical motifs that find their first textual attestations in the Protevangelium of James are most famous today from their iterations in Renaissance painting such as Giotto's scenes from the life of Mary in the Arena Chapel in Padua (1305) and Titian's *Presentation of the Virgin Mary* (1534–1538). Yet Mary is depicted as weaving already in a fifth-century mosaic in Santa Maria Maggiore in Rome, and one finds multiple scenes from her early life depicted in a manner akin to the narrative of the Protevangelium of James in the Kariye Djami mosaics in Istanbul (ca. 1320), possibly based on a now-lost illuminated manuscript. Contemporaneous examples from manuscripts include Morgan Library M.268, fol. 24r, 26r, etc.

[89] Kathryn A. Smith, *Art, Identity, and Devotion in Fourteenth-Century England: Three Women and Their Books of Hours* (Toronto: University of Toronto Press, 2003), 269–77.

[90] Ibid., 269.

[91] Mary Dzon, "Jesus and the Birds in Medieval Abrahamic Traditions," *Traditio* 66 (2011): 189–230, http://dx.doi.org/10.1353/trd.2011.0008; see also Dzon, "Joseph and the Amazing Christ-Child of Late-Medieval Legend," in *Childhood in the Middle Ages and the Renaissance: The Results of a Paradigm Shift in the History of Mentality*, ed. Albrecht Classen (Berlin: de Gruyter, 2005), 135–57; Dzon, "Boys Will Be Boys: The Physiology of Childhood and the Apocryphal Christ Child in the Later Middle Ages," *Viator* 42 (2011): 179–225.

denounce Pseudo-Matthew, but—as Dzon has demonstrated—these and related texts seem to have inspired much literary creativity, likely because they provided models for producing "devotional reading for the pious" in a manner known to and permitted by clerics.[92] And just as there is evidence for the movement of motifs between literary and artistic domains, so too from East to West—with some, such as the motif of Jesus and the clay birds, even serving as a "shared feature of religious culture" between Christians, Muslims, and Jews.[93]

Nor are the afterlives of apocryphal motifs limited to one setting or topic. The literature and illuminated manuscripts of upper-class readers or clerics form one crucible for the intensification of medieval interest in the childhood of Christ, but the afterlives of the apocryphal lives of the apostles play out in more public settings, such as in the case of the surprising prominence of the Acts of Thomas in thirteenth-century French stained glass and cathedral architecture.[94] Infancy material is notably lacking, in fact, in the most prominent example of the repurposing and hagiographical extension of apocryphal acts, namely, Jacobus de Voragine's popular compilation *Legenda Aurea* (1260–1275).[95]

Examples could be multiplied from the rich medieval afterlives of the Gospel of Nicodemus, for instance, or from the Faustus and other legends growing up from around the Pseudo-Clementine corpus. What is clear, in any case, is that "apocryphal" texts and traditions circulated in the Middle Ages in a variety of settings—mostly unhindered by the canonical controversies that sometimes placed some parabiblical works on this or that list of forbidden documents. Categorical denigration of apocrypha is certainly a recurring theme among Christian theologians, as we have seen above. When placed in broader perspective, however, even canon lists are revealed as being far from determinative for late antique and medieval attitudes toward the texts that we now call NT apocrypha—and definitely nowhere close to the sum total of premodern perspectives on the apostolic past in relation to the bounds of Scripture. What we find in our evidence, rather, is a remarkable degree of cultural creativity surrounding apocrypha, neither isolated from

---

[92] Dzon, "Jesus and the Birds," 201, also 204–5.

[93] Ibid.; also Davis, *Christ Child,* 129–92; Sarit Kattan Gribetz, "Jesus and the Clay Birds: Reading *Toledot Yeshu* in Light of the Infancy Gospels," in *Envisioning Judaism: Studies in Honor of Peter Schäfer on the Occasion of His Seventieth Birthday,* ed. R. S. Boustan, R. Leicht, A. Y. Reed, and G. Veltri, with Alex Ramos, 2 vols. (Tübingen: Mohr Siebeck, 2013), 2:1021–48.

[94] Not only is there an entire window dedicated to the story in Cathédrale Notre-Dame de Chartres, but Thomas and Gundaphoras, for example, are illustrated in the ambulatory, window 9 (ca. 1210–1215), in the Cathédrale Saint-Étienne de Bourges, and the image of Gad and the heavenly palace shown appears in a thirteenth-century window in the portal of the Cathédrale Saint-Pierre de Poitiers. Interest in such works in thirteenth-century France is attested also by the illustrations of the Apocalypse of Paul in Bibliothèque Municipale of Toulouse MS 815.

[95] Jacobus de Voragine, *The Golden Legend: Readings on the Saints,* trans. William Granger Ryan, 2 vols. (Princeton: Princeton University Press, 1993); Rémi Gounelle, "Sens et usage d'apocryphus dans la Légende Dorée," *Apocrypha* 5 (1994): 189–210.

literature nor subordinated to it, but forming a vital part of a living complex of practices at the interface of past and present, shaping cultural memory in ways that were simultaneously intensively local and surprisingly interconnected. Both in premodern and modern times, the afterlives of these writings are not limited to the notion of a secret history of Christian origins or to the allure of potential relics of a suppressed esotericism: NT apocrypha continue to exhibit a remarkable elasticity, ensuring their continued vitality in changing times and settings.

III. Conclusion

In pulling together such varied data for the afterlives of NT apocrypha, my aim is not to argue for a single answer or programmatic path, but instead to open up a conversation on the present state and future prospects of scholarship on parabiblical literature and its place in biblical studies. From even a quick survey of the some of the relevant evidence, it is possible to get some feel for just how much is missed when NT apocrypha are analyzed primarily in relation to the NT. Some are obviously relevant for the reconstruction of Christian origins, but there is also much of interest to see when we direct our gaze to the more expansive horizons in which the apostolic past has been remembered, retold, and repurposed from late antiquity to the present. In the process, fresh attention to the afterlives of NT apocrypha (both "early" and "late") helps us to notice neglected elements of these works, as we glimpse them anew through the eyes of readers in various times and through the lens of specialists in different fields.

Part of what is so exciting about recent specialist research along these lines is that it brings biblical studies into conversation with new interlocutors, including experts in medieval and early modern materials. Attention to apocrypha and their afterlives, in turn, can complement the history of the biblical text and its interpretation while also contributing to the new concern in the humanities for tracing cultural memory across different times and locales. We may wish further to ask whether such conversations can help us to shift the interface of scholarly and popular perspectives, or at least to expand it beyond a largely confessional axis predicated on the prioritization of origins. After all, even the medieval afterlives of NT apocrypha attest the appeal of some of these narratives beyond the bounds of Christianity and the West, and this is certainly the case today. Far from diluting the value of biblical studies, a sense of the stunningly broad reach of NT apocrypha may aid in illuminating neglected elements of the "Bible as It Was." The result may not be quite as dramatic as the promise to reveal lost secrets about Jesus himself, but it does result in the recovery of some of the dynamics, trajectories, and connections that shaped the worlds of late antiquity and the Middle Ages—and also continue to shape our own.

In Search for Aram and Israel
Politics, Culture, and Identity
Edited by Omer Sergi, Manfred Oeming and Izaak J. de Hulster

2015. 400 pages (est.)
(Orientalische Religionen in der Antike).
ISBN 978-3-16-153803-2
cloth (August)

Throughout its history, the Kingdom of Israel had strong connections with the Aramaean world. Constantly changing relations, from rivalry and military conflicts to alliances and military cooperation, affected the history of the whole Levant and left their marks on both Biblical and extra-Biblical sources. New studies demonstrate that Israelite state formation was contemporaneous with the formation of the Aramaean polities (11th–9th centuries BCE). Consequently, the Jordan Valley (and especially its northern parts and its extension to the valley of Lebanon) was a constantly changing border zone between different Iron Age polities. In light of that, there is a need to study the history of Ancient Israel not only from the »Canaanite« point of view but also within the political and cultural context of the Aramaean world. This volume brings together experts working in different fields to address the relations and interactions between Aram and Israel during the Early Iron Age (12th to 8th centuries BCE).

The authors of this volume address the interactions between the Aramaean kingdoms and the Israelite Northern Kingdom during the Early Iron Age (12th–8th century BCE) focusing on archaeology and material culture vis-à-vis textual sources and historical memory.

Mohr Siebeck
Tübingen
info@mohr.de
www.mohr.de

Custom made information: *www.mohr.de*

"I Will Become Him": Homology and Deification in the Gospel of Thomas

M. DAVID LITWA
mdl2dj@virginia.edu
University of Virginia, Charlottesville, VA 22904

This article argues that many of the disparate soteriological themes in the Gospel of Thomas can be united under the category of deification. Strikingly, the Gospel of Thomas presents an early Christian form of deification parallel to the deification of Jesus in the Gospel of John. Like John's Gospel, the Gospel of Thomas presents a Jesus who is fully divine. Unlike in John, however, Jesus's distinctively divine traits and predicates are applied also to the elect in the Gospel of Thomas. The homology of Jesus and the Thomasine Christian indicates a soteriology of gemination—a scenario in which the elect realize their identity with Jesus and thus their status as spiritual "twins." Since Jesus is presented as a divine figure in the Gospel of Thomas, Thomasine gemination is simultaneously a form of deification.

The term "deification," occasionally used though rarely defined, has been employed periodically by scholars as an important concept for understanding early Jewish and Christian forms of transcendence.[1] Typically, deification means that a human comes to possess a divine status by sharing in qualities that, in the

---

[1] See Matthew Black, "The Throne Theophany Prophetic Commission and the 'Son of Man': A Study in Tradition-History," in *Jews, Greeks and Christians: Religious Cultures in Late Antiquity: Essays in Honor of William David Davies*, ed. Robert Hamerton-Kelly and Robin Scroggs, SJLA 21 (Leiden: Brill, 1976), 57–73; James Tabor, "Paul's Notion of Many 'Sons of God' and Its Hellenistic Contexts," *Helios* 13 (1986): 87–97; John J. Collins, "A Throne in the Heavens: Apotheosis in Prechristian Judaism," in *Death, Ecstasy, and Otherworldly Journeys*, ed. John J. Collins and Michael Fishbane (Albany: State University of New York Press, 1995), 43–58; Philip Alexander, "From Son of Adam to Second God: Transformations of the Biblical Enoch," in *Biblical Figures outside the Bible*, ed. Michael E. Stone and Theodore A. Bergren (Harrisburg, PA: Trinity Press International, 1998), 87–122; Naomi Janowitz, *Magic in the Roman World: Pagans, Jews and Christians*, Religion in the First Christian Centuries, http://dx.doi.org/10.4324/9780203457641 (London: Routledge, 2001), 70–85; M. David Litwa, *We Are Being Transformed: Deification in Paul's Soteriology*, BZNW 187 (Berlin: de Gruyter, 2012), 37–116.

ancient Mediterranean world, constituted a divine identity. These qualities usually include immortality and superhuman power, but others (e.g., wisdom, virtue) are also prominent.

Deification as a soteriological theory has long had a home in patristic theology but has only fairly recently appeared as an academic category useful for historians interested in an earlier and broader range of ancient thought.[2] As a category of thought, deification involves four basic ideas: (1) there is no infinite difference between the divine and humans; (2) divinity is manifested across a range of beings and qualities; (3) humans can participate in these qualities and even share the identity of a particular divine being; and (4) this participation is "realistic" in the sense that humans truly come to be part of the class "god/divine being."[3]

In this article, I contend that the Gospel of Thomas (hereafter, Thomas) presents an early form of Christian deification parallel to the discursive deification of Jesus in the Gospel of John (hereafter, John).[4] Although scholars have recognized that Thomas speaks of an internal divine nature,[5] few have used the terminology

---

[2] For patristic deification, see Norman Russell, *The Doctrine of Deification in the Greek Patristic Tradition*, OECS (Oxford: Oxford University Press, 2004). For deification as a modern academic category, see Dietrich Roloff, *Gottähnlichkeit, Vergöttlichung und Erhöhung zu seligem Leben: Untersuchungen zur Herkunft der platonischen Angleichung an Gott*, Untersuchungen zur antiken Literatur und Geschichte 4 (Berlin: de Gruyter, 1970); Richard Bodéüs, *Aristotle and the Theology of the Living Immortals*, trans. Jan Edward Garrett, SUNY Series in Ancient Greek Philosophy (Albany: State University of New York Press, 2000); Salvatore Lavecchia, "Die Ὁμοίωσις Θεῷ in Platons Philosophie," in *Perspektiven der Philosophie*, ed. Wiebke Schrader et al. (Amsterdam: Rodopi, 2005), 321–94; Miguel Herrero de Jáuregui, "Orphic Ideas of Immortality," in *Lebendige Hoffnung–ewiger Tod?! Jenseitsvorstellungen im Hellenismus, Judentum und Christentum*, ed. Michael Labahn and Manfred Lang, Arbeiten zur Bibel und ihrer Geschichte (Leipzig: Evangelische Verlagsanstalt, 2007), 289–314; Patrick Lee Miller, *Becoming God: Pure Reason in Early Greek Philosophy* (London: Continuum, 2011).

[3] Realistic participation is a Platonic theme. Although Plato himself seems only to have envisioned humans as entering the society of the gods (*Phaed.* 69c6–d3, 81a9–10, 82b10–c1), his idea of participatory likeness to God gave a rational basis to deification in the ancient world. See further David Sedley, "The Ideal of Godlikeness," in *Plato 2: Ethics, Politics, Religion, and the Soul*, ed. Gail Fine (Oxford: Oxford University Press, 1999), 309–28; Julia Annas, *Platonic Ethics, Old and New*, CSCP 57 (Ithaca, NY: Cornell University Press, 1999), 52–71; J. M. Armstrong, "After the Ascent: Plato on Becoming like God," *OSAP* 26 (2004): 171–83.

[4] Discursive deification refers to the historical process whereby ancient authors creatively apply distinctive traits of divinity to human beings. See further M. David Litwa, *Iesus Deus: The Early Christian Depiction of Jesus as a Mediterranean God* (Minneapolis: Fortress, 2014), 1–6.

[5] April D. DeConick, *The Original Gospel of Thomas in Translation: With a Commentary and New English Translation of the Complete Gospel*, LNTS 287 (London: T&T Clark, 2006), 5, 225, 248; DeConick, *Recovering the Original Gospel of Thomas: A History of the Gospel and Its Growth*, LNTS 286 (London: T&T Clark, 2005), 74, 170, 196, 212, 237; Stephen Patterson, "Jesus Meets Plato: The Theology of the *Gospel of Thomas* and Middle Platonism," in *Das Thomasevangelium: Entstehung-Rezeption-Theologie*, ed. Jörg Frey et al., BZNW 157 (Berlin: de Gruyter, 2008),

of deification, and virtually no one (to my knowledge) has holistically expounded Thomasine soteriology in terms of the category of deification.[6] Instead, other frameworks have been used.

April D. DeConick, for instance, has approached Thomasine soteriology under the category of "vision mysticism."[7] In Christian history, the *visio dei* has sometimes been associated with deification.[8] Deification might also be called a mystical theme, especially when it involves union with a divine being.[9] In modern scholarship, however, it is best not to view deification under the category of mysticism, since mysticism is often associated with experiences that are exclusive, individual (or subjective), and nonconceptual, and which involve indistinct fusion with deity.[10] To be sure, DeConick defines mysticism in terms of personal, immediate experience of the divine, but Thomas offers something more specific: *identification*

181-205, esp. 183; idem, "The View from across the Euphrates," *HTR* 104 (2011): 411-31, esp. 417-18.

[6] DeConick is comfortable with the language of deification (in Hermetic thought, for instance) in *Seek to See Him: Ascent and Vision Mysticism in the Gospel of Thomas*, VCSup 33 (Leiden: Brill, 1996); and DeConick, *Voices of the Mystics: Early Christian Discourse in the Gospels of John and Thomas and Other Ancient Christian Literature*, JSNTSup 157 (Sheffield: Sheffield Academic, 2001). Yet she does not apply the language to Thomas. Enno Edzard Popkes has recently mentioned Thomasine deification (*Vergöttlichung*) in passing, with no definition or development (*Das Menschenbild des Thomasevangeliums: Untersuchungen zu seiner religionsgeschichtlichen und chronologischen Einordnung*, WUNT 206 [Tübingen: Mohr Siebeck, 2007], 354).

[7] See esp. DeConick, *Voices of the Mystics*, 42, 110.

[8] Augustine preached that the mind, when it is lost in wonder at the sight of God, "becomes divine" (*fit divina*) (*Enarrat. Ps.* 35.14).

[9] See, e.g., Thomas Merton, *An Introduction to Christian Mysticism: Initiation into the Monastic Tradition 3*, ed. Patrick F. O'Connell, Monastic Wisdom 13 (Kalamazoo, MI: Cistercian Publications, 2008), 58-96. A standard list of early Christian parallels that involve identification with the Savior or another divine being is sometimes used to illuminate Thomas (especially log. 108) (e.g., in Thomas Zöckler, *Jesu Lehren im Thomasevangelium*, NHMS 47 [Leiden: Brill, 1999], 245). Heading the list is often the so-called Gospel of Eve, quoted by Epiphanius, "And I heard as it were the sound of thunder and drew near to hear, and he spoke with me and said, I am you and you are I [Ἐγὼ σύ καὶ σὺ ἐγώ]" (*Pan.* 26.3.1). Cf. also Irenaeus, *Haer.* 1.13.3 (Marcus the Valentinian); Acts John 100; Corp. herm. 5.11. See further Pheme Perkins, "Identification with the Savior in Coptic Texts from Nag Hammadi," in *The Jewish Roots of Christological Monotheism: Papers from the St. Andrews Conference on the Historical Origins of the Worship of Jesus*, ed. Carey C. Newman et al., JSJSup 63 (Leiden: Brill, 1999), 166-86.

[10] William James noted long ago that the words "mysticism" and "mystical" are "often used as terms of mere reproach, to throw at any opinion which we regard as vague and vast and sentimental" (*The Varieties of Religious Experience: A Study in Human Nature* [New York: Macmillan, 1961], 299). His four characteristics of mysticism—ineffability, noetic quality, transiency, and passivity (pp. 299-300)—would not be accepted by all scholars of mysticism today. Indeed, there is no current consensus among scholars on how to define "mysticism."

with the divine Jesus.[11] In my view, deification (which can manifest itself in political, mythological, Orphic, Hermetic, Christian, and philosophical contexts) bursts the bounds of mysticism and should be viewed as a category in its own right.[12]

Using the category of deification opens up new vistas concerning how first- and early-second-century Christians conceived of the nature of divinity and humanity, the relation between God and human beings, how humans were thought to share a divine identity, and the role of Jesus in attaining this identity. Deification unites under one umbrella themes in Thomas that would otherwise remain disparate, including the inward light, Christians' preexistence, identification with the Savior, oneness or equality with God, and the transformative ascent to see God. In short, deification offers an integrative framework for thinking about salvation in Thomas and other documents of earliest Christianity.

The argument of this essay is carried out through two simultaneous comparisons: internal and external. Internal to Thomas itself, the divine nature of Jesus is compared with the nature of Thomasine Christians in an attempt to show their implicit and explicit identity.[13] Externally, the divine christology of John's Gospel is compared with Thomas's depiction of the ideal Christian to show how the discursive deification of Jesus in John parallels the discursive deification of Christians

---

[11] April D. DeConick, "Mysticism and the *Gospel of Thomas*" in Frey et al., *Das Thomasevangelium*, 206–21, esp. 214.

[12] See further M. David Litwa, *Becoming Divine: An Introduction to Deification in Western Culture* (Eugene, OR: Cascade, 2013).

[13] In this essay, "the Thomasine Christian" refers to the ideal Christian reader of the Gospel of Thomas and does not assume a theory about an actual Thomasine community (or communities) in Edessa or elsewhere. On a possible community, see Risto Uro, *Thomas: Seeking the Historical Context of the Gospel of Thomas* (London: T&T Clark, 2003), 25–30; DeConick, *Recovering the Original*, 231–37; William Arnal, "Blessed Are the Solitary: Textual Practices and the Mirage of a Thomas 'Community,'" in *"The One Who Sows Bountifully": Essays in Honor of Stanley K. Stowers*, ed. Caroline Johnson Hodge et al., BJS 356 (Providence, RI: Brown Judaic Studies, 2013), 271–82. Although interest has surged in the tradition history of Thomas—and in particular the dependence of individual sayings on Synoptic traditions—I am interested solely in the soteriology of its "final form" as it appears in NHC II 2, and will study it as a (relatively coherent) piece of early Christian literature. Although various attempts have been made to date earlier layers of Thomas to the first century CE (e.g., Helmut Koester, *Ancient Christian Gospels: Their History and Development* [Philadelphia: Trinity Press International, 1990], 84–112; DeConick, *Recovering the Original*, 38–155), the finished document is widely believed to stem from the early second century. This dating is supported by the manuscripts of the Greek fragments, which date from the early third century (Harold W. Attridge, "Appendix: The Greek Fragments," in *Nag Hammadi Codex II,2–7*, ed. Bentley Layton, 2 vols., NHS 20–21 [Leiden: Brill, 1989], 96–99), as well as possible Synoptic influence (Simon Gathercole, *The Composition of the Gospel of Thomas: Original Language and Influences*, SNTSMS 151 [Cambridge: Cambridge University Press, 2012], 127–224; Mark Goodacre, *Thomas and the Gospels: The Case for Thomas's Familiarity with the Synoptics* [Grand Rapids: Eerdmans, 2012]).

in Thomas.[14] In short, both the Johannine Jesus and the Thomasine Christian share many of the same divine predicates and prerogatives. The application of such divine prerogatives constitutes in both documents a discursive form of deification. In essence, John presents a picture of what a deified human looks like (Jesus), and thus a roughly contemporary early Christian model for understanding the divinity of other human beings.[15] The comparison is executed in two parts: the first focusing on the divine nature of Jesus and Thomasine Christians, and the second on their divine destiny.

I. Divine Nature

Preexistent Light

In log. 77 of the Gospel of Thomas, Jesus identifies himself with the divine light: "It is I who am the light that is above them all." Stephen Patterson observes that light is "that most quintessentially divine quality."[16] The psalmist declared "YHWH is my light" (27:1). Commenting on this passage, Philo calls the Logos the archetype of every other light (*Somn.* 1.75). For Platonists in general, light

---

[14] Raymond E. Brown was the first to compare Thomas and John systematically ("The Gospel of Thomas and St. John's Gospel," *NTS* 9 [1962]: 155–77). He concluded that Thomas was indirectly dependent on John but introduced some "Gnostic" modifications to the Johannine material (pp. 176–77). Koester held a nearly opposite view (*Ancient Christian Gospels*, 122). Recently, John's Gospel has been viewed as in critical dialogue with Thomas (Gregory J. Riley, *Resurrection Reconsidered: Thomas and John in Controversy* [Minneapolis: Fortress, 1995]; April D. DeConick, "John Rivals Thomas: From Community Conflict to Gospel Narrative," in *Jesus in Johannine Tradition: New Directions*, ed. Tom Thatcher and Robert T. Fortna [Louisville: Westminster John Knox, 2001], 303–11; Elaine Pagels, *Beyond Belief: The Secret Gospel of Thomas* [New York: Random House, 2003], 30–73). For criticism of this view, see Ismo Dunderberg, *The Beloved Disciple in Conflict? Revisiting the Gospels of John and Thomas* (Oxford: Oxford University Press, 2006), 14–67, http://dx.doi.org/10.1093/0199284962.003.0002; and Christopher W. Skinner, *John and Thomas—Gospels in Conflict? Johannine Characterization and the Thomas Question*, Princeton Theological Monograph Series 115 (Eugene, OR: Pickwick, 2009).

[15] Most scholars agree that John's Gospel is the first explicitly to call Jesus a god both at the beginning (1:1) and at the end (20:28) (see further Gilbert Van Belle, "Christology and Soteriology in the Fourth Gospel: The Conclusion to the Gospel of John Revisited," in *Theology and Christology in the Fourth Gospel: Essays by Members of the SNTS Johannine Writings Seminar*, ed. G. Van Belle et al., BETL 184 [Leuven: Leuven University Press, 2005], 435–62, esp. 443–52). In between, Jesus is consistently depicted as a divine being who holds awesome power (e.g., 5:27) and dispenses immortality (e.g., 5:21; 11:26). By using the Johannine Christ as a means of comparison, I do not wish to imply that John's Christ was directly in mind when the composer(s) of Thomas depicted the true nature of Christians. Thomasine Christians identify with Jesus by identifying with Thomas, Jesus's spiritual twin.

[16] Patterson, "Jesus Meets Plato," 196.

symbolized the intellectual and incorporeal aspects of the divine.[17] In Johannine literature, both God and the Logos are directly called "light" (1 John 1:5, John 1:9).[18]

According to Elaine Pagels, the idea of Jesus as a being of light probably emerged from a reading of Gen 1:3 LXX: γενηθήτω φῶς ("let light exist!").[19] In an unaccented text, ΦΩΣ ("light") could be read as a reference to a primordial Human (φώς). The meanings of φῶς and φώς could then readily bleed into one another, so that the "light"/"human" became a "Light Human." This interpretation probably preceded Thomas and appears, Pagels thinks, in John's prologue.[20] Thomas's contribution is to identify the divine Light Human with Jesus.

Yet Jesus's divine status in and as preexistent light is not unique to him. In Thomas, humans also preexisted as luminous beings living in union with God. For the notion of human preexistence, log. 19 is most clear: "Blessed is the one who came into being before coming into being." Jesus, who speaks this verse, is almost certainly not merely blessing himself but is referring to others.

In the Gospel of John, the preexistent one is Jesus himself. He is the Logos in the Beginning (1:1) who declares, "Before Abraham was, I am" (8:58). In this latter passage, Jesus clearly makes a divine claim (as evidenced by his narrow escape from stoning).

Although in John, Jesus alone is preexistent, for Thomas both Jesus and the elect share a luminous preexistence. In log. 49, the elect are said to be "from the kingdom." "The kingdom" is soon identified as "the light" (log. 50): "Jesus said, 'If they say to you, "From whom [or what] did you come?" say to them, "We came from the light, the place where the light exists through itself alone, established [itself] and appeared in their image."'" According to this logion, the preexistent state of human beings is the location and origin of light.[21] As those who "came from the [preexistent] light" (log. 50), Thomasine Christians could rightfully say with the Johannine Christ, "And now glorify me alongside yourself, Father, with the glory that I had by your side before the world began" (John 17:5).[22]

In log. 50, the light appeared in "their image" (ⲧⲟⲩϩⲓⲕⲱⲛ). "Their" image

---

[17] The sun is Plato's image for the Good (*Resp.* 507b–509c). On the sun image, cf. Philo, *Virt.* 164 (God is ὁ νοητὸς ἥλιος), Plutarch, *Def. orac.* 433d–e, Alcinous, *Epit.* 10.2, 5.

[18] Cf. Corp. herm. 1.9, 12, 21; Sent. Sextus 30. See further Patterson, "Jesus Meets Plato," 196–99.

[19] Elaine Pagels, "Exegesis of Genesis 1 in the Gospels of Thomas and John," *JBL* 118 (1999): 477–96, esp. 479–80.

[20] Ibid., 481.

[21] See further Gerard Luttikhuizen, "The Hidden Meaning of 'The Kingdom Inside You and Outside You' in the *Gospel of Thomas*," in *The Apocryphal Gospels within the Context of Early Christian Theology*, ed. Jens Schröter, BETL 260 (Leuven: Peeters, 2013), 539–47.

[22] See further Zöckler, *Jesu Lehren im Thomasevangelium*, 127–28.

could be taken to refer to angels.²³ It seems preferable, however, to see the exegetical origin of "their" image in Gen 1:26: "Let *us* make humankind in *our* image." In the Epistle of Barnabas, this statement is understood to be spoken by the Father to the Son (5.5, 6.12). The image has reference to two divine beings: God and Jesus. Applied to Thomas, this interpretation would indicate that humans come from a divine light modeled on the dual image of Father and Son.

Sonship

Thomasine Christians do not directly identify themselves with the light in log. 50; rather, they are its children. As children of the light, they are children of God. Earlier the elect are called "children of the Living Father" (ⲛ̄ϣⲏⲣⲉ ⲙ̄ⲡⲉⲓⲱⲧ ⲉⲧⲟⲛϩ, log. 3). Elsewhere Jesus refers to himself as "the child of the Living One" (ⲡϣⲏⲣⲉ ⲙ̄ⲡⲉⲧⲟⲛϩ, log. 37; cf. 65). There is little indication in Thomas that Jesus (as the child of God) and Christians (as the children of God) are unequally ranked. This parity accords with the sense of equality between the elect and Jesus found elsewhere (e.g., log. 13: "I am not your master"; cf. John 15:15).

In the Gospel of John, Jesus is God's only-begotten or unique Son (τὸν υἱὸν τὸν μονογενῆ, 3:16).²⁴ John's prologue calls Jesus "the only-born god" (μονογενὴς θεός, 1:18). A pervasive textual variant reads "only-born Son" (ὁ μονογενὴς υἱός).²⁵ In John, the "sonship" relation is reduced to one man. Members of the Johannine community become "children" (τέκνα) of God, apparently a meaningful but secondary kind of kinship (John 1:12, 1 John 3:1).

Knowledge

Like Jesus in John, the Thomasine elect not only share a divine origin; they *know* their origin and destination. In John 8:14, Jesus directly claims that he knows "from where I came and where I am going" (cf. 13:3, 16:28). Such knowledge is also

---

²³ DeConick, *Seek to See Him*, 68–70; cf. Pagels, "Exegesis of Genesis 1," 487 n. 29. It is unlikely that "their" image refers to "the [gnostic] inferior god and his entourage" (Uwe-Karsten Plisch, *The Gospel of Thomas: Original Text with Commentary*, trans. Gesine Schenke Robinson [Stuttgart: Deutsche Bibelgesellschaft, 2008], 130).

²⁴ For the sense of μονογενής as "unique" or "only," see Gerard Pendrick, "ΜΟΝΟΓΕΝΗΣ," *NTS* 41 (1995): 587–600; John F. McHugh, "Von Sinn des μονογενής in John 1,14.18," in *Von der Suche nach Gott: Helmut Riedlinger zum 75. Geburtstag*, ed. Margot Schmidt and Fernando Domínguez Reboiras, Mystik in Geschichte und Gegenwart: Christliche Mystik 15 (Stuttgart-Bad Cannstatt: Frommann-Holzboog, 1998), 339–49.

²⁵ The variant occurs in Codex Alexandrinus, the "Family 1 and 13" group of manuscripts, the majority of later Byzantine manuscripts, as well as several early church fathers including Irenaeus, Clement, Hippolytus, and Origen. See the apparatus in Barbara Aland et al., eds., *The Greek New Testament*, 4th ed. (Stuttgart: Deutsche Bibelgesellschaft, 2012), 314.

the privilege of Thomasine Christians: they are from the kingdom (or light), and to it they will return (log. 49–50).²⁶

Stevan L. Davies points out that the interrogation in log. 50 ("Where do you come from? … Is it you? … What is the sign of your Father in you?") is similar to the interrogations of Jesus in John's Gospel: "They said to him, 'Where is your father?'" (8:19), "Who are you?" (8:25), and "What sign are you going to give us…?" (6:30; cf. 2:18).²⁷ Like Jesus, Thomasine Christians are persecuted in the world because—unlike their opponents—they know who and whence they are.

Light Within

In log. 50, the opponents demand a sign for the Father "in" (ϩⲛ̄) the elect. These elect persons not only came from the divine light; they have light abiding within themselves. It was a common teaching in ancient philosophy that divinity existed within the human person, typically in or as the mind (νοῦς, λόγος).²⁸ Sometimes this divinity was metaphorized as light.²⁹

Earlier, in log. 24, Jesus says that "there is light existing within a person of light [ⲟⲩⲣⲙ̄ⲟⲩⲟⲉⲓⲛ], and it enlightens the whole world. If he does not shine, he [or it, i.e., the world] is darkness [ⲟⲩⲕⲁⲕⲉ ⲡⲉ]."³⁰ More clearly than in any other text in Thomas, this saying indicates that divine light exists not only within Jesus but also within

---

²⁶ For the idea of kingdom in Thomas, see Patterson, "View from across the Euphrates," 427–28.

²⁷ Stevan L. Davies, "The Christology and Protology of the Gospel of Thomas," *JBL* 111 (1992): 663–82, esp. 670–71.

²⁸ Plato depicted the divine mind as sown within humans by the Demiurge (*Tim.* 41c; cf. 45a1–2, 69d6, 73a7–8, 88b2, 90a2–b1); cf. *Prot.* 322a (ἄνθρωπος θείας μετέσχε μοίρας); [*Alc.*] 1.133c1–6; Plutarch, *Fac.* 926c–d (νοῦν, χρῆμα θεῖον). Aristotle taught the divinity of mind (νοῦς) in *De an.* 1.4, 408b29; *Eth. nic.* 10.7, 1177a16, b28–32. Zeno of Citium believed that humans "have in themselves as it were a god" (ἔχειν … ἐν ἑαυτοῖς οἱονεὶ θεόν) (Diogenes Laertius 7.119). For later Stoic teaching, see Cicero, *Tusc.* 1.65 (*animus … divinus est*); cf. *Leg.* 1.59; Seneca, *Ep.* 41.1 (*deus tecum est, intus est*); Epictetus, *Diatr.* 1.14.6 (ψυχαὶ … αὐτοῦ [= θεοῦ] μόρια οὖσαι καὶ ἀποσπάσματα).

²⁹ For Plutarch, the soul is the light within (φῶς γάρ ἐστιν ἡ ἐντὸς ψυχή) (*Quaest. rom.* 281b). The sun provides the mind (νοῦς) to the human being (*Fac.* 943a), and souls resemble a ray of light (943d). "The lamp [of the body] is the mind," according to a saying of Jesus in Dial. Sav. (NHC III 5) 125.18–19. Cf. Teach. Silv. (NHC VII 4) 99.15–16. Paul-Hubert Poirier comments on the Greek fragment of the Book of Watchers 5:8, "and there will be in the illuminated human a light" (ἔσται ἐν ἀνθρώπῳ πεφωτισμένῳ φῶς) ("Un parallèle grec partiel au logion 24 de l'Évangile selon Thomas," in *For the Children, Perfect Instruction: Studies in Honor of Hans-Martin Schenke on the Occasion of the Berliner Arbeitskreis für koptisch-gnostische Schriften's Thirtieth Year*, ed. Hans-Gebhard Bethge et al., NHMS 54 [Leiden: Brill, 2002], 95–100).

³⁰ Cf. Matt 5:14. See further Thomas Zöckler, "Light within a Human Person: A Comparison of Matthew 6:22–23 and Gospel of Thomas 24," *JBL* 120 (2001): 487–99, here 491.

human beings.[31] What signals its divine character is that it enlightens the entire world (ⲡⲕⲟⲥⲙⲟⲥ ⲧⲏⲣϥ).

In John 8:12, Jesus declares, "I am the light of the world" (cf. 9:5, 12:35).[32] By making this remark, Jesus positions himself as God's unique revelation. Humans do not have the light. Instead, Jesus the true Light enlightens every human coming into the world (1:9). What John reserves for Jesus alone—divine light—is the present possession of all Thomasine Christians.

If in log. 24 the final ⲡⲉ refers to the world, the whole world is darkness without the Thomasine Christian.[33] Compare John 12:46: "I [Jesus] have come as light into the world, so that everyone who believes in me should not remain in the darkness."[34] In log. 24, then, Thomasine Christians function very much like the Johannine Christ. The function that they share is an extraordinary and divine one: they illumine the entire world.

Primal Unity

Finally, log. 50 says that the sign of the Father within is "motion and repose." The words are mysterious but can helpfully be explained in light of ancient philosophy. Platonists told a story of salvation wherein the soul, first resting in the divine, wandered and fell. The destiny of the soul was to rediscover its repose by returning to the light.[35]

---

[31] Pagels connects the inward light in humans to their creation in the image of God (*Beyond Belief*, 40–41). The light-filled human must be modeled after the Human of Light. Humans are images of the primordial light, for this light was already in human form (p. 55). Humans are, in this way, light from light, true divine beings from a true divine (light) being.

[32] For the motif of light in John, see Jey J. Kanagaraj, *'Mysticism' in the Gospel of John: An Inquiry into Its Background*, JSNTSup 158 (Sheffield: Sheffield Academic, 1998), 282–309. For the relation of light imagery in John and Thomas, see Enno Edzard Popkes, "'Ich bin das Licht': Erwägungen zur Verhältnisbestimmung des Thomasevangeliums und der johanneischen Schriften anhand der Lichtmetaphorik," in *Kontexte des Johannesevangeliums: Das vierte Evangelium in religions- und traditionsgeschichtlicher Perspective*, ed. Jörg Frey and Udo Schnelle, WUNT 175 (Tübingen: Mohr Siebeck, 2004), 641–74, esp. 653–55, 663–67.

[33] For this interpretation, see Zöckler, "Light within a Human Person," 495; and Richard Valantasis, *The Gospel of Thomas*, New Testament Readings (London: Routledge, 1997), 98.

[34] Zöckler argues that in Gos. Thom. 24, the light within a human person can turn to darkness. In Thomas, "one cannot rely on the light as one's essence or divine principle residing unalterably inside oneself" ("Light within a Human Person," 492). This interpretation is unnecessary. If ⲡⲉ in ⲟⲩⲕⲁⲕⲉ ⲡⲉ refers to the world (ⲡⲕⲟⲥⲙⲟⲥ)—as Zöckler believes (p. 495)—then the world, not the person, turns dark. If ⲡⲉ refers to the person, it only means that the person of light may not shine, not that the internal light can be "replaced" by darkness. The light abides, though it may be covered.

[35] See, e.g., Plato, *Phaedr.* 247a–250c. Plutarch offered several mythic variants (*Def. orac.*

The repose indicates a primal unity with the divine. Such primal unity is hinted at in log. 11. There was a day, Jesus says to his disciples, "when you were one [ⲉⲧⲉⲧⲛ̄ⲟ ⲛ̄ⲟⲩⲁ]." The saying may recall the primeval unity of Adam before the split into male and female.[36] Yet it also brings to mind the eternal unity enjoyed by the Johannine Jesus with God: "I and the Father are one" (John 10:30).[37] In John 17:21, Jesus prays "that they [Christian disciples] may all be one, as you, Father, are in me and I am in you, may they also be in us."[38] Other—largely Alexandrian—witnesses (ℵ A C³ L Θ Ψ *f*¹·¹³ 33 sy^{p.h} bo; Cl Or) read the last phrase as "may they also be one [ἕν] in us." Assuming the correctness of this reading, Thomasine Christians, like the Johannine Christ, will share a oneness with God. Significantly, the divine-human union that John envisions for the future, Thomas places in the past. But the past oneness of Thomasine Christians makes them appear all the more like the Johannine Christ who, as Logos, was eternally with the Father.[39]

II. Divine Destiny

Return to the Light

Thomasine soteriology involves a return to the primal state of light. In Thomas, Jesus assumes that a return to the light is the fate of his followers: "When you come to be [ϩⲟⲧⲁⲛ ⲉⲧⲉⲧⲛ̄ϣⲁⲛϣⲱⲡⲉ] in the light [ϩⲙ̄ ⲡⲟⲩⲟⲉⲓⲛ]…" (log. 11). Miroslav Marcovich pointed out that the language of "coming to be in the light" (ἐν τῷ φωτί) may have been inspired by 1 John 1:7, where Jesus is "in the light" (ἐν τῷ φωτί) (2:9; cf. John 12:36).[40] The ϩⲟⲧⲁⲛ in log. 11 makes clear that arriving in the light is not a matter of "if" but "when." Thomasine Christians came from the light (log. 50), and to it they will return. "For where the beginning is, there will the end be. Blessed is the one who will take his place in the beginning" (log. 18; cf. 49).

This *egressus-regressus* pattern is reminiscent of the Johannine Christ, who was "in the beginning" with God (John 1:1). In time, he descended in flesh to reveal the Father (1:14). When his mission was complete, he hastened to return above

---

415a–c, *Fac.* 943a–945d, *Gen. Socr.* 591d–592e). The Hymn of the Pearl is a Christian adaptation of the same mythic pattern. See further Patterson, "Jesus Meets Plato," 200–204.

[36] DeConick, *Original Gospel of Thomas*, 79. Cf. Plato, *Symp.* 189d–193b.

[37] See further Klaus Scholtissek, "'Ich und der Vater, wir sind eins' (John 10,30): Zum theologischen Potential und zur hermeneutischen Kompetenz der johanneischen Christologie," in Van Belle et al., *Theology and Christology in the Fourth Gospel*, 315–46, esp. 337–39.

[38] See ibid., 342–44.

[39] A. F. J. Klijn relates the soteriological idea of oneness to Philo's depiction of the one God ("The Single One in the Gospel of Thomas," *JBL* 81 [1962]: 271–78, esp. 276–77). In this case as well, being or becoming one assimilates the elect to God.

[40] Miroslav Marcovich, "The Text of the Gospel of Thomas (Nag Hammadi II,2)," in idem, *Studies in Graeco-Roman Religions and Gnosticism*, SGRR 4 (Leiden: Brill, 1988), 55–79, esp. 77.

(16:28). The Johannine Jesus evidently envisioned some kind of ascent for believers, "that where I am you may be also" (14:3). Nevertheless this ascent does not occur until after death. Jesus firmly states: "No one has ascended into heaven except the one who descended from heaven—the Son of the Human" (3:13).[41]

In Thomas, however, the elect seem to ascend—like the Son of the Human—in their lifetime. DeConick argues that log. 50 reflects a premortem apocalyptic ascent tradition in which the (angelic) gatekeepers ask the ascenders about their origin, knowledge, and purity.[42] The goal of the Thomasine mystic, in her view, is to see God while still alive (log. 59).[43] If her interpretation is correct, this is another instance wherein the Thomasine Christian appears homologous with the Johannine Christ. Yet, as we have come to expect, there remains a difference: whereas John's Jesus alone sees the Father (1:18, 6:46), Thomas offers the vision to all.[44]

Assimilation

The return to the light also involves assimilation to it. The view that there were heavenly archetypes or Ideas was a common Platonic notion.[45] The idea that an image could conform to the archetype was the presupposition of Platonic "assimilation to God" (ὁμοίωσις θεῷ) (Plato, *Theaet.* 176b).[46] Such assimilation seems to be appealed to in a central statement of Thomasine soteriology:

> Jesus said to them [his disciples], "When you make the two one, and when you make the inside like the outside and the outside like the inside, and the above like the below, and when you make the male and the female one and the same, so that the male not be male nor the female female; and when you fashion eyes in place of an eye, and a hand in place of a hand, and a foot in place of a foot, and an image in place of an image [ογϩικων επμα ñογϩικω(ν)], then you will come into [the kingdom]." (log. 22)

Transformation from one image into another is reminiscent of Pauline transformation, or "iconification," language. In 2 Cor 3:18, Paul speaks of being

---

[41] For the motif of ascent in John, see Kanagaraj, *'Mysticism' in the Gospel of John*, 186–213.

[42] DeConick, *Seek to See Him*, 50–63; DeConick, *Voices of the Mystics*, 93–94.

[43] DeConick, *Seek to See Him*, 123–25; DeConick, *Voices of the Mystics*, 88–89; eadem, *Original Gospel of Thomas*, 197.

[44] Cf. Sent. Sextus 417, 420. On Jesus as the sole seer of God in John, see Marianne Meye Thompson, "Jesus: 'The One Who Sees God,'" in *Israel's God and Rebecca's Children: Christology and Community in Early Judaism and Christianity: Essays in Honor of Larry W. Hurtado and Alan F. Segal*, ed. David B. Capes et al.; Waco, TX: Baylor University Press, 2007), 215–26, esp. 225–26.

[45] Alcinous, *Epit.* 9; Ps.-Plutarch, *Plac.* 1.10 (882d–e); Apuleius, *Plat.* 1.6 §§192–93.

[46] See further Lavecchia, "Die Ὁμοίωσις Θεῷ," 326–31; Patterson, "Jesus Meets Plato," 190–96, and the sources cited in n. 3 above.

transformed into "the same image" (ἡ αὐτή εἰκών) as Christ. The exact correspondence of eye to eye, hand to hand, and foot to foot reminds one of the Pauline emphasis on "the same" image—*same*, that is, in every respect.[47]

John never calls Jesus the image of God, but the idea is at the heart of the Fourth Gospel: "He who has seen me has seen the Father" (John 14:9). For John, Jesus is the eternal image of God. Yet when he comes in flesh, he does not cease to be the image. His glory (or divinity) can be seen through the flesh (as vividly illustrated in the story of "doubting" Thomas, John 20:19–28; cf. 1:14). It would seem, then, that Jesus alone is the image. Believers are never invited to become "the same image" as Christ.

For Thomas, however, Christians and Christ do end up as the same image. In log. 22, the reader is not directly told *to* whose image one is being conformed. If humans were made in the image of the Light Human, then perhaps they are being conformed to Jesus, the Light above the universe (log. 77). In this interpretation, we have to understand the "image" as functioning like an archetype. Jesus (or the Logos) is an image of God, while believers are an image of Jesus. Thus, one conforms to an archetype that is itself the image of a greater (divine) archetype.[48] Since Jesus's image (= archetype) is luminous (as we shall see), transformation into this image indirectly conforms the elect to the Light Human. They are both called "images," and in effect become "the same image."

Being "the same image" results in a sharing of the same title. "When you make the two one" opens the conditional statement in log. 22. The same words are found in log. 106, with a different result: "Jesus said, 'When you make the two one, you will become the children of the Human.'" In log. 22, making the two one means being conformed to the archetypal Light. As a result of being conformed to this archetype, Christians can become the "children of the Human" (ⲛ̄ϣⲏⲣⲉ ⲙ̄ⲡⲣⲱⲙⲉ). The "Human" is apparently God (the elect, as we saw, are *God's* children). Yet being "children of the Human" means more than being children of God, since "the Son of the Human" (ὁ υἱός τοῦ ἀνθρώπου) is also a standard designation of Jesus in the Gospels.

Jesus as "the Son of the Human" plays a particularly exalted role in John's Gospel. He has charge of angels (1:51), he ascends to heaven (3:13, 6:62), he has authority to judge (5:27), he is sealed by the Father (6:27), and he is glorified (12:23, 13:31). Benjamin E. Reynolds rightly concludes that the expression "the Son of the Human" in John "draws attention to the heavenly nature of Jesus."[49]

---

[47] See further Litwa, *We Are Being Transformed*, 216–23.

[48] Cf. Philo, who views the Logos as the true image of God (*Conf.* 146), making humanity the image of the image. Alternatively, DeConick interprets the "image" in log. 22 to refer to the preexistent, divine self (*Voices of the Mystics*, 95–96). See further Patterson, "Jesus Meets Plato," 192–93.

[49] Benjamin E. Reynolds, "The Use of the Son of Man Idiom in the Gospel of John," in '*Who*

As "children of the Human," Thomasine Christians also possess a "heavenly"—indeed, divine—nature. They have an internal light (log. 24). They ascend to heaven (log. 50, 59). They will come to dwell in divine light (log. 11). These are traits of the Johannine "Son of the Human." In John, being "the Son of the Human" is Jesus's unique appointment. In Thomas, that extraordinary designation—and status—belongs to the elect. Once again, Jesus and the elect end up as "the same image."

There is more image language in Thomas. In log. 84, Jesus says, "When you see your likeness, you rejoice. But when you see your images which came into being before you, and which neither die nor become manifest, how much will you have to bear!'" The human "likeness" (ⲉⲓⲛⲉ) is probably a reference to the human body seen in any reflective surface (such as a mirror). The human "image" (ϩⲓⲕⲱⲛ), as several interpreters have argued, refers to the preexistent divine self.[50] This preexistent divine self is not independent, in my view. It is the image conformed to the archetypal light, namely, Jesus.

The suffering that the elect will bear is caused by the contrast of their present sarkic state with their preexistent divine state. What must be tolerated is the awareness of how far one's current self (the "likeness") falls short of one's true self (conformed to the archetype). What log. 84 describes, then, is a troubling encounter with one's archetypal, divine identity, who is ultimately Jesus himself.[51]

Logion 83 can be interpreted in a similar way.

Jesus said:
a. "The images [ⲛϩⲓⲕⲱⲛ] are manifest to people,
b. but the light in them remains concealed in the image [ⲉⲓⲕⲱⲛ] of the light of the Father.
c. He [or: the light] [ϥ] will become manifest,
d. but his image [ⲧⲉϥϩⲓⲕⲱⲛ] will remain concealed by his light."

Uwe-Karsten Plisch calls this saying "utterly incomprehensible" and resorts to emendation.[52] Is there another solution?

Is This Son of Man?' The Latest Scholarship on a Puzzling Expression of the Historical Jesus, ed. Larry Hurtado and Paul Owen, LNTS 390 (London: T&T Clark, 2011), 101–29, here 122.

[50] DeConick, *Recovering the Original*, 216; Patterson, "Jesus Meets Plato," 194; Popkes, *Das Menschenbild des Thomasevangeliums*, 254. For background on the preexistent divine self, see DeConick, *Seek to See Him*, 150–57. For historical *comparanda* of the image character of human existence, see Popkes, 255–347. Popkes's claim that "likeness" (ⲉⲓⲛⲉ) "marks the likeness of humankind to Yaldabaoth and his archons" seems forced (pp. 314–25, here 322).

[51] The distress is reminiscent of log. 2. Once the conformation to the image is complete (log. 22), however, distress will presumably lead to rule and (as the Greek fragment of log. 2 indicates) repose.

[52] Plisch, *Gospel of Thomas*, 191. For various interpretations of this logion, see Stevan L. Davies, *The Gospel of Thomas and Christian Wisdom* (New York: Seabury, 1983), 63–66; idem,

"The images are manifest to people." The "images"—or "image"—met in log. 84 refer to one's own ideal, divine self conformed to the archetype (Jesus).[53] The elect can come to view themselves in their divine form (this is what causes them pain—at least initially). But the light in them is concealed in the image of the Father's light. One's own luminous divinity, apparently, is wrapped up in the light image of the Father. The image (or rather Image) of the Father's light is likely Jesus himself, who has already identified himself with divine light (log. 77). Whether the ч in log. 83c refers to Jesus or the light ultimately makes no difference, since Jesus *is* the light.

Jesus/the light will become manifest. "But his image will remain concealed by his light." Jesus's true divine form, in other words, remains hidden above in divine light.[54] In this interpretation, the nature of both Jesus and the Thomasine Christian is conceived of as light and image—or as a luminous image. Both parties have hidden and revealed aspects. In the case of the elect, their light is hidden in Jesus (the Image of the Father's light); in the case of Jesus, his light-image is hidden in God. The light of Christians is buried in the light Image that is Jesus. The light of both is the same divine light; the image of both is the same divine image. Again, we see that what in John is reserved for Jesus alone (identity as the light and image of God) becomes the prerogative of all Christians.

Equality

In the end, the one fully conformed to the archetype becomes equal to it. Logion 61 offers a profound statement about equality:

Salome said, "Who are you, man? As being from One [oyλ], you have come up on my couch and eaten from my table."[55] Jesus said to her, "I am he who exists

---

"Christology and Protology," 669; Valantasis, *Gospel of Thomas*, 162–63; DeConick, *Seek to See Him*, 101–5; DeConick, *Original Gospel of Thomas*, 247–48; Pagels, "Exegesis of Genesis 1," 488; Jon Ma. Asgeirsson, "Conflicting Epic Worlds," in *Thomasine Traditions in Antiquity: The Social and Cultural World of the Gospel of Thomas*, ed. Jon Ma. Asgeirsson et al., NHMS 59 (Leiden: Brill, 2006), 155–74, esp. 164–67.

[53] DeConick understands the images in log. 83 to refer to human bodies (*Voices of the Mystics*, 92). This position is in tension with her view that the image in log. 84, the very next saying, is a reference to the ideal, divine self (ibid., 94). It seems best to be consistent and to understand both cases of "image" (εικων) to be referring to the divine self.

[54] For texts depicting God's true form (or nature) hidden by light, see DeConick, *Seek to See Him*, 104–5.

[55] I take the word oyλ to refer to God in primordial unity. Although Attridge denied that oyλ (representing ἑνός) can be anarthrous ("Greek Equivalents of Two Coptic Phrases: CG I,1.65,9–10 and CG II,2.43.26," *BASP* 18 [1981]: 27–32, here 31), Dunderberg shows an anarthrous usage in Clement of Alexandria, *Exc.* 36.1 (*Beloved Disciple in Conflict?* 94–95). Taking oyλ as a reference to God indicates that Salome already has some intimation of Jesus's true divine nature.

from he who is equal [ⲡⲉⲧϣⲏϣ]. I was given some of the things of [*or:* some who belong to] my father." [Salome said,] "I am Your disciple." [Jesus said to her,] "Therefore I say, if one is equal [ϣⲏϣ], that one will be filled with light, but if one is divided, that one will be filled with darkness."

In this logion, Jesus claims that he was given select disciples (cf. John 17:24). Salome claims to be one of these disciples. Jesus then remarks on the nature of discipleship; it means being equal and filled with light. "Equal" (ϣⲏϣ) is a widely accepted emendation for the manuscript reading ϣⲏϥ ("destroyed"). In its stative form, ϣⲏϣ means "to be equal, level, straight," and frequently translates ἴσος εἶναι. The question is, to whom are the disciples equal? The correspondence of ϣⲏϣ to ⲡⲉⲧϣⲏϣ earlier suggests that they are equal like the Equal One, who is presumably God.[56] If they are equal in the same respect as the Equal One, by implication the elect are equal to God.

The claim thus resembles the situation in John 5:18: "So on this account the Jews all the more were seeking to kill him [Jesus],… [because] he was calling God his own father, making himself equal with God [ἴσον ἑαυτὸν ποιῶν τῷ θεῷ]" (cf. 10:33).[57] In an interesting study, Jesse Sell emphasizes the importance of John 5:18 for log. 61.[58] Problematically, he makes both passages say more or less the same thing: Jesus is equal to God. The meaning of log. 61, however, is that the *elect* are equal to God. Thomasine Christians become conscious of their equality when they realize their own internal light. In Thomas, this realization does not necessarily occur through the mediation of Jesus. At best, Jesus and the elect share a similar nature and destiny. Those who are equal to God are also equal to each other.

Identification

Radical conformation to the archetype (Jesus) leads to equality with it. Radical equality with Jesus, in turn, leads to identification. No saying in Thomas more starkly expresses identification with the divine Jesus than log. 108: "Jesus said, 'He who will drink from my mouth will become as I am [ϥⲛⲁϣⲱⲡⲉ ⲛ̄ⲧⲁϩⲉ]. I myself shall become he [ⲁⲛⲟⲕ ϩⲱ ϯⲛⲁϣⲱⲡⲉ ⲉⲛⲧⲟϥ ⲡⲉ], and the things that are hidden will be revealed to him.'" Here the identification between Jesus and the elect occurs through a kind of intimate kiss whereby the waters of life flow from Jesus's mouth to the mouth of the disciple.[59] The kiss imagery may hint at the bridal chamber:

---

[56] Cf. Dunderberg, *Beloved Disciple in Conflict?* 91, 97.

[57] See further Wayne A. Meeks, "Equal to God," in *The Conversation Continues: Studies in Paul and John in Honor of J. Louis Martyn*, ed. Robert T. Fortna and Beverly R. Gaventa (Nashville: Abingdon, 1990), 309–21.

[58] Jesse Sell, "Johannine Traditions in Logion 61," *PRSt* 7 (1980): 24–37, esp. 30–32.

[59] For drinking and eternal life, see John 4:13–14. These themes are related to the Spirit in

"Many are standing at the door, but it is the solitary who will enter the bridal chamber" (log. 75; cf. 104).

The union envisioned with Jesus has some similarity to the union portrayed in John 17:21: "may they also be one [ἓν] in us" (the Alexandrian reading).[60] In Thomas, the union seems more radical, and more mutual: Jesus will become like the disciple just as the disciple becomes like Jesus. But "like" language is too pale to redescribe deification in log. 108; this passage indicates a striking identification of the elect with the divine Jesus.

The language of log. 108 helps to make plausible Marco Frenschkowski's reading of log. 13.[61] In this saying, Jesus reveals three words (ϣⲟⲙⲧⲉ ⲛ̄ϣⲁϫⲉ) to Thomas. When the other disciples urge Thomas to disclose the words, Thomas warns them that if he makes known what Jesus said to him, they will stone him (Thomas). The stones will then take vengeance (apparently to defend the truth of the saying) by breathing out fire and consuming the disciples. Frenschkowski argues that the three words revealed to Thomas are ἐγώ σύ εἰμί, or "I am you," and comments, "Thomas … is actually identical with the revealer, though he does not yet know it."[62] This explanation has the advantage of explaining why the disciples would stone *Thomas*, rather than Jesus, given the fact that Jesus originated the saying.[63]

In log. 13, Jesus says to Thomas that he has become drunk from the bubbling spring that Jesus has measured out. Jesus declares in log. 108 that whoever drinks from his mouth will become "like me; I myself shall become he, and what is hidden will be revealed to him."[64] Thomas receives a revelation in log. 13. Whatever the revelation was, it likely confirms the content of log. 108: Thomas has become like

---

7:37–39. For drink imagery related to mystical transformation, see DeConick, *Voices of the Mystics*, 96.

[60] Cf. also Paul: "The one who cleaves to the Lord is one spirit [ἓν πνεῦμα] with him" (1 Cor 6:17). On this, see Litwa, *We Are Being Transformed*, 166–69.

[61] Marco Frenschkowski, "The Enigma of the Three Words of Jesus in Gospel of Thomas Logion 13," *JHC* 1 (1994): 73–84.

[62] Ibid., 77. Other suggestions for the content of the three words can be found in Martina Janßen, "Evangelium des Zwillings? Das *Thomasevangelium* als Thomas-Schrift," in Frey et al., *Das Thomasevangelium*, 222–48, esp. 234 n. 71; Riley, *Resurrection Reconsidered*, 113 n. 42. Riley's own position is similar to Frenschkowski's. Riley believes that the three words can be taken from the Book of Thomas 138.8, 10: ⲡⲁⲥⲟⲉⲓϣ, ⲡⲁϣⲃⲣ̄ ⲙ̄ⲙⲉ, and ⲡⲁⲥⲟⲛ ("my twin, my true companion, and my brother") (pp. 112–13). In this interpretation, Thomas also appears on a par with Jesus.

[63] DeConick's explanation, that Jesus said אהיה אשר אהיה ("I am who I am"), does not explain why the disciples would stone Thomas specifically (*Original Gospel of Thomas*, 85). The upshot of her interpretation, however, ends up very similar to Frenschkowski's: "Thomas, by drinking from Jesus' bubbling fount, has been transformed into Jesus' equal" (DeConick, p. 85). In John 8:58–59, the Jews pick up stones in response to Jesus claiming Ἐγώ εἰμι. Now Thomas—identified with the divine Jesus—falls under the same threat.

[64] For drink related to knowledge of spiritual mysteries, note 4 Ezra 14:38–40; Odes Sol. 11:6–7.

Jesus, and Jesus has become Thomas. Thomas's equality with Jesus is implied in what Jesus said to him before: "I am not your master [or teacher]" (log. 13).[65] Frenschkowski notes, "Thomas remains in the act of understanding this mystery no longer a disciple, but becomes an equal of Jesus."[66] But the destiny of Thomas is not for him alone; he is a prototype for all Thomasine Christians called to realize their own identity with the divine Jesus.[67]

III. Results

The data presented above indicate a dual underpinning for a Thomasine version of deification: (1) the fact that Thomasine Christians share many of the same divine predicates and traits of Jesus as he is depicted in both Thomas and John, and (2) the direct identification of Thomasine Christians with the divine Jesus. The divinity of Jesus, although contested for many first-century Christian documents, is widely acknowledged by the early second century (when many believe that the complete Gospel of Thomas emerged). In Thomas, Jesus is surely a divine being: he is the preexistent light of the Father (log. 77); his existence stems directly from God (log. 61); he is transcendent (log. 13, 77); and he is the son of God (log. 37).

Intriguingly, these same divine traits and qualities make Thomasine Christians divine as well: they are preexistent (log. 49, 50); they are "the children of the Living Father" (log. 3); they are people of light (log. 24); and they are called to perfect unity (log. 22, 108) and equality (log. 61) with God. "Christology" has become anthropology. What is predicated of the divine Jesus to highlight his divinity is predicated also of the elect.

This *communicatio idiomatum* (sharing of properties) between Jesus and Thomasine Christians becomes especially pronounced when we compare Thomas with John's Gospel. Over and over again we have seen that what Thomas claims for Christians, John reserves for Christ. The significance of this point for Thomasine deification cannot be overestimated. Just as Christ is preexistent (John 1:1, 8:58), so are Thomasine Christians (log. 19). Just as Jesus speaks of his preexistent glory (John 17:5), so the elect come from the light (log. 50). Both have knowledge of their destiny (John 8:14; log. 11, 49). Both are privileged with a direct vision of God (John 1:18, 6:46; log. 59). Each party functions as the light of the world (John 8:12; log. 24). Each possesses a oneness (with God) (John 17:21; log. 11, 61), bears the exalted title "the Son (or Child) of the Human" (John 5:27, 12:23, etc.; log. 106), and exists

---

[65] Stephen J. Patterson, *The Gospel of Thomas and Jesus*, FF: Reference Series (Sonoma, CA: Polebridge, 1993), 206.
[66] Frenschkowski, "Enigma of the Three Words," 81; cf. Davies, "Christology and Protology," 676.
[67] Patterson, *Gospel of Thomas and Jesus*, 206; Davies, "Christology and Protology," 678–79; Janßen, "Evangelium des Zwillings?" 235 n. 78.

as a child of God the Father (John 10:36; log. 3). Finally, just as Jesus is equal to God (John 5:18), so are Thomasine Christians (log. 61). When arranged cumulatively, this striking homology between John's divine Jesus and Thomasine Christians more than hints at the divinity of the elect. The same discursive strategies used by the writer(s) of John to deify Jesus are used by the writer(s) of Thomas to deify Christians. If John deifies Jesus with a chain of awesome traits and predicates, Thomas deifies Christians using an almost identical strategy and understanding of divinity.

The fact that Thomasine Christians are homologous with John's Christ does not necessarily, in my view, represent a theological conflict between communities.[68] It does indicate, however, that both communities shared similar views of what constitutes divinity and of the ability of select humans to share in it. In essence, both communities adapt a preexisting Christian intuition: the joining of the human and the divine to achieve transcendence. The difference is chiefly one of focalization. For John, Jesus is the nodal point of divinity—the human who is fully divine and thus provides access to God. In Thomas, the scope of divinity is widened—divine light shines in every Christian heart. The end result of each theology is different, but perhaps not radically so. The Johannine Jesus calls his disciples to eternal life, light, and divinity through him: "that where I am you may be also" (John 14:3; cf. 17:21–22). The Thomasine Jesus calls his followers to realize that his life and divinity are already within.

If we take at face value that the sayings in Thomas are words of the living Jesus (Gos. Thom. prologue), then Thomas constitutes a gospel in which deification is a basic element in the teaching of Jesus.[69] To be sure, deification in the mouth of Jesus sounds foreign to moderns and may represent a departure from the "original" teachings of Jesus. Nevertheless, we have reason to believe that Christians who read Thomas from the second to the fourth centuries were reading what they believed to be genuine Jesus traditions. This Jesus, far from making his divinity separate from his disciples, invited them to realize their own deity within.

Thomasine deification is both similar to and different from other early Christian forms of deification. It is similar in that deification is ultimately a form of

---

[68] Pagels, for example, understands John's restriction of the light to Jesus as a response to Thomas's "claim that this light may be present in everyone" (*Beyond Belief*, 41). Cf. DeConick, *Voices of the Mystics*, 131–32.

[69] See, recently, Stephen Finlan, "Deification in Jesus' Teaching," in *Theōsis: Deification in Christian Theology*, ed. Stephen Finlan and Vladimir Kharlamov, 2 vols., Princeton Theological Monograph Series 156 (Eugene, OR: Pickwick, 2006–2011), 2:21–41. He uses Thomas only to shed light on Luke 17:21 (the kingdom within) and treats Thomas as valuable only for material related to the "historical [= canonical] Jesus" (p. 38). Finlan concludes that, because Thomas log. 3 and 113 mitigate inwardness, they are more or less "gnosticizing" and thus cannot derive from the historical Jesus [!] (p. 39). For Thomas as relating authentic Jesus traditions, see DeConick, "The Original *Gospel of Thomas*," *VC* 56 (2002): 167–99, esp. 199.

assimilation to and identification with the divine Jesus. Among ancient Christians, it was out of reflection on Christ's incarnate (or human) divinity that there arose the idea of the deification of human beings. In Paul, Thomas, and arguably John, Jesus is the archetype for the deified human being.[70]

Unlike John, however, Thomas does not envision a strict dependence on Jesus. As Pagels points out, "He [Jesus] directs the disciple not toward himself (as does the Jesus of John 14:6) but toward the light hidden within."[71] Salvation is the realization that one's inner light is the same light as the light that is Jesus himself (log. 77). This realization leads to an identification with Jesus's divine nature.[72]

In the end, it is difficult to distinguish the divine Jesus from the elect. They are truly "the same image." Like "Didymus Judas Thomas" (Coptic Gos. Thom. prologue)—whose name contains a double affirmation of his twin status—all the elect have the inner potential to become Jesus's "twins."[73] "Gemination" is thus an appropriate and realistic description of Thomasine identification with Jesus. This striking

---

[70] Koester is right to conclude that Jesus in John is not a soteriological paradigm (*Ancient Christian Gospels*, 119). Nevertheless, there is assimilation to him. His disciples do his works (John 14:12), come to see and know the Father (14:9; 17:3, 26; cf. 1:18, 6:46), and ascend to the place where Jesus goes (13:36, 14:2-3). For comparisons of Pauline and Thomasine soteriology, see Davies, "Christology and Protology," 668-69, 677; Uro, *Thomas: Seeking the Historical Context*, 74-77; Joshua W. Jipp, "Death and the Human Predicament, Salvation as Transformation, and Bodily Practices in 1 Corinthians and the *Gospel of Thomas*," in *Paul and the Gospels: Christologies, Conflicts, and Convergences*, ed. Michael F. Bird and Joel Willitts, LNTS 411 (London: T&T Clark, 2011), 242-66, esp. 249-58. The relation between Paul and Thomas has been recently explored by Christopher Skinner, who argues that Thomas depended on, adapted, and even rejected Pauline ideas ("The Gospel of Thomas's Rejection of Paul's Theological Ideas," in Bird and Willitts, *Paul and the Gospels*, 220-41). Gathercole argues for a more limited literary influence of Paul on Thomas, specifically Thomas's use of Pauline language for "un-Pauline ends" (*Composition of the Gospel of Thomas*, 227-49).

[71] Pagels, "Exegesis of Genesis 1," 487; cf. Davies, "Christology and Protology," 664-65.

[72] The fundamental similarity between Jesus and the elect in Thomas is commonly recognized, most recently by Antti Marjanen, "The Portrait of Jesus in the *Gospel of Thomas*," in Asgeirsson et al., *Thomasine Traditions in Antiquity*, 209-20, esp. 213-17; Popkes, *Das Menschenbild des Thomasevangeliums*, 355; and Janßen, "Evangelium des Zwillings?" 236-37.

[73] On the twin motif, see Uro, *Thomas: Seeking the Historical Context*, 10-15; Janßen, "Evangelium des Zwillings?" 222-48; Marco Frenschkowski, "Zwillingsmythologie in der Thomastradition," in Schröter, *Apocryphal Gospels within the Context of Early Christian Theology*, 509-28. Wilfried Eisele accepts spiritual identification with Jesus in Thomas but rejects the twin motif (*Welcher Thomas? Studien zur Text- und Überlieferungsgeschichte des Thomasevangeliums*, WUNT 259 [Tübingen: Mohr Siebeck, 2010], 66-68). Cf. Paul-Hubert Poirier, "The Writings Ascribed to Thomas and the Thomas Tradition," in *The Nag Hammadi Library after Fifty Years: Proceedings of the 1995 Society of Biblical Literature Commemoration*, ed. John D. Turner and Anne McGuire, NHMS 44 (Leiden: Brill, 1997), 295-307, esp. 301-2. That "Didymus" is placed before "Judas Thomas" in the prologue of NHC II 2 may indicate *not* that the tradents of the Coptic version have forgotten the sense of Didymus (*pace* Poirier) but the very fact that they wish to highlight Thomas's status as Jesus's twin.

identification of the divine Jesus and the elect constitutes one of the earliest forms of Christian deification.

One of the main differences between Thomasine and later patristic forms of deification is that Thomasine deification seems to require little or no application of external divine aid. In the late second century, Irenaeus asserted, "For those in the light do not themselves illumine the light, but are illumined and brightened by it [*sed illuminantur et illustrantur ab eo*]. In themselves, they offer nothing to it [*ipsi quidem nihil ei praestant*], but receiving his [the Savior's] benefaction they are illuminated by light" (*Haer.* 4.14.1). Irenaeus's observation follows from John's Gospel, where the life that is the light of human beings originated only in the Word (John 1:4; cf. 1:9). This light can go away from people, and only by believing in it can one become its child (12:35–36; cf. 11:10).

Nevertheless, the Irenaean (and later Augustinian) insistence on external grace is not fully representative of patristic forms of deification. Many Christian fathers acknowledged something analogous to a divine core within the human soul, often identified with the νοῦς and interpreted to be the image of God. Roughly contemporaneous with Irenaeus, Clement of Alexandria writes:

> For the Word of God is intelligible [νοερός], according to which the image of the mind [νοῦς] is seen in the human being alone, by which also the good man is deiform and dei-similar [θεοειδὴς καὶ θεοείκελος] in his soul, and God, in turn, is anthropoform [ἀνθρωποειδής]. For the form of both is the mind [ὁ νοῦς], by which we are fashioned. (*Strom.* 6.9.72.2; my translation)[74]

Like deification in Clement, Thomasine deification is a form that acknowledges one's own internal resources in the journey toward transcendence. "Jesus said, 'When you produce that [which is] in you [ϩⲟⲧⲁⲛ ⲉⲧⲉⲧⲛ̅ϣⲁⲝⲡⲉ ⲡⲏ ϩⲛ̅ ⲑⲏⲩⲧⲛ], what you have will save you'" (log. 70). Divine grace is active, to be sure, but present as a light within the self. Such internal light, although coterminous with the light of Jesus (the light over all, log. 77), is not centralized in or restricted to a "unique" mediating deity (μονογενὴς θεός, John 1:18). Instead, the light is the root of every Christian's deity and the cause of their identification with the divine light, the living Jesus.[75]

Finally, there is an important implication for early Christians' understanding of divinity. John presents an ultimately dualistic, albeit dialectical, notion of God.[76] Thomas, by contrast, appears frankly panentheistic. Future research should explore how widespread panentheistic thinking was in earliest Christianity. In this

---

[74] See further Patterson, "Jesus Meets Plato," 184–93. DeConick presents a fuller comparison of Clement and Thomas in *Recovering the Original*, 225–31.

[75] See further Davies, "Christology and Protology," 679.

[76] Cf. the Christian theological terminology of Larry Hurtado, "The Binitarian Shape of Early Christian Worship," in Newman et al., *Jewish Roots of Christological Monotheism*, 187–213.

discussion, implicit apologetic models of "orthodoxy vs. heresy," or "Gnostic(ism) vs. Christian(ity)," must be abandoned.

In the end, deification as a category of thought is both old and new. Its (new) use as an academic category helps bring together many of Thomas's themes that otherwise float disconnectedly. This use suggests that deification was a key part of Christian myth earlier than was previously thought (namely, in the early second century CE). It shows that Christians saw deification as a teaching of Jesus. It reveals the intimate connection between christological and anthropological reflection. It indicates that Christians could conceive of their divine nature as an innate gift. Finally, it suggests that some Christians saw little contradiction between God's singular deity and divine omnipresence in every human heart. Thomas's similarities to the Gospel of John highlight the differences between an inclusive and an exclusive Christology. In Thomas, Christology has become anthropology—or rather, anthropology has become Christology.

fp fortress press
scholarship that matters

fresh possibilities!

 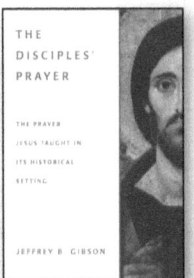  

Power and Politics in the Book of Judges
Men and Women of Valor
JOHN C. YODER

Considers the variety of strategies the men and women of valor used to gain their power, from the use of violence to cultivating a reputation for reliability and honor, and positioning themselves as skillful mediators between the realms of earth and heaven.
9781451496420 192 pp pbk $44

The Disciples' Prayer
The Prayer Jesus Taught in Its Historical Setting
JEFFREY B. GIBSON

Gibson reviews scholarship that derives the Lord's Prayer from Jewish synagogal prayers and refutes it. The genre of the prayer, he shows, is petitionary, and understanding its intent requires understanding Jesus' purpose in calling disciples as witnesses against "this generation."
9781451490251 192 pp pbk $44

The Origin of Evil Spirits
The Reception of Genesis 6:1-4 in Early Jewish Literature Revised Edition
ARCHIE T. WRIGHT

Wright traces the concept of evil spirits from the Hebrew Bible through postbiblical Jewish literature. He suggests that the nonspecificity inherent in the biblical text of Genesis 6:1–4 opened the basis for the emergence of an etiology of evil spirits as Jewish authors engaged with the text.
9781451490329 247 pp pbk $44

The Jewish Pseudepigrapha
An Introduction to the Literature of the Second Temple Period
SUSAN DOCHERTY

"A clear and concise introduction, based on impeccable scholarship, which opens this fascinating world to students and general readers."
—PHILIP ALEXANDER
Emeritus, University of Manchester
9781451490282 208 pp pbk $49

Available wherever books are sold or
800-328-4648
fortresspress.com

scholarship that matters

surprising insights!

The Social World of the Sages
An Introduction to Israelite and Jewish Wisdom Literature
MARK R. SNEED

Sneed produces a surprising new picture of the authors and tradents of the wisdom materials by exploring archaeological and literary data illustrating scribal culture and pedagogy in the ancient Near East. Includes sidebars, photos, diagrams, and maps.
9781451470369   224 pp   pbk $44

My Flesh Is Meat Indeed
A Nonsacramental Reading of John 6:51-58
MEREDITH J. C. WARREN

Warren argues that the "bread of life" discourse in John 6:51c-58 does not bear any Eucharistic overtones. Rather, John plays on shared cultural expectations in the ancient Mediterranean world about the nature of heroic sacrifice and the accompanying sacrificial meal, which established the identification of a hero with a deity.
9781451490244   304 pp   pbk $44

James and Paul
The Politics of Identity at the Turn of the Ages
V. GEORGE SHILLINGTON

"Provocative exegesis and readable prose... Shillington develops a fresh portrait of James, and shows how reconceiving Jesus' brother exerts a profound influence on how we see Paul."   —BRUCE CHILTON, Bard College
9781451482133   288 pp   pbk $44

Available wherever books are sold or
800-328-4648
fortresspress.com

Evangelically Rooted. *Critically Engaged.*

NEW FROM IVP ACADEMIC

xxxii + 394 pages, hardcover, 978-0-8308-2912-5, $60.00

184 pages, paperback, 978-0-8308-2469-4, $22.00

COMMENTARY ON JOHN, VOLUME 2

Cyril of Alexandria

Translated by David R. Maxwell, edited by Joel C. Elowsky

In the latest addition to the Ancient Christian Texts series, David Maxwell renders a service to students of patristics and New Testament studies alike. The first complete English translation of Cyril of Alexandria's *Commentary on John* since the nineteenth century, this volume unveils one of the brightest lights in the Alexandrian tradition.

DO WE NEED THE NEW TESTAMENT?

Letting the Old Testament Speak for Itself

John Goldingay

"Goldingay turns our modern thinking on its head and exposes the weaknesses in the way contemporary Christians understand the Old Testament—and the New. With thought-provoking ideas on every page, this book will help readers look at the Old and New Testaments in new and exciting ways."

Nathan MacDonald,
University of Cambridge

Visit *ivpacademic.com/examcopy* to request an exam copy.

 Follow us on Twitter Join us on Facebook   800.843.9487 | ivpacademic.com

Evangelically Rooted. *Critically Engaged.*

A FRESH VIEW OF THE PAST

A Week in the Life of a Roman Centurion

Gary M. Burge

"Masterfully written and extensively researched, this fast-paced account invites the reader into the first-century world of the Gospels even while intriguing the reader as a good story should."

Craig Keener,
Asbury Theological Seminary, author, The IVP Bible Background Commentary: New Testament

Interpreting the Prophets
Reading, Understanding and Preaching from the Worlds of the Prophets

Aaron Chalmers

"Happy are the students who take Aaron Chalmers's classes! He has assimilated a vast and complex range of materials from the Old Testament and from the scholarly world, and has formulated a coherent and intelligible account of the Prophets for his readers."

John Goldingay,
David Allen Hubbard Professor of Old Testament School of Theology, Fuller Theological Seminary

Visit **ivpacademic.com** to request an exam copy.

 Follow us on Twitter   Join us on Facebook   800.843.9487 | ivpacademic.com

J. Patout Burns Jr. and Robin M. Jensen

CHRISTIANITY IN ROMAN AFRICA

the development of its practices and beliefs

"This is an astonishing compendium integrating history, theology, and material culture. It is really unprecedented. The theology illuminates the art, and the art in turn illuminates the theology — and both make the history come alive, almost right before the reader's eyes. A truly amazing achievement!"
— John C. Cavadini

"Especially valuable for its treatment of archeological and material-culture remains, *Christianity in Roman Africa* provides a valuable resource for recent scholarship on this important center of early Christianity."
— Elizabeth A. Clark

"A fascinating and very readable contribution to the understanding of Christian North African culture as found in texts (both pastoral and polemical), liturgical artifacts, architecture, iconography, and epigraphy. . . . Provides sweeping yet keenly perceptive and balanced overviews."
— Allan Fitzgerald

ISBN 978-0-8028-6931-9 • 724 pages • hardcover • $55.00

At your bookstore,
or call 800-253-7521
www.eerdmans.com

Wm. B. Eerdmans Publishing Co.
2140 Oak Industrial Dr NE
Grand Rapids, MI 49505

FRAMING PAUL
An Epistolary Biography

DOUGLAS A. CAMPBELL

"Through careful argumentation, laced with a mass of radically new suggestions, Campbell builds an original case for a ten-letter corpus of authentic Pauline letters in a historical sequence never before proposed. All Pauline scholars, whether convinced or not, will need to give this book the careful attention it deserves."

— JOHN BARCLAY

"At once brilliant, bold, provocative, maddening, Campbell's work will require careful attention, not least because of his insistence that the chronological framing of the letters matters — and crucially so — for any responsible historical interpretation of Paul."

— DAVID G. HORRELL

ISBN 978-0-8028-7151-0 • 490 pages • paperback • $39.00

At your bookstore,
or call 800-253-7521
www.eerdmans.com

4533

WM. B. EERDMANS
PUBLISHING CO.
2140 Oak Industrial Drive NE
Grand Rapids, MI 49505

SBL PRESS New and Recent Titles

PAUL AS INFANT AND NURSING MOTHER
Metaphor, Rhetoric, and Identity in 1 Thessalonians 2:5–8
Jennifer Houston McNeel
Paper $29.95, 978-1-58983-966-3   216 pages, 2014   Code: 064512
Hardcover $44.95, 978-1-58983-968-7   E-book $29.95, 978-1-58983-967-0
Early Christianity and Its Literature 12

COMMUNITIES IN DISPUTE
Current Scholarship on the Johannine Epistles
R. Alan Culpepper and Paul N. Anderson, editors
Paper $39.95, 978-1-62837-015-7   316 pages, 2014   Code: 064513
Hardcover $54.95, 978-1-62837-017-1   E-book $39.95, 978-1-62837-016-4
Early Christianity and Its Literature 13

UNTOLD TALES FROM THE BOOK OF REVELATION
Sex and Gender, Empire and Ecology
Stephen D. Moore
Paper $39.95, 978-1-58983-990-8   302 pages, 2014   Code: 060379
Hardcover $54.95, 978-1-58983-991-5   E-book $39.95, 978-1-58983-992-2
Resources for Biblical Study 79

MEMORY AND IDENTITY IN ANCIENT JUDAISM AND EARLY CHRISTIANITY
A Conversation with Barry Schwartz
Tom Thatcher, editor
Paper $40.95, 978-1-58983-952-6   372 pages, 2014   Code: 060678
Hardcover $55.95, 978-1-58983-953-3   E-book $40.95, 978-1-58983-954-0
Semeia Studies 78

"YOU ARE A PRIEST FOREVER"
Second Temple Jewish Messianism and the
Priestly Christology of the Epistle to the Hebrews
Eric F. Mason
Paper $31.95   244 pages, 2014   Code: 069563
STDJ 74, Brill Reprints 63

SBL Press • P.O. Box 2243 • Williston, VT 05495-2243
Phone: 877-725-3334 (toll-free) or 802-864-6185 • Fax: 802-864-7626
Order online at www.sbl-site.org/publications

SBL PRESS New and Recent Titles

PROVERBS
An Eclectic Edition with Introduction and Textual Commentary
Michael V. Fox
Hardcover $69.95, 978-1-62837-020-1   500 pages, 2015   Code: 062401
E-book $69.95, 978-1-62837-021-8
The Hebrew Bible: A Critical Edition 1

THE WRITINGS AND LATER WISDOM BOOKS
Christl M. Maier and Nuria Calduch-Benages, editors
Paper $44.95, 978-1-62837-057-7   344 pages, 2014   Code: 066003
Hardcover $59.95, 978-1-62837-059-1   E-book $44.95, 978-1-62837-058-4
Bible and Women 3

LATINO/A BIBLICAL HERMENEUTICS
Problematics, Objectives, Strategies
Francisco Lozada Jr. and Fernando F. Segovia, editors
Paper $46.95, 978-1-58983-654-9   386 pages, 2014   Code: 060668P
Hardcover $61.95, 978-1-58983-927-4   E-book $46.95, 978-1-58983-655-6
Semeia Studies 68

THE SHAPE AND SHAPING OF THE BOOK OF PSALMS
The Current State of Scholarship
Nancy L. deClaissé-Walford, editor
Paper $36.95, 978-1-62837-001-0   284 pages, 2014   Code: 062620
Hardcover $51.95, 978-1-62837-003-4   E-book $36.95, 978-1-62837-002-7
Ancient Israel and Its Literature 20

HISTORICAL ROOTS OF THE OLD TESTAMENT (1200–63 BCE)
Richard D. Nelson
Paper $38.95, 978-1-62837-005-8   314 pages, 2014   Code: 063213
Hardcover $53.95, 978-1-62837-007-2   E-book $38.95, 978-1-62837-006-5
Biblical Encyclopedia 13

SBL Press • P.O. Box 2243 • Williston, VT 05495-2243
Phone: 877-725-3334 (toll-free) or 802-864-6185 • Fax: 802-864-7626
Order online at www.sbl-site.org/publications

NOW AVAILABLE FROM SBL PRESS
THE SBL HANDBOOK OF STYLE, SECOND EDITION

"Every graduate program should make *The SBL Handbook of Style* a required text."
— Carol A. Newsom, Candler School of Theology, Emory University

The SBL Handbook of Style has been thoroughly updated to reflect the latest practices among scholars, editors, and publishers as well as to take into account current trends in scholarly publishing. This edition has been meticulously supplemented with important new subject matter that fills gaps in the first edition. Chapters and sections have been reorganized and restructured to be more intuitive and logical.

Hardcover $39.95, 978-1-58983-964-9
E-book $39.95, 978-1-58983-965-6

Instructors may request a complimentary copy of the *Handbook* when it is adopted for a course and ten or more copies are ordered.

New Material in the Second Edition includes
- Clearer and more comprehensive guidelines for authors in preparing manuscripts for publication, including a discussion of Unicode fonts
- A list of ancient Near Eastern archaeological site names
- An expansive discussion of the treatment of qur'anic sources
- An expanded and improved list of capitalization and spelling examples
- Addition of a section on Islamic dates
- An introduction on the principles of transliteration and transcription
- A substantially revised and updated discussion of Akkadian transliteration
- Addition of Sumerian, Hittite, Old Persian, Moabite, Edomite, Ammonite, Syriac, Mandaic, Ethiopic, Arabic, and Turkish to the list of ancient languages treated
- A more complete discussion of the rules of citation
- New rules for the treatment of Latin titles
- A comprehensive list of publishers and their places of publication
- Detailed guidelines for citing a variety of electronic sources
- Expanded coverage of rabbinic works and ancient codices
- A thoroughly updated and expanded list of secondary sources

SBL PRESS

SBL Press • P.O. Box 2243 • Williston, VT 05495-2243
Phone: 877-725-3334 (toll-free) or 802-864-6185 • Fax: 802-864-7626
Order online at www.sbl-site.org/publications

www.ingramcontent.com/pod-product-compliance
Lightning Source LLC
Chambersburg PA
CBHW021826300426
44114CB00009BA/344